POSUKA DEMIZU

The vampiric plant vida was featured beautifully in the anime.

Vida is a fictitious flower, but...

"The way the small flowers come together to bloom symbolizes families and unity." These were the words for the flower verbena, and I really liked them. So I used them as reference for the design of vida.

Spring is just about starting. For those of you who are interested, you can try growing some verbena.

Please look forward to the next volume! I'm so inspired by the exciting plot developments that I've already thought of what to do for the next cover!

KAIU SHIRAI

Writer Shirai's personal highlights for *The Promised Neverland* fanatics, part 9!

1. The grave of Kaiu Shirai (I wonder where it would be?)

2. Don is sensitive to heat (he was like that in volumes 5 and 6 too...)

3. The voice in the first panel on page 117... Whose voice is it?

By the way, according to Demizu Sensei, the motifs of volumes 1 through 12 are hidden in the volume 13 cover! Try looking for them!

Please enjoy this volume!

Posuka Demizu debuted as a manga artist with the 2013 *CoroCoro* series *Oreca Monster Bouken Retsuden*. A collection of illustrations, *The Art of Posuka Demizu*, was released in 2016 by PIE International.

Kaiu Shirai debuted in 2015 with *Ashley Gate no Yukue* on the *Shonen Jump+* website. Shirai first worked with Posuka Demizu on the two-shot *Poppy no Negai*, which was released in February 2016.

THE PROMISED NEVERLAND

VOLUME 13
SHONEN JUMP Manga Edition

STORY BY KAIU SHIRAI
ART BY POSUKA DEMIZU

Translation/Satsuki Yamashita
Touch-Up Art & Lettering/Mark McMurray
Design/Julian [JR] Robinson
Editor/Alexis Kirsch

YAKUSOKU NO NEVERLAND © 2016 by Kaiu Shirai, Posuka Demizu
All rights reserved.
First published in Japan in 2016 by SHUEISHA Inc., Tokyo.
English translation rights arranged by SHUEISHA Inc.

Printed in Italy

Published by VIZ Media, LLC
P.O. Box 77010
San Francisco, CA 94107

10 9 8 7 6 5 4 3
First printing, January 2020
Third printing, February 2022

PARENTAL ADVISORY
THE PROMISED NEVERLAND is rated T+
and is recommended for ages 16 and up.
This volume contains fantasy violence and
adult themes.

THE PROMISED NEVERLAND

13

The King of Paradise

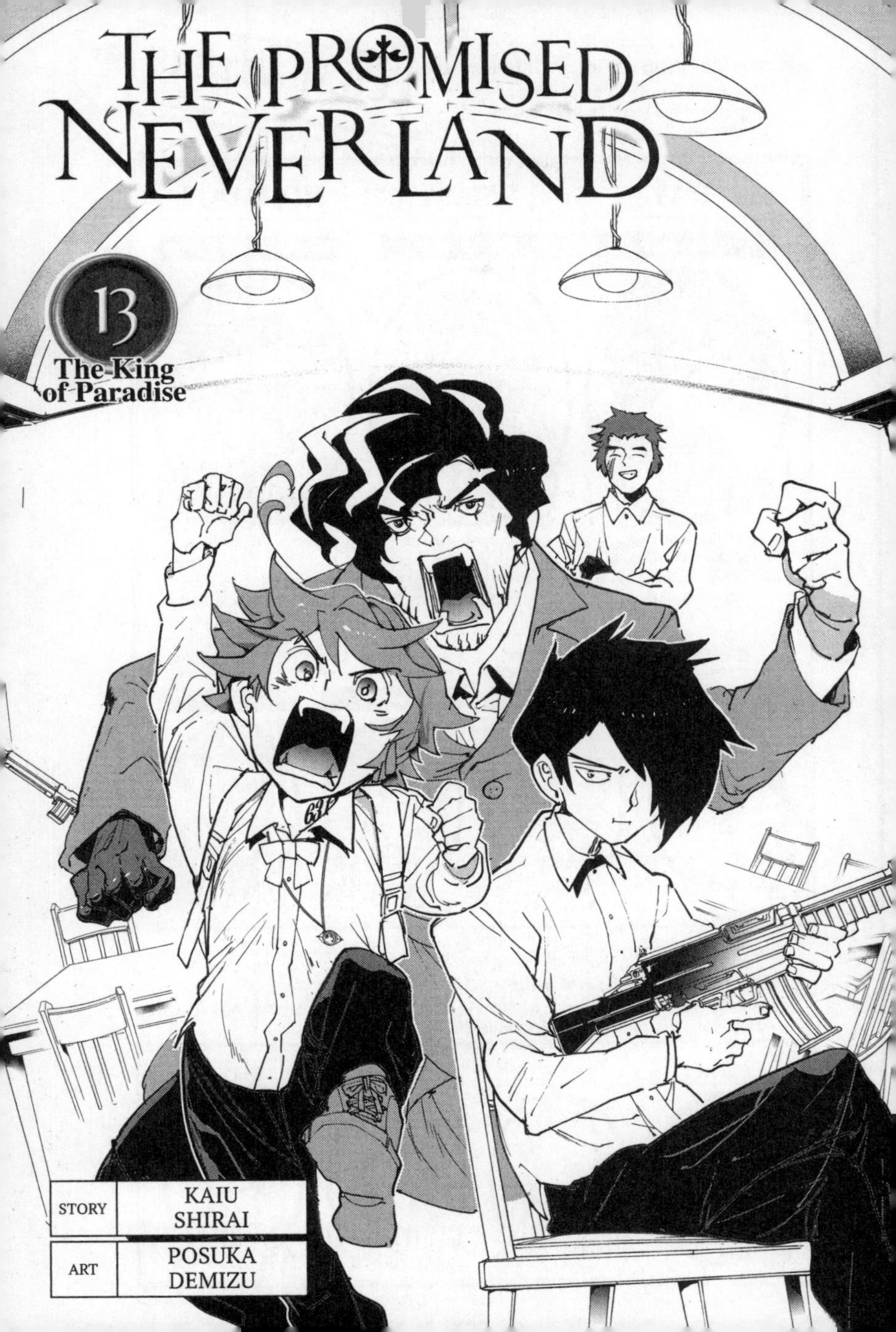

STORY	KAIU SHIRAI
ART	POSUKA DEMIZU

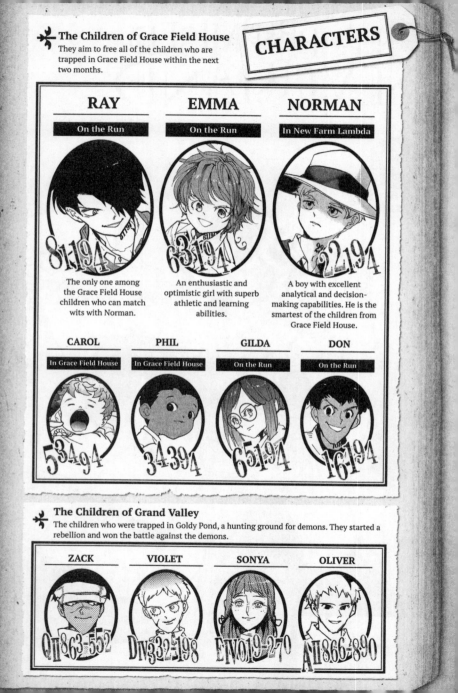

The Children of Grace Field House

They aim to free all of the children who are trapped in Grace Field House within the next two months.

RAY
On the Run

The only one among the Grace Field House children who can match wits with Norman.

EMMA
On the Run

An enthusiastic and optimistic girl with superb athletic and learning abilities.

NORMAN
In New Farm Lambda

A boy with excellent analytical and decision-making capabilities. He is the smartest of the children from Grace Field House.

CAROL
In Grace Field House

PHIL
In Grace Field House

GILDA
On the Run

DON
On the Run

The Children of Grand Valley

The children who were trapped in Goldy Pond, a hunting ground for demons. They started a rebellion and won the battle against the demons.

ZACK

VIOLET

SONYA

OLIVER

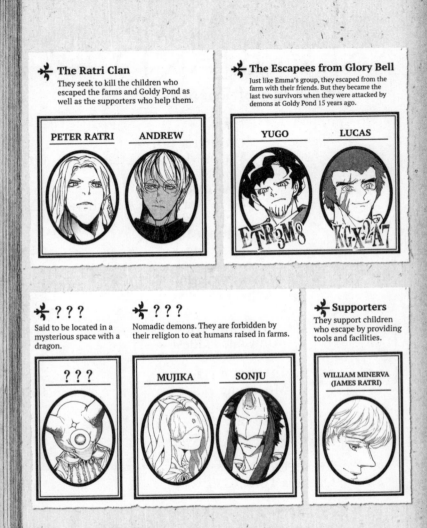

The Ratri Clan
They seek to kill the children who escaped the farms and Goldy Pond as well as the supporters who help them.

PETER RATRI

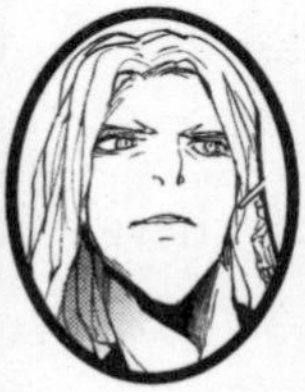

ANDREW

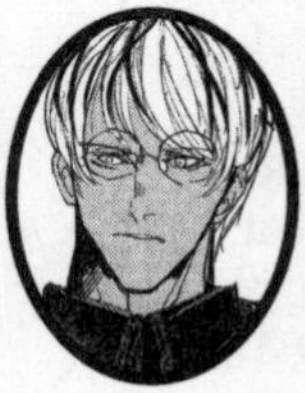

The Escapees from Glory Bell
Just like Emma's group, they escaped from the farm with their friends. But they became the last two survivors when they were attacked by demons at Goldy Pond 15 years ago.

YUGO

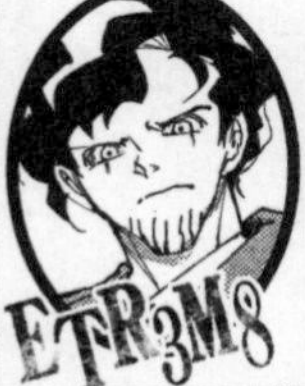
ETR3M8

LUCAS

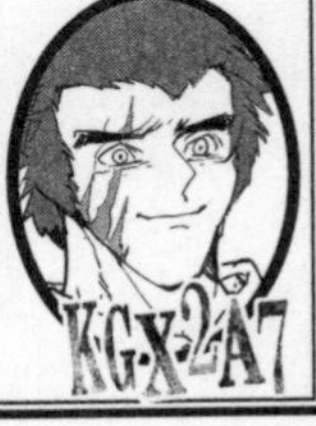
KG-X-2A7

? ? ?
Said to be located in a mysterious space with a dragon.

? ? ?

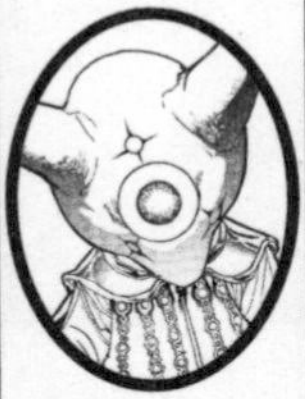

? ? ?
Nomadic demons. They are forbidden by their religion to eat humans raised in farms.

MUJIKA

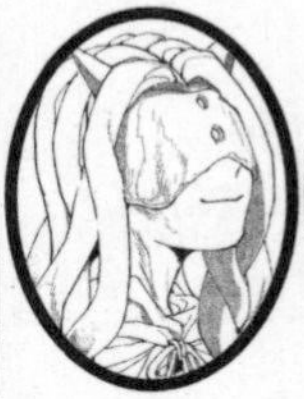

SONJU

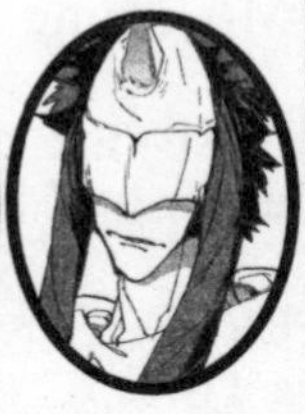

Supporters
They support children who escape by providing tools and facilities.

WILLIAM MINERVA (JAMES RATRI)

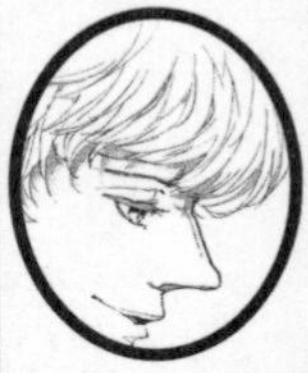

The Story So Far

Emma is living happily at Grace Field House with her foster siblings. One day, she realizes that they are being bred as food for demons and decides to escape with a group of other children. At a safe shelter, she meets Yugo, who guides her and Ray to Goldy Pond, a location Minerva indicated in a letter. There she meets other humans and joins their fight to annihilate the demons. After they return to the shelter, Emma reveals to everyone her intention to free all of the children in the farms using the information she obtained at Goldy Pond. She finds a clue about how to make a new promise to replace the one made between humans and demons 1,000 years ago, but then Andrew and his men attack the shelter.

THE PROMISED NEVERLAND 13

The King of Paradise

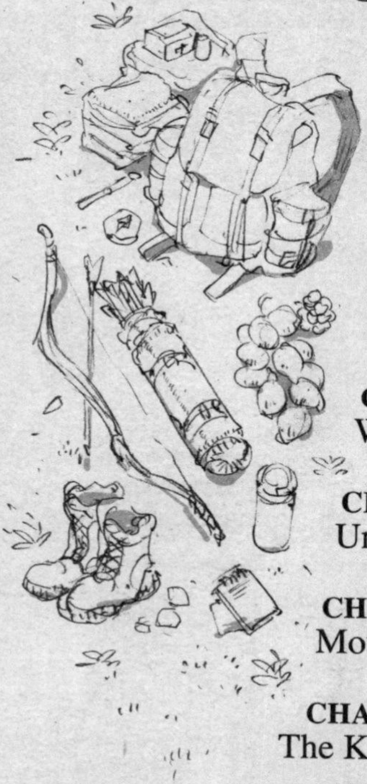

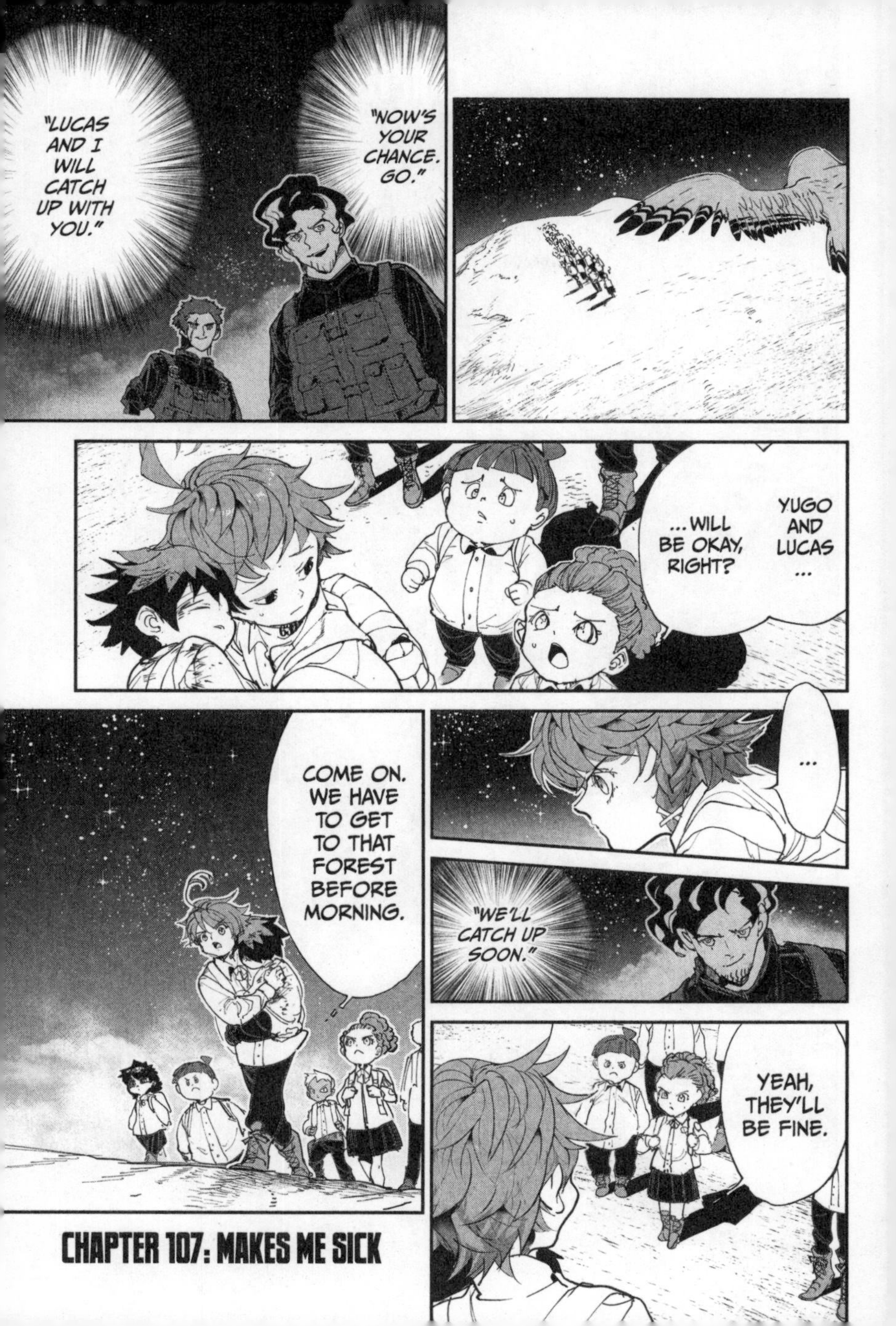
"NOW'S YOUR CHANCE. GO."
"LUCAS AND I WILL CATCH UP WITH YOU."
YUGO AND LUCAS ...
... WILL BE OKAY, RIGHT?
...
"WE'LL CATCH UP SOON."
YEAH, THEY'LL BE FINE.
COME ON. WE HAVE TO GET TO THAT FOREST BEFORE MORNING.
CHAPTER 107: MAKES ME SICK

CHAPTER 107: MAKES ME SICK

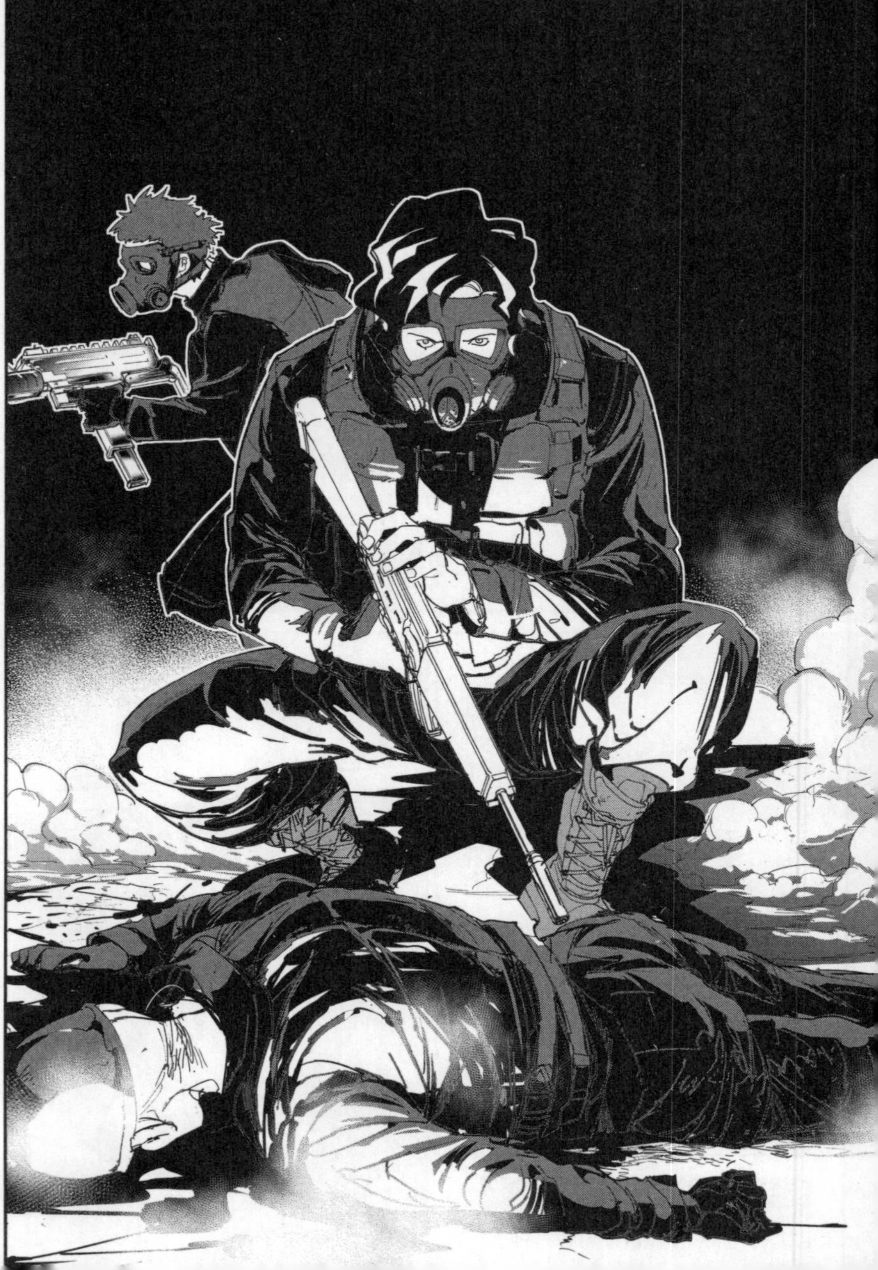

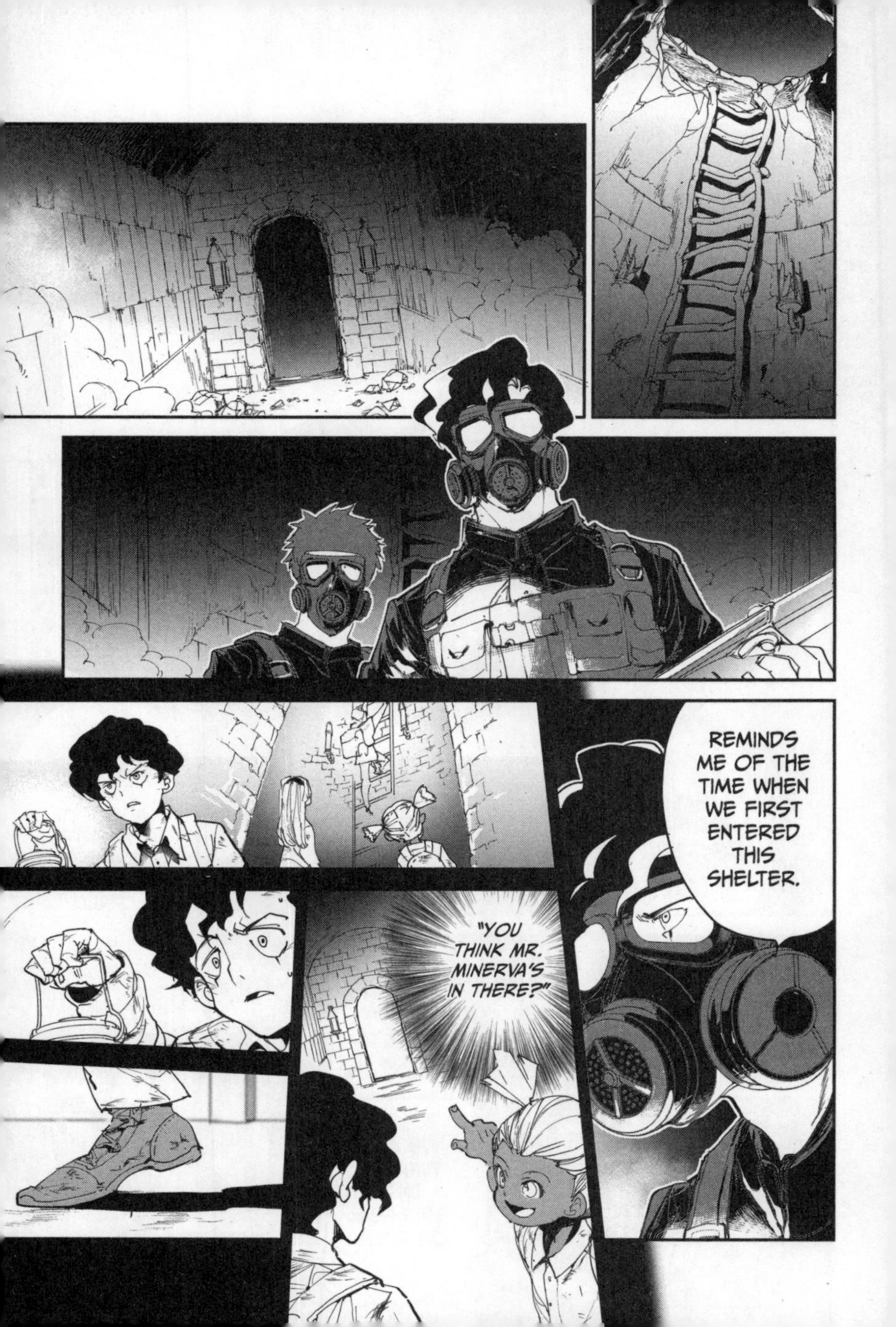
REMINDS ME OF THE TIME WHEN WE FIRST ENTERED THIS SHELTER.
"YOU THINK MR. MINERVA'S IN THERE?"

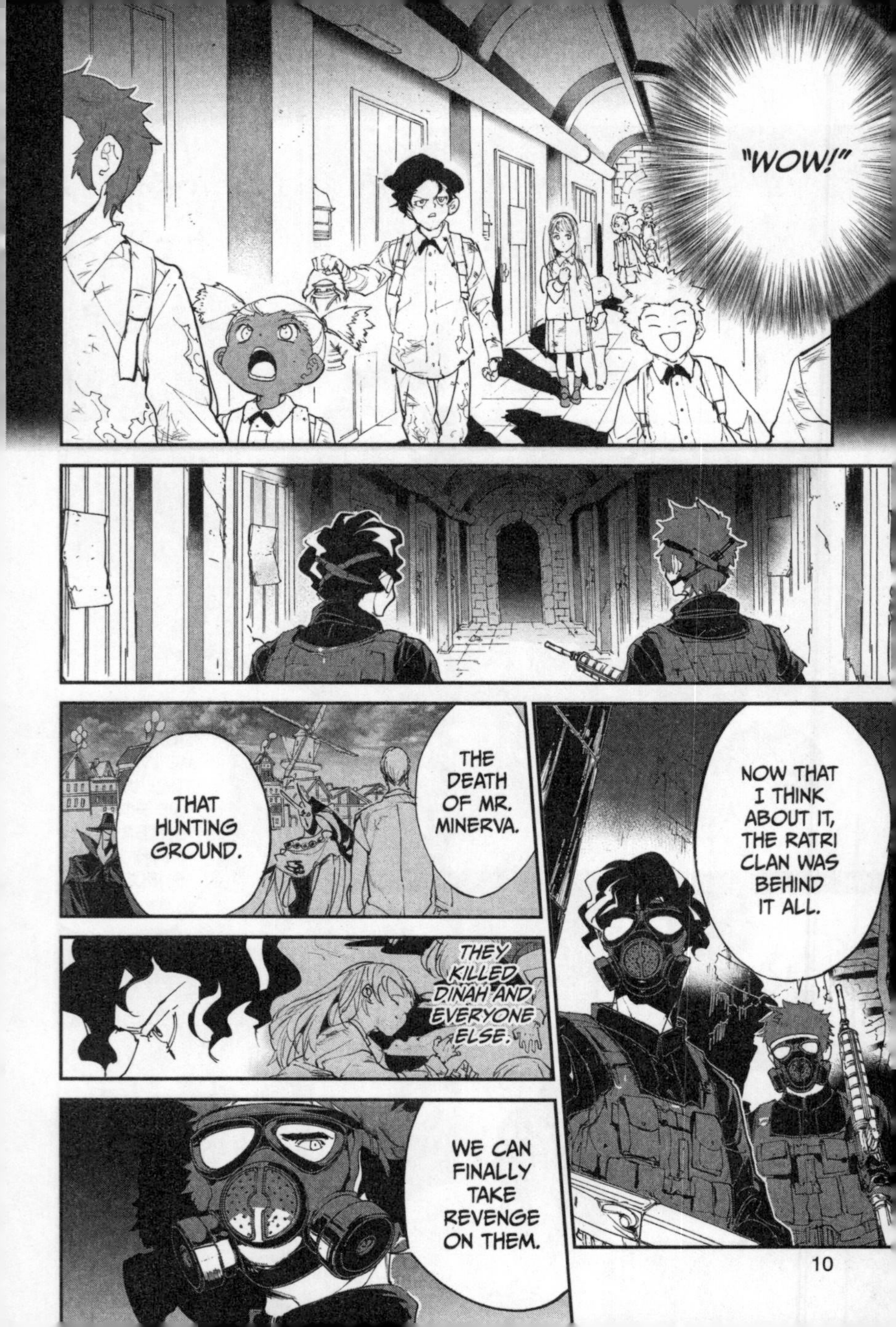
"WOW!"
NOW THAT I THINK ABOUT IT, THE RATRI CLAN WAS BEHIND IT ALL.
THE DEATH OF MR. MINERVA.
THAT HUNTING GROUND.
THEY KILLED DINAH AND EVERYONE ELSE.
WE CAN FINALLY TAKE REVENGE ON THEM.

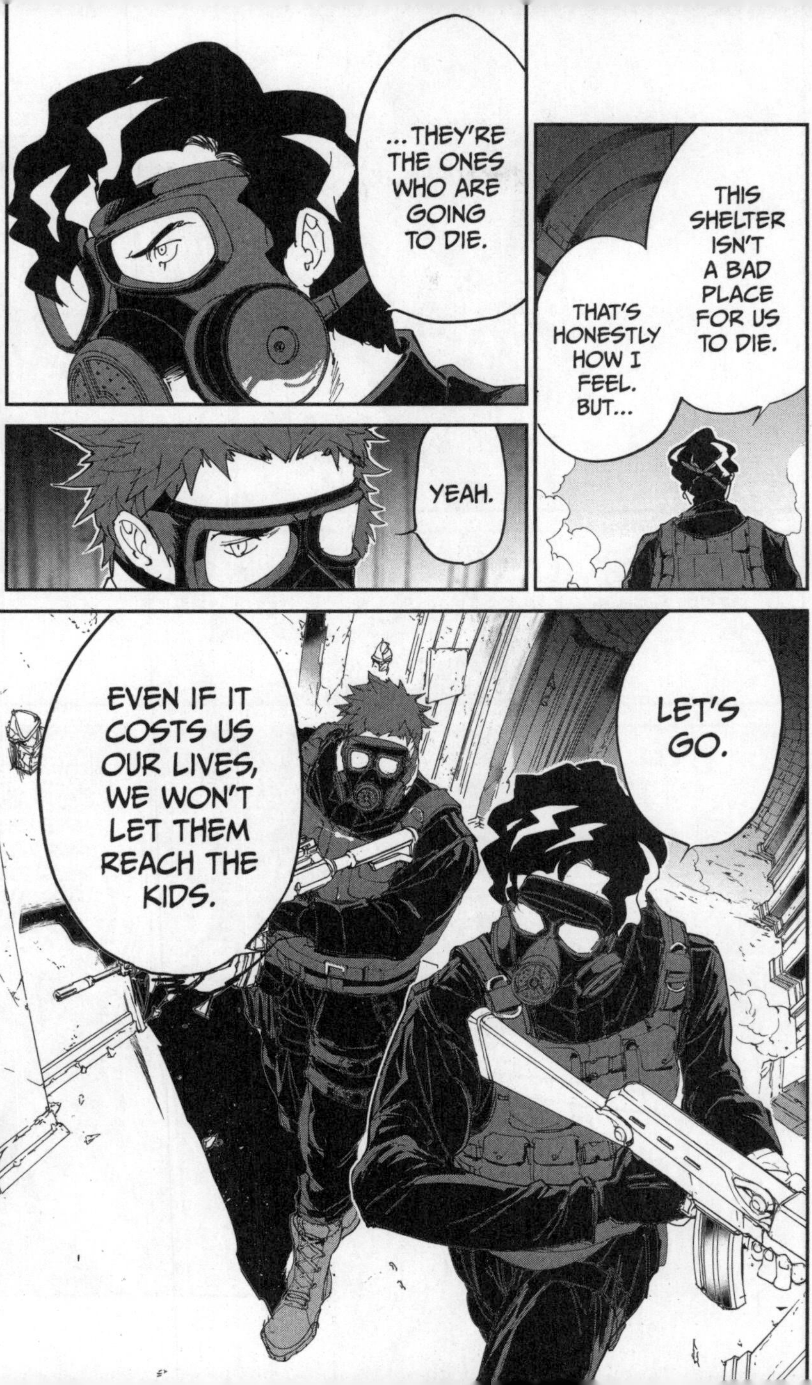

THIS SHELTER ISN'T A BAD PLACE FOR US TO DIE.
THAT'S HONESTLY HOW I FEEL. BUT...
...THEY'RE THE ONES WHO ARE GOING TO DIE.
YEAH.
LET'S GO.
EVEN IF IT COSTS US OUR LIVES, WE WON'T LET THEM REACH THE KIDS.

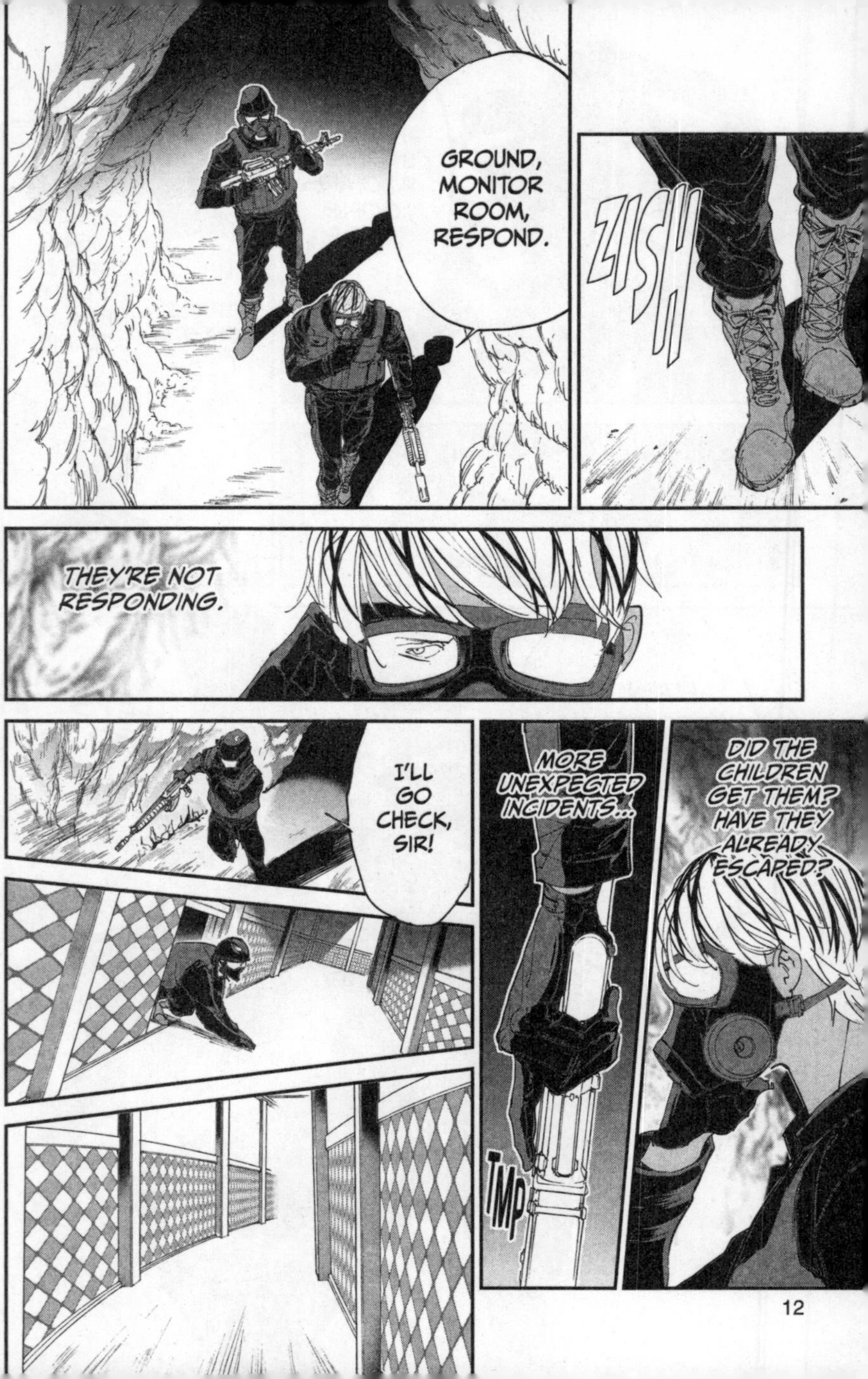
ZISH
GROUND, MONITOR ROOM, RESPOND.
THEY'RE NOT RESPONDING.
DID THE CHILDREN GET THEM? HAVE THEY ALREADY ESCAPED?
MORE UNEXPECTED INCIDENTS...
TMP
I'LL GO CHECK, SIR!

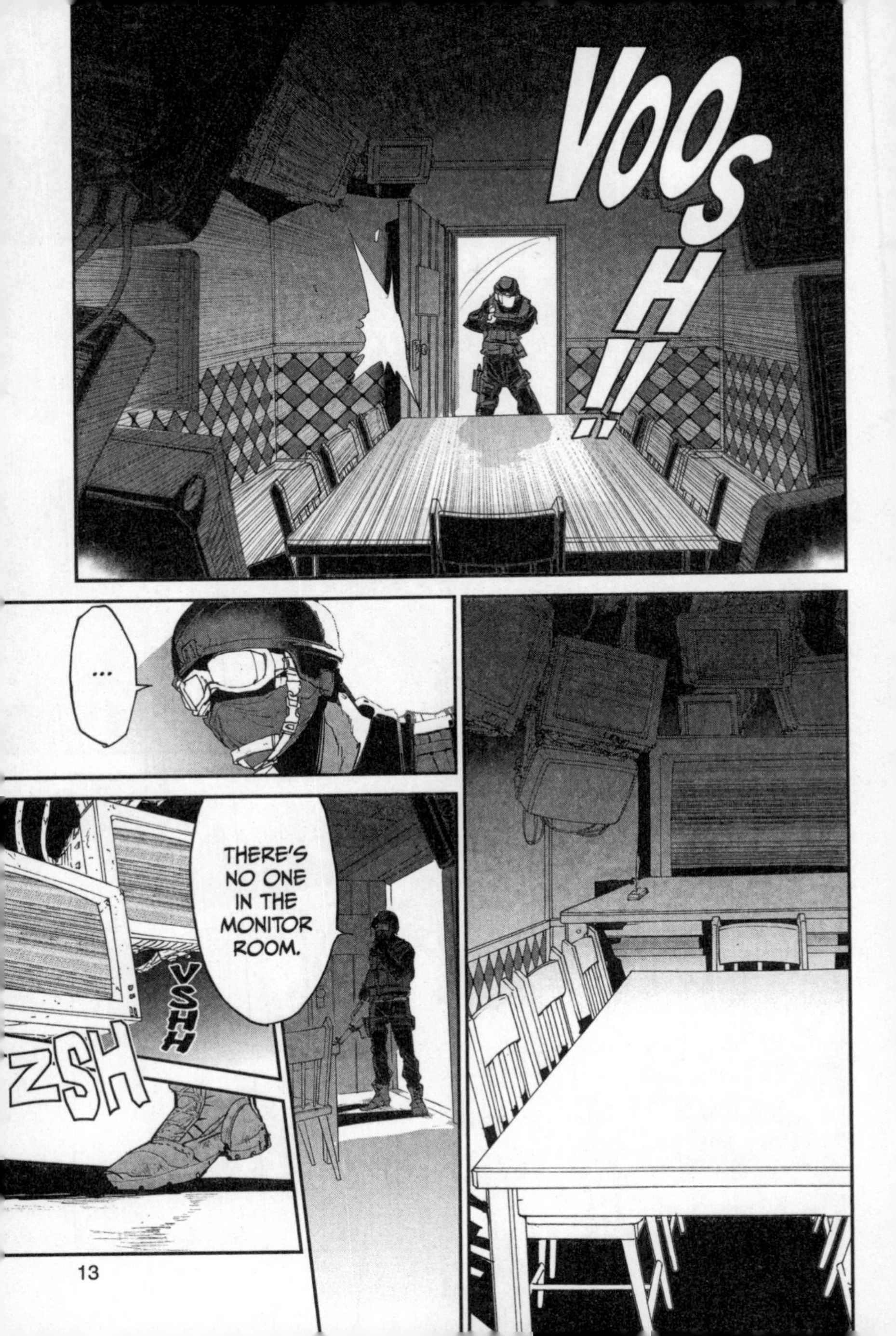
VOOSH!!
...
THERE'S NO ONE IN THE MONITOR ROOM.
VSHH
ZSH

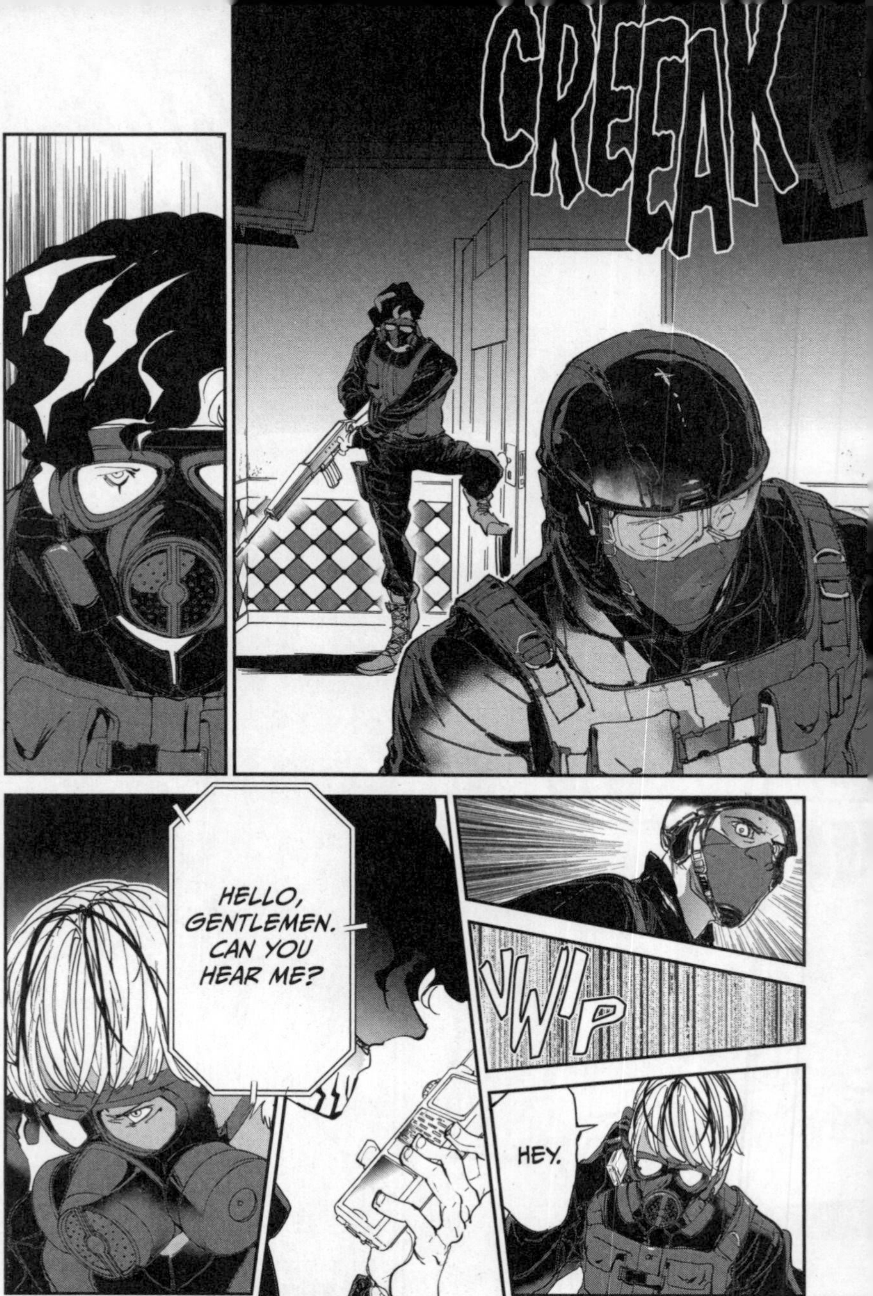
CREEAK
VWIP
HEY.
HELLO, GENTLEMEN. CAN YOU HEAR ME?

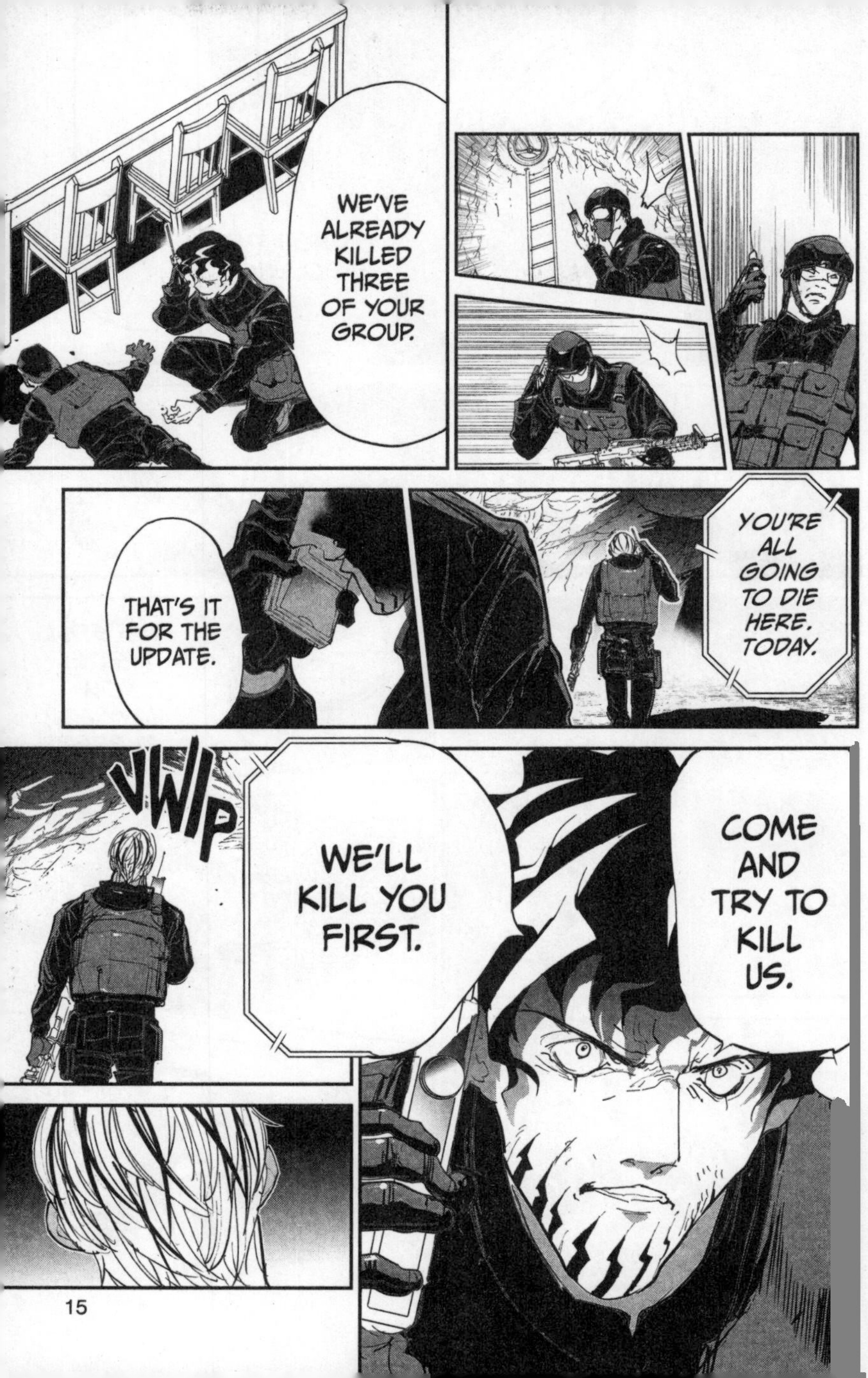
WE'VE ALREADY KILLED THREE OF YOUR GROUP.
YOU'RE ALL GOING TO DIE HERE. TODAY.
THAT'S IT FOR THE UPDATE.
COME AND TRY TO KILL US.
WE'LL KILL YOU FIRST.
VWIP

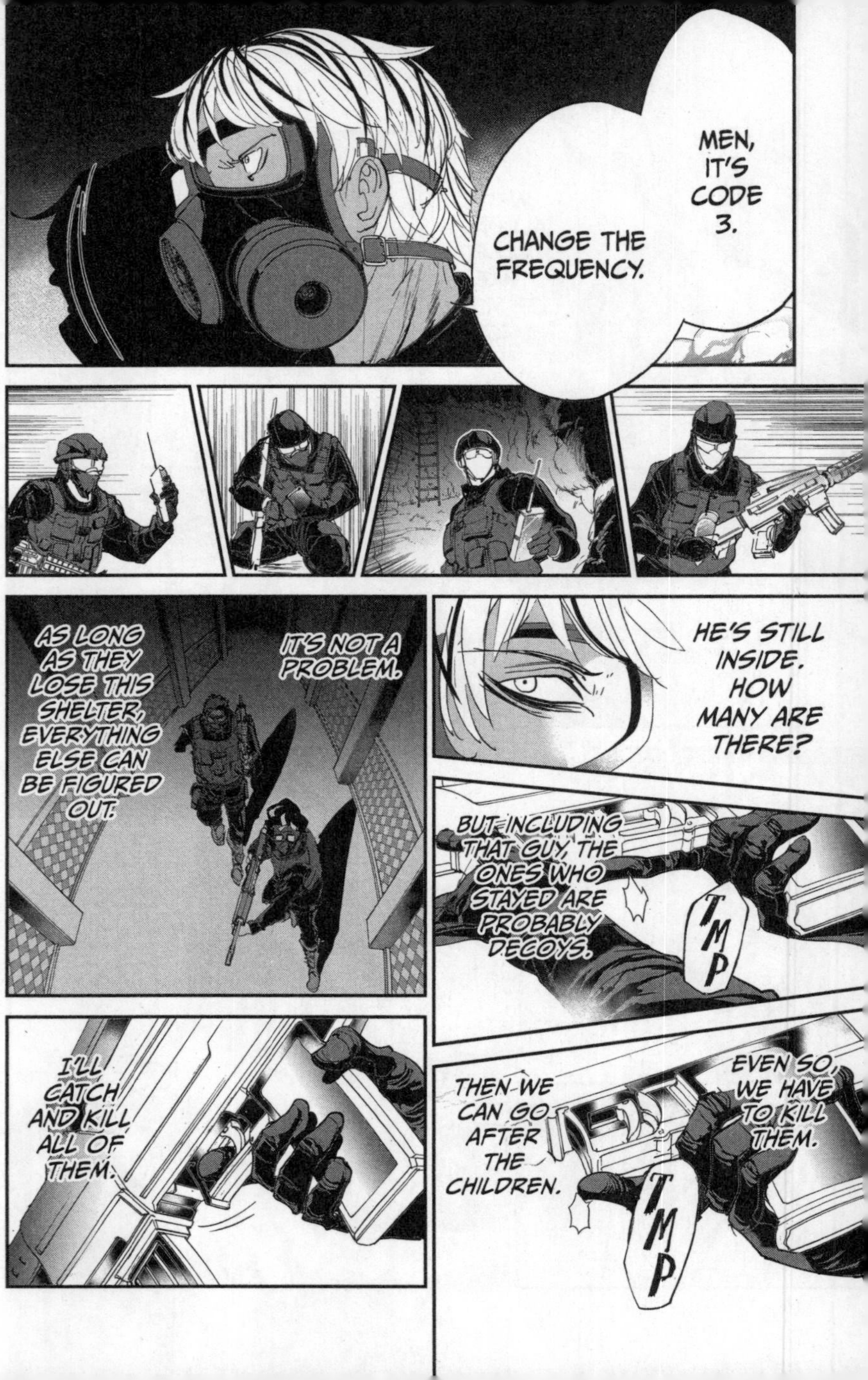
MEN, IT'S CODE 3.
CHANGE THE FREQUENCY.
HE'S STILL INSIDE. HOW MANY ARE THERE?
BUT INCLUDING THAT GUY, THE ONES WHO STAYED ARE PROBABLY DECOYS.
TMP
IT'S NOT A PROBLEM.
AS LONG AS THEY LOSE THIS SHELTER, EVERYTHING ELSE CAN BE FIGURED OUT.
EVEN SO, WE HAVE TO KILL THEM.
THEN WE CAN GO AFTER THE CHILDREN.
TMP
I'LL CATCH AND KILL ALL OF THEM.

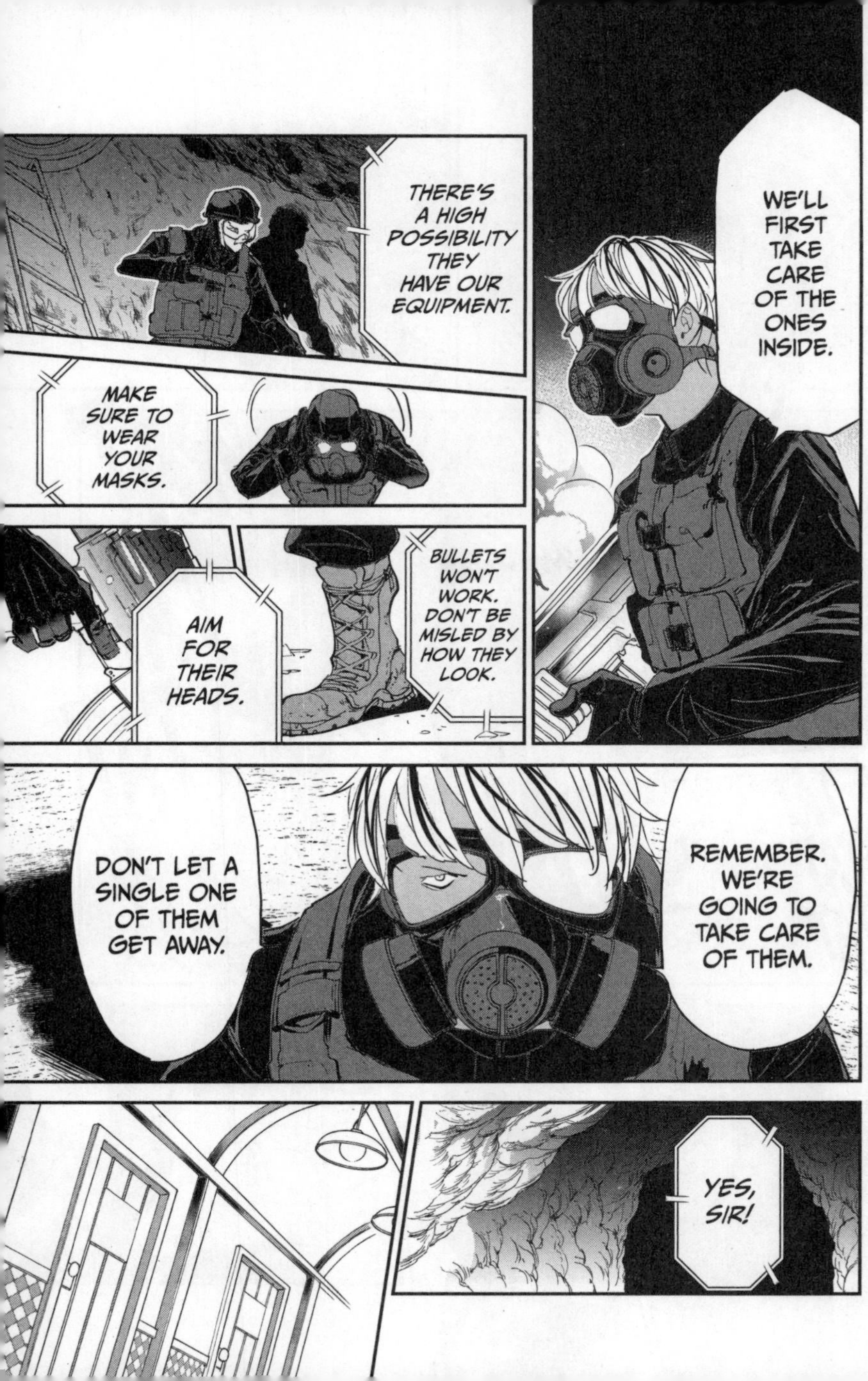
WE'LL FIRST TAKE CARE OF THE ONES INSIDE.
THERE'S A HIGH POSSIBILITY THEY HAVE OUR EQUIPMENT.
MAKE SURE TO WEAR YOUR MASKS.
BULLETS WON'T WORK. DON'T BE MISLED BY HOW THEY LOOK.
AIM FOR THEIR HEADS.
REMEMBER. WE'RE GOING TO TAKE CARE OF THEM.
DON'T LET A SINGLE ONE OF THEM GET AWAY.
YES, SIR!

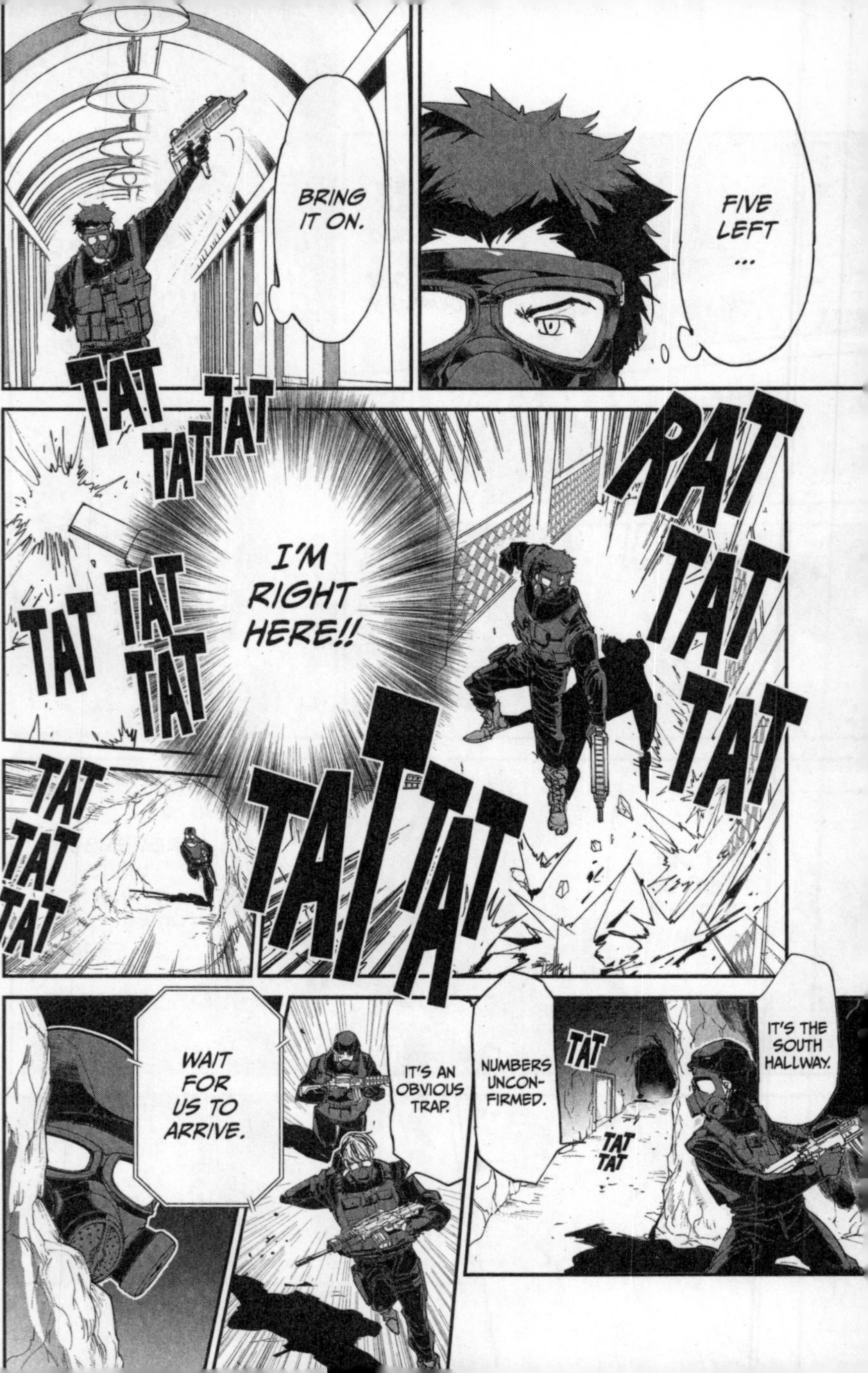
FIVE LEFT ...
BRING IT ON.
TAT TAT TAT
RAT TAT TAT TAT
I'M RIGHT HERE!!
TAT TAT TAT
TAT
TATATAT
TAT TAT TAT TAT
IT'S THE SOUTH HALLWAY.
TAT
TAT TAT
NUMBERS UNCON-FIRMED.
IT'S AN OBVIOUS TRAP.
WAIT FOR US TO ARRIVE.

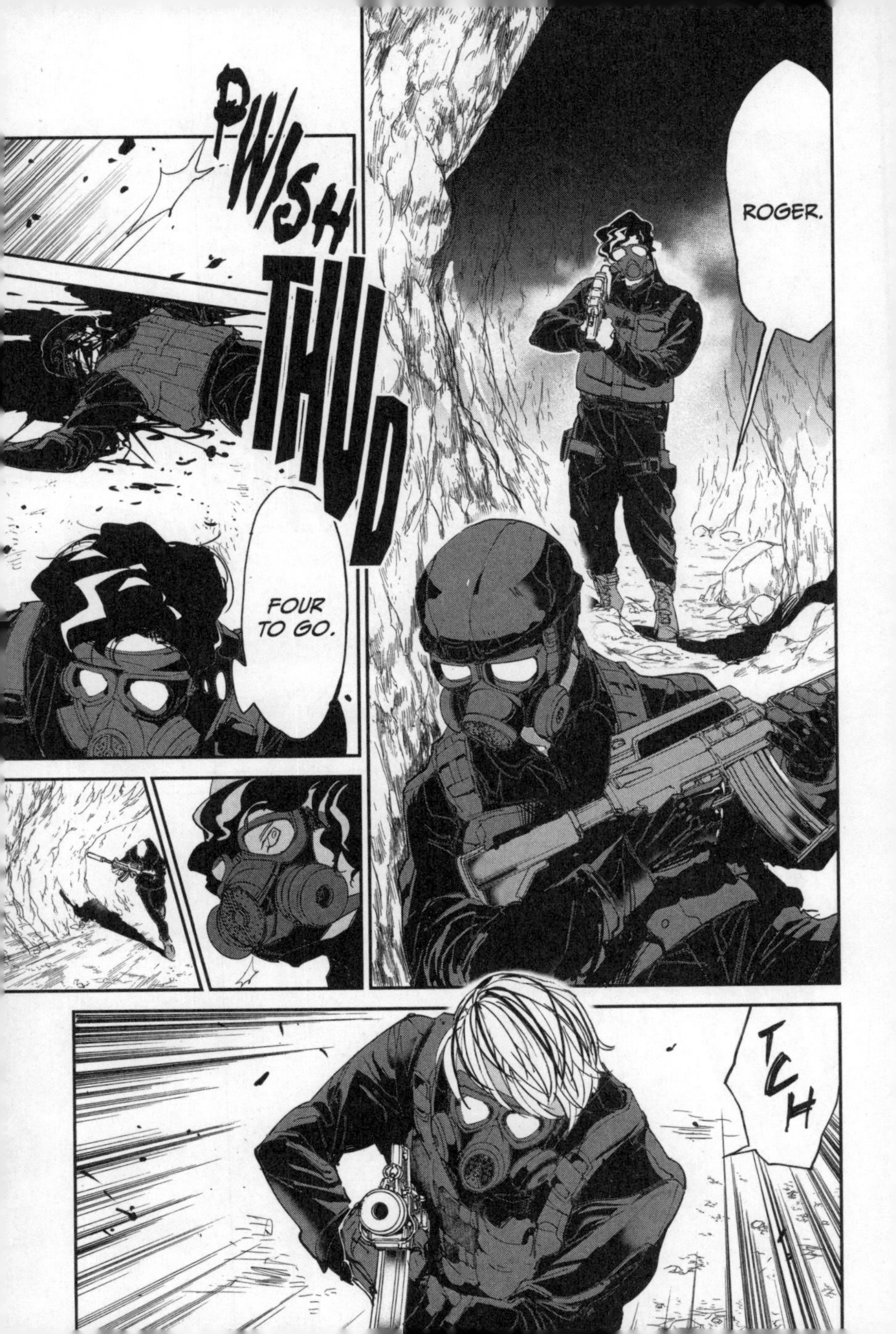
ROGER.
PWISH
THUD
FOUR TO GO.
TCH

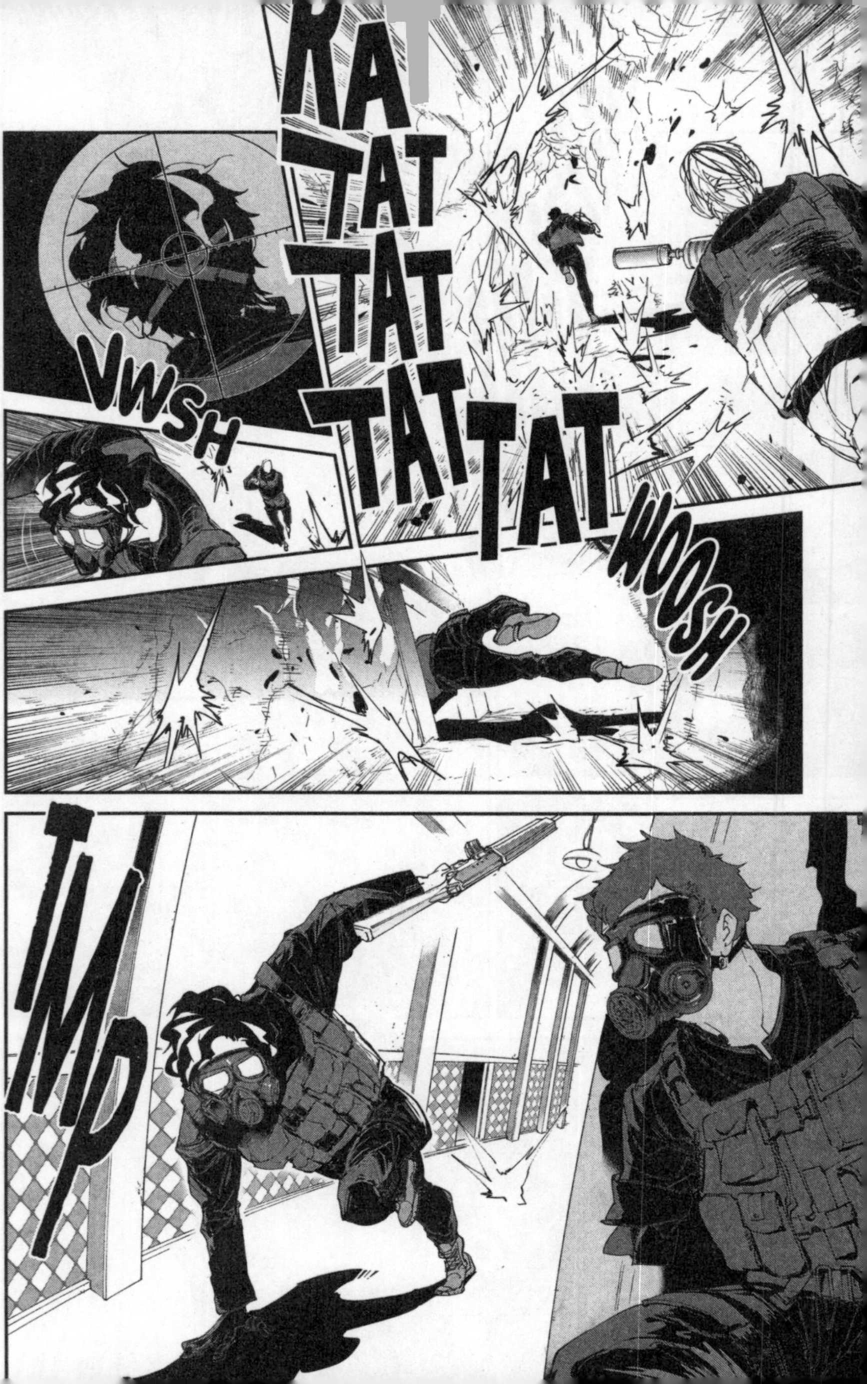
KA TAT TAT TAT TAT
VWSH
WOOSH
TMP

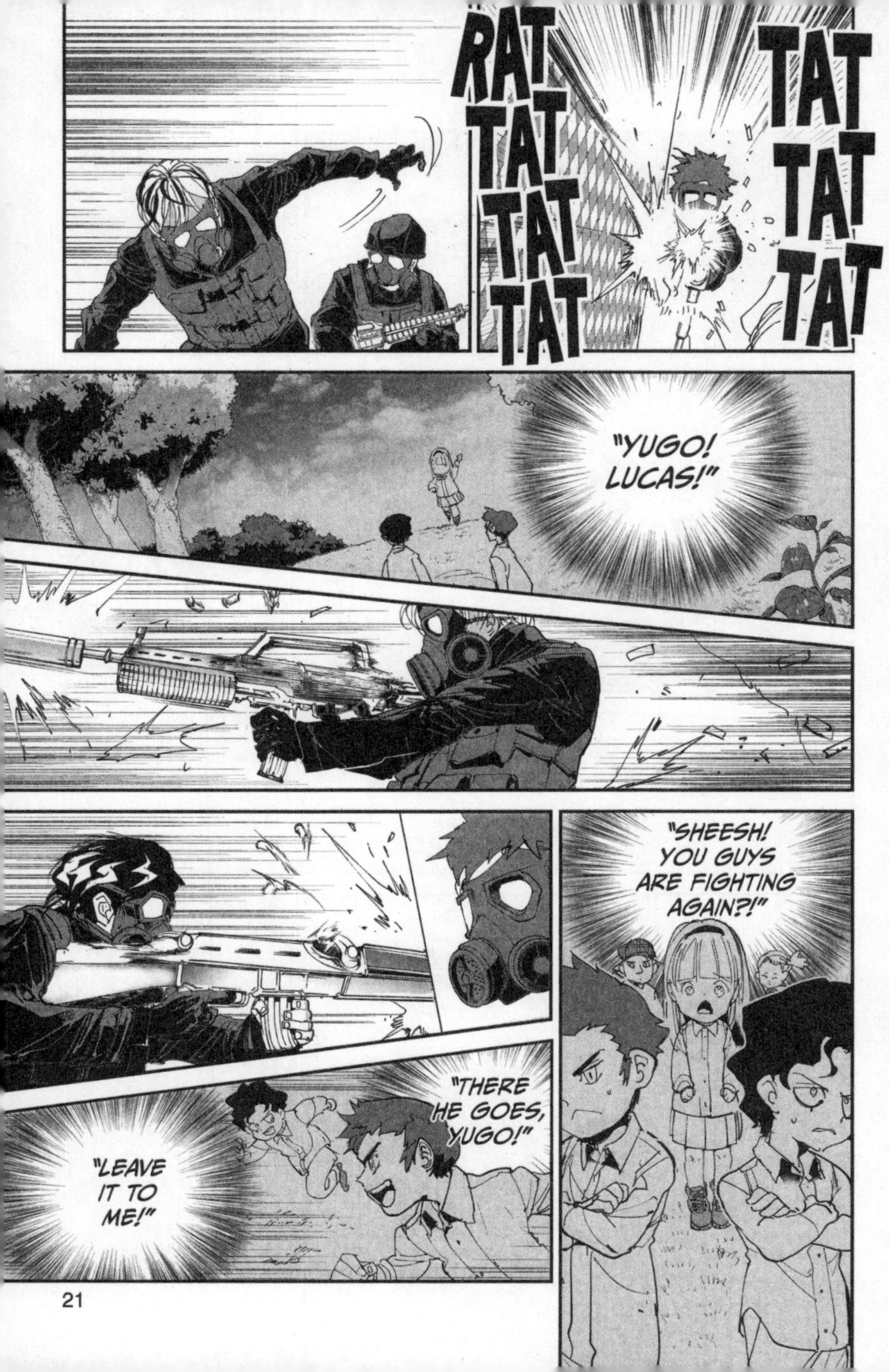
TAT TAT TAT TAT
RAT TAT TAT TAT TAT
"YUGO! LUCAS!"
"SHEESH! YOU GUYS ARE FIGHTING AGAIN?!"
"THERE HE GOES, YUGO!"
"LEAVE IT TO ME!"

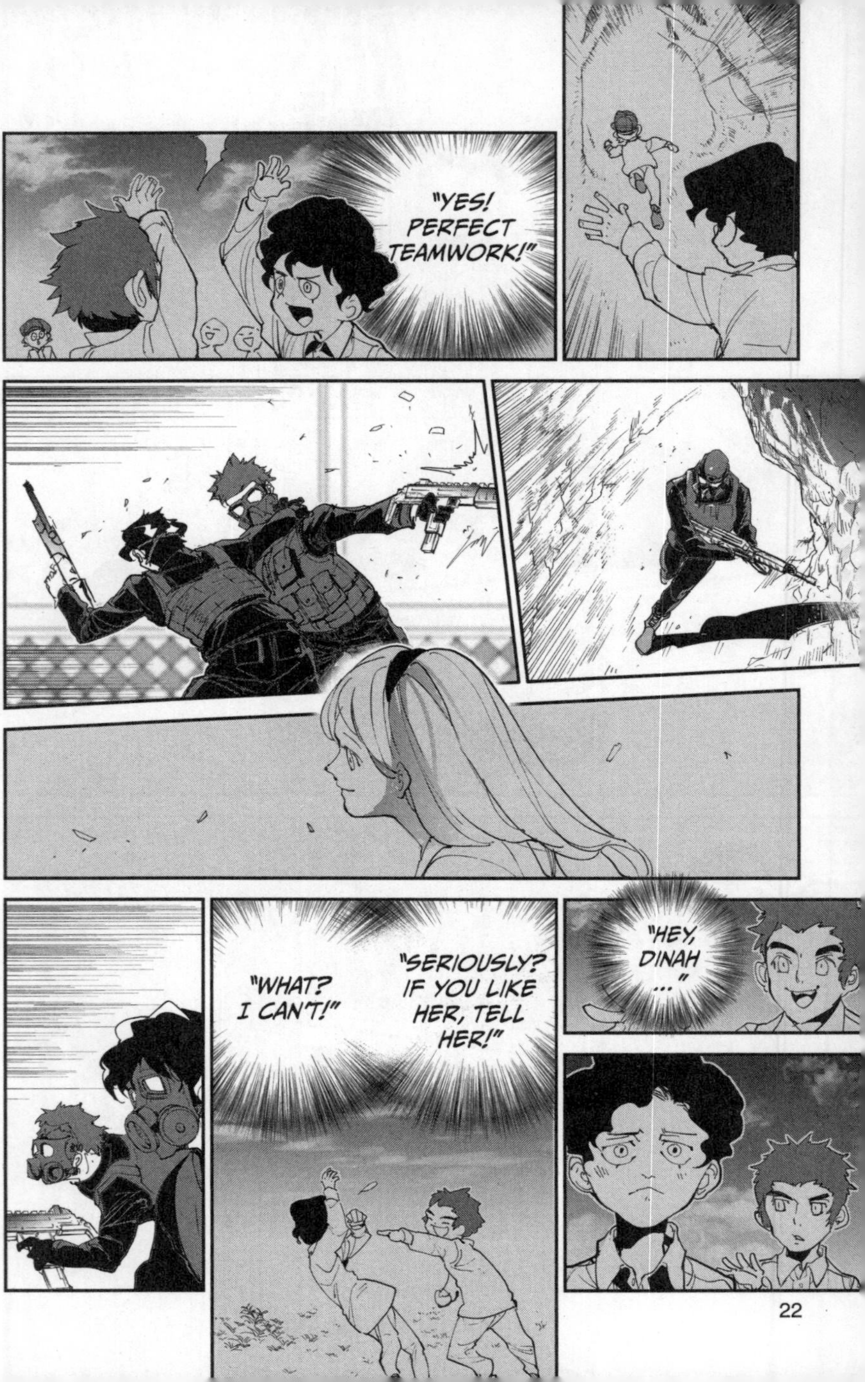
"YES! PERFECT TEAMWORK!"
"HEY, DINAH ..."
"SERIOUSLY? IF YOU LIKE HER, TELL HER!"
"WHAT? I CAN'T!"

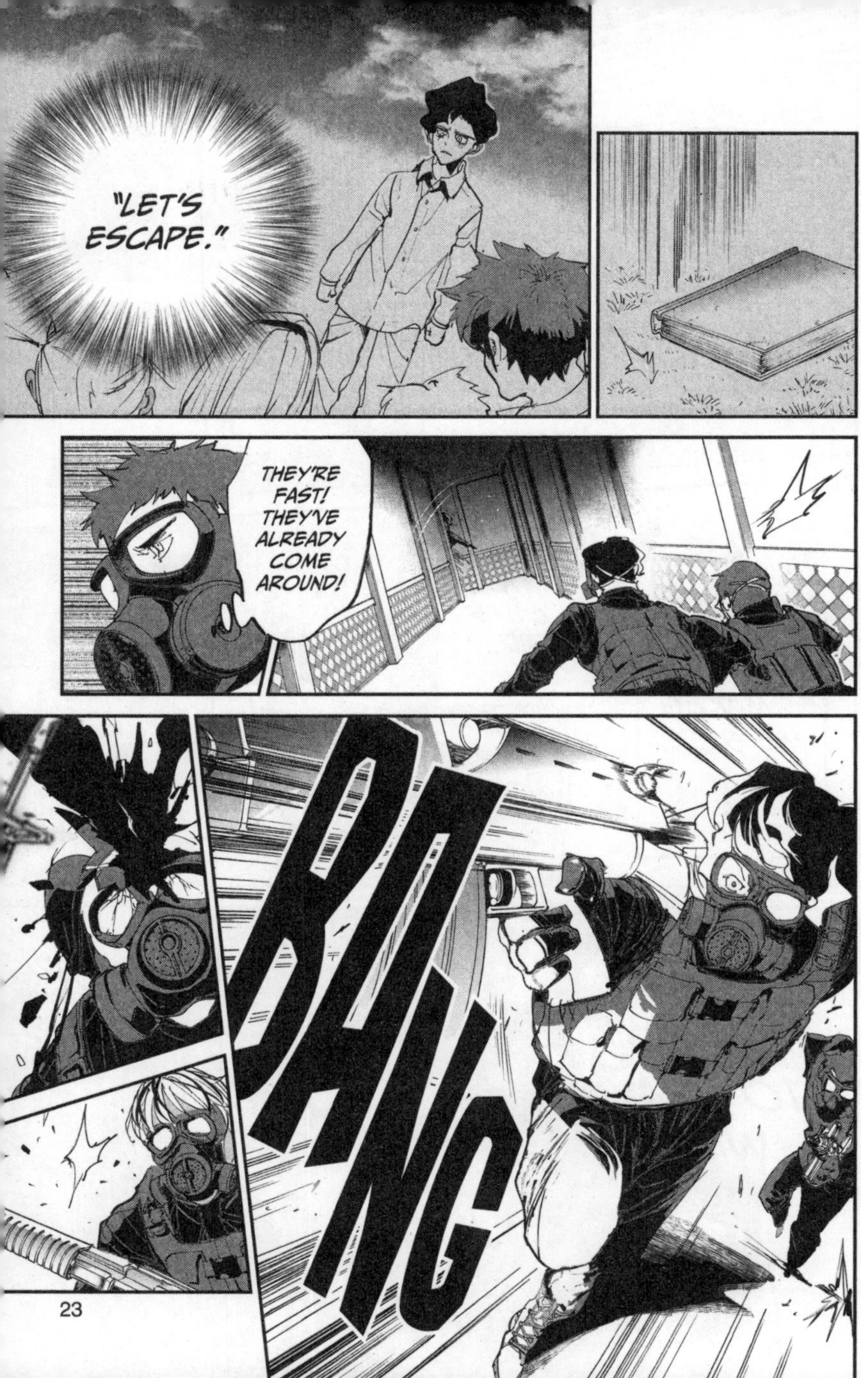
"LET'S ESCAPE."
THEY'RE FAST! THEY'VE ALREADY COME AROUND!
BANG

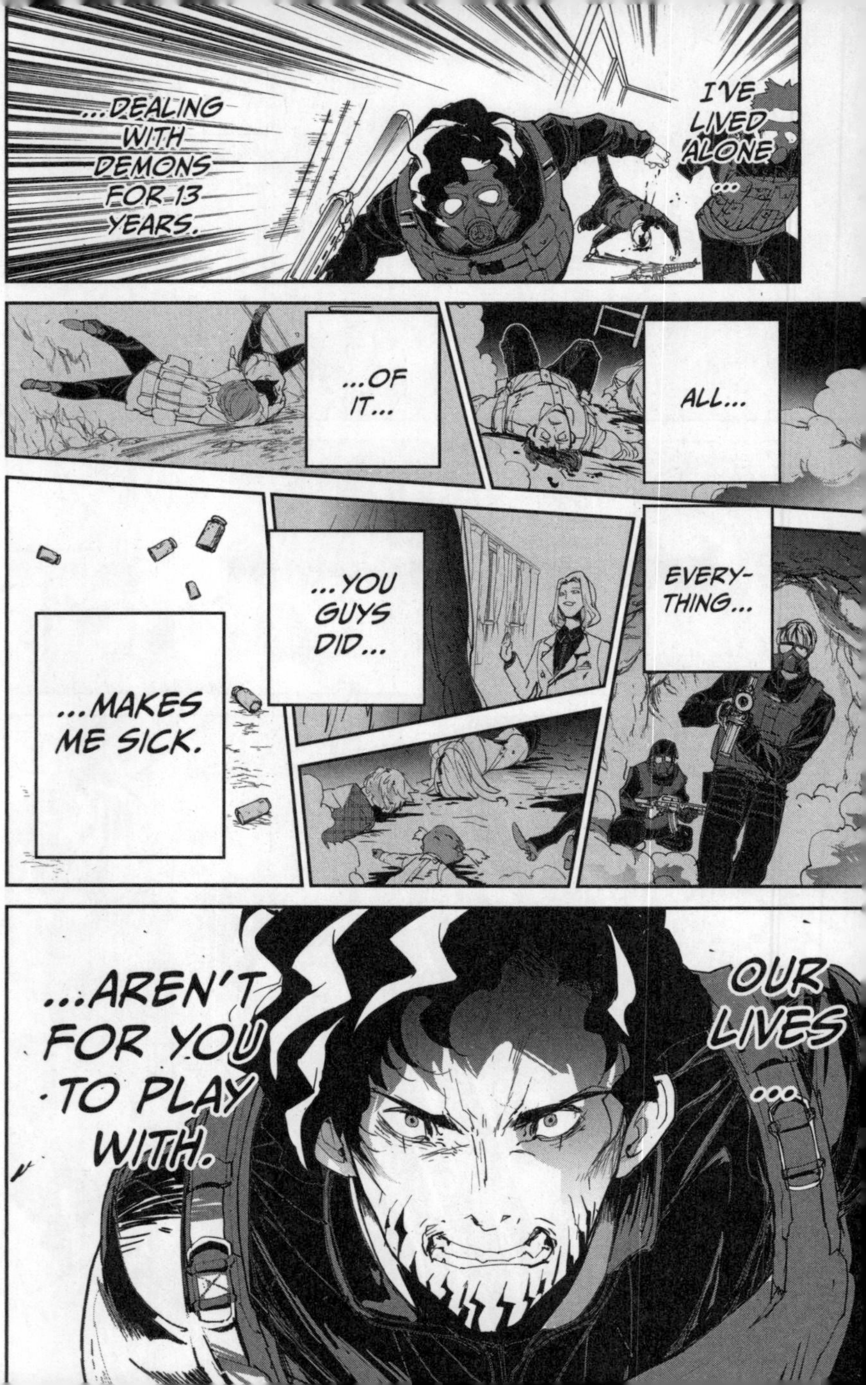
I'VE LIVED ALONE...
...DEALING WITH DEMONS FOR 13 YEARS.
ALL...
...OF IT...
EVERY-THING...
...YOU GUYS DID...
...MAKES ME SICK.
OUR LIVES...
...AREN'T FOR YOU TO PLAY WITH.

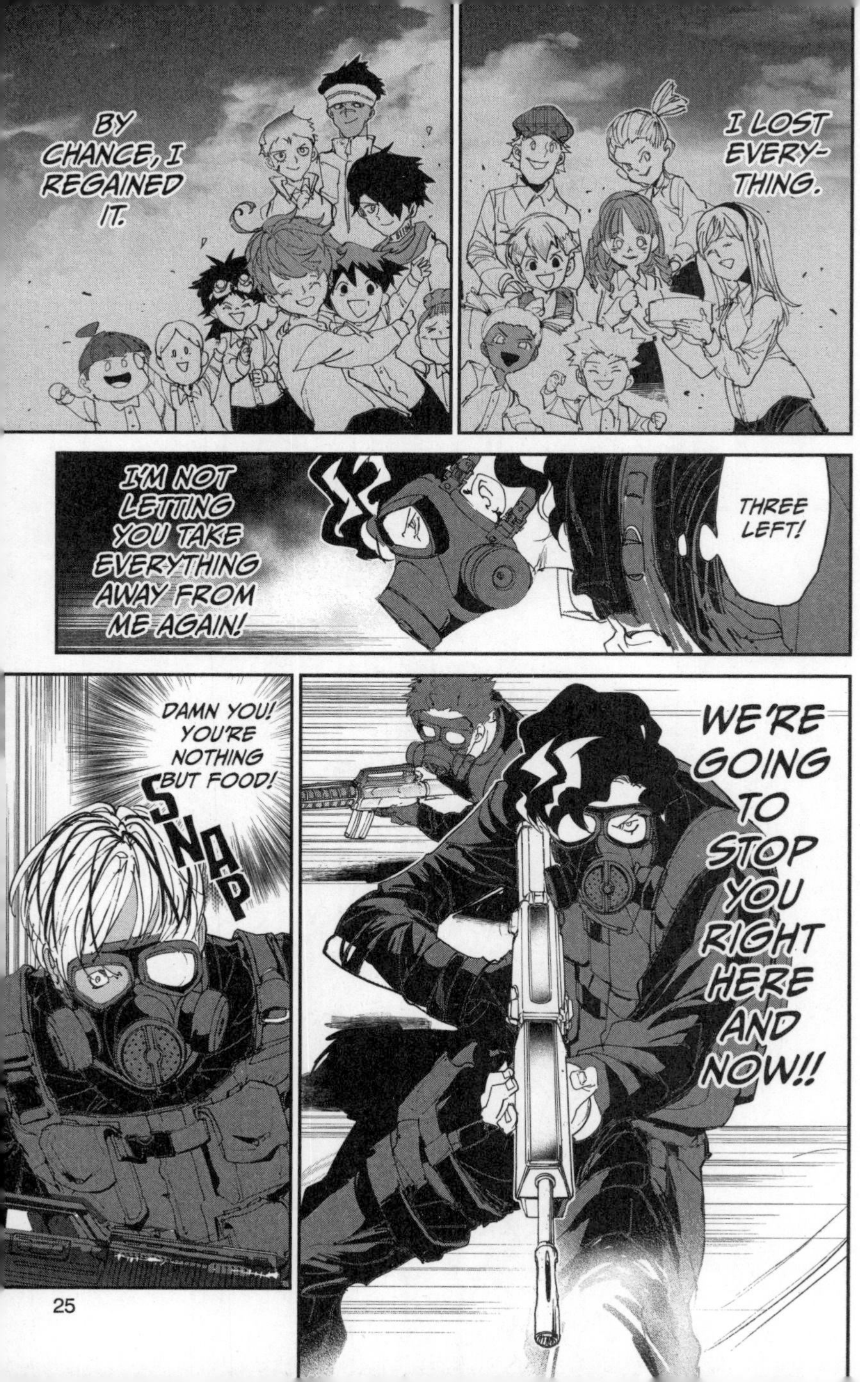
I LOST EVERY-THING.
BY CHANCE, I REGAINED IT.
THREE LEFT!
I'M NOT LETTING YOU TAKE EVERYTHING AWAY FROM ME AGAIN!
WE'RE GOING TO STOP YOU RIGHT HERE AND NOW!!
DAMN YOU! YOU'RE NOTHING BUT FOOD!
SNAP

CHAPTER 108: YOU'RE NOT GOING ANYWHERE

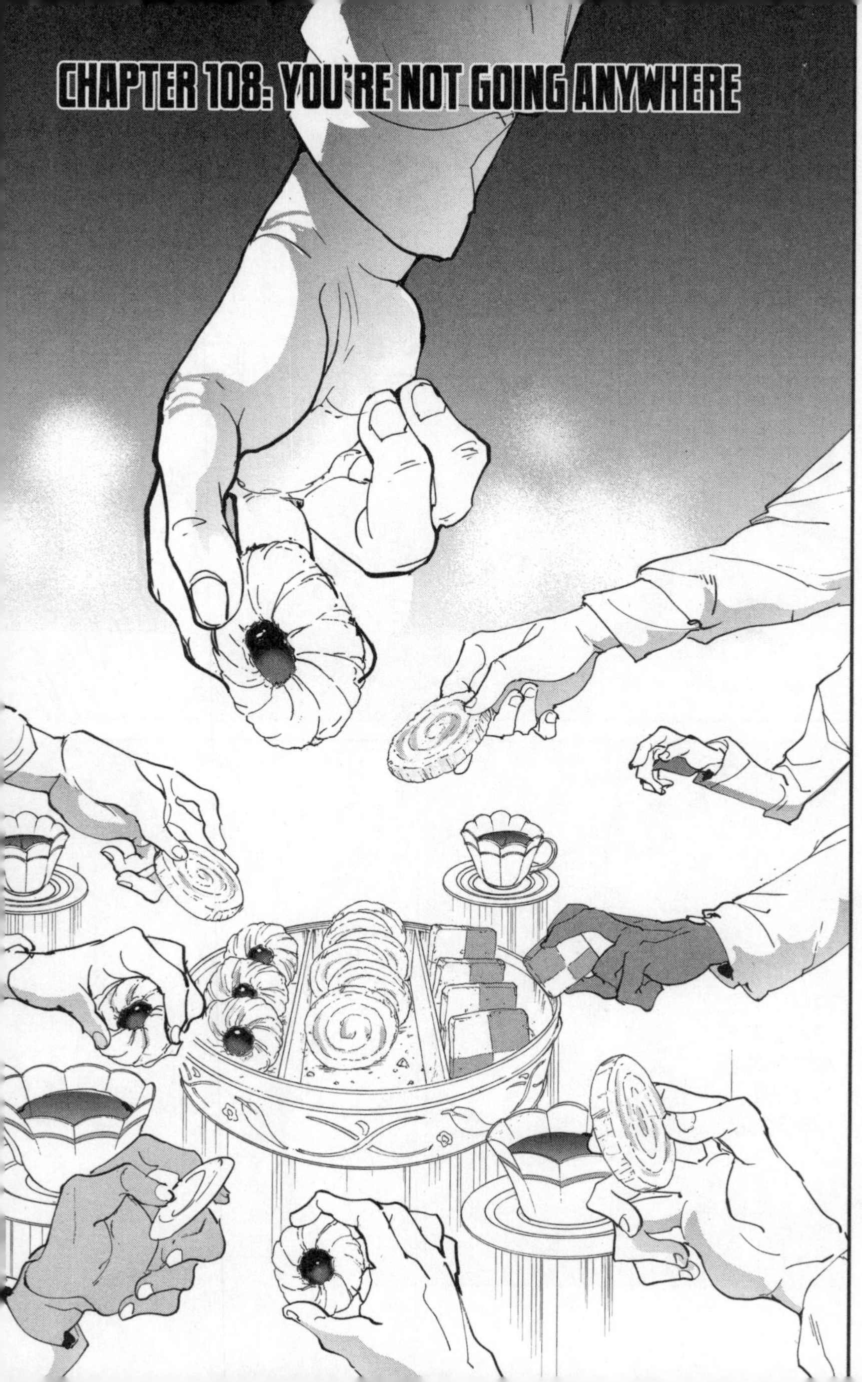

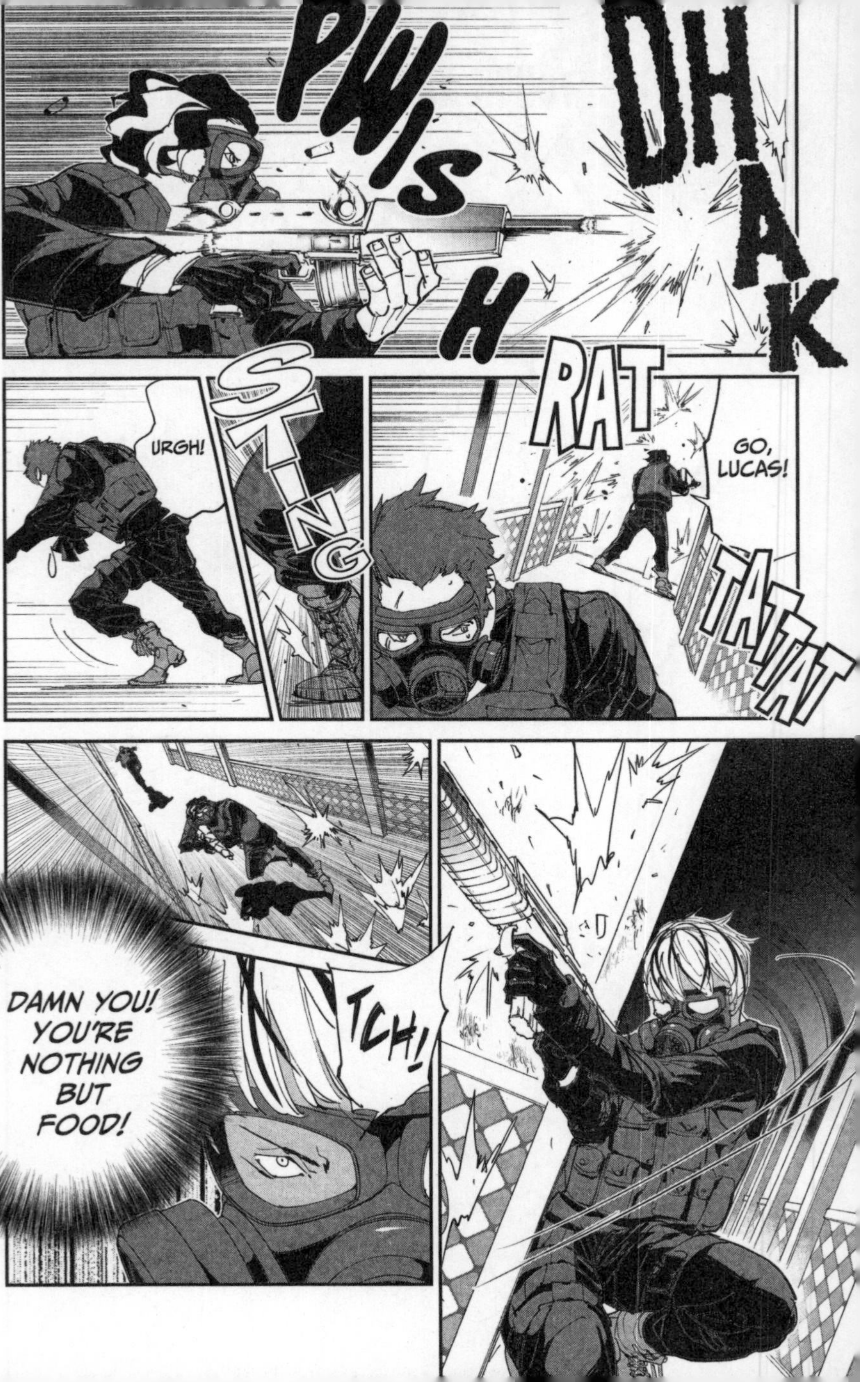
DHAK
PWISH
RAT
GO, LUCAS!
TATATAT
STING
URGH!
DAMN YOU! YOU'RE NOTHING BUT FOOD!
TCH!

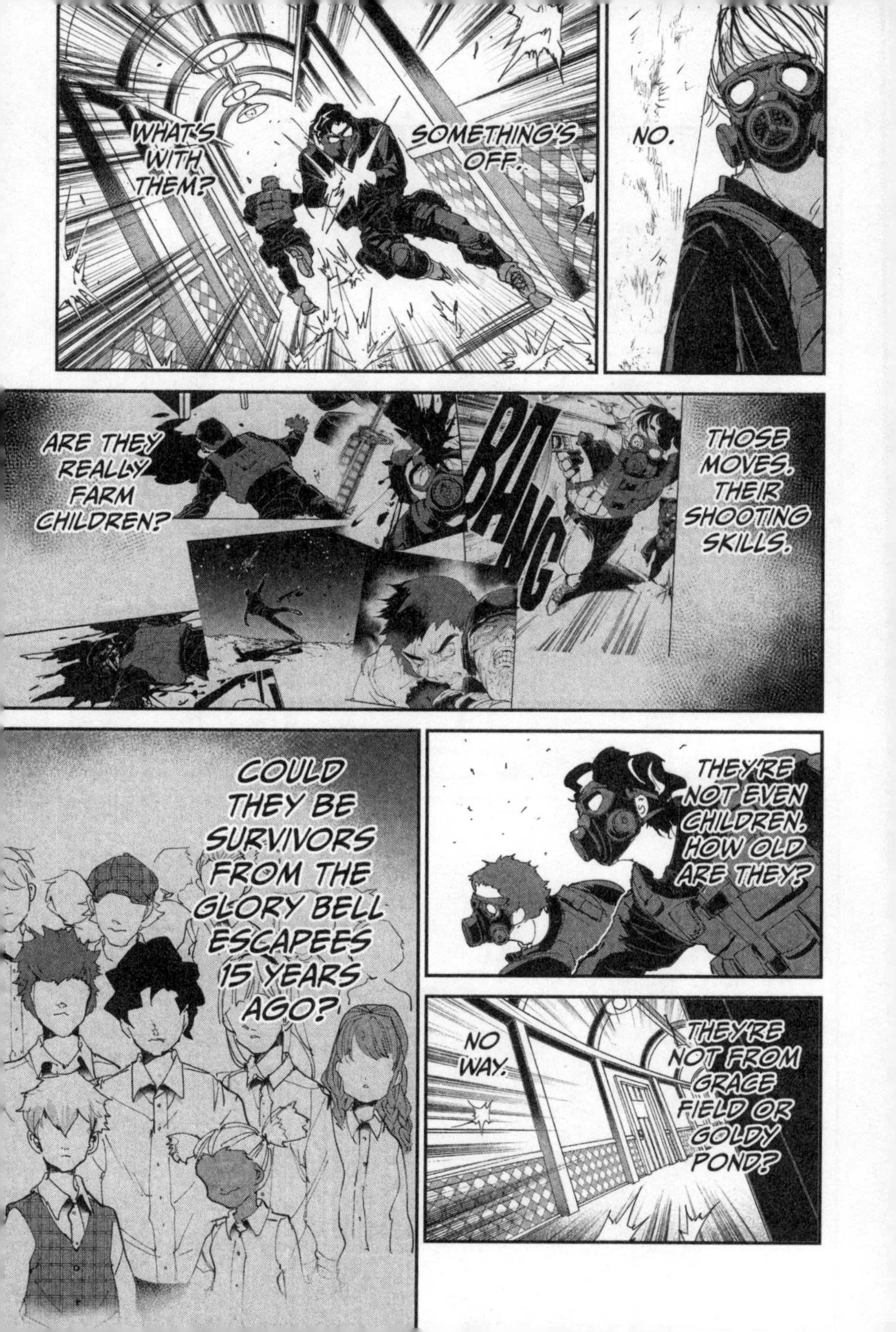
NO.
SOMETHING'S OFF.
WHAT'S WITH THEM?
THOSE MOVES. THEIR SHOOTING SKILLS.
BANG
ARE THEY REALLY FARM CHILDREN?
THEY'RE NOT EVEN CHILDREN. HOW OLD ARE THEY?
THEY'RE NOT FROM GRACE FIELD OR GOLDY POND?
NO WAY.
COULD THEY BE SURVIVORS FROM THE GLORY BELL ESCAPEES 15 YEARS AGO?

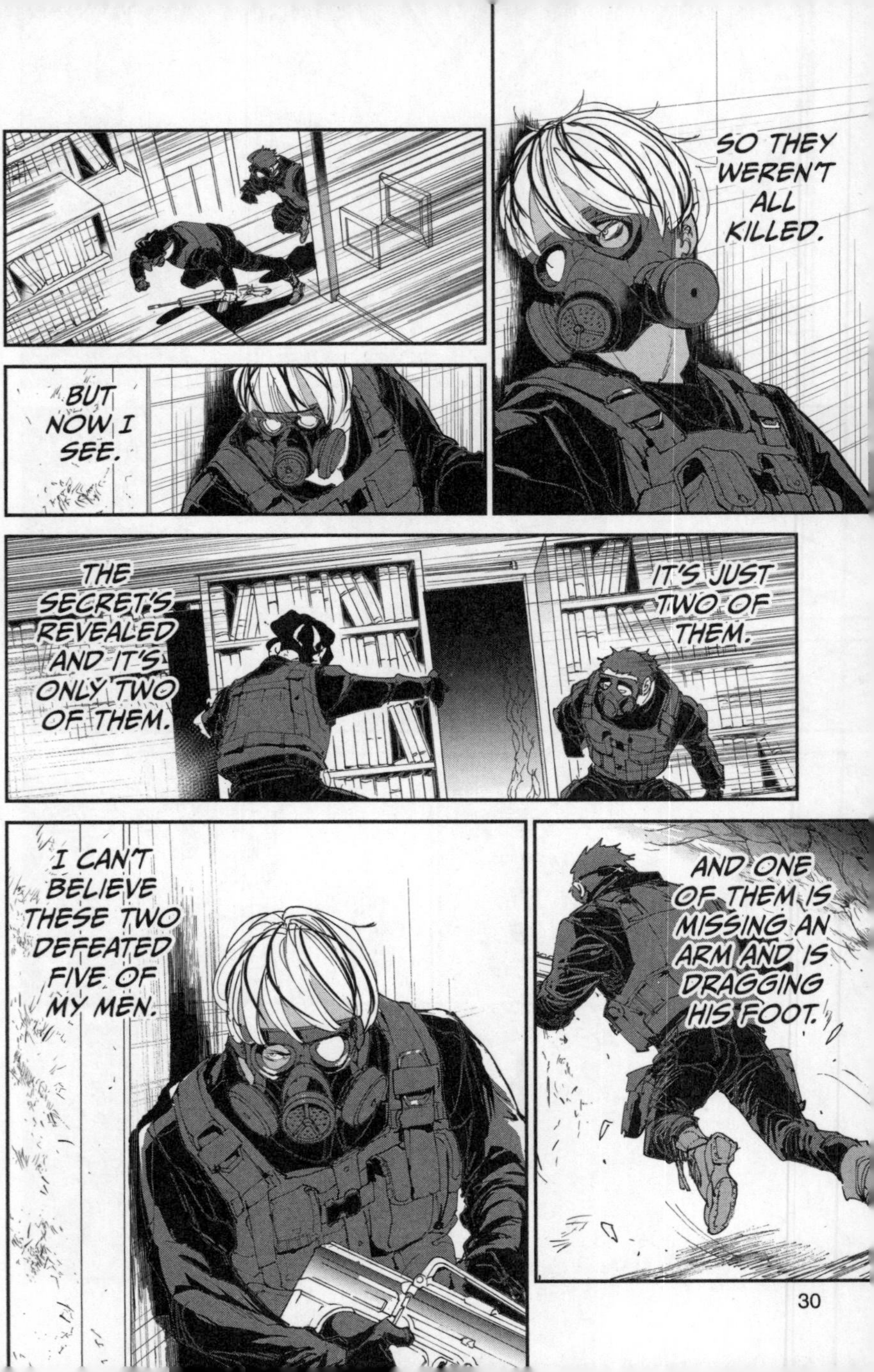
SO THEY WEREN'T ALL KILLED.
BUT NOW I SEE.
IT'S JUST TWO OF THEM.
THE SECRET'S REVEALED AND IT'S ONLY TWO OF THEM.
AND ONE OF THEM IS MISSING AN ARM AND IS DRAGGING HIS FOOT.
I CAN'T BELIEVE THESE TWO DEFEATED FIVE OF MY MEN.

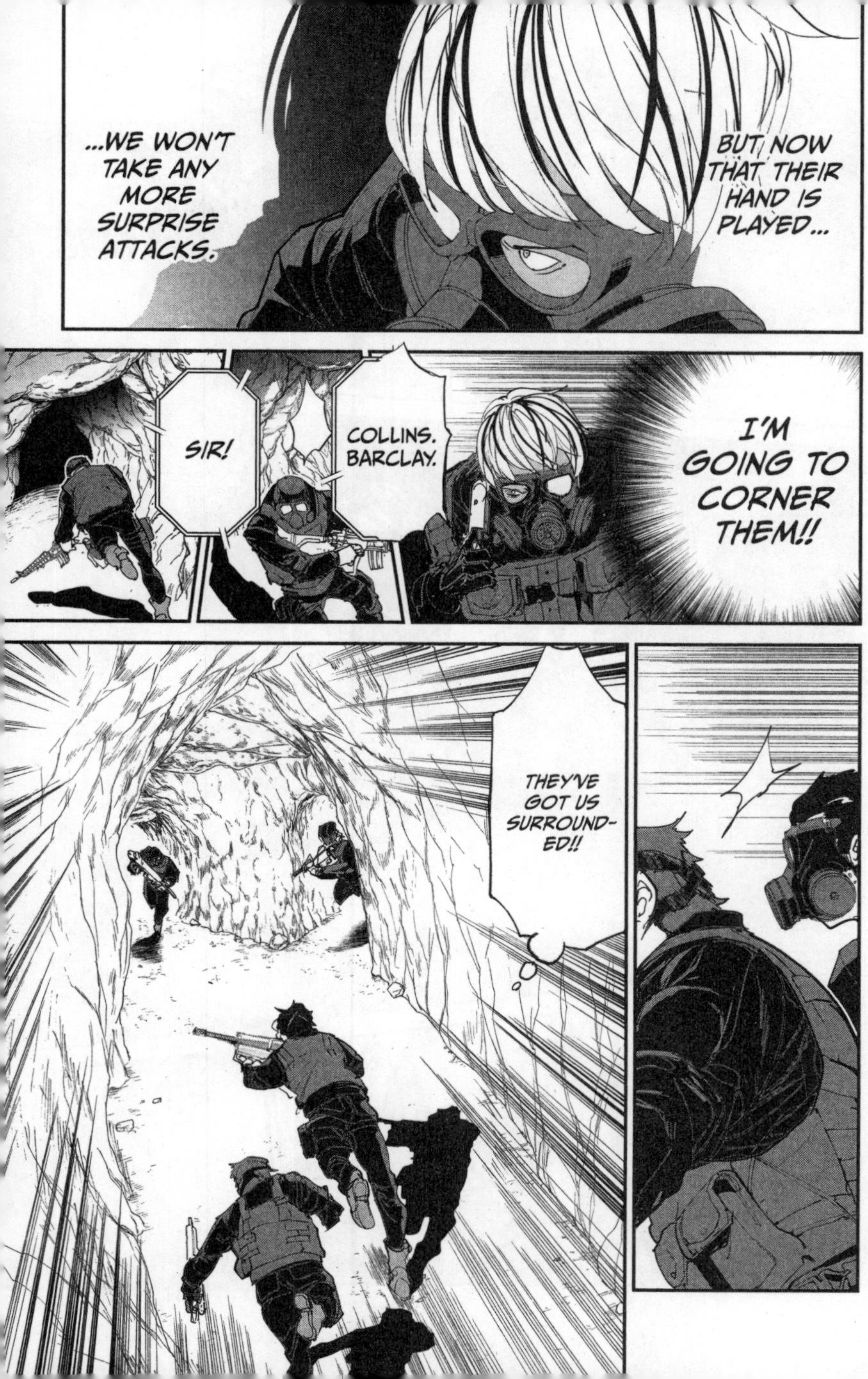
BUT NOW THAT THEIR HAND IS PLAYED...
...WE WON'T TAKE ANY MORE SURPRISE ATTACKS.
I'M GOING TO CORNER THEM!!
COLLINS. BARCLAY.
SIR!
THEY'VE GOT US SURROUND-ED!!

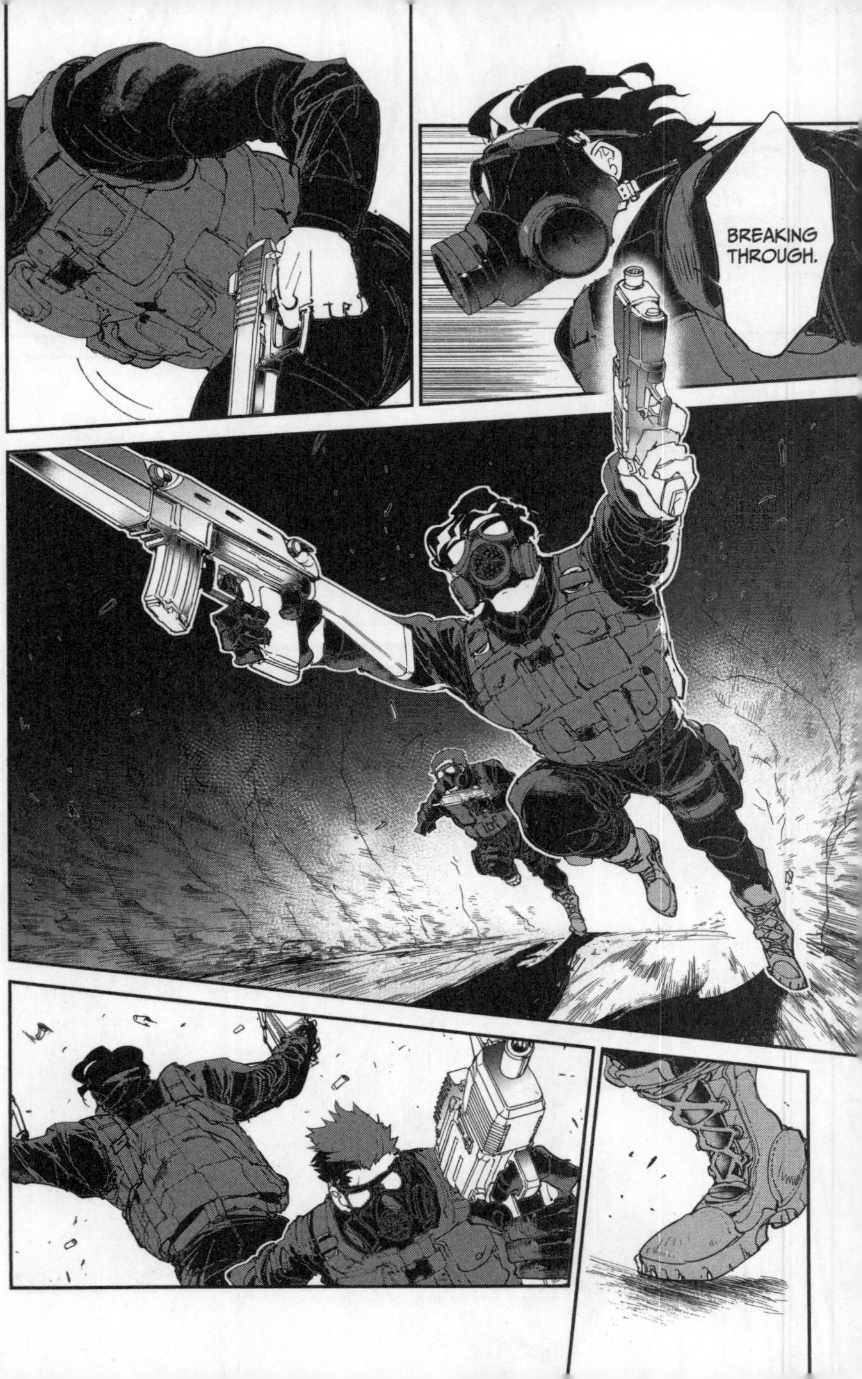
BREAKING THROUGH.

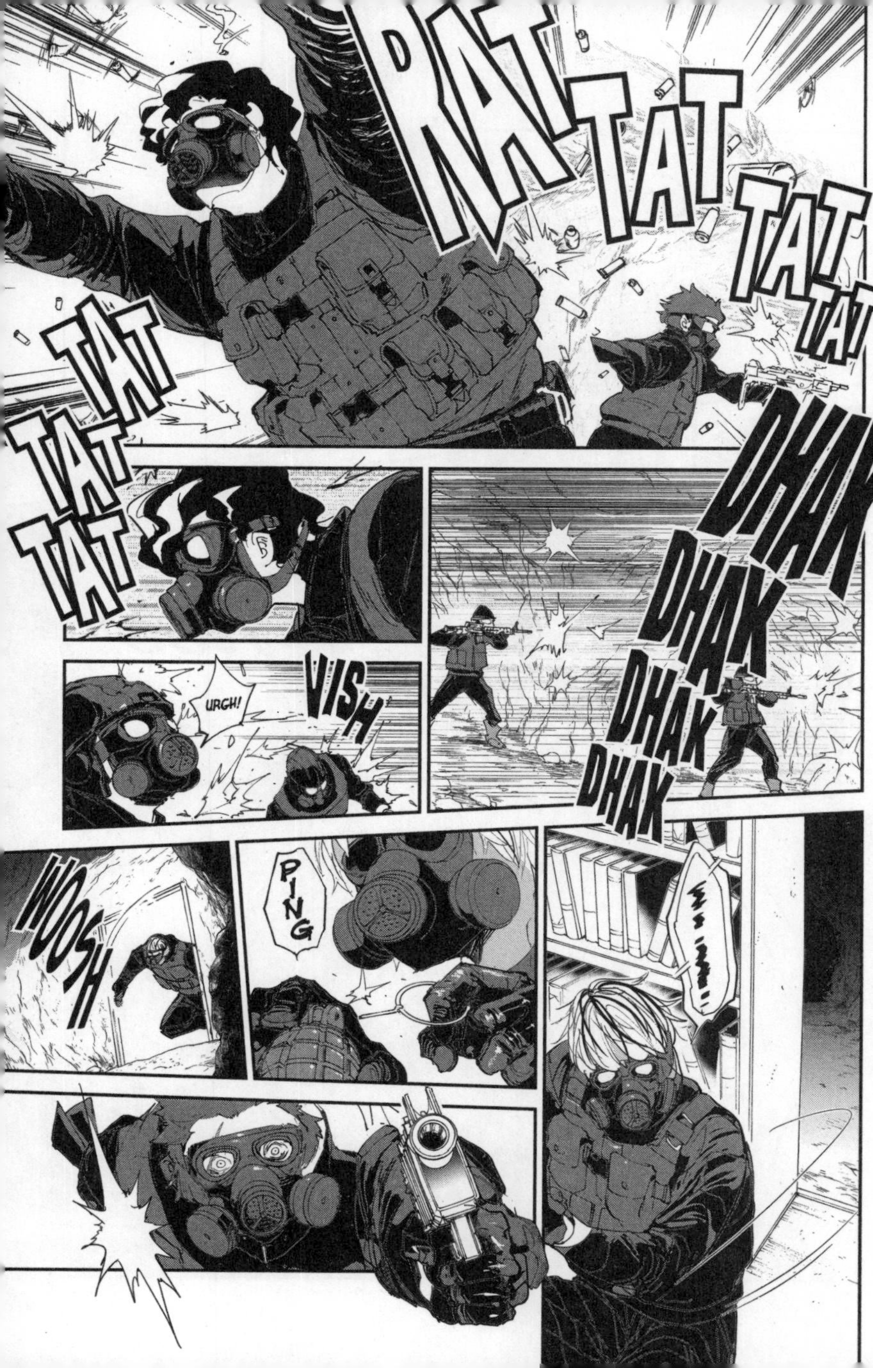
RAT-TAT
TAT TAT TAT
TAT TAT TAT TAT
DHAK DHAK DHAK DHAK
VISH
URGH!
PING
WOOSH

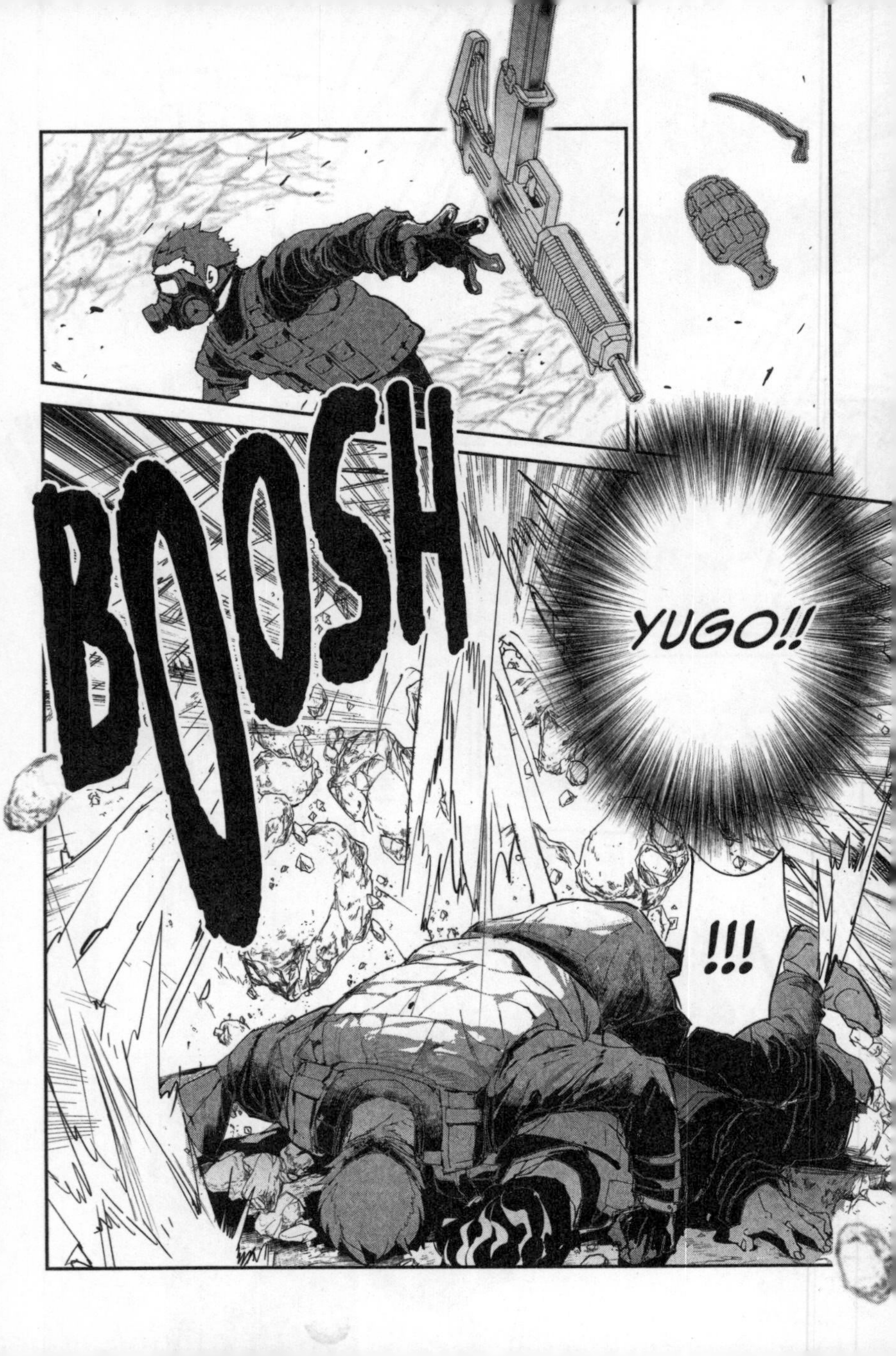
YUGO!!
BOOSH
!!!

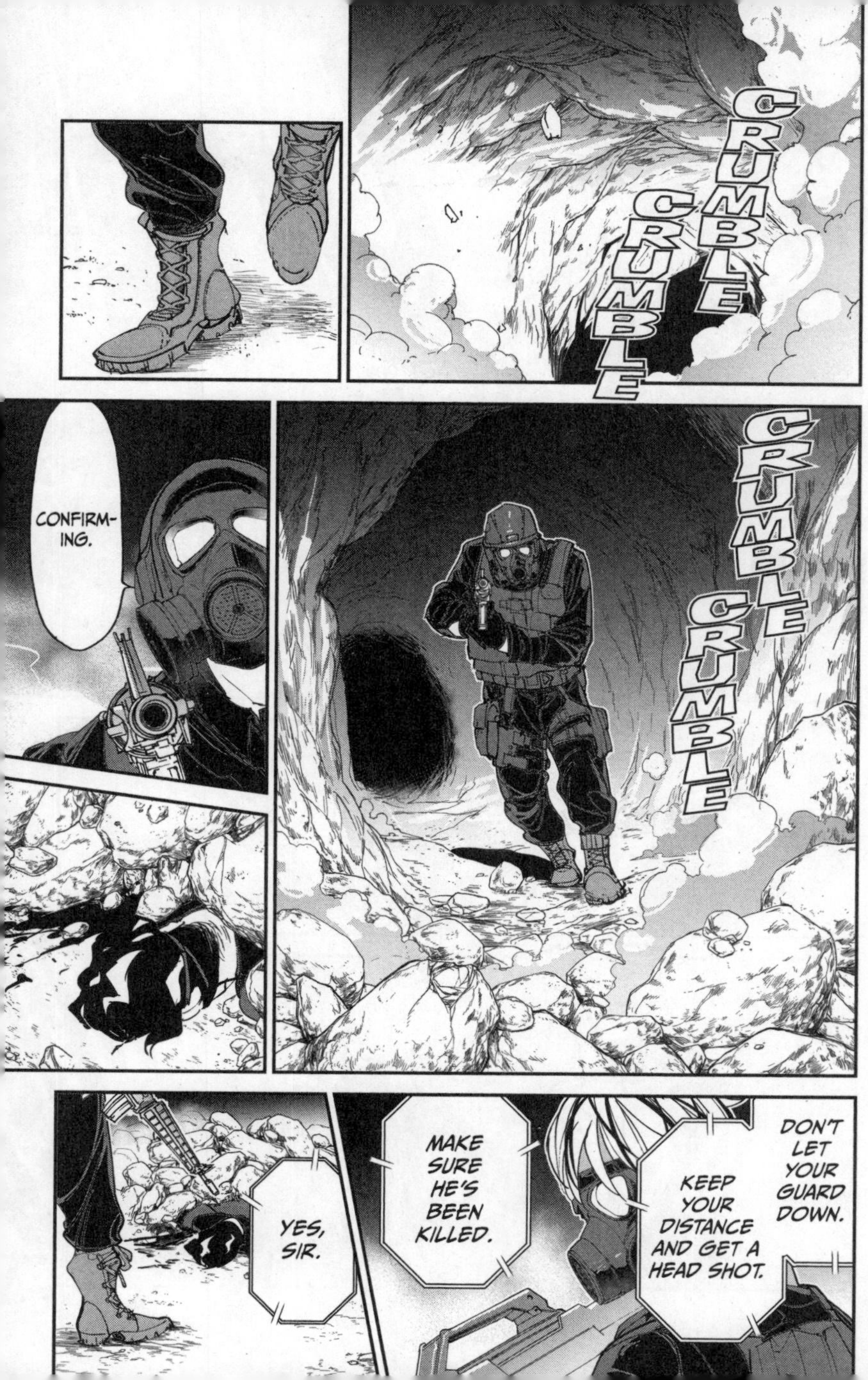
CRUMBLE
CRUMBLE
CRUMBLE
CRUMBLE
CONFIRMING.
DON'T LET YOUR GUARD DOWN.
KEEP YOUR DISTANCE AND GET A HEAD SHOT.
MAKE SURE HE'S BEEN KILLED.
YES, SIR.

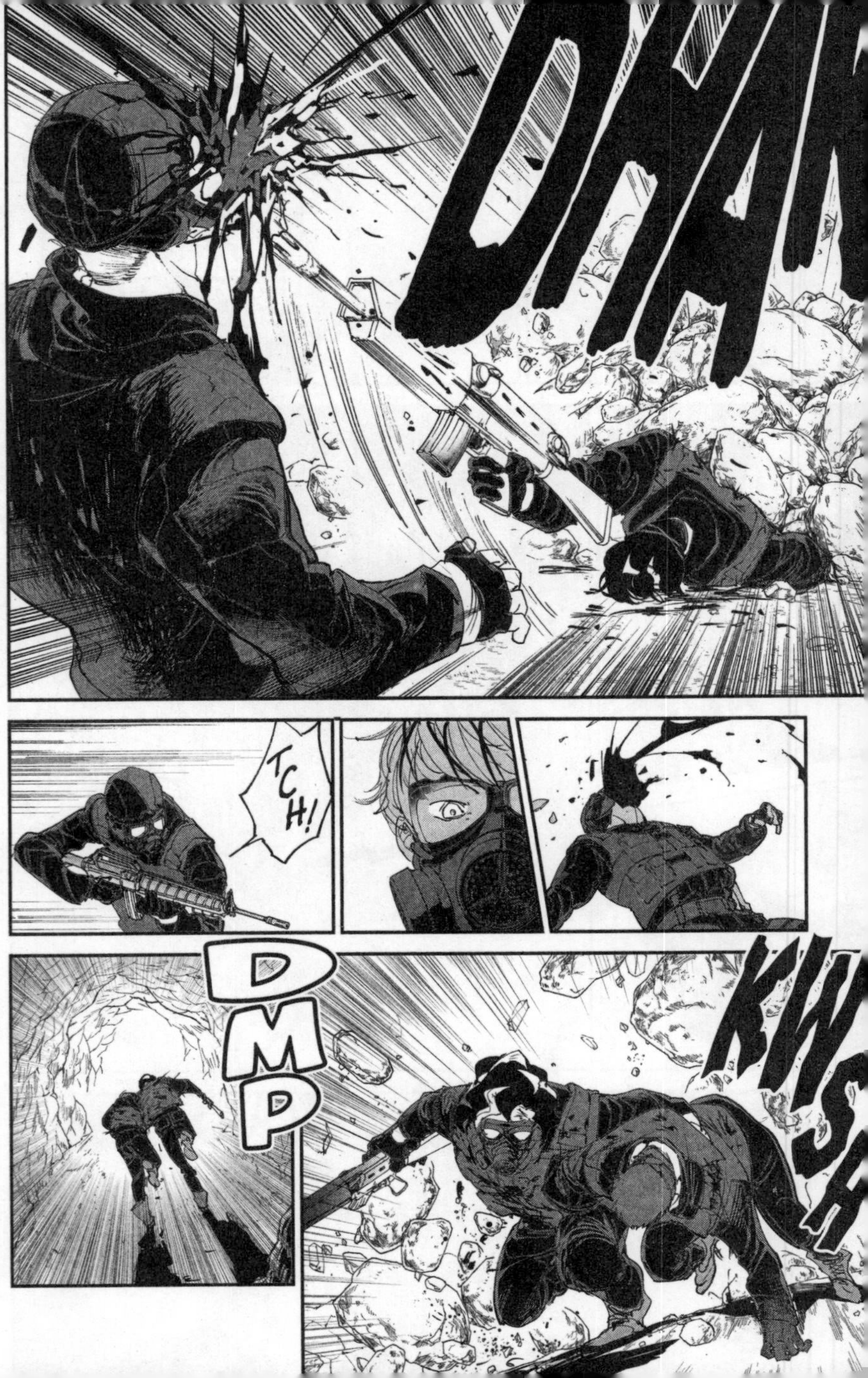
DHA
TCH!
KWSH
DMP

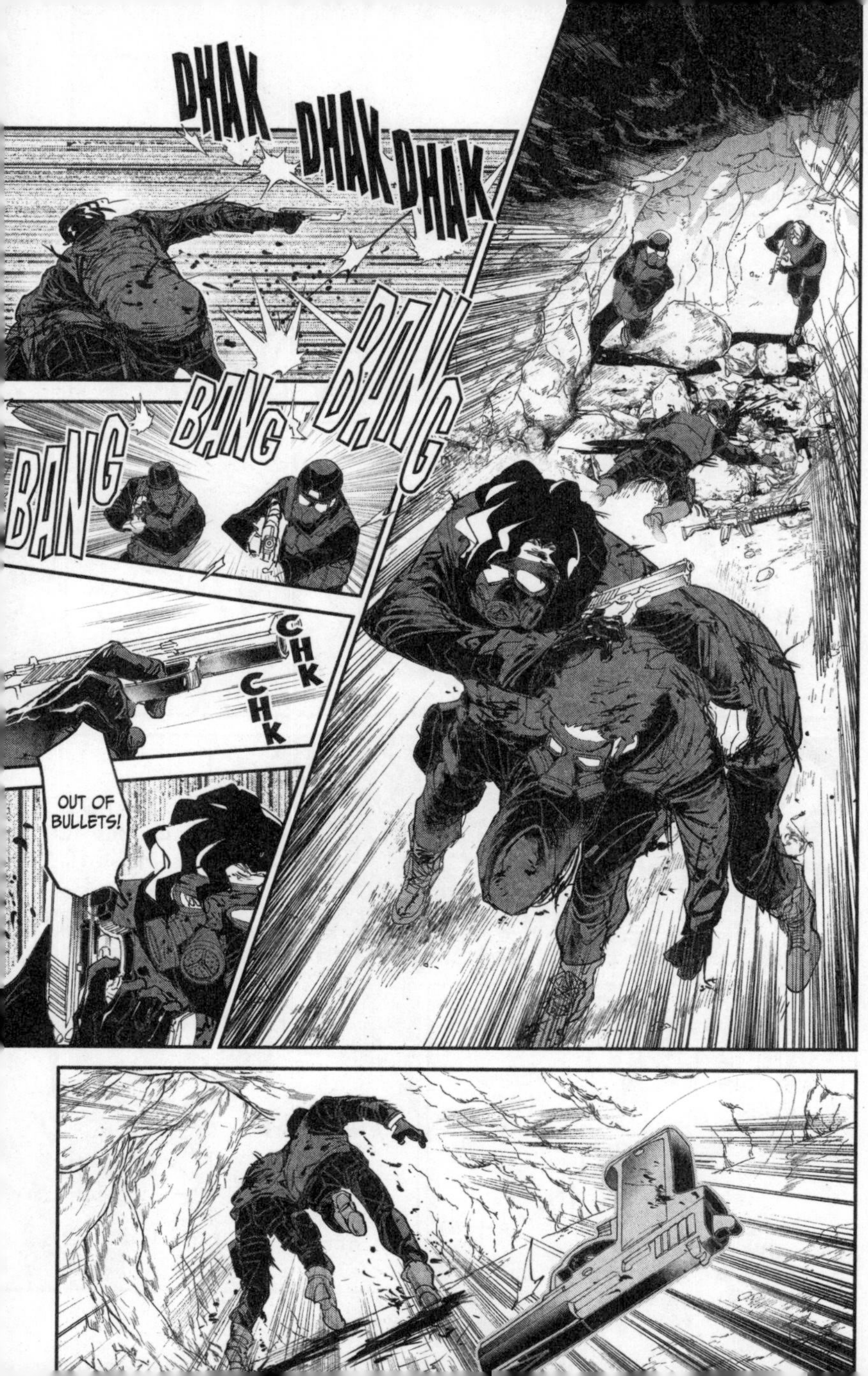
DHAK DHAK DHAK DHAK
BANG BANG BANG
CHK CHK
OUT OF BULLETS!

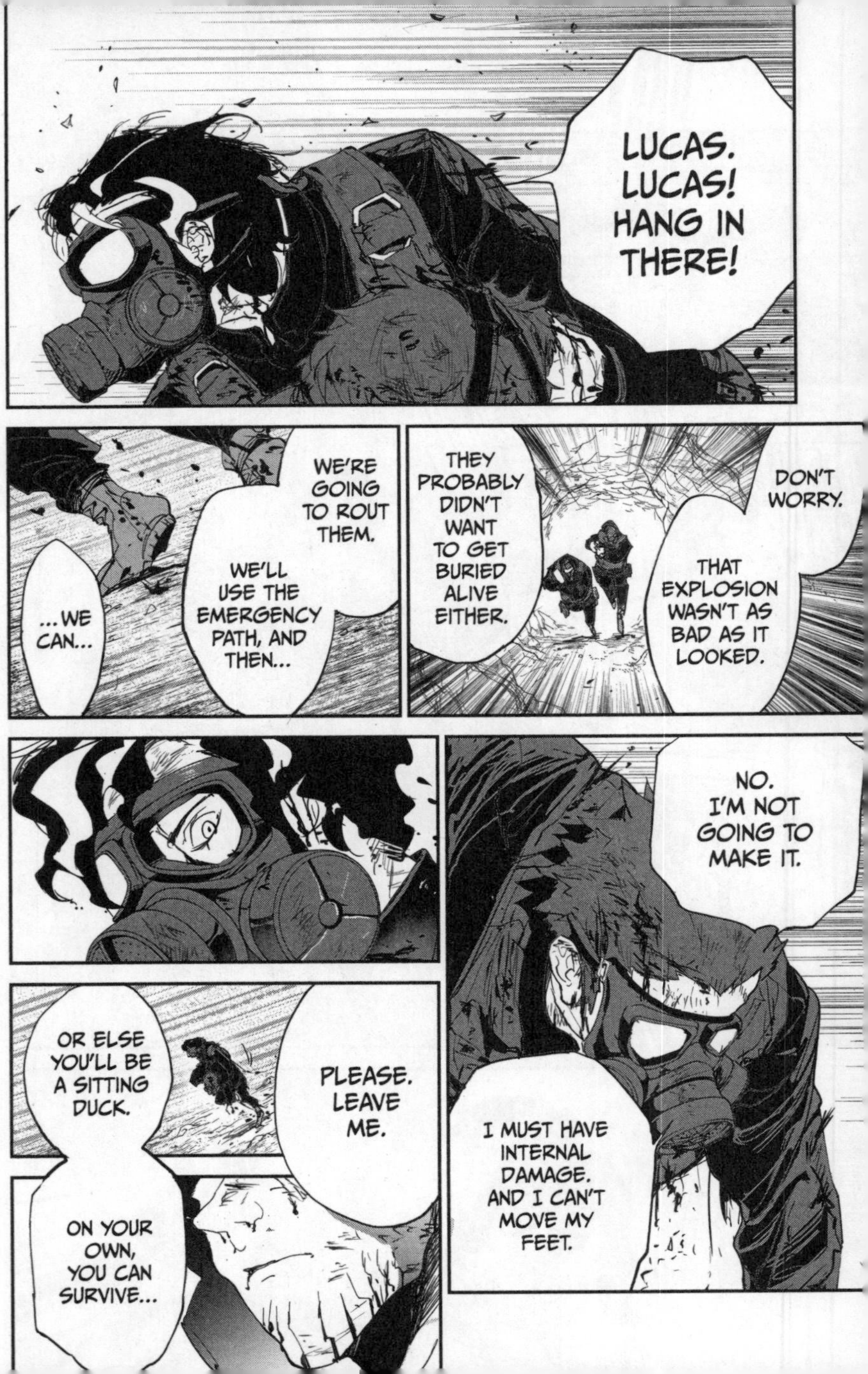
LUCAS. LUCAS! HANG IN THERE!
DON'T WORRY.
THAT EXPLOSION WASN'T AS BAD AS IT LOOKED.
THEY PROBABLY DIDN'T WANT TO GET BURIED ALIVE EITHER.
WE'RE GOING TO ROUT THEM.
WE'LL USE THE EMERGENCY PATH, AND THEN...
...WE CAN...
NO. I'M NOT GOING TO MAKE IT.
I MUST HAVE INTERNAL DAMAGE. AND I CAN'T MOVE MY FEET.
PLEASE. LEAVE ME.
OR ELSE YOU'LL BE A SITTING DUCK.
ON YOUR OWN, YOU CAN SURVIVE...

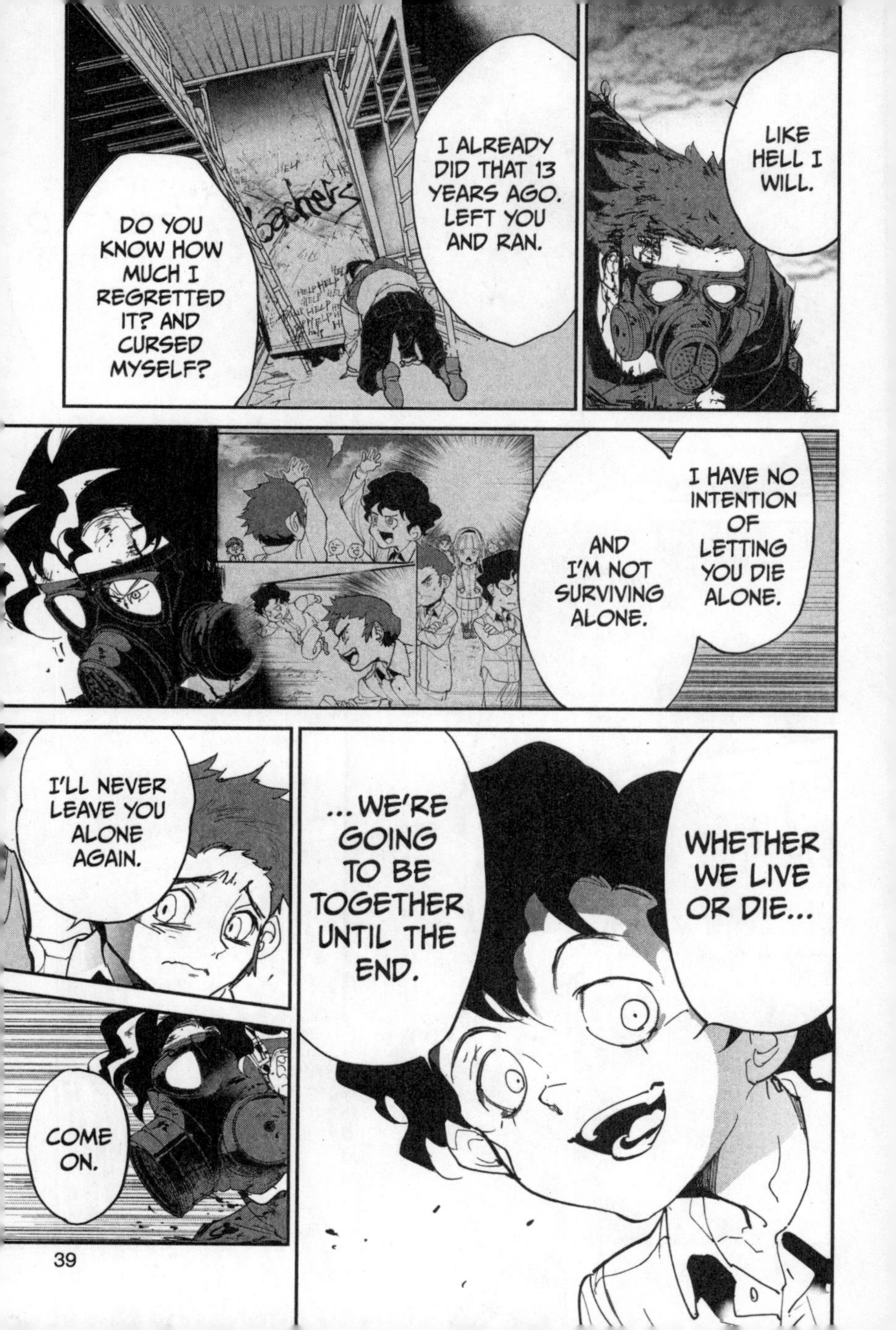
LIKE HELL I WILL.
I ALREADY DID THAT 13 YEARS AGO. LEFT YOU AND RAN.
DO YOU KNOW HOW MUCH I REGRETTED IT? AND CURSED MYSELF?
I HAVE NO INTENTION OF LETTING YOU DIE ALONE.
AND I'M NOT SURVIVING ALONE.
WHETHER WE LIVE OR DIE...
...WE'RE GOING TO BE TOGETHER UNTIL THE END.
I'LL NEVER LEAVE YOU ALONE AGAIN.
COME ON.

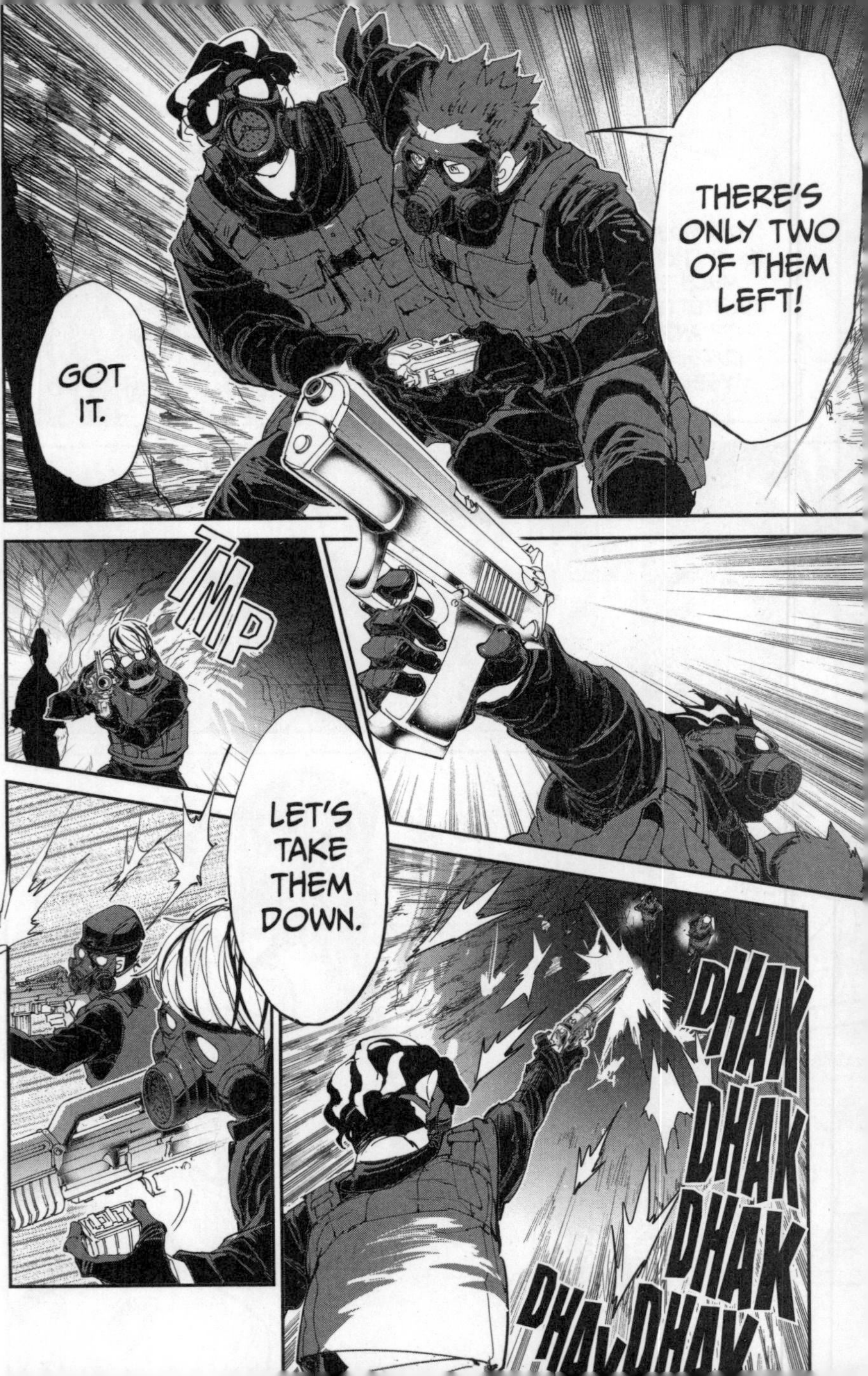
THERE'S ONLY TWO OF THEM LEFT!
GOT IT.
TMP
LET'S TAKE THEM DOWN.
DHAK DHAK DHAK DHAK

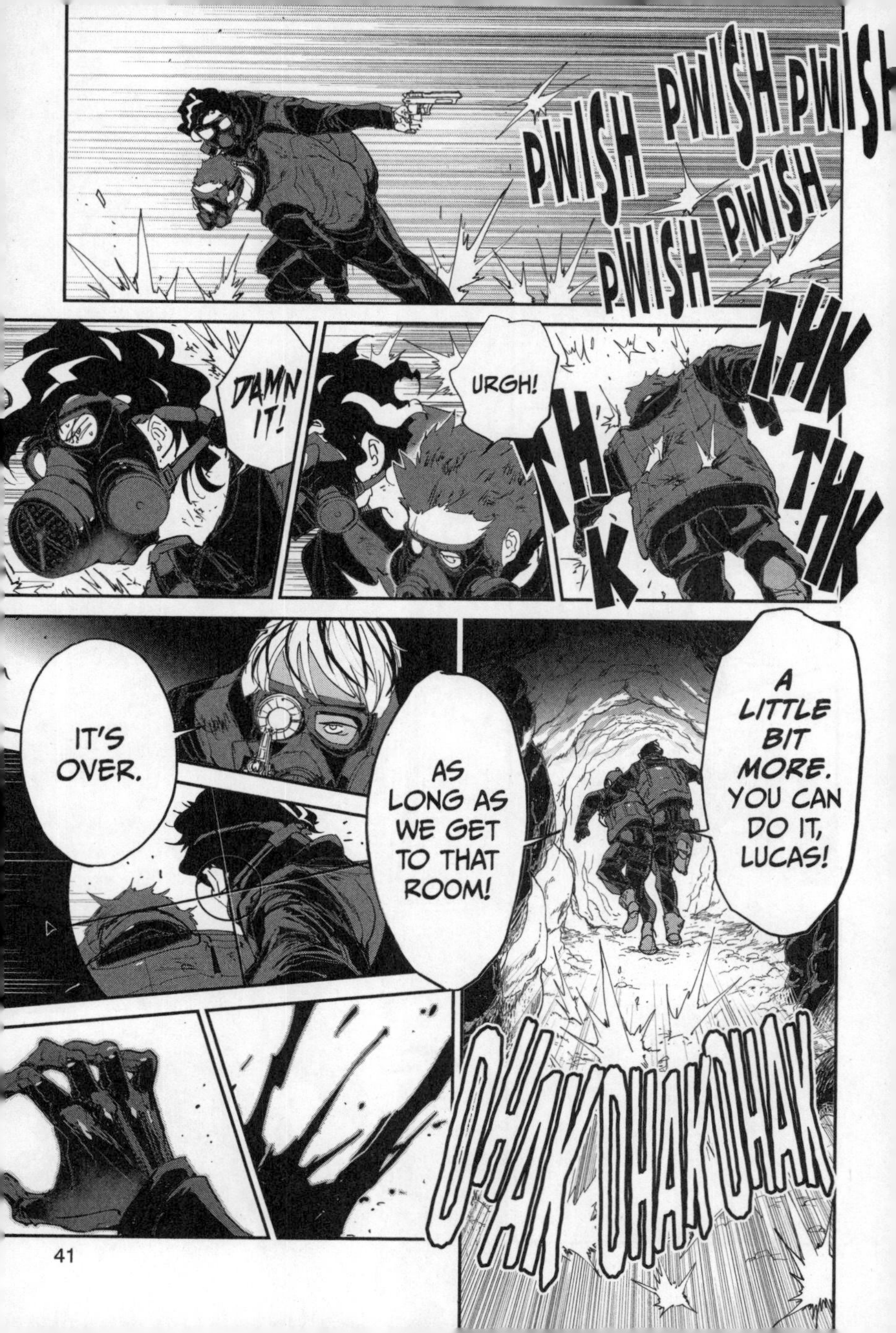
PWISH PWISH PWISH PWISH
PWISH PWISH
THK THK
URGH!
THK
DAMN IT!
A LITTLE BIT MORE. YOU CAN DO IT, LUCAS!
AS LONG AS WE GET TO THAT ROOM!
CHAK CHAK CHAK CHAK
IT'S OVER.

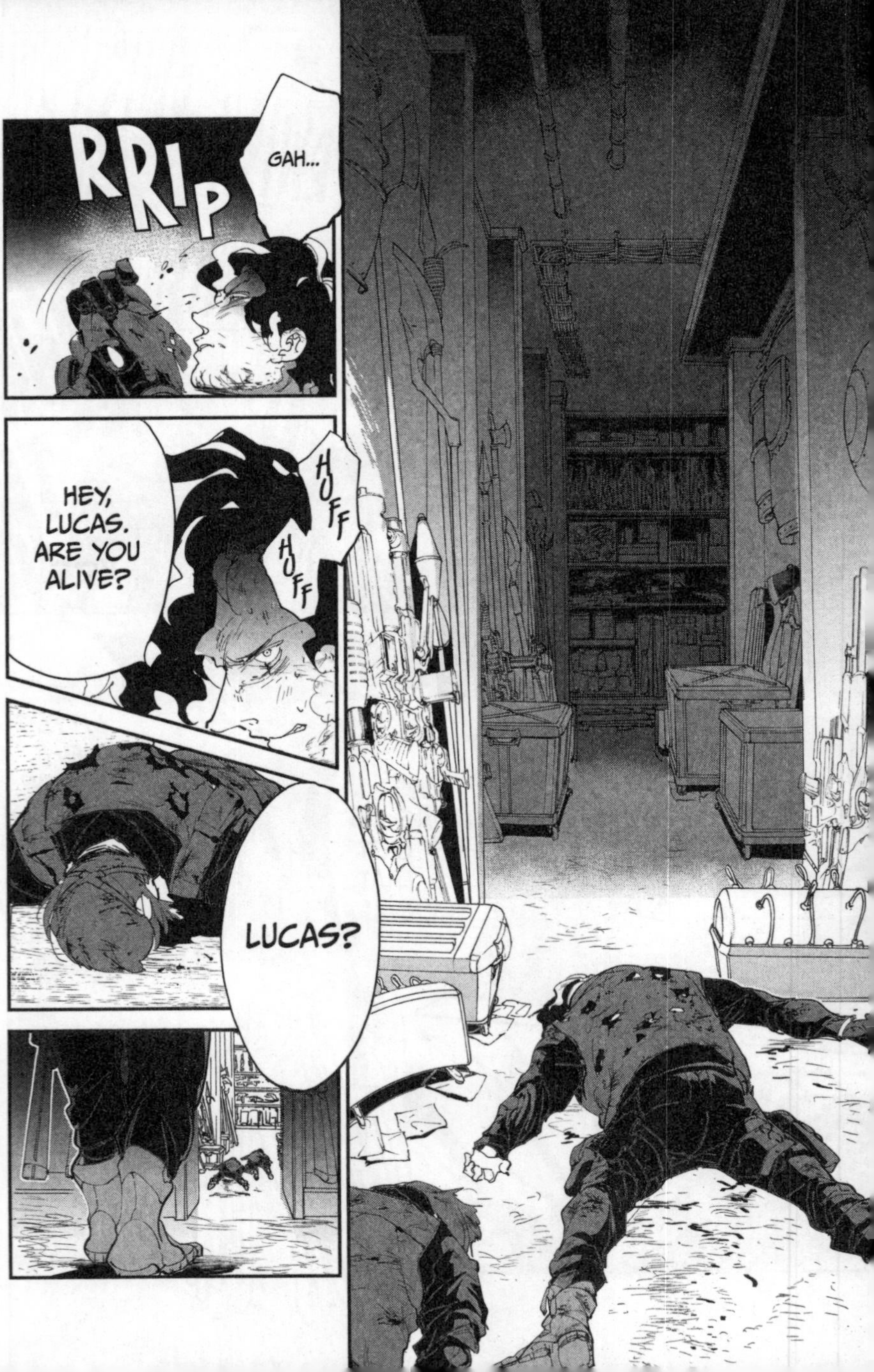
GAH...
RRIP
HUFF
HUFF
HEY, LUCAS. ARE YOU ALIVE?
LUCAS?

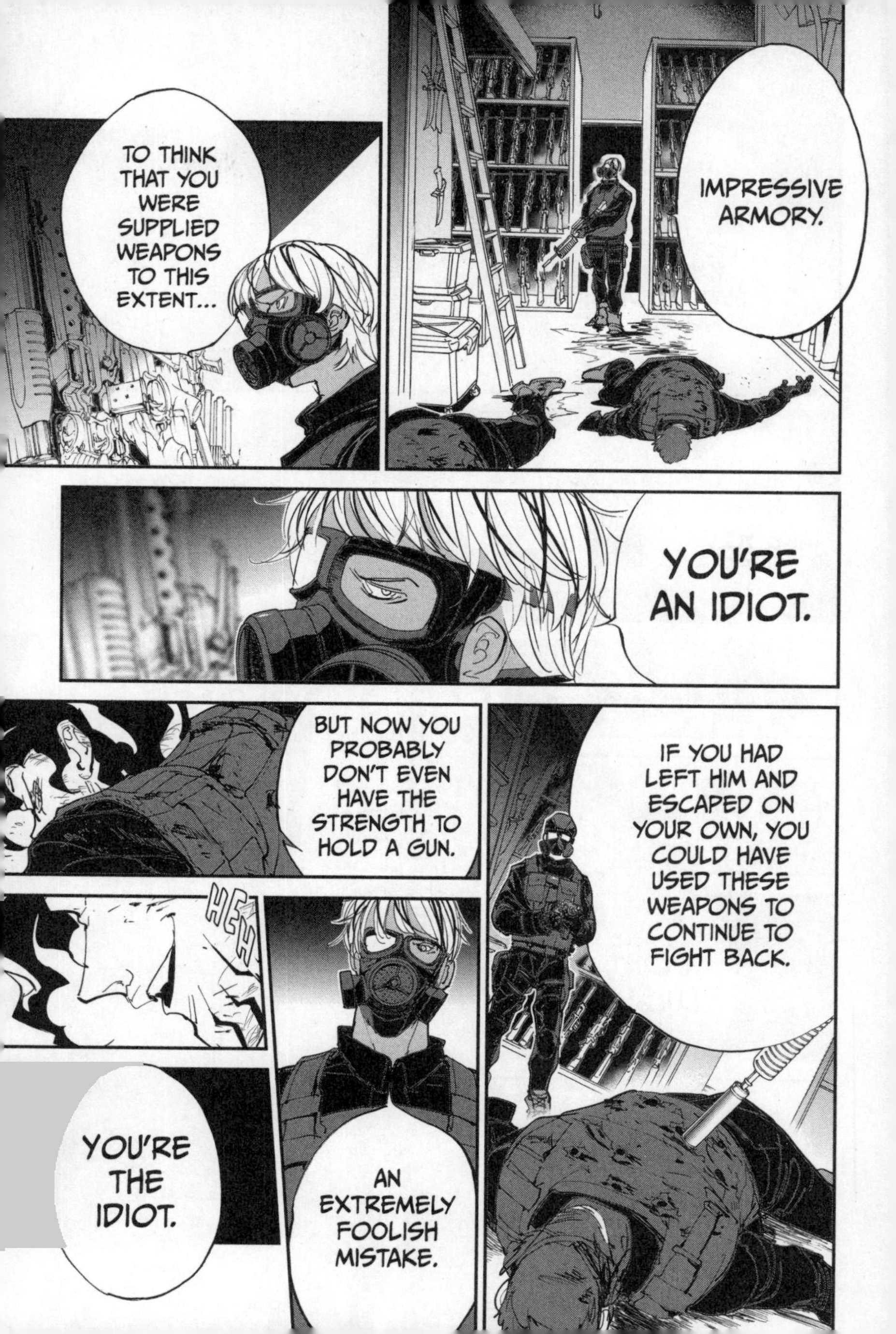
IMPRESSIVE ARMORY.
TO THINK THAT YOU WERE SUPPLIED WEAPONS TO THIS EXTENT...
YOU'RE AN IDIOT.
IF YOU HAD LEFT HIM AND ESCAPED ON YOUR OWN, YOU COULD HAVE USED THESE WEAPONS TO CONTINUE TO FIGHT BACK.
BUT NOW YOU PROBABLY DON'T EVEN HAVE THE STRENGTH TO HOLD A GUN.
AN EXTREMELY FOOLISH MISTAKE.
HEH
YOU'RE THE IDIOT.

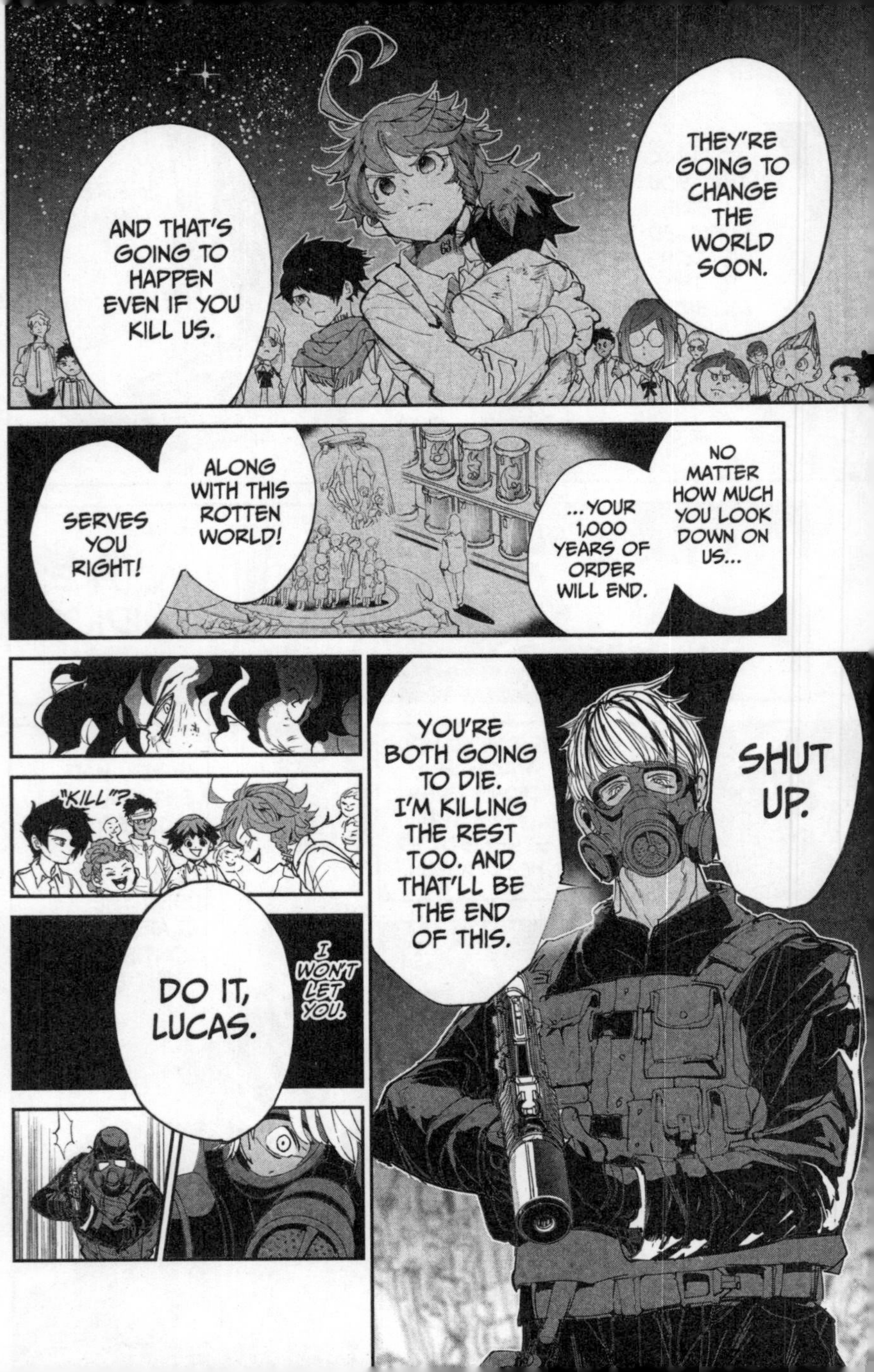
THEY'RE GOING TO CHANGE THE WORLD SOON.
AND THAT'S GOING TO HAPPEN EVEN IF YOU KILL US.
NO MATTER HOW MUCH YOU LOOK DOWN ON US...
...YOUR 1,000 YEARS OF ORDER WILL END.
ALONG WITH THIS ROTTEN WORLD!
SERVES YOU RIGHT!
SHUT UP.
YOU'RE BOTH GOING TO DIE. I'M KILLING THE REST TOO. AND THAT'LL BE THE END OF THIS.
"KILL"?
I WON'T LET YOU.
DO IT, LUCAS.

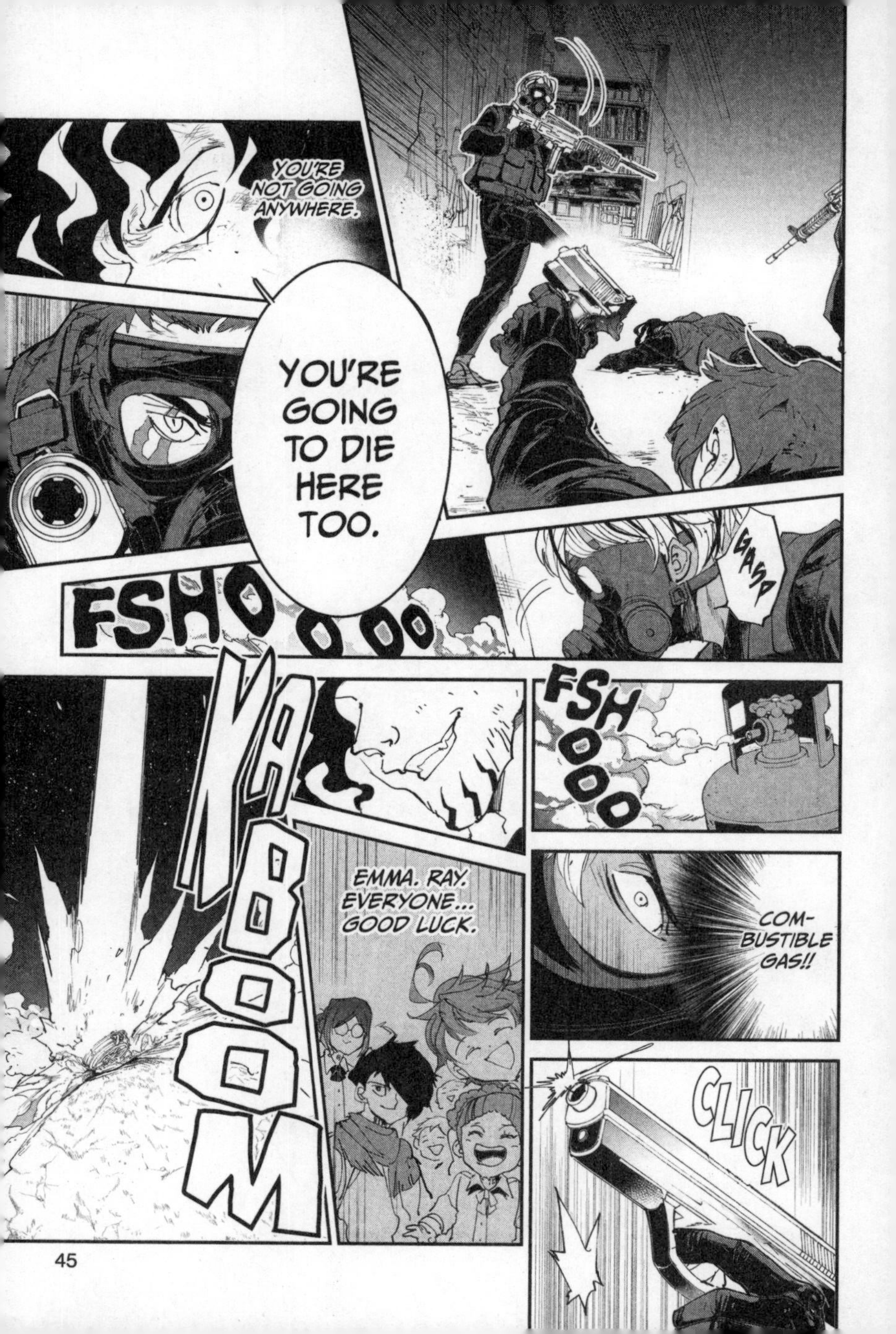
YOU'RE NOT GOING ANYWHERE.
YOU'RE GOING TO DIE HERE TOO.
GASP
FSHOOOO
FSHOOOO
COM-BUSTIBLE GAS!!
CLICK
EMMA. RAY. EVERYONE... GOOD LUCK.
KABOOOM

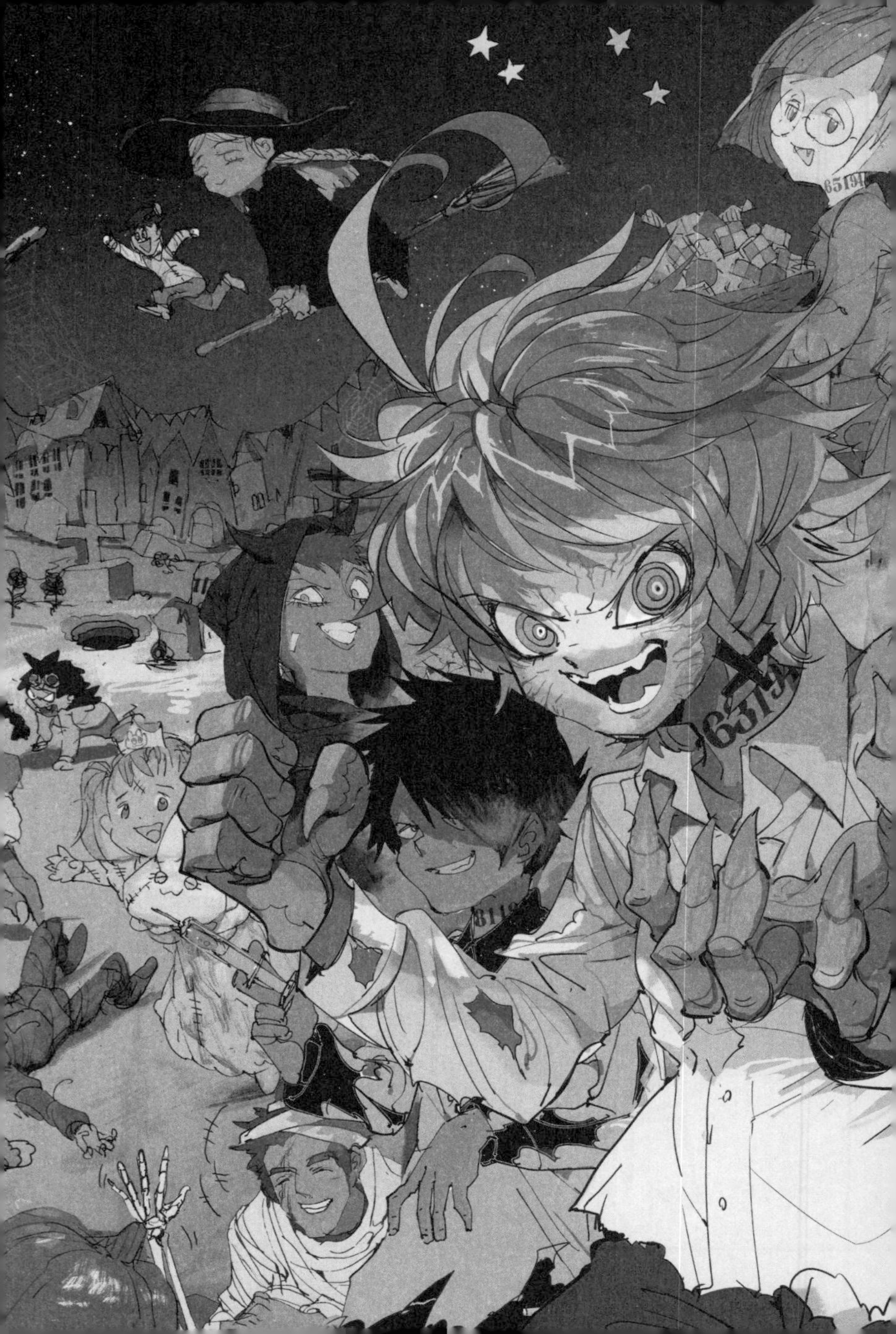

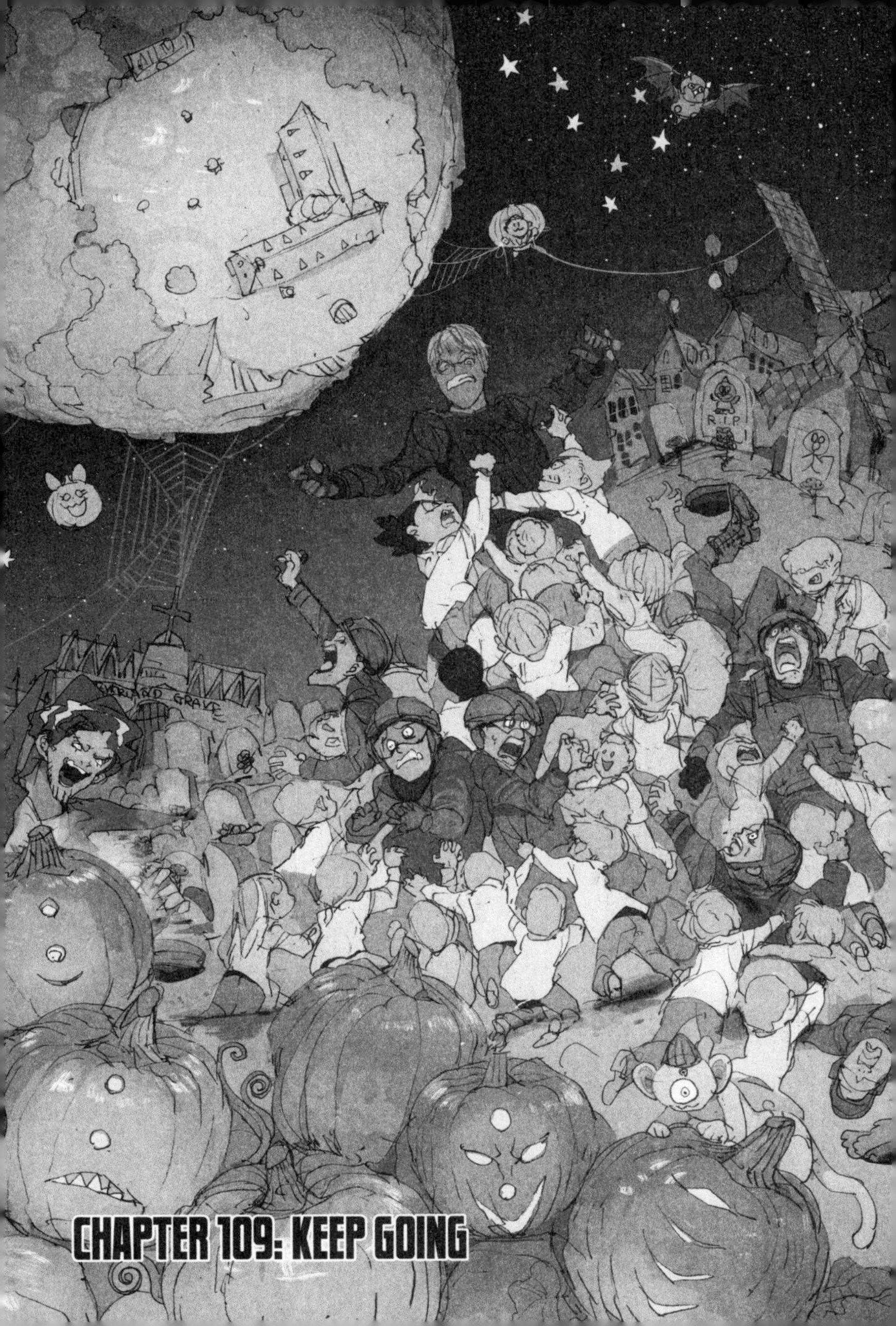
R.I.P.
GRAVE

CHAPTER 109: KEEP GOING

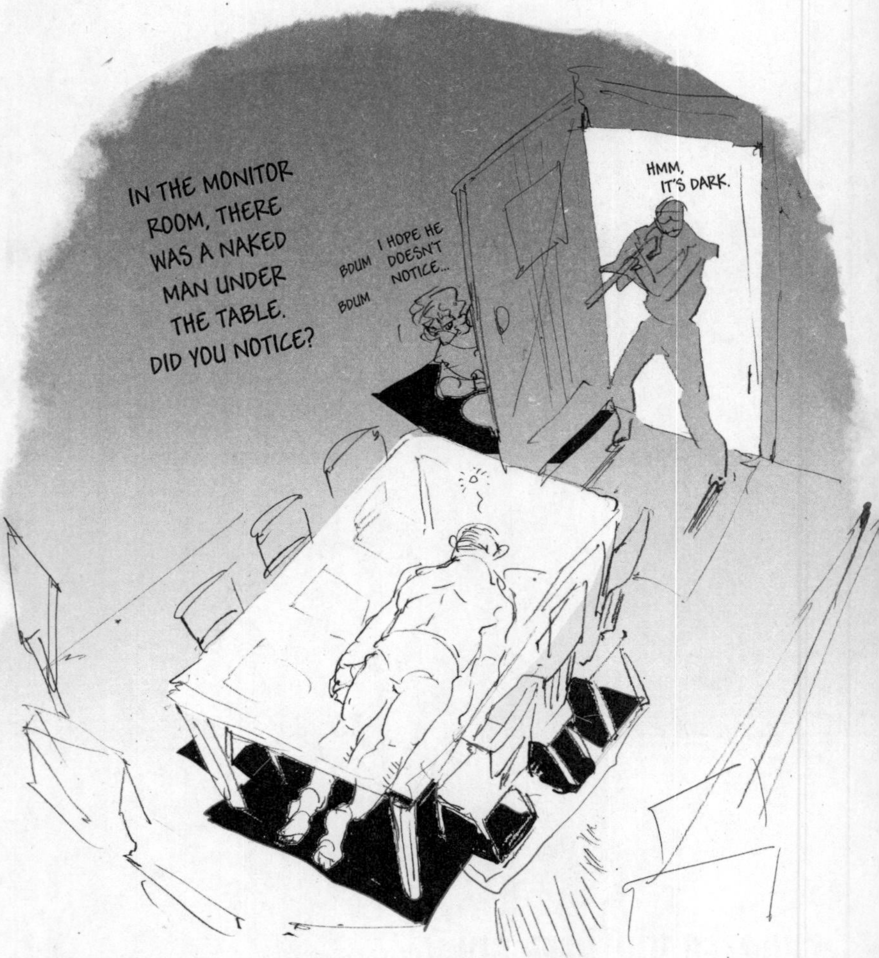
HMM, IT'S DARK.
I HOPE HE DOESN'T NOTICE...
BDUM BDUM
IN THE MONITOR ROOM, THERE WAS A NAKED MAN UNDER THE TABLE. DID YOU NOTICE?

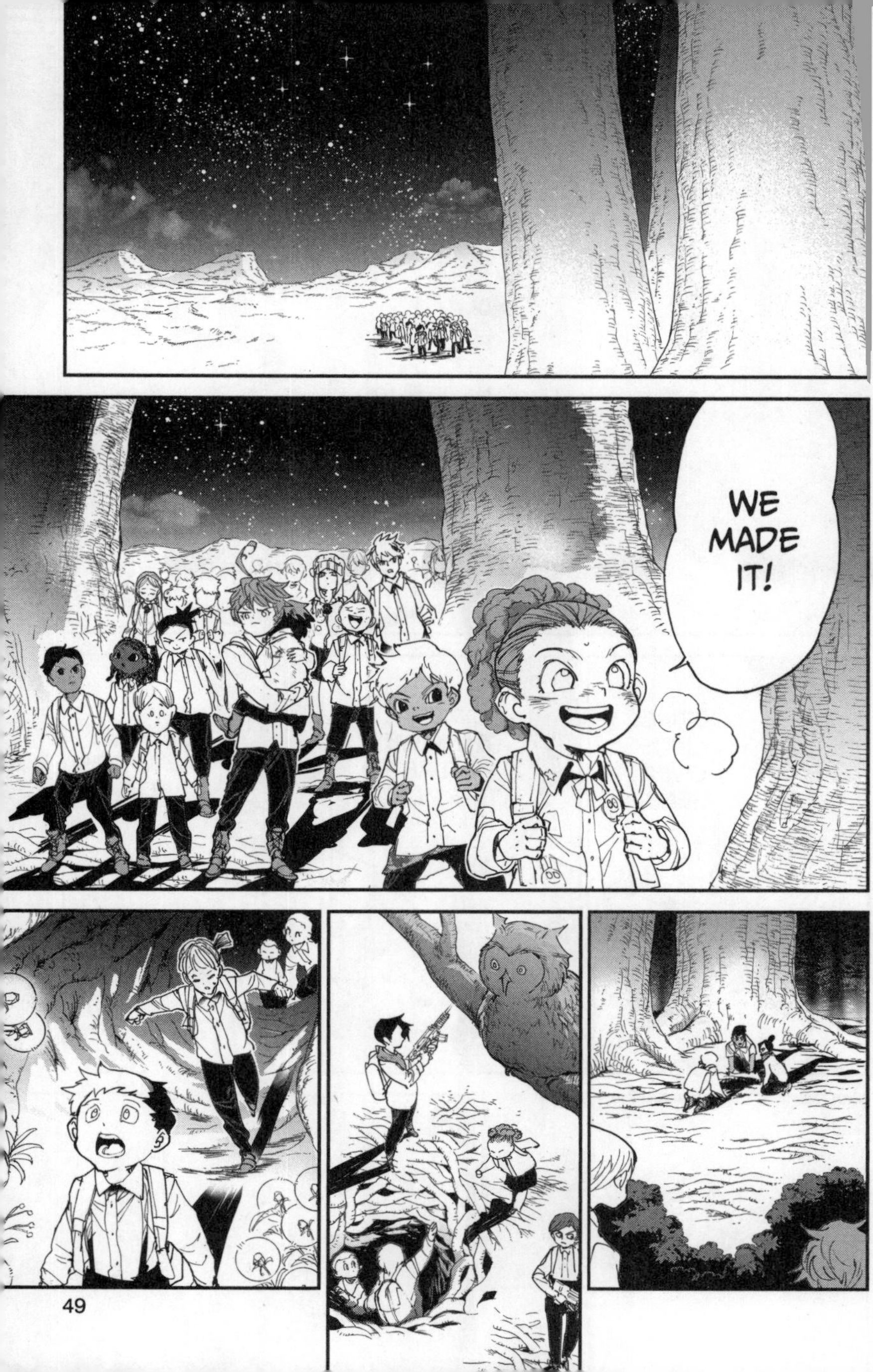
WE MADE IT!

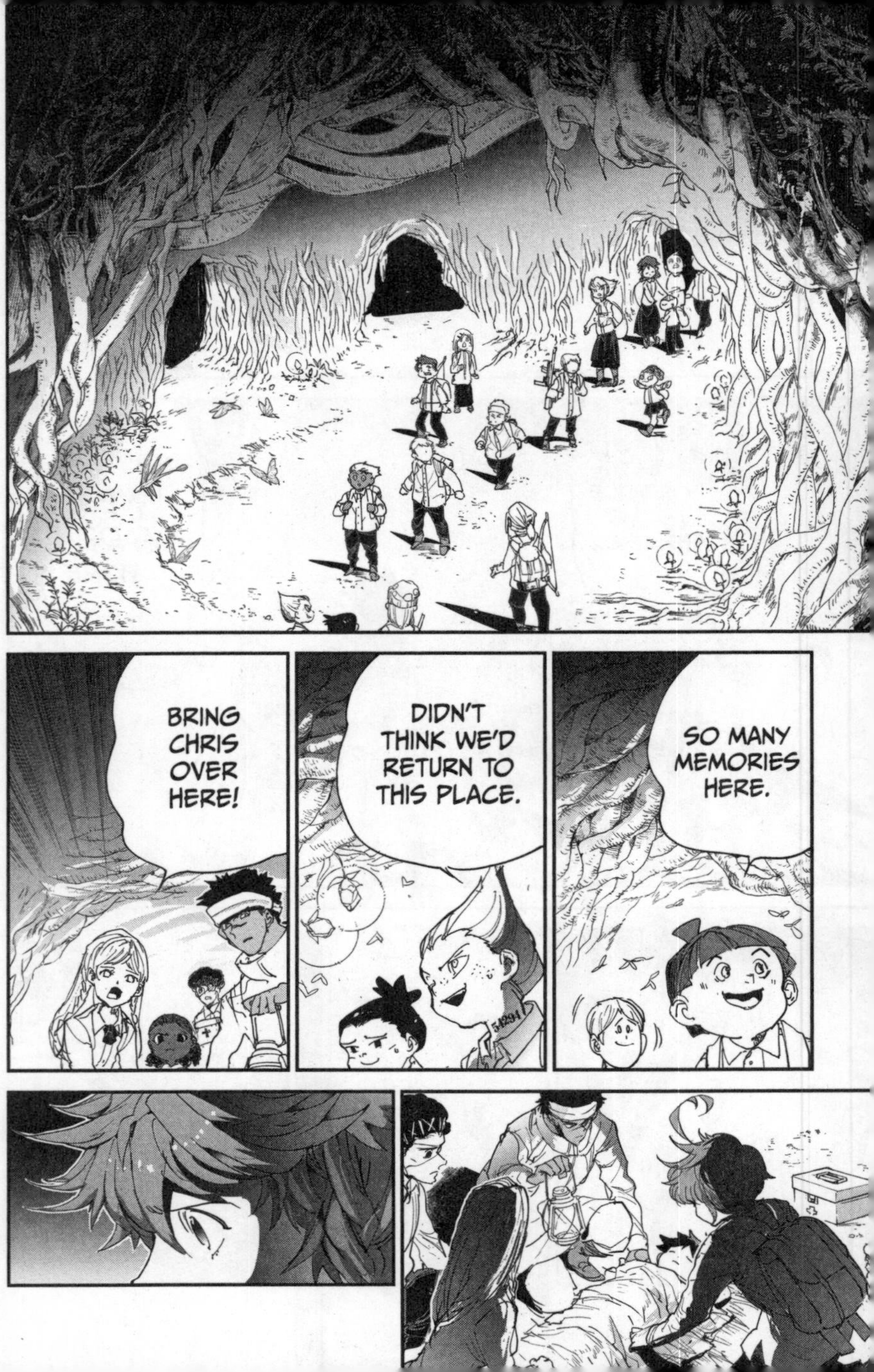
SO MANY MEMORIES HERE.
DIDN'T THINK WE'D RETURN TO THIS PLACE.
BRING CHRIS OVER HERE!

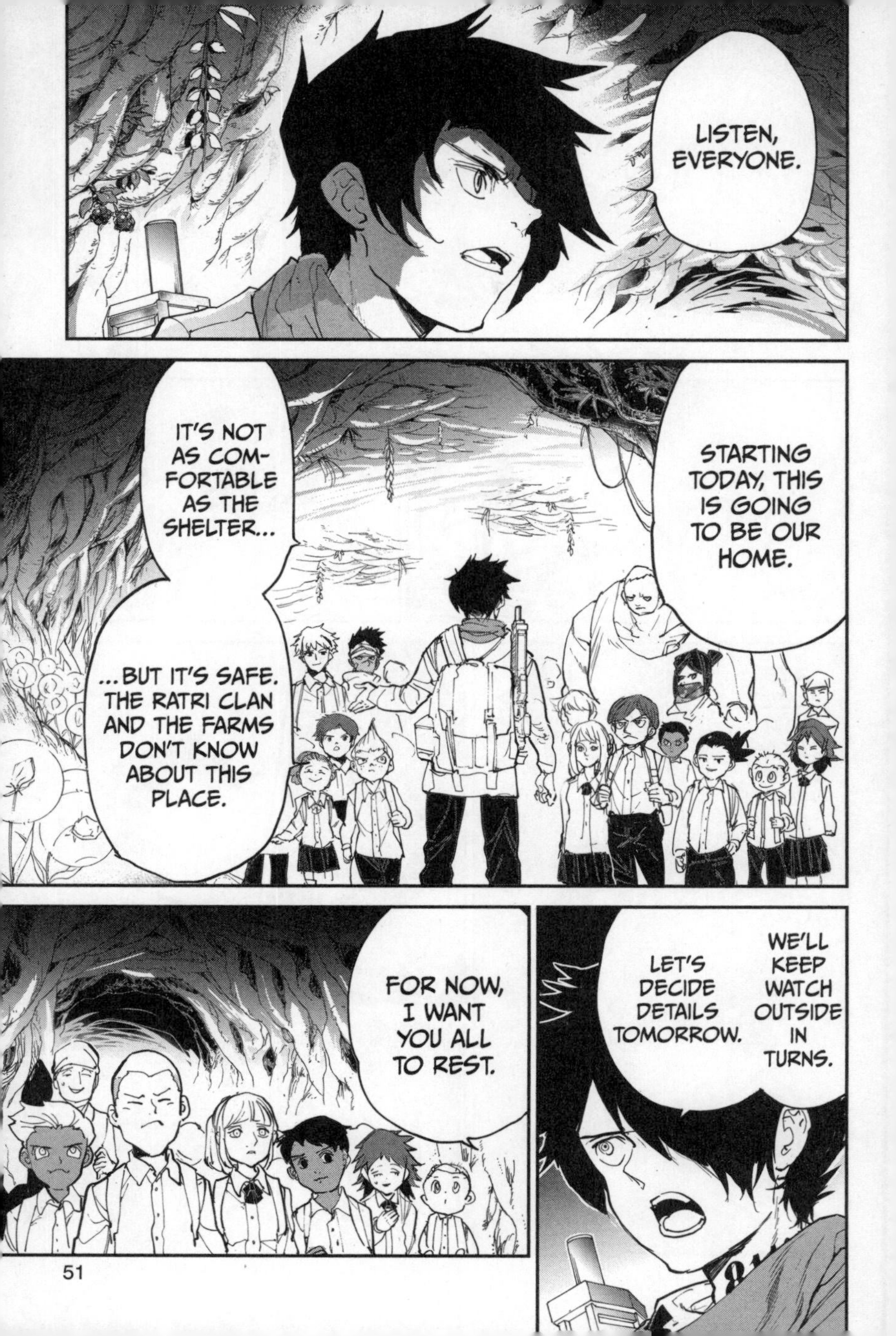
LISTEN, EVERYONE.
STARTING TODAY, THIS IS GOING TO BE OUR HOME.
IT'S NOT AS COM-FORTABLE AS THE SHELTER...
...BUT IT'S SAFE. THE RATRI CLAN AND THE FARMS DON'T KNOW ABOUT THIS PLACE.
WE'LL KEEP WATCH OUTSIDE IN TURNS.
LET'S DECIDE DETAILS TOMORROW.
FOR NOW, I WANT YOU ALL TO REST.

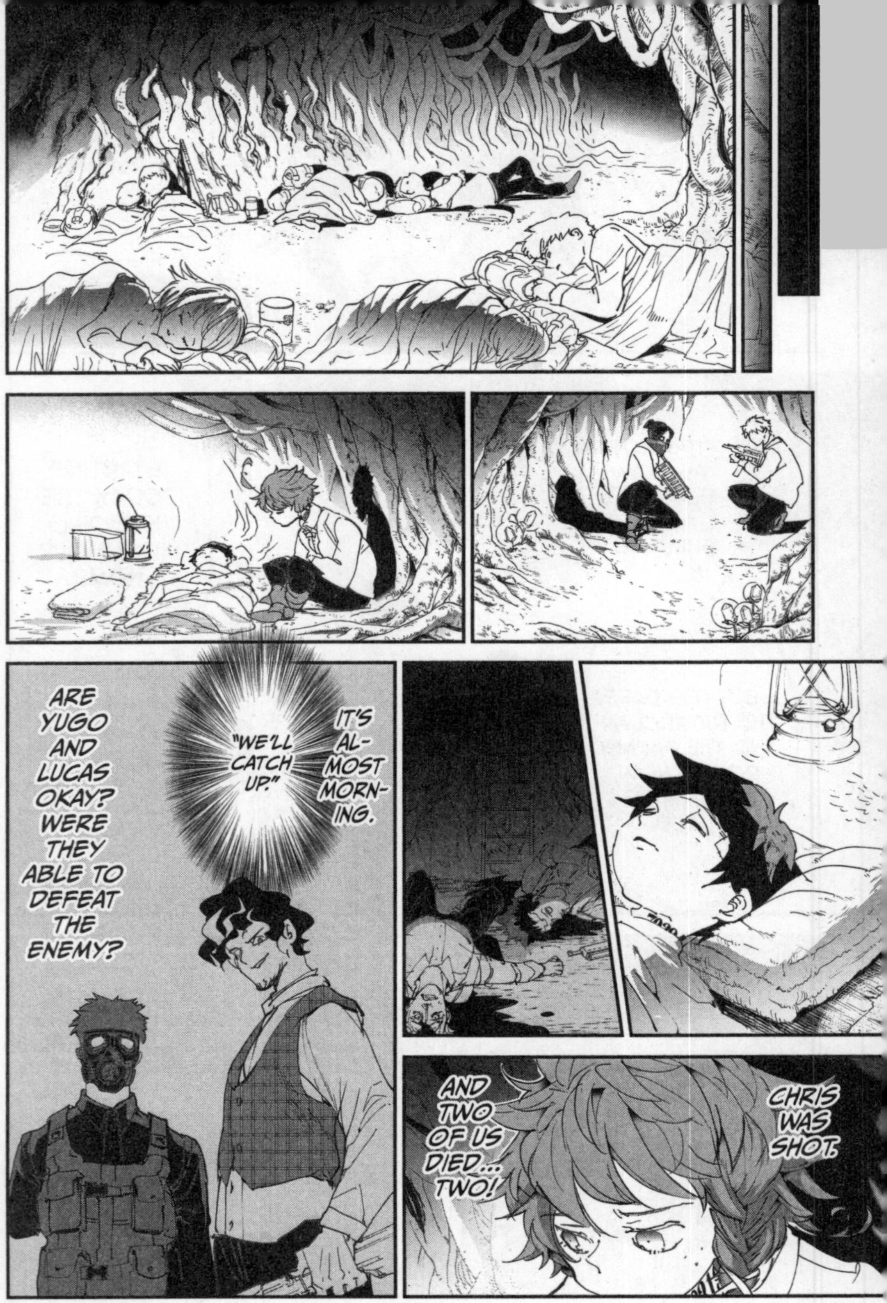
CHRIS WAS SHOT.
AND TWO OF US DIED... TWO!
IT'S AL-MOST MORN-ING.
"WE'LL CATCH UP."
ARE YUGO AND LUCAS OKAY? WERE THEY ABLE TO DEFEAT THE ENEMY?

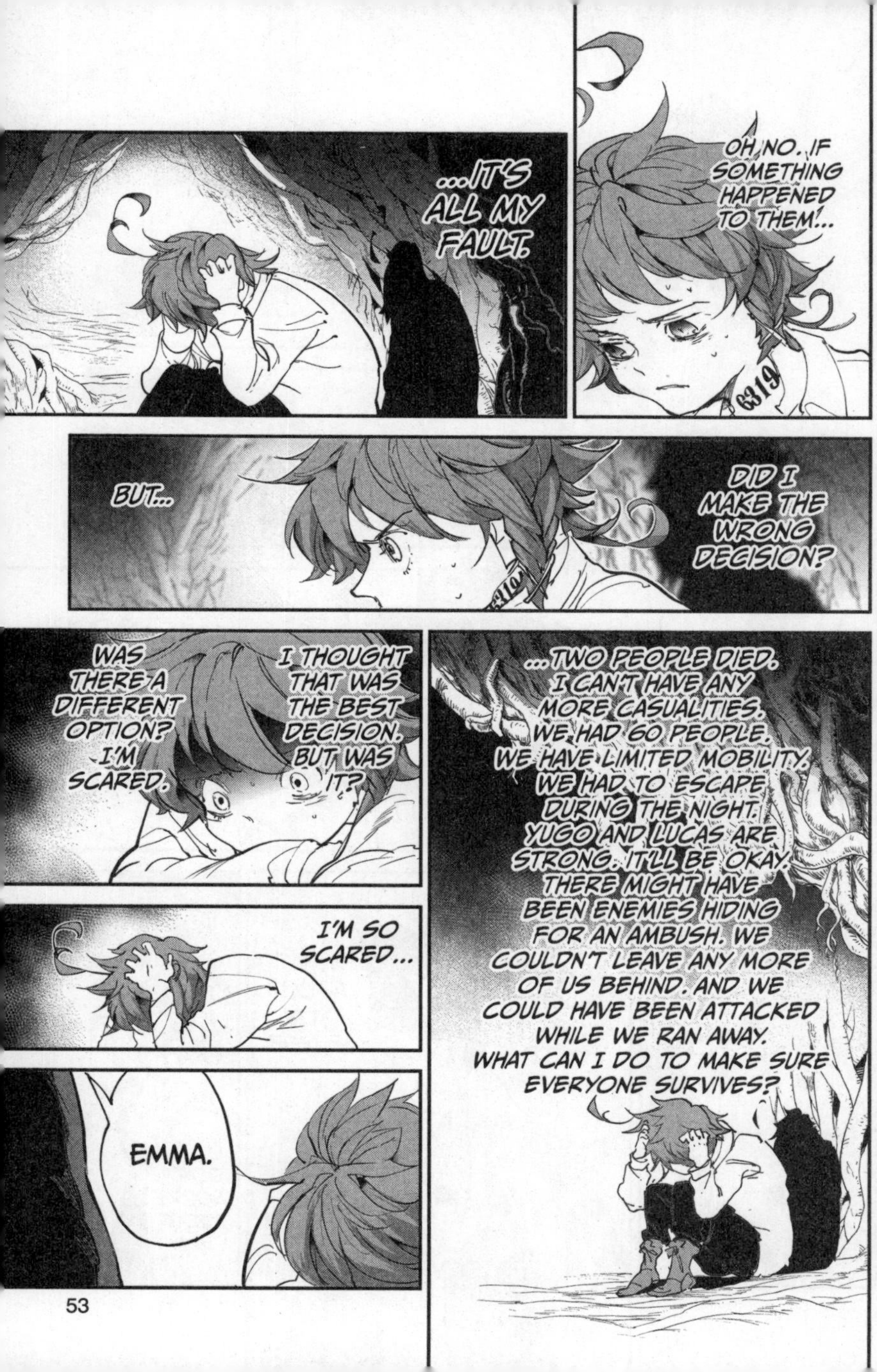
OH NO. IF SOMETHING HAPPENED TO THEM...
...IT'S ALL MY FAULT.
DID I MAKE THE WRONG DECISION?
BUT...
...TWO PEOPLE DIED. I CAN'T HAVE ANY MORE CASUALITIES. WE HAD 60 PEOPLE. WE HAVE LIMITED MOBILITY. WE HAD TO ESCAPE DURING THE NIGHT. YUGO AND LUCAS ARE STRONG. IT'LL BE OKAY. THERE MIGHT HAVE BEEN ENEMIES HIDING FOR AN AMBUSH. WE COULDN'T LEAVE ANY MORE OF US BEHIND. AND WE COULD HAVE BEEN ATTACKED WHILE WE RAN AWAY. WHAT CAN I DO TO MAKE SURE EVERYONE SURVIVES?
I THOUGHT THAT WAS THE BEST DECISION. BUT WAS IT?
WAS THERE A DIFFERENT OPTION? I'M SCARED.
I'M SO SCARED...
EMMA.

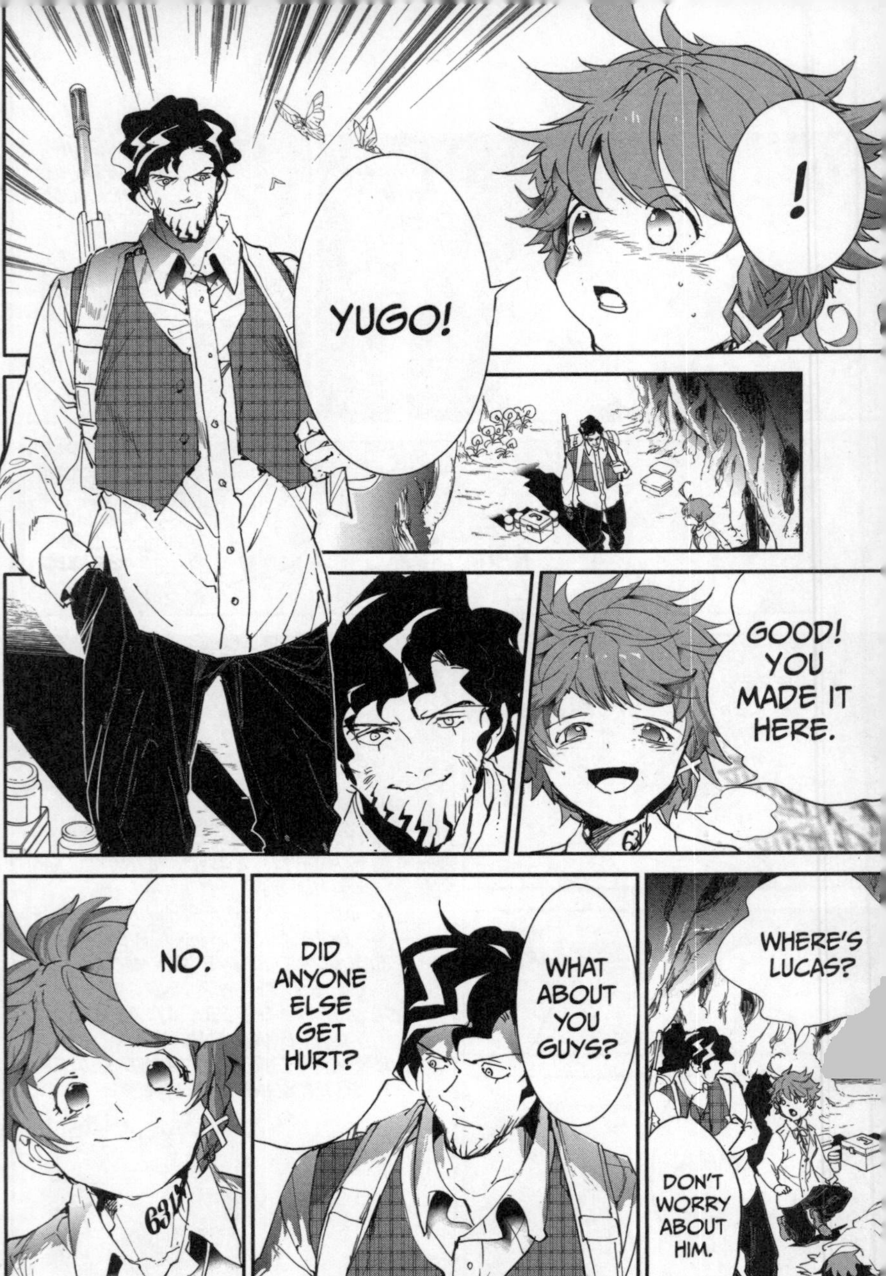
!
YUGO!
GOOD! YOU MADE IT HERE.
WHERE'S LUCAS?
DON'T WORRY ABOUT HIM.
WHAT ABOUT YOU GUYS?
DID ANYONE ELSE GET HURT?
NO.

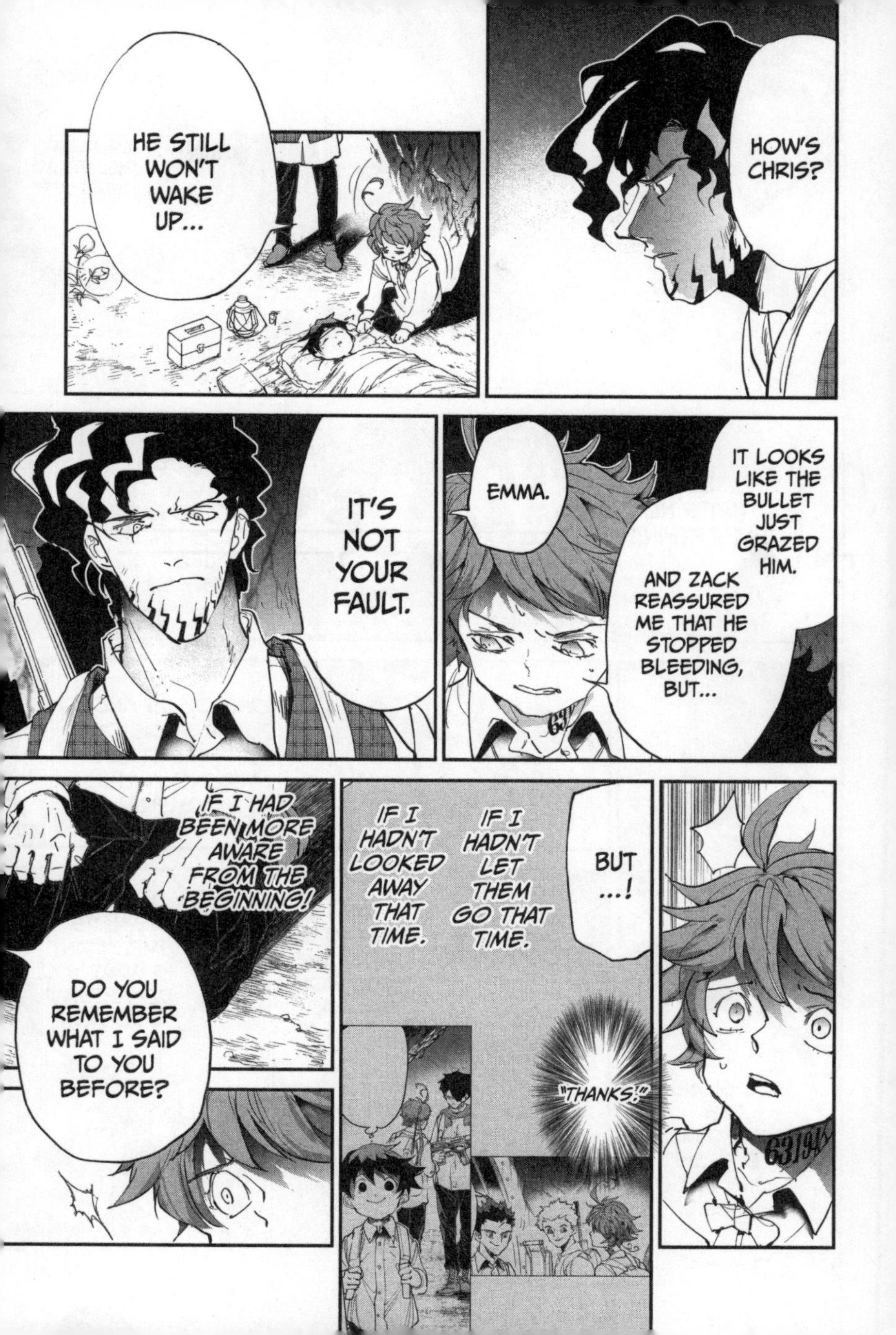
HOW'S CHRIS?
HE STILL WON'T WAKE UP...
IT LOOKS LIKE THE BULLET JUST GRAZED HIM.
AND ZACK REASSURED ME THAT HE STOPPED BLEEDING, BUT...
EMMA.
IT'S NOT YOUR FAULT.
BUT ...!
IF I HADN'T LET THEM GO THAT TIME.
IF I HADN'T LOOKED AWAY THAT TIME.
IF I HAD BEEN MORE AWARE FROM THE BEGINNING!
DO YOU REMEMBER WHAT I SAID TO YOU BEFORE?
"THANKS!"

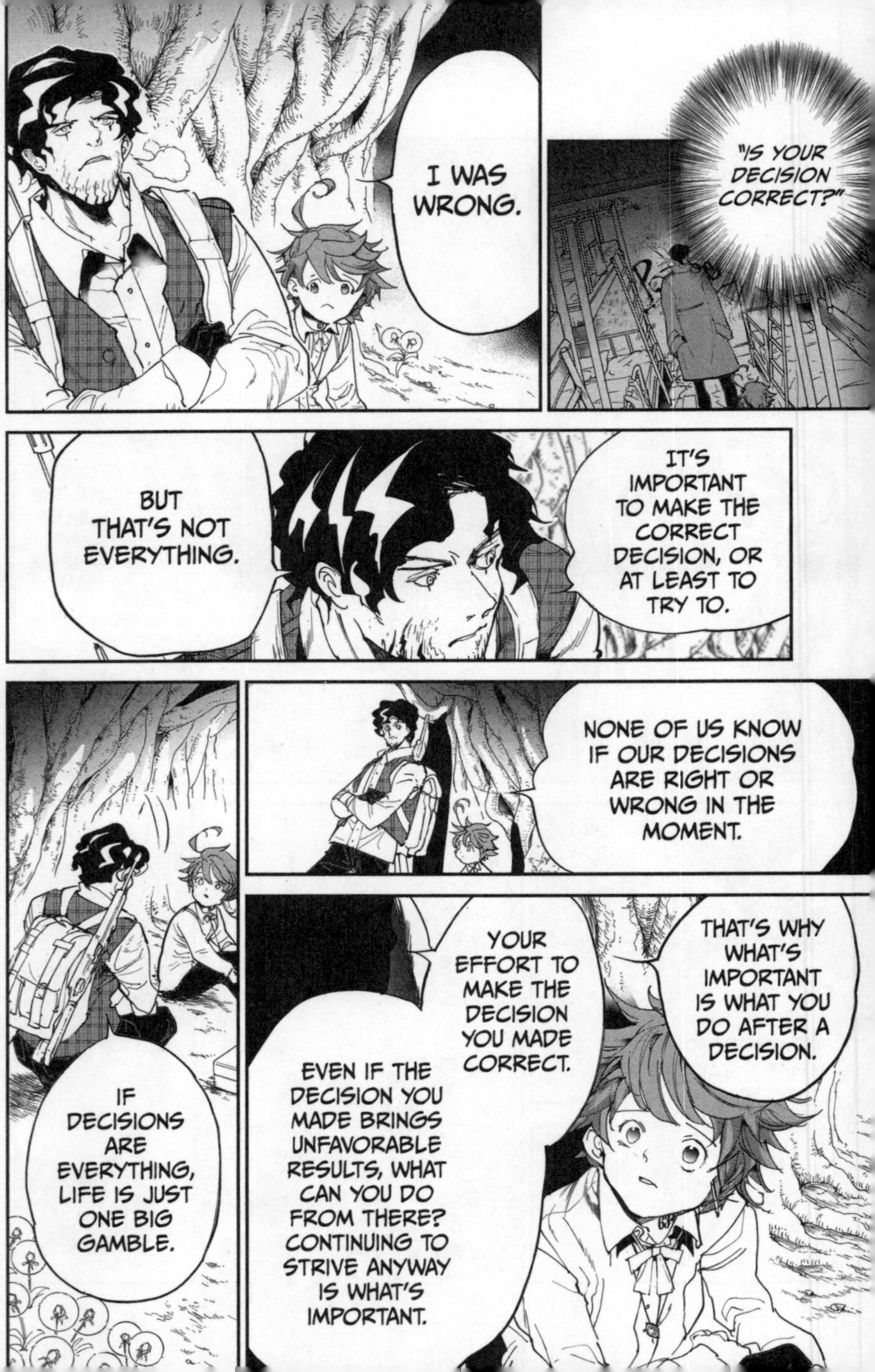
"IS YOUR DECISION CORRECT?"
I WAS WRONG.
IT'S IMPORTANT TO MAKE THE CORRECT DECISION, OR AT LEAST TO TRY TO.
BUT THAT'S NOT EVERYTHING.
NONE OF US KNOW IF OUR DECISIONS ARE RIGHT OR WRONG IN THE MOMENT.
THAT'S WHY WHAT'S IMPORTANT IS WHAT YOU DO AFTER A DECISION.
YOUR EFFORT TO MAKE THE DECISION YOU MADE CORRECT.
EVEN IF THE DECISION YOU MADE BRINGS UNFAVORABLE RESULTS, WHAT CAN YOU DO FROM THERE? CONTINUING TO STRIVE ANYWAY IS WHAT'S IMPORTANT.
IF DECISIONS ARE EVERYTHING, LIFE IS JUST ONE BIG GAMBLE.

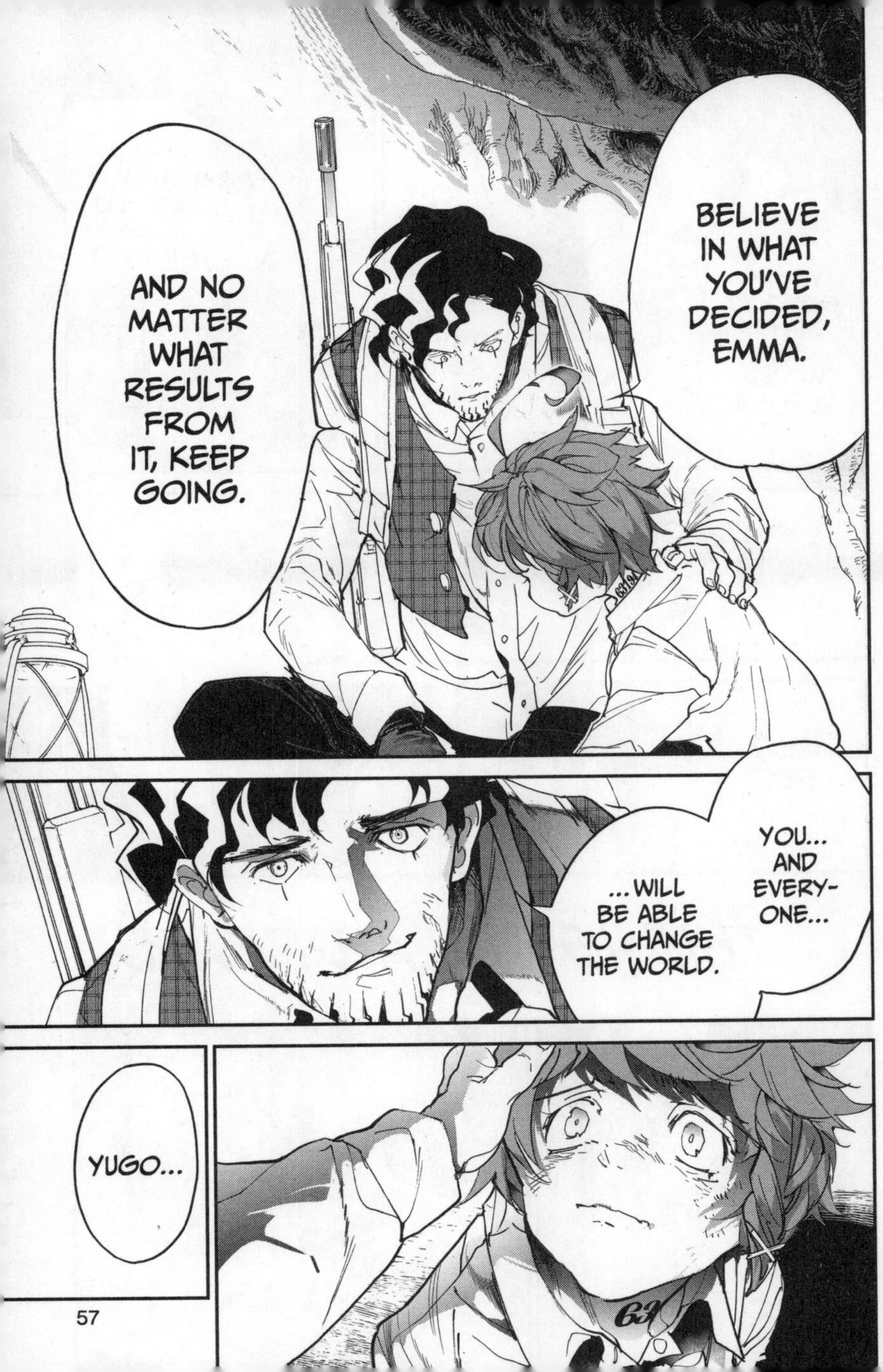
BELIEVE IN WHAT YOU'VE DECIDED, EMMA.
AND NO MATTER WHAT RESULTS FROM IT, KEEP GOING.
YOU... AND EVERY-ONE...
...WILL BE ABLE TO CHANGE THE WORLD.
YUGO...

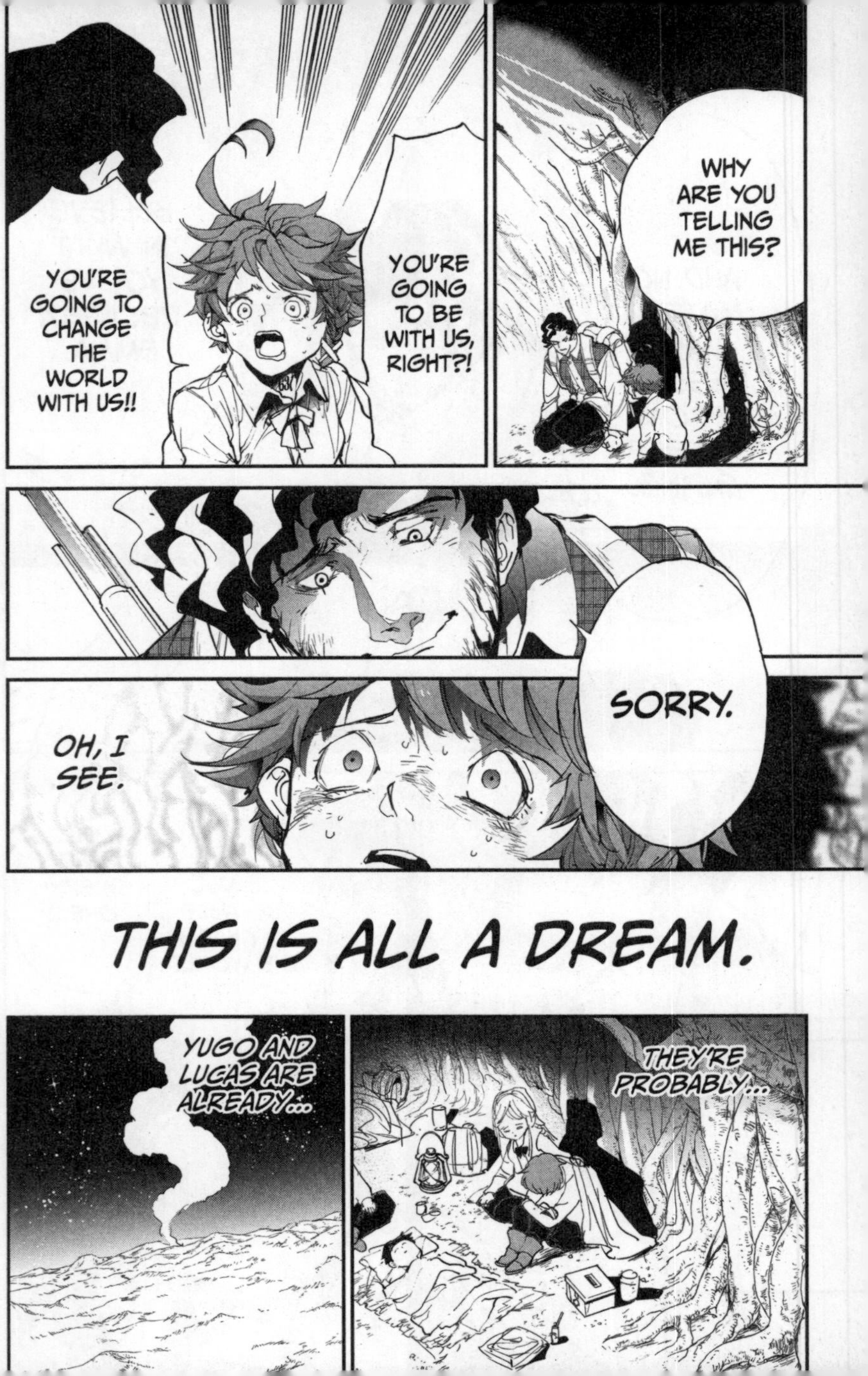
WHY ARE YOU TELLING ME THIS?
YOU'RE GOING TO BE WITH US, RIGHT?!
YOU'RE GOING TO CHANGE THE WORLD WITH US!!
SORRY.
OH, I SEE.
THIS IS ALL A DREAM.
THEY'RE PROBABLY...
YUGO AND LUCAS ARE ALREADY...

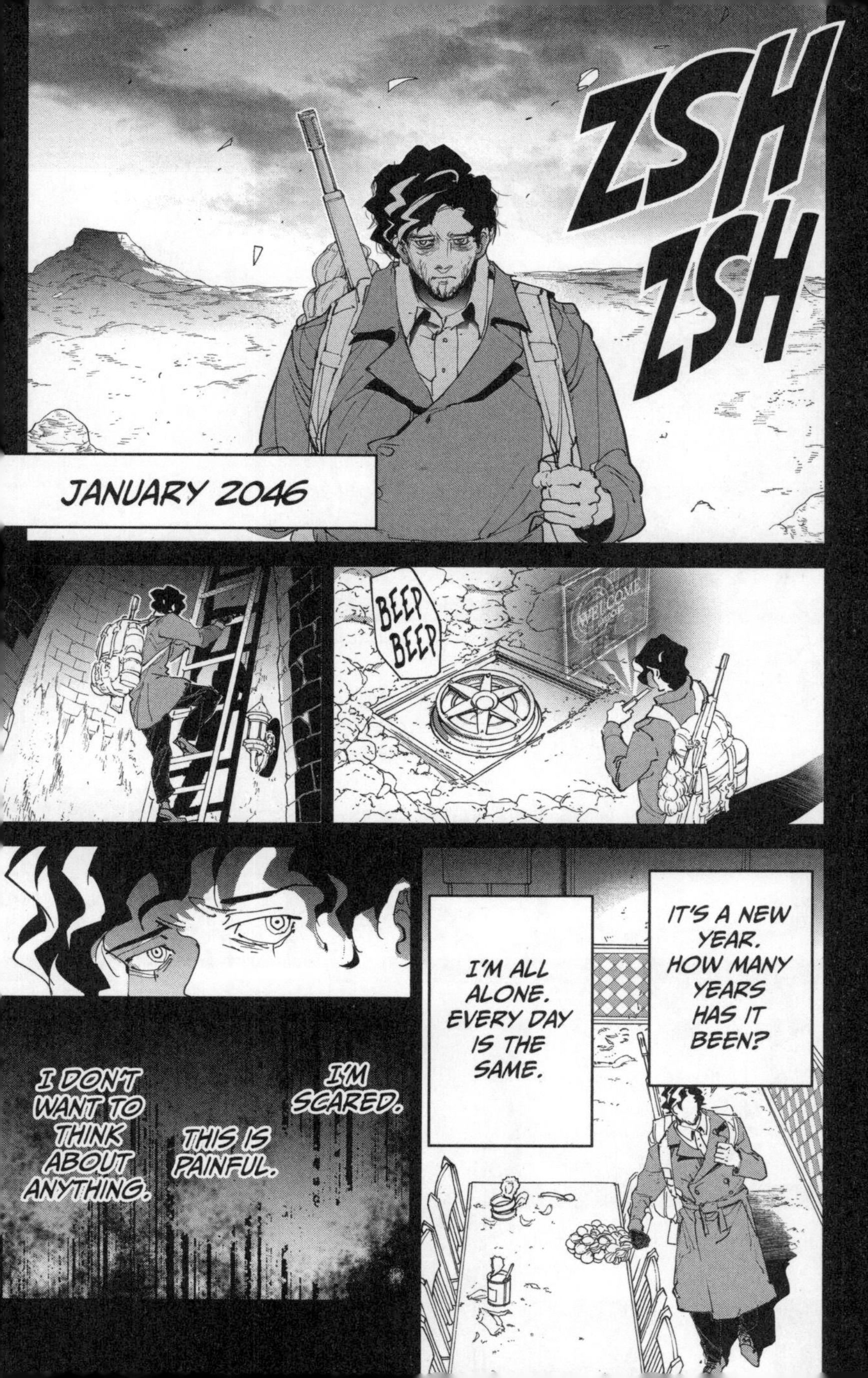
ZSH ZSH
JANUARY 2046
BEEP BEEP
IT'S A NEW YEAR. HOW MANY YEARS HAS IT BEEN?
I'M ALL ALONE. EVERY DAY IS THE SAME.
I'M SCARED.
THIS IS PAINFUL.
I DON'T WANT TO THINK ABOUT ANYTHING.

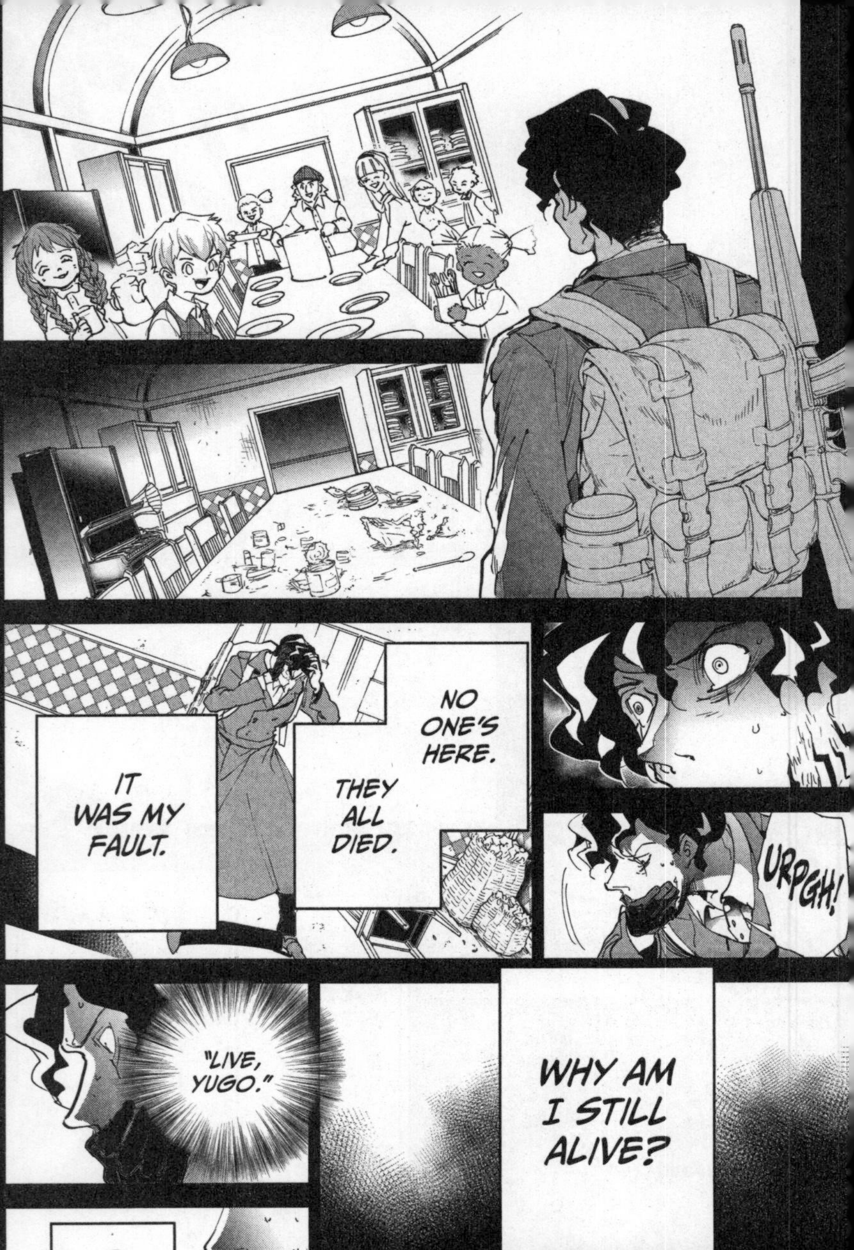
URPGH!
NO ONE'S HERE.
THEY ALL DIED.
IT WAS MY FAULT.
WHY AM I STILL ALIVE?
"LIVE, YUGO."

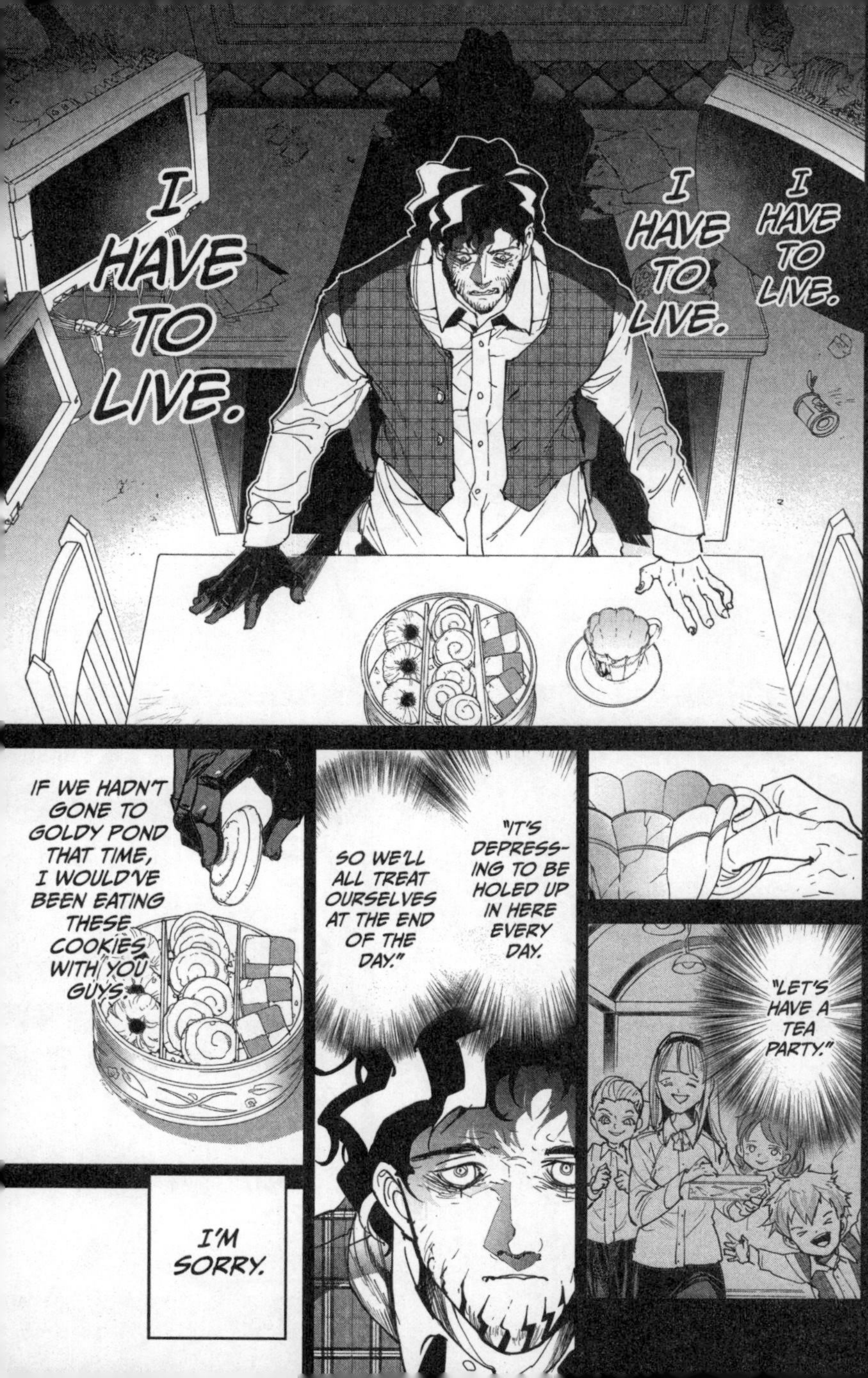
I HAVE TO LIVE.
I HAVE TO LIVE.
I HAVE TO LIVE.
"LET'S HAVE A TEA PARTY."
"IT'S DEPRESSING TO BE HOLED UP IN HERE EVERY DAY.
SO WE'LL ALL TREAT OURSELVES AT THE END OF THE DAY."
IF WE HADN'T GONE TO GOLDY POND THAT TIME, I WOULD'VE BEEN EATING THESE COOKIES WITH YOU GUYS.
I'M SORRY.

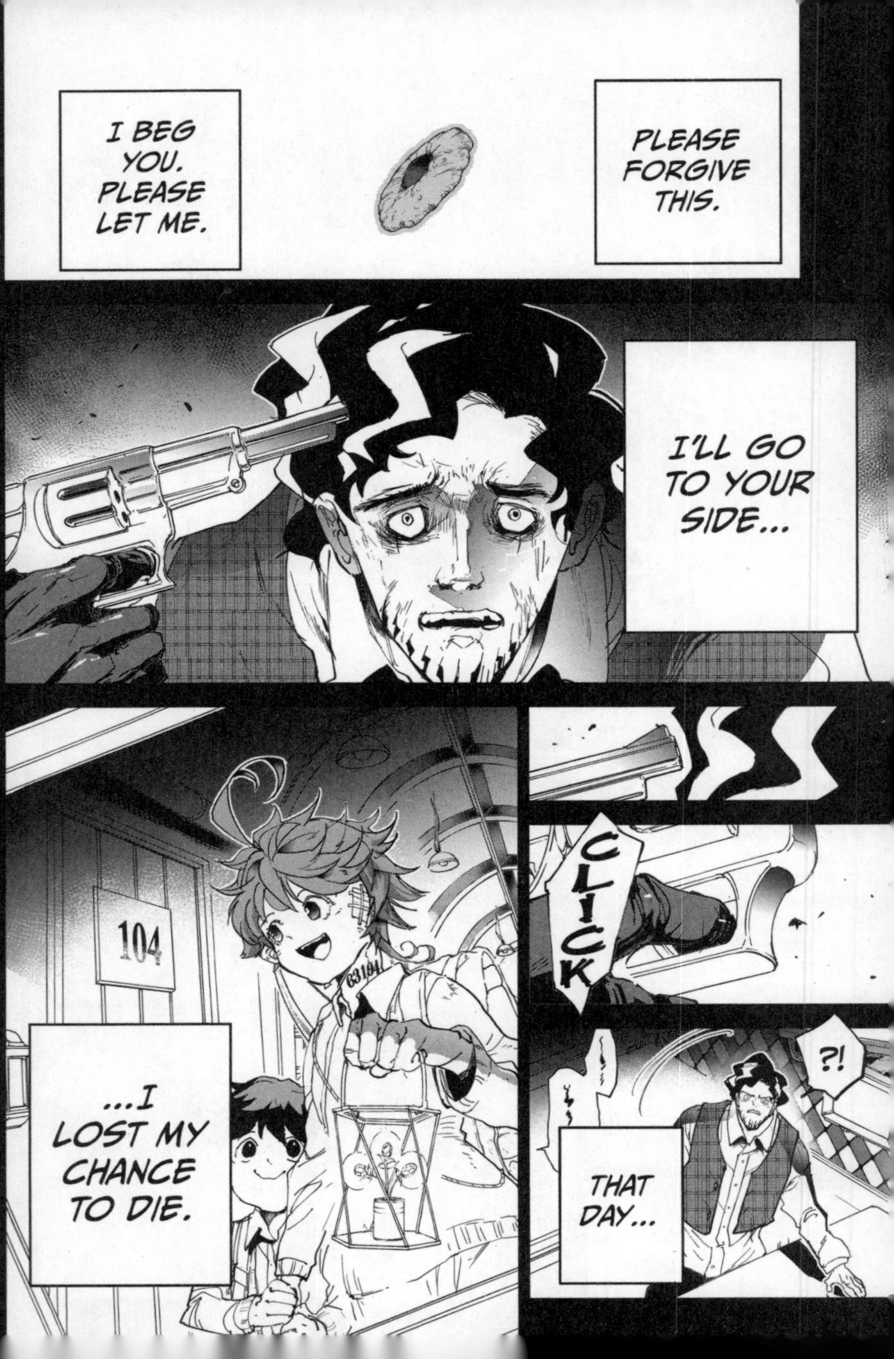
PLEASE FORGIVE THIS.
I BEG YOU. PLEASE LET ME.
I'LL GO TO YOUR SIDE...
CLICK
?!
THAT DAY...
104
...I LOST MY CHANCE TO DIE.

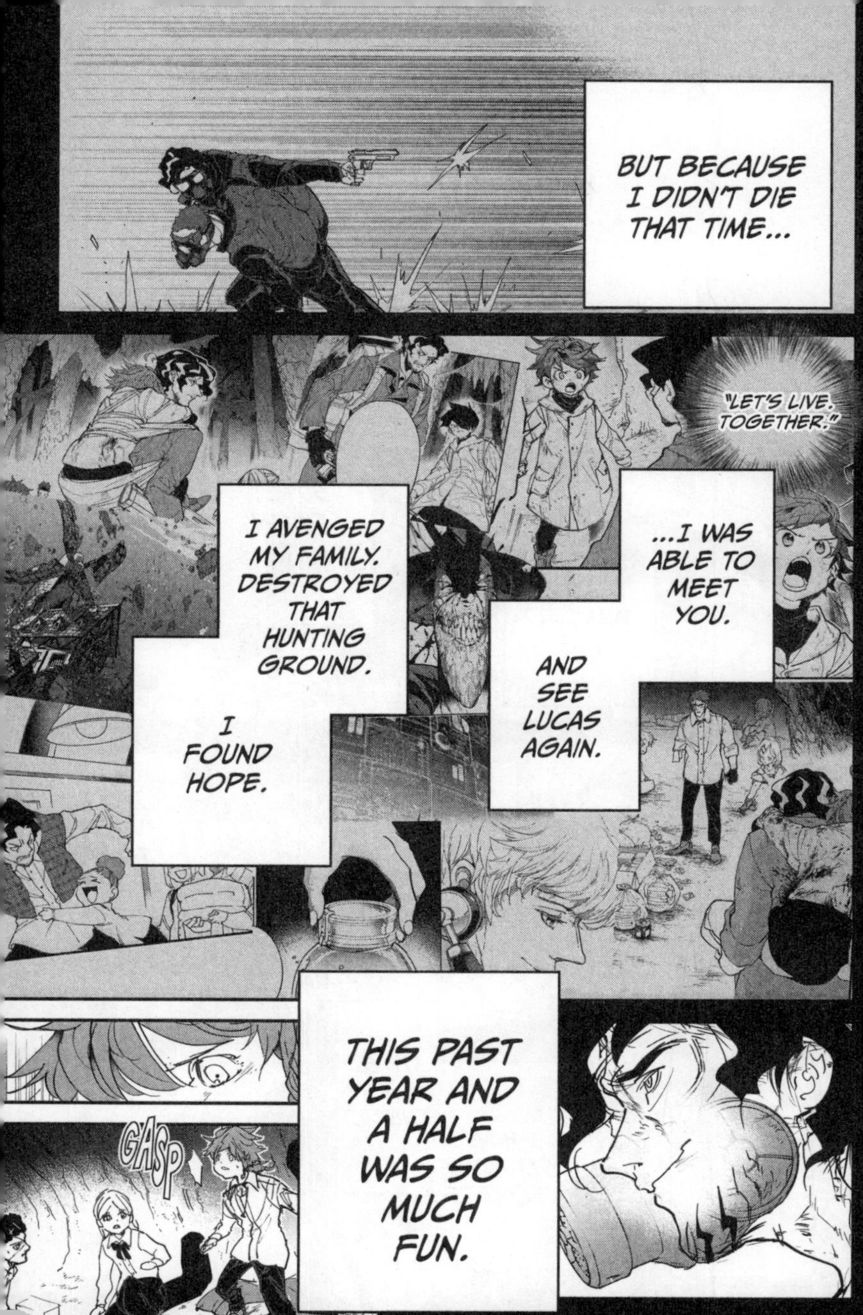
BUT BECAUSE I DIDN'T DIE THAT TIME...
"LET'S LIVE. TOGETHER."
...I WAS ABLE TO MEET YOU.
AND SEE LUCAS AGAIN.
I AVENGED MY FAMILY. DESTROYED THAT HUNTING GROUND.
I FOUND HOPE.
THIS PAST YEAR AND A HALF WAS SO MUCH FUN.
GASP

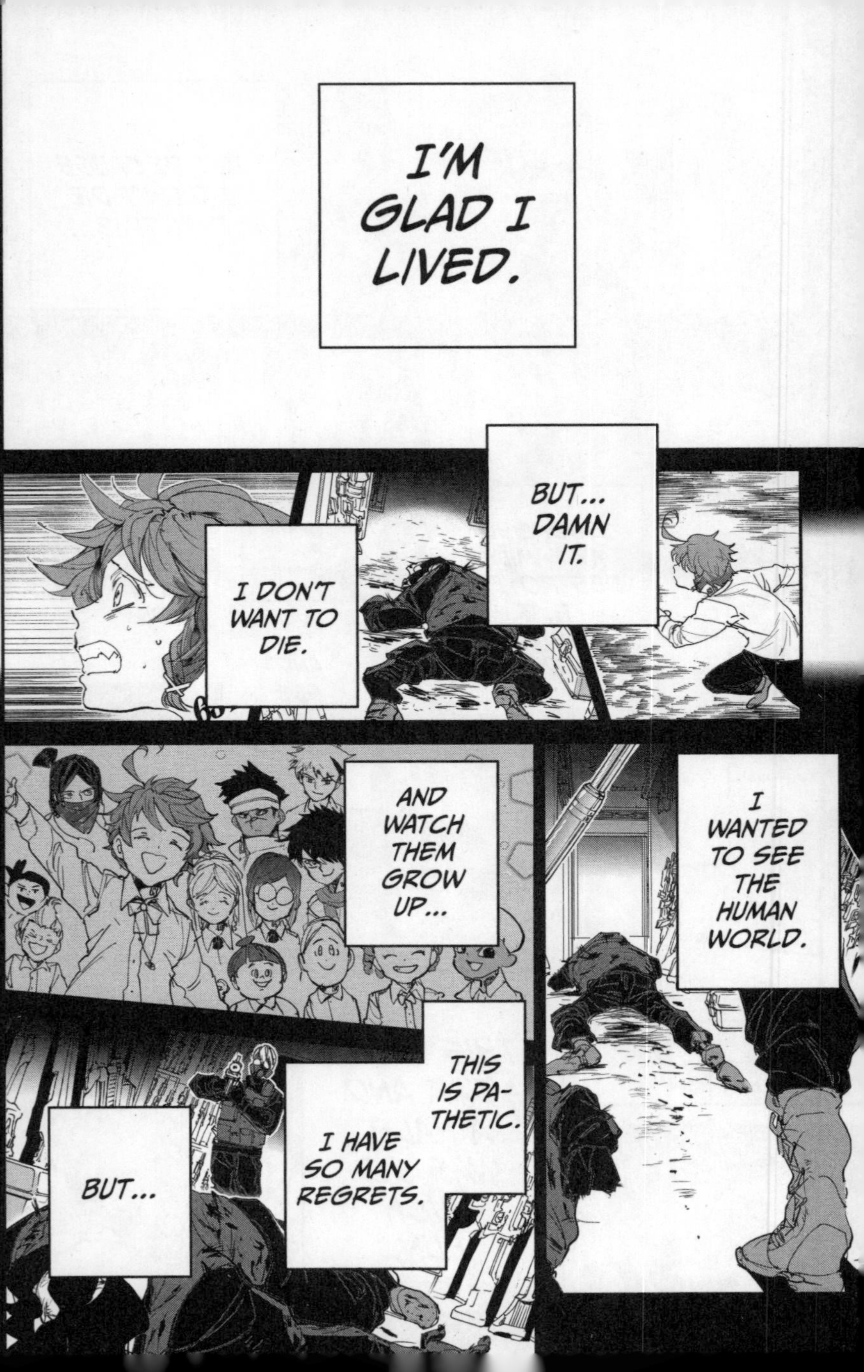
I'M GLAD I LIVED.
BUT... DAMN IT.
I DON'T WANT TO DIE.
I WANTED TO SEE THE HUMAN WORLD.
AND WATCH THEM GROW UP...
THIS IS PA-THETIC.
I HAVE SO MANY REGRETS.
BUT...

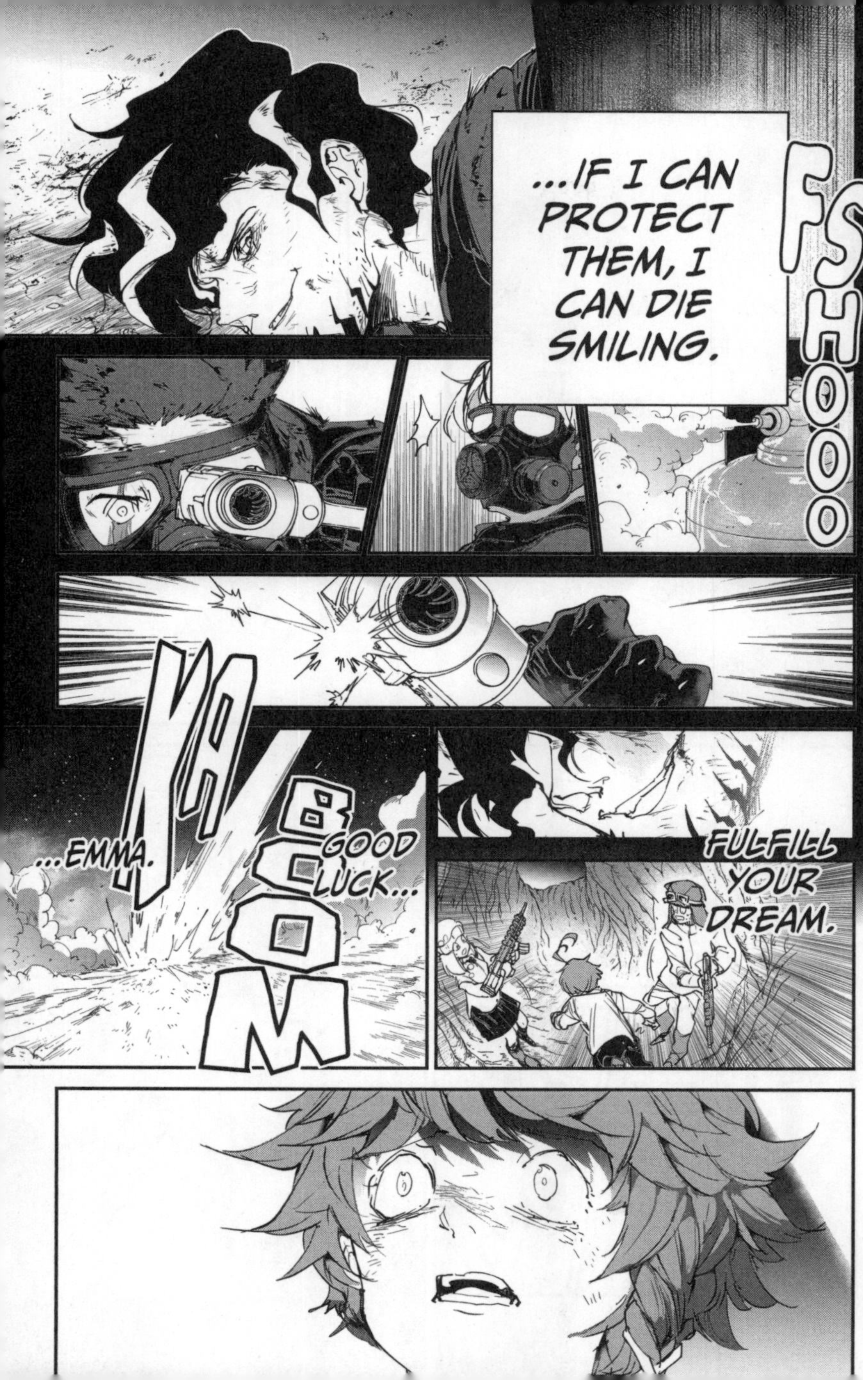
...IF I CAN PROTECT THEM, I CAN DIE SMILING.
FSHOOO
FULFILL YOUR DREAM.
GOOD LUCK...
...EMMA.
KA
BOOM

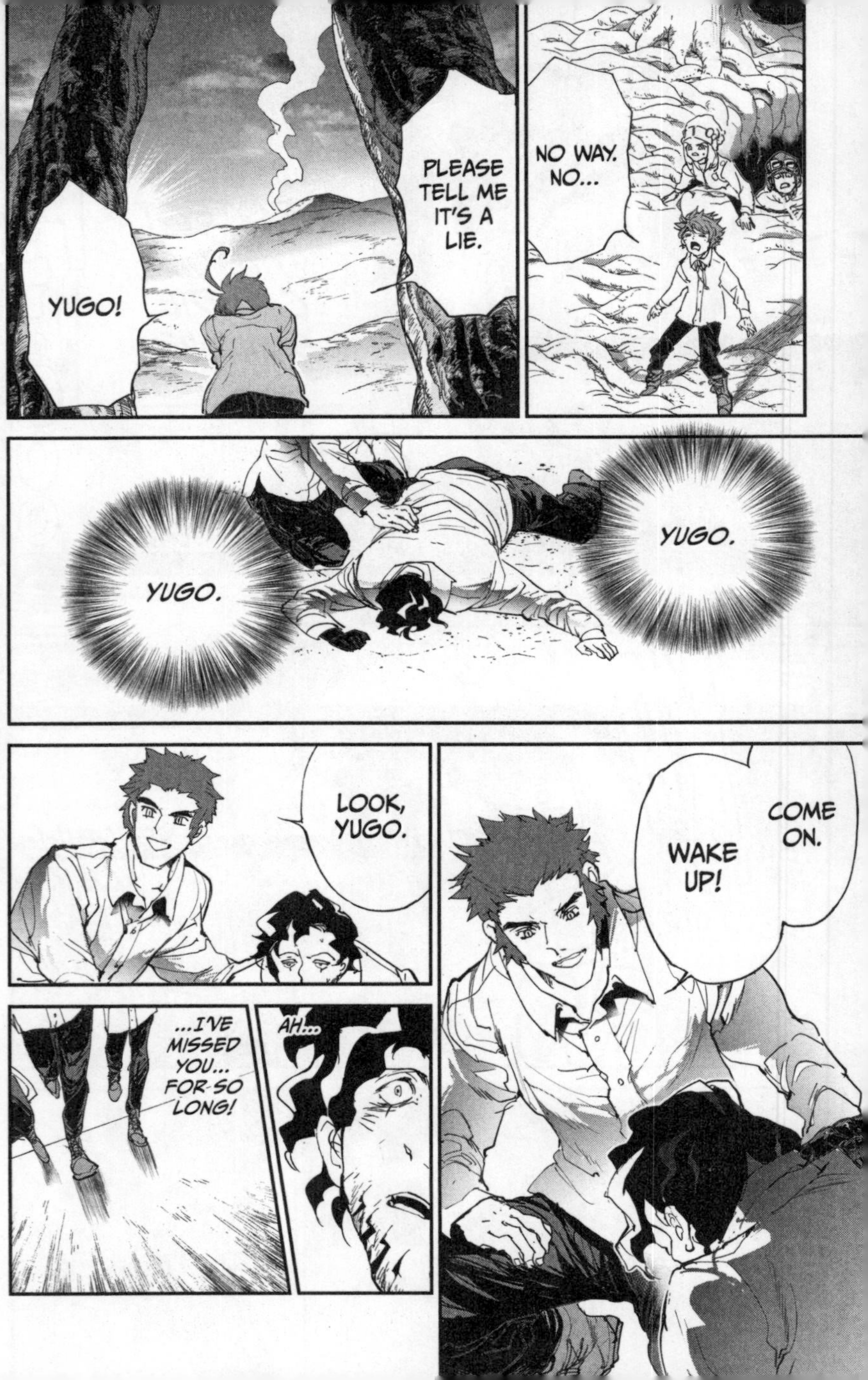
NO WAY. NO...
PLEASE TELL ME IT'S A LIE.
YUGO!
YUGO.
YUGO.
COME ON.
WAKE UP!
LOOK, YUGO.
AH...
...I'VE MISSED YOU... FOR SO LONG!

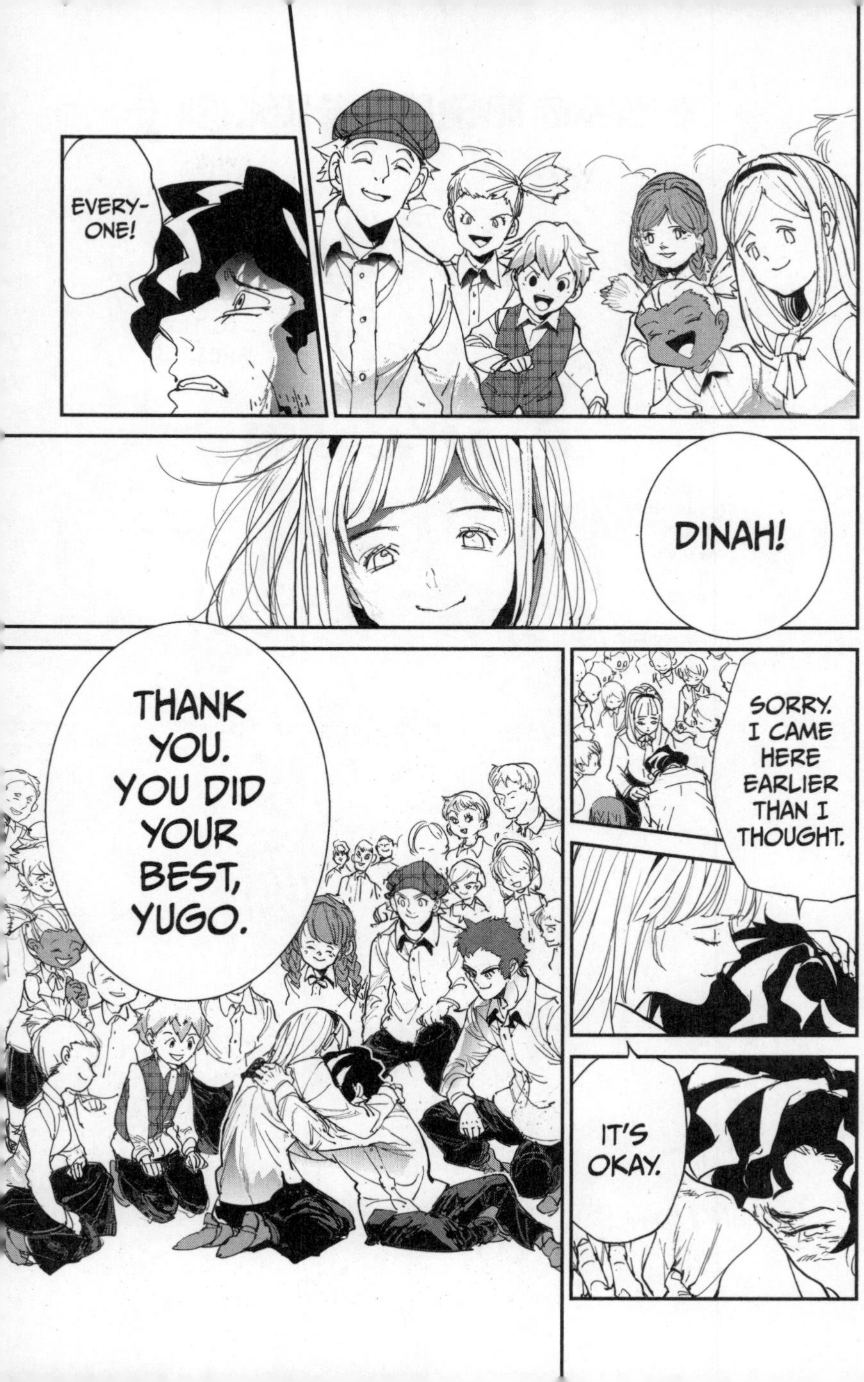
EVERY-ONE!
DINAH!
SORRY. I CAME HERE EARLIER THAN I THOUGHT.
IT'S OKAY.
THANK YOU. YOU DID YOUR BEST, YUGO.

THE PROMISED NEVERLAND SIDE SCENE 020

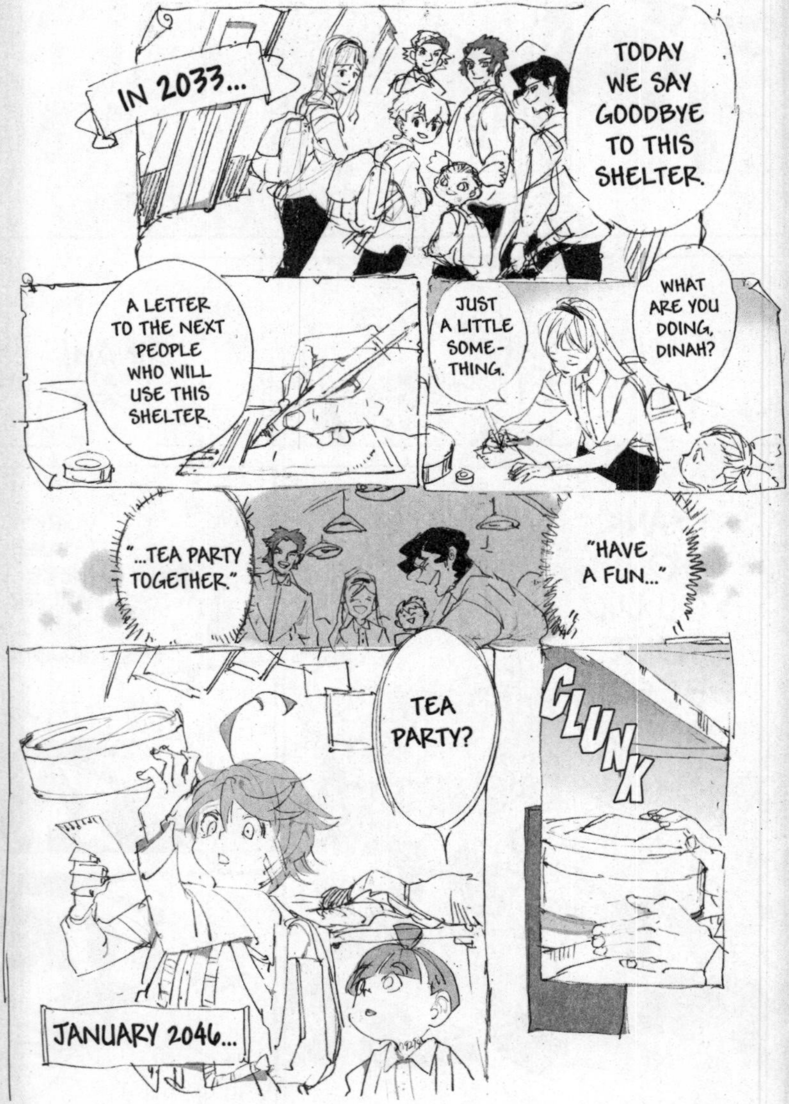

TODAY WE SAY GOODBYE TO THIS SHELTER.
IN 2033...
WHAT ARE YOU DOING, DINAH?
JUST A LITTLE SOME-THING.
A LETTER TO THE NEXT PEOPLE WHO WILL USE THIS SHELTER.
"HAVE A FUN..."
"...TEA PARTY TOGETHER."
CLUNK
TEA PARTY?
JANUARY 2046...

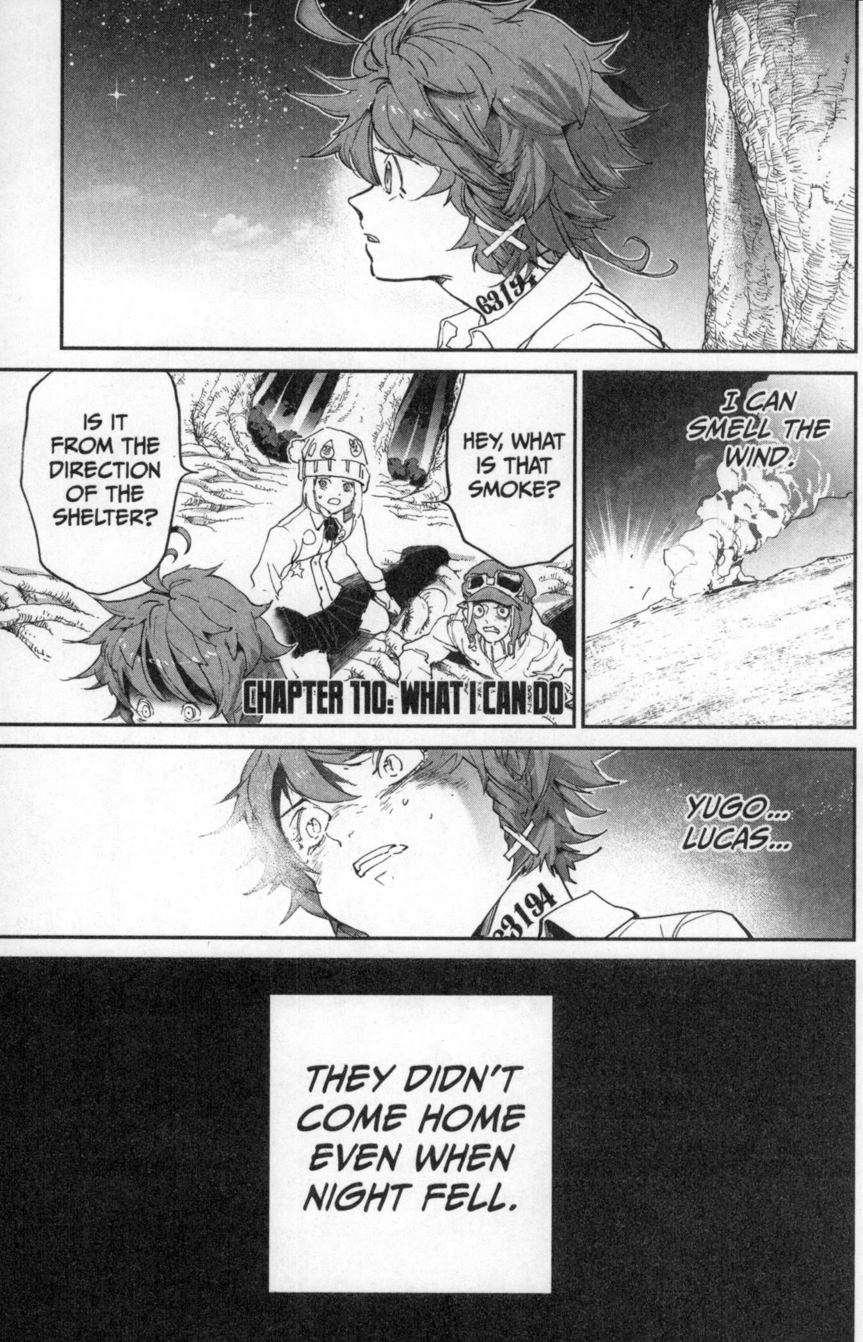
I CAN SMELL THE WIND.
HEY, WHAT IS THAT SMOKE?
IS IT FROM THE DIRECTION OF THE SHELTER?
CHAPTER 110: WHAT I CAN DO
YUGO... LUCAS...
THEY DIDN'T COME HOME EVEN WHEN NIGHT FELL.

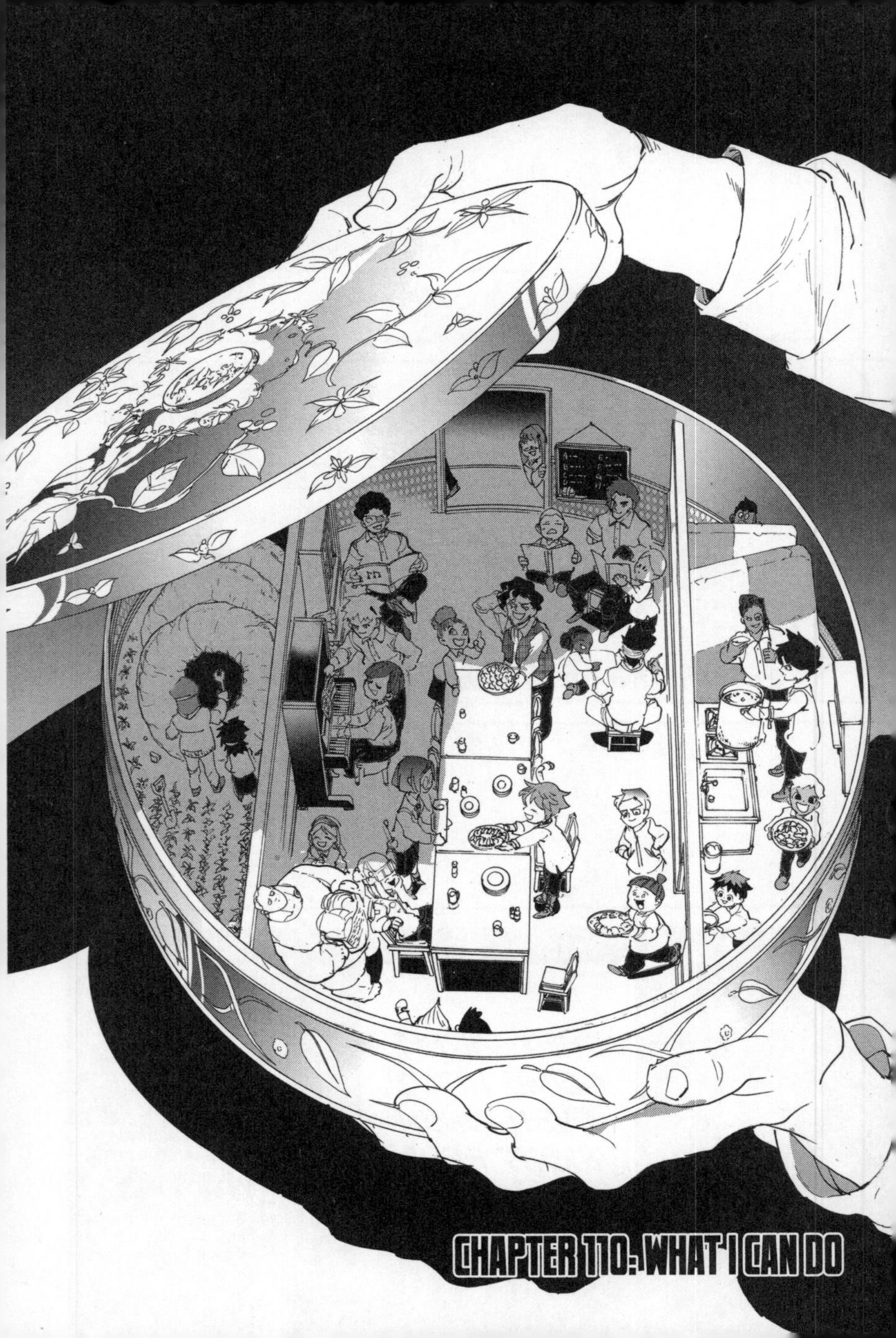

CHAPTER 110: WHAT I CAN DO

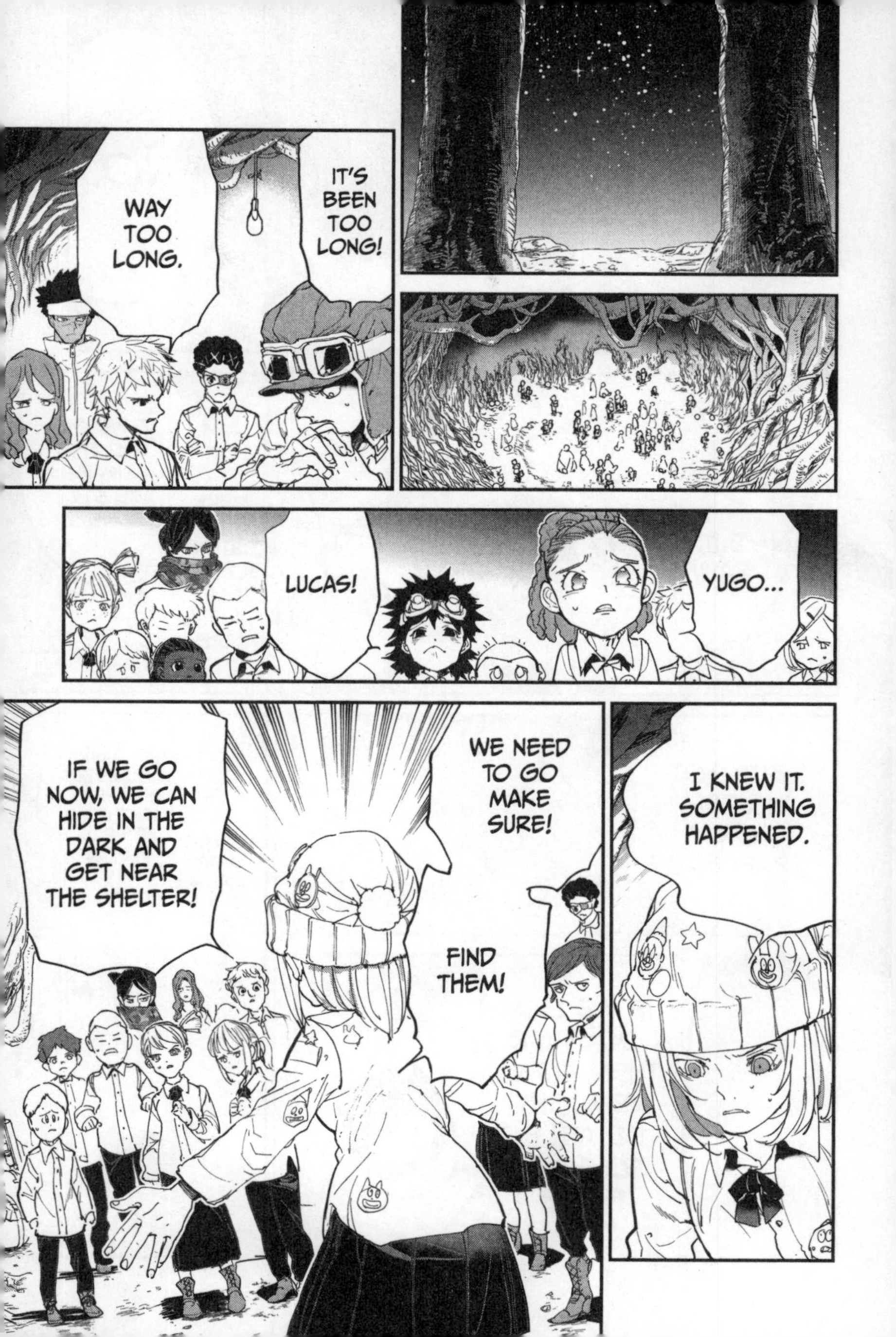
IT'S BEEN TOO LONG!
WAY TOO LONG.
YUGO...
LUCAS!
I KNEW IT. SOMETHING HAPPENED.
WE NEED TO GO MAKE SURE!
FIND THEM!
IF WE GO NOW, WE CAN HIDE IN THE DARK AND GET NEAR THE SHELTER!

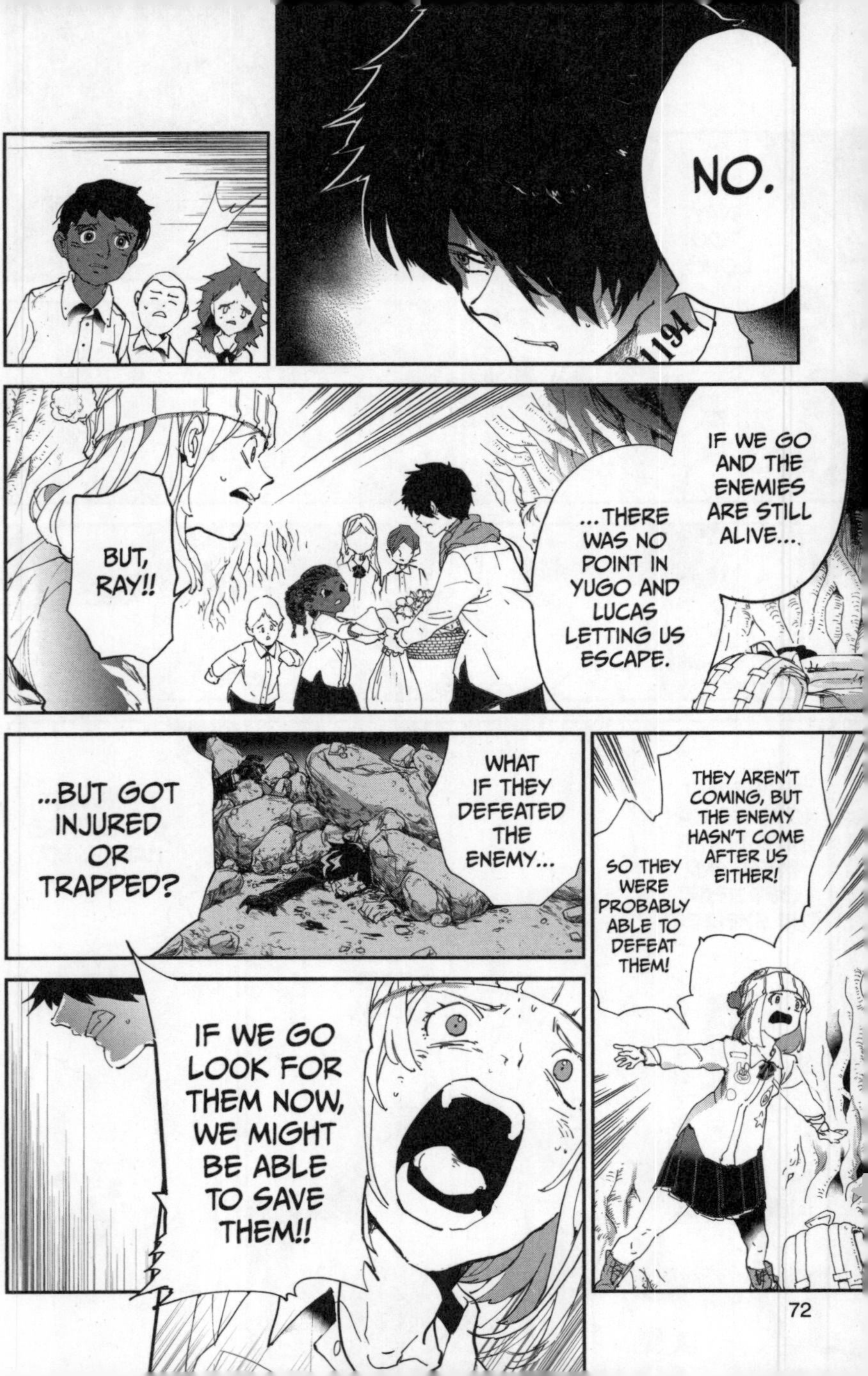
NO.
IF WE GO AND THE ENEMIES ARE STILL ALIVE...
...THERE WAS NO POINT IN YUGO AND LUCAS LETTING US ESCAPE.
BUT, RAY!!
THEY AREN'T COMING, BUT THE ENEMY HASN'T COME AFTER US EITHER!
SO THEY WERE PROBABLY ABLE TO DEFEAT THEM!
WHAT IF THEY DEFEATED THE ENEMY...
...BUT GOT INJURED OR TRAPPED?
IF WE GO LOOK FOR THEM NOW, WE MIGHT BE ABLE TO SAVE THEM!!

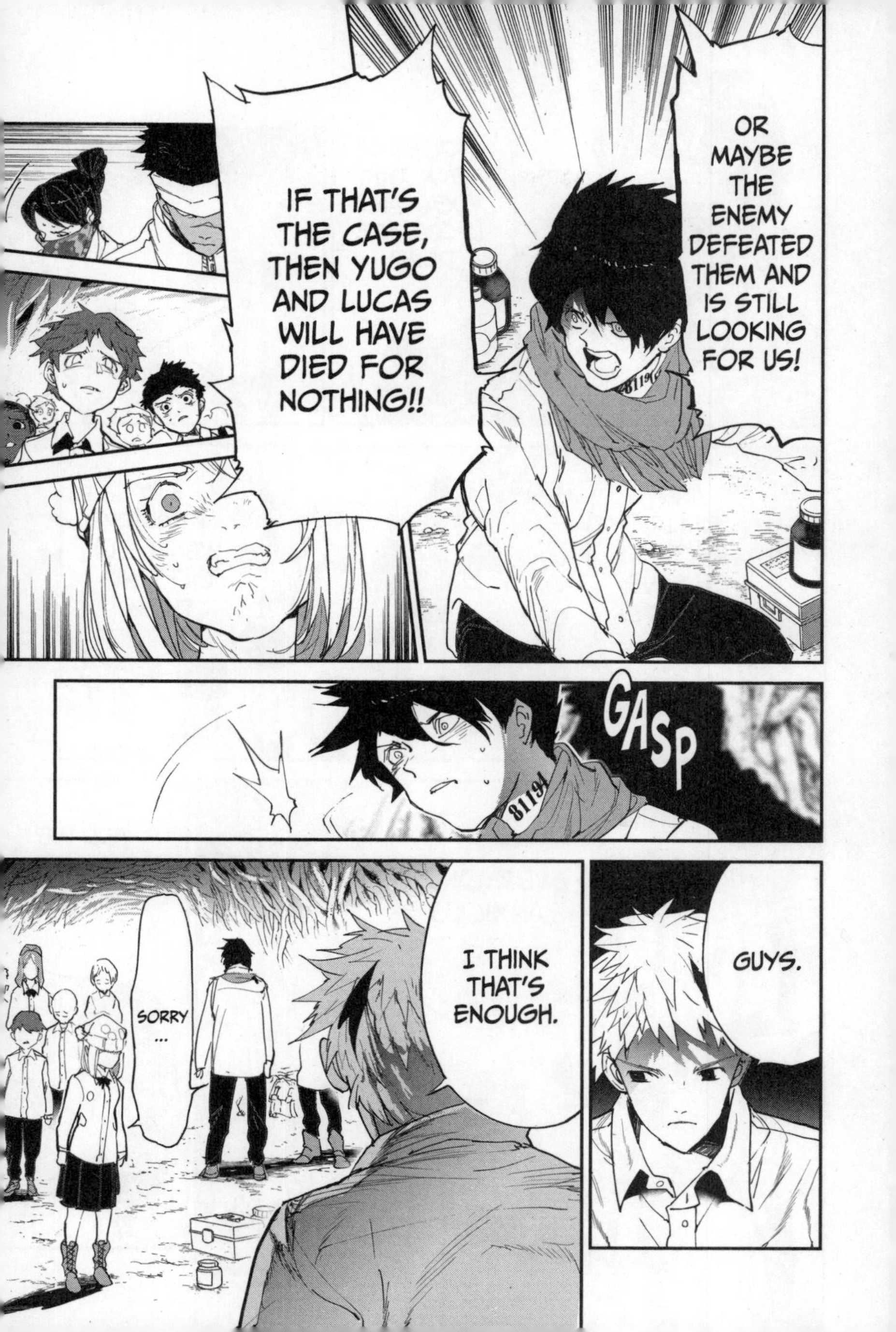
OR MAYBE THE ENEMY DEFEATED THEM AND IS STILL LOOKING FOR US!
IF THAT'S THE CASE, THEN YUGO AND LUCAS WILL HAVE DIED FOR NOTHING!!
GASP
GUYS.
I THINK THAT'S ENOUGH.
SORRY ...

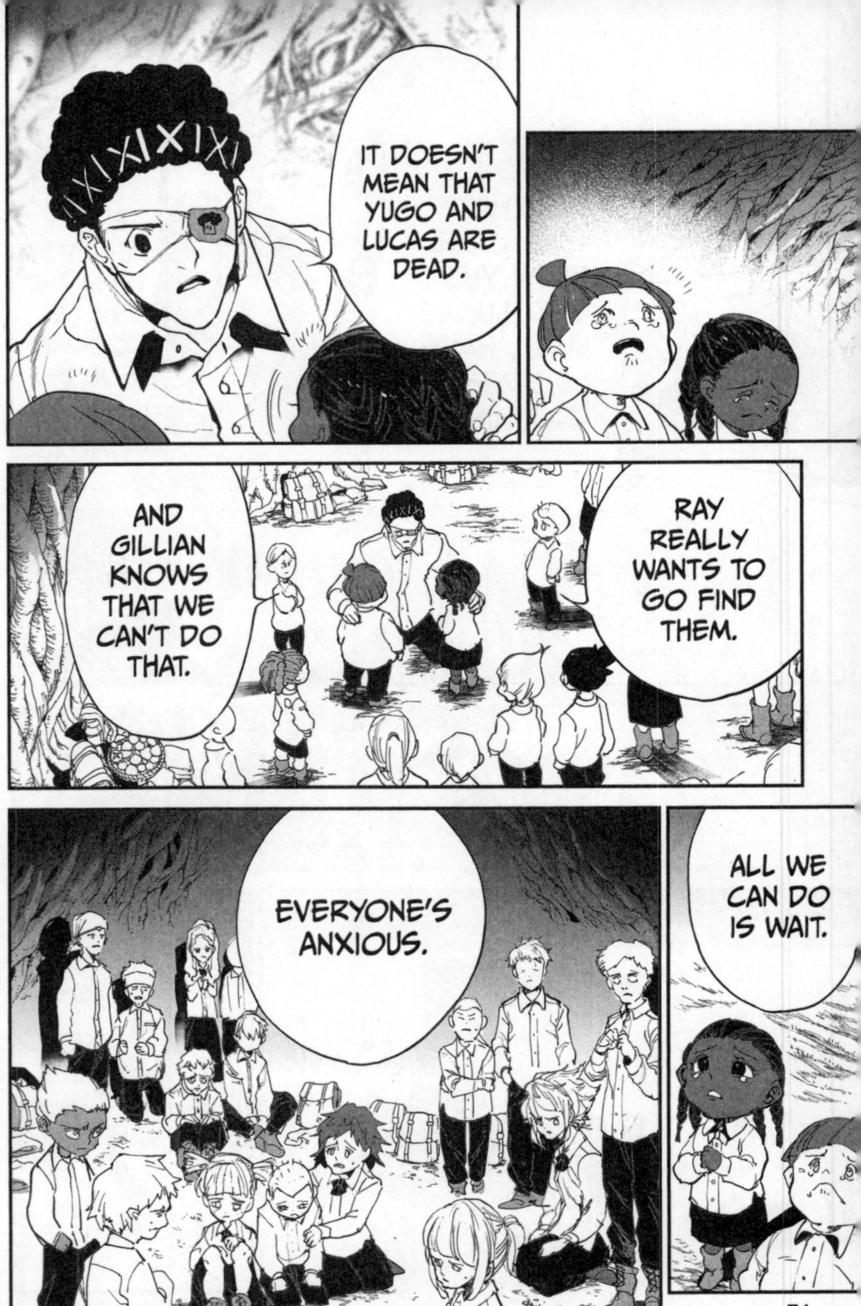
IT DOESN'T MEAN THAT YUGO AND LUCAS ARE DEAD.
RAY REALLY WANTS TO GO FIND THEM.
AND GILLIAN KNOWS THAT WE CAN'T DO THAT.
ALL WE CAN DO IS WAIT.
EVERYONE'S ANXIOUS.

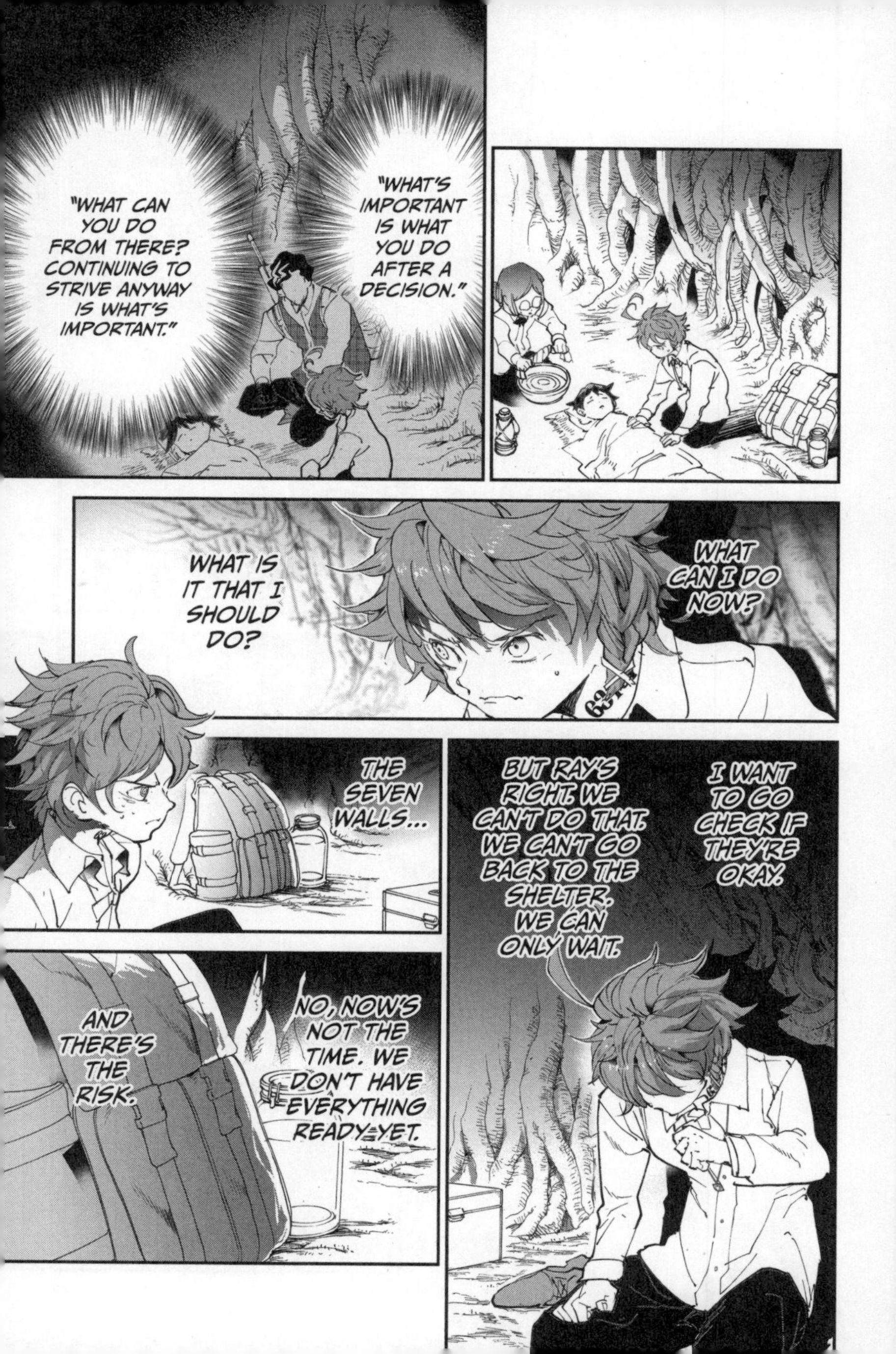
"WHAT'S IMPORTANT IS WHAT YOU DO AFTER A DECISION."
"WHAT CAN YOU DO FROM THERE? CONTINUING TO STRIVE ANYWAY IS WHAT'S IMPORTANT."
WHAT CAN I DO NOW?
WHAT IS IT THAT I SHOULD DO?
I WANT TO GO CHECK IF THEY'RE OKAY.
BUT RAY'S RIGHT. WE CAN'T DO THAT. WE CAN'T GO BACK TO THE SHELTER. WE CAN ONLY WAIT.
THE SEVEN WALLS...
NO, NOW'S NOT THE TIME. WE DON'T HAVE EVERYTHING READY YET.
AND THERE'S THE RISK.

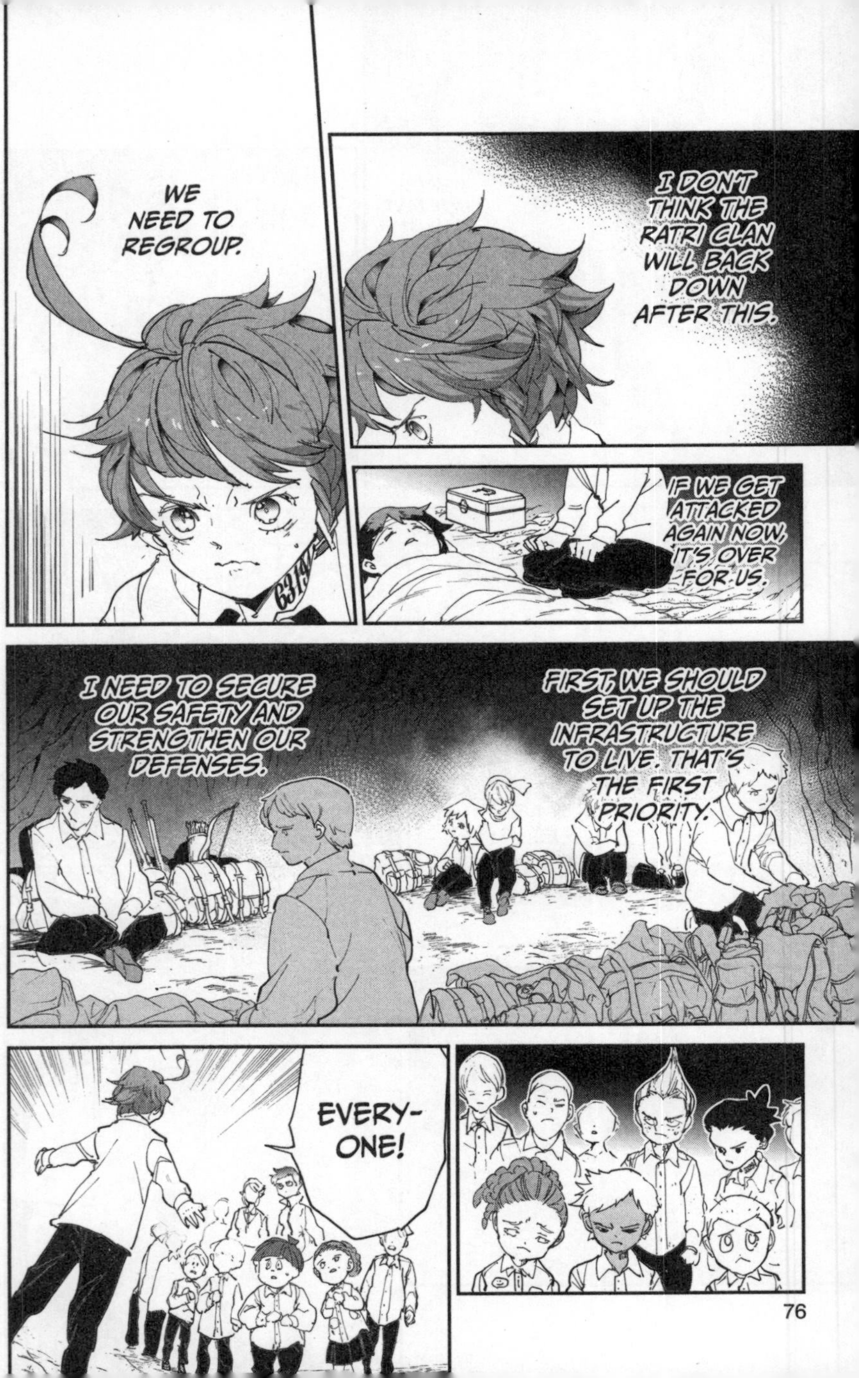
I DON'T THINK THE RATRI CLAN WILL BACK DOWN AFTER THIS.
IF WE GET ATTACKED AGAIN NOW, IT'S OVER FOR US.
WE NEED TO REGROUP.
FIRST, WE SHOULD SET UP THE INFRASTRUCTURE TO LIVE. THAT'S THE FIRST PRIORITY.
I NEED TO SECURE OUR SAFETY AND STRENGTHEN OUR DEFENSES.
EVERY-ONE!

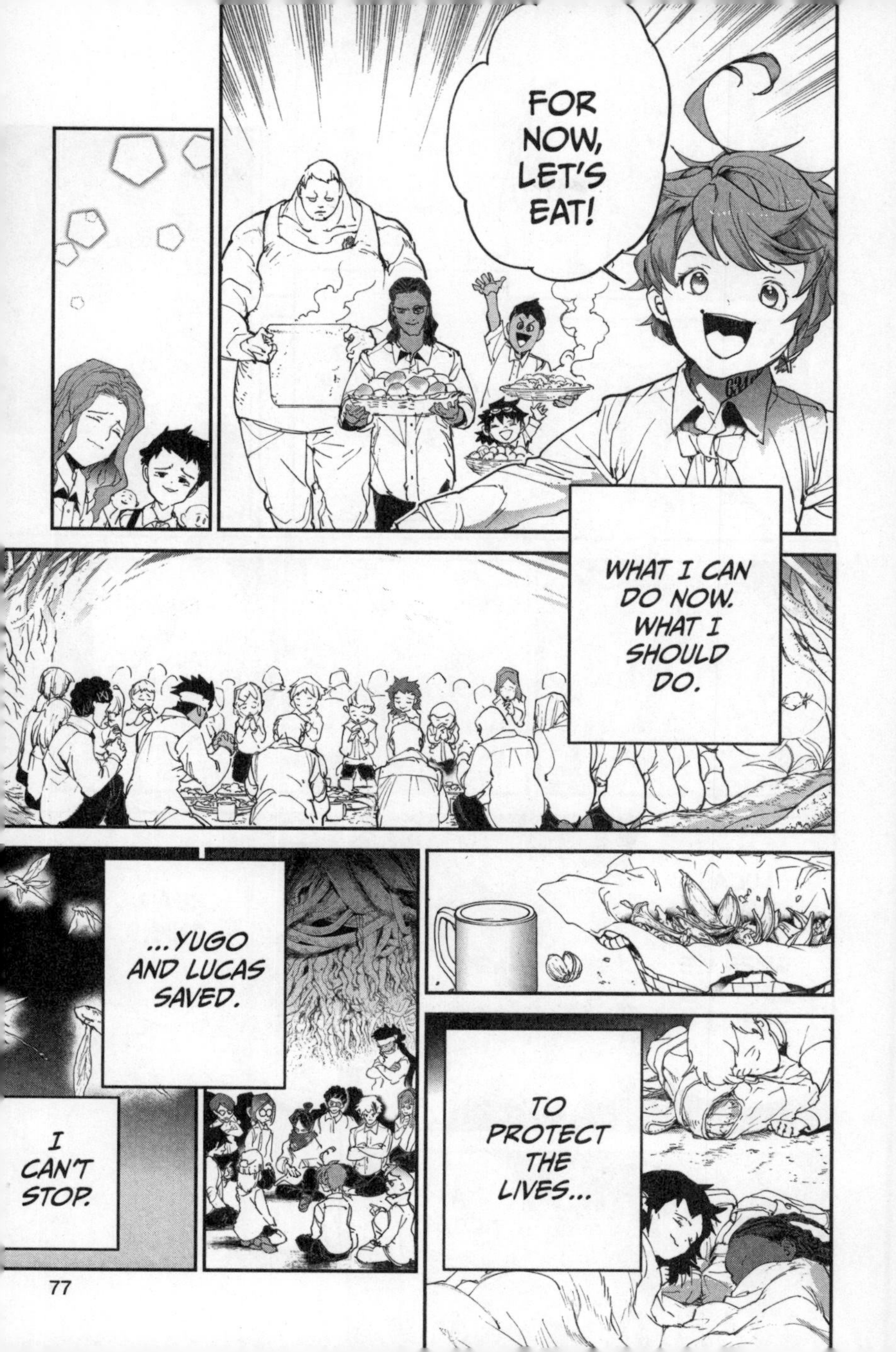

FOR NOW, LET'S EAT!
WHAT I CAN DO NOW. WHAT I SHOULD DO.
TO PROTECT THE LIVES...
...YUGO AND LUCAS SAVED.
I CAN'T STOP.

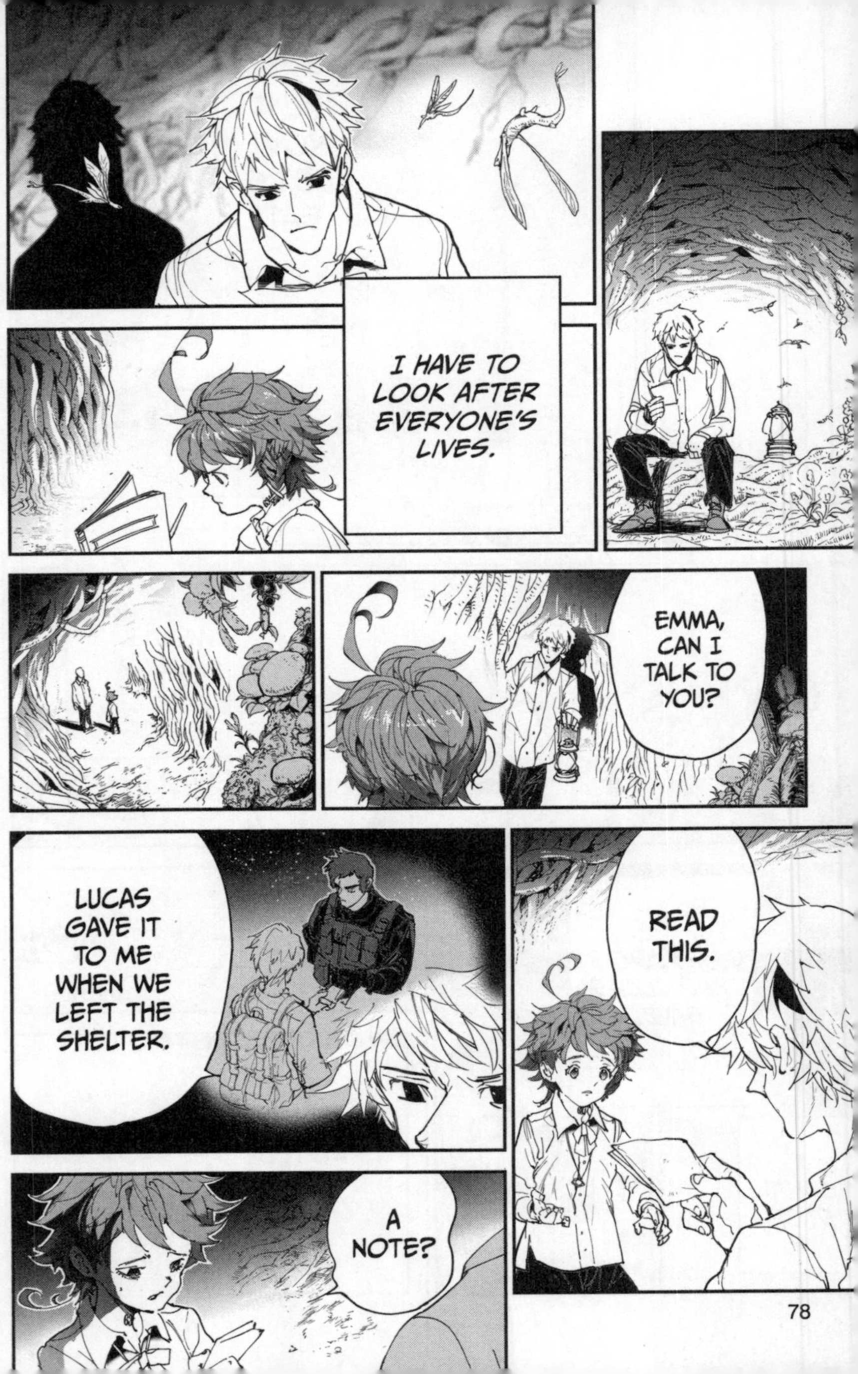
I HAVE TO LOOK AFTER EVERYONE'S LIVES.
EMMA, CAN I TALK TO YOU?
READ THIS.
LUCAS GAVE IT TO ME WHEN WE LEFT THE SHELTER.
A NOTE?

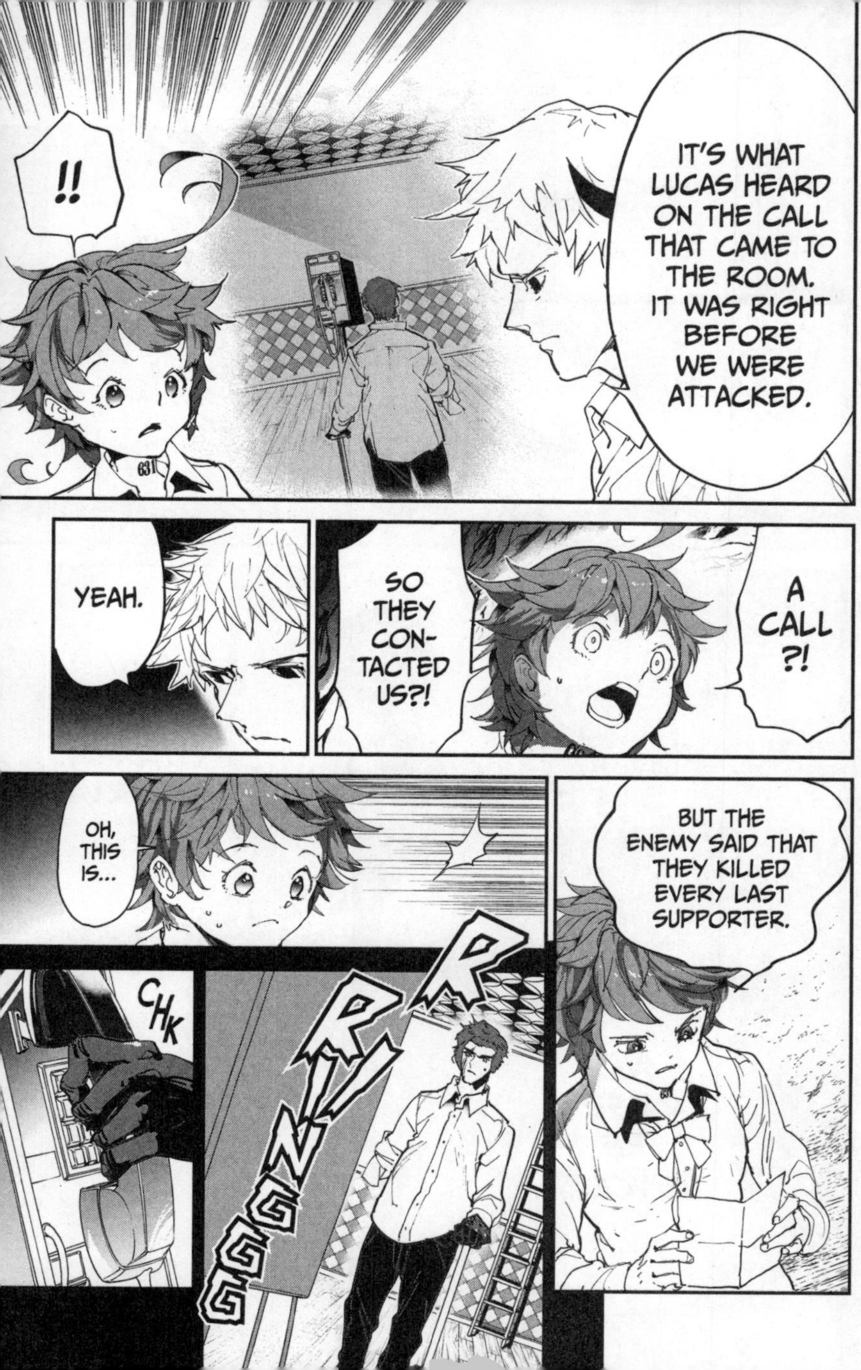
IT'S WHAT LUCAS HEARD ON THE CALL THAT CAME TO THE ROOM. IT WAS RIGHT BEFORE WE WERE ATTACKED.
!!
A CALL?!
SO THEY CON- TACTED US?!
YEAH.
BUT THE ENEMY SAID THAT THEY KILLED EVERY LAST SUPPORTER.
OH, THIS IS...
RRINGGG
CHK

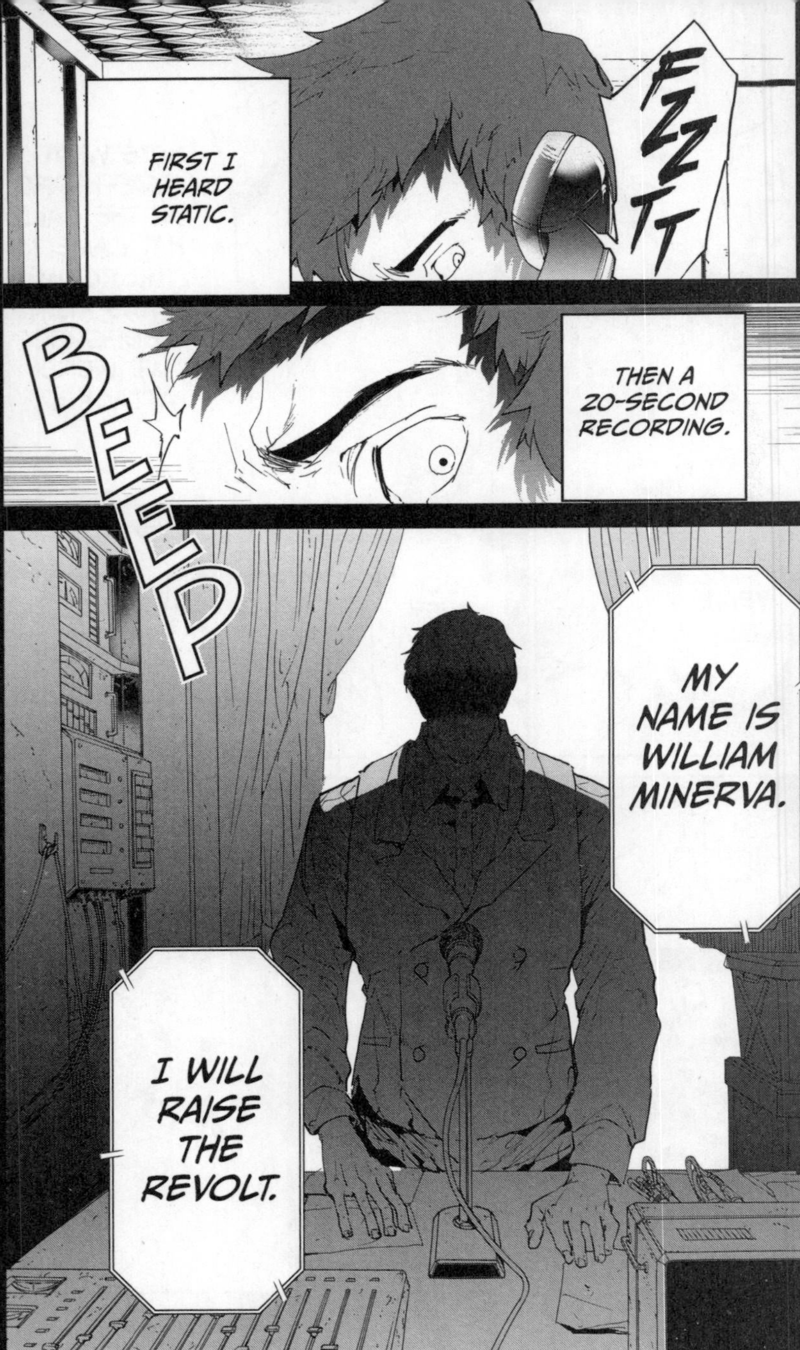
FZZTT
FIRST I HEARD STATIC.
THEN A 20-SECOND RECORDING.
BEEP
MY NAME IS WILLIAM MINERVA.
I WILL RAISE THE REVOLT.

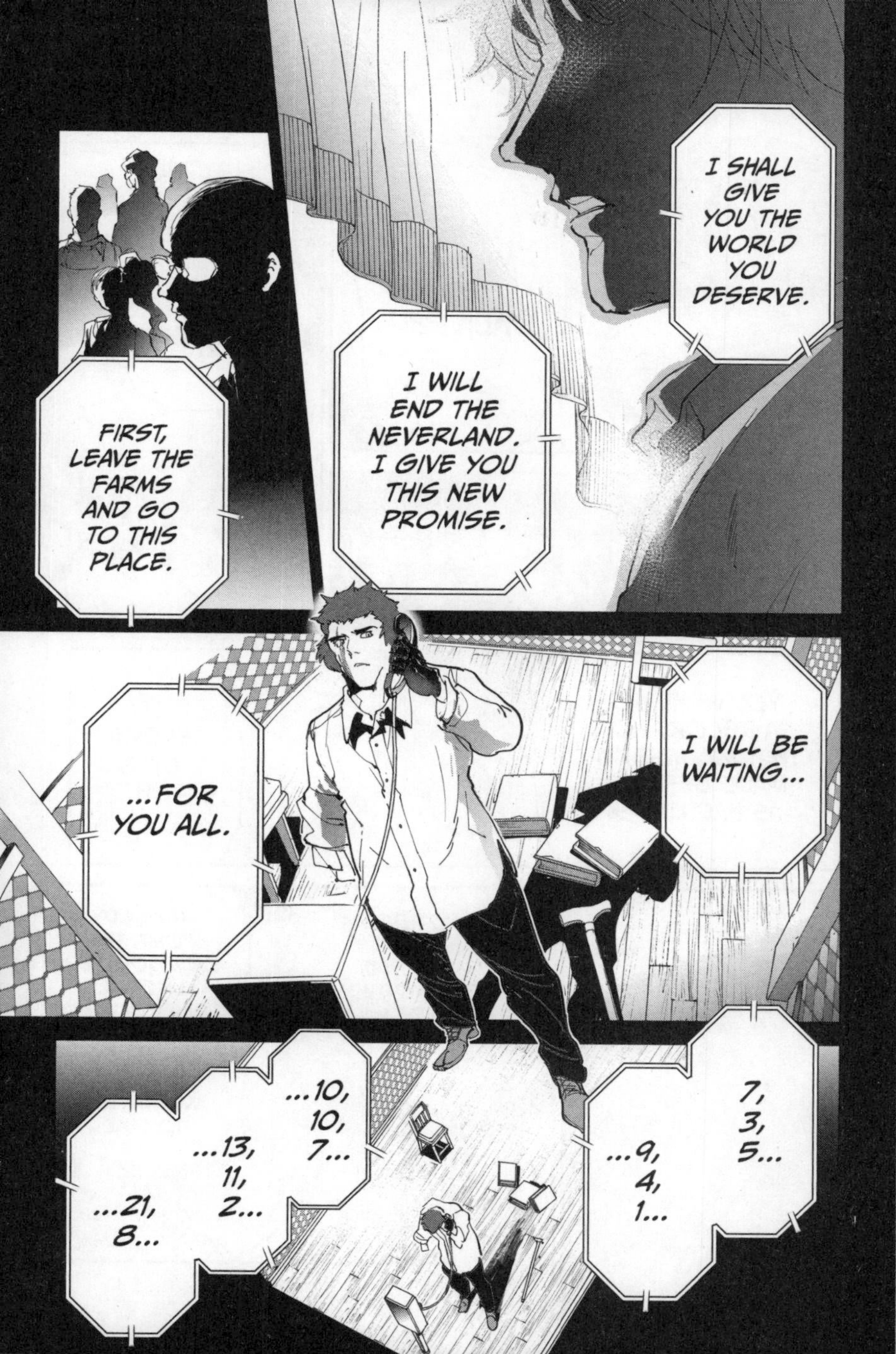
I SHALL GIVE YOU THE WORLD YOU DESERVE.
I WILL END THE NEVERLAND. I GIVE YOU THIS NEW PROMISE.
FIRST, LEAVE THE FARMS AND GO TO THIS PLACE.
I WILL BE WAITING...
...FOR YOU ALL.
7, 3, 5...
...9, 4, 1...
...10, 10, 7...
...13, 11, 2...
...21, 8...

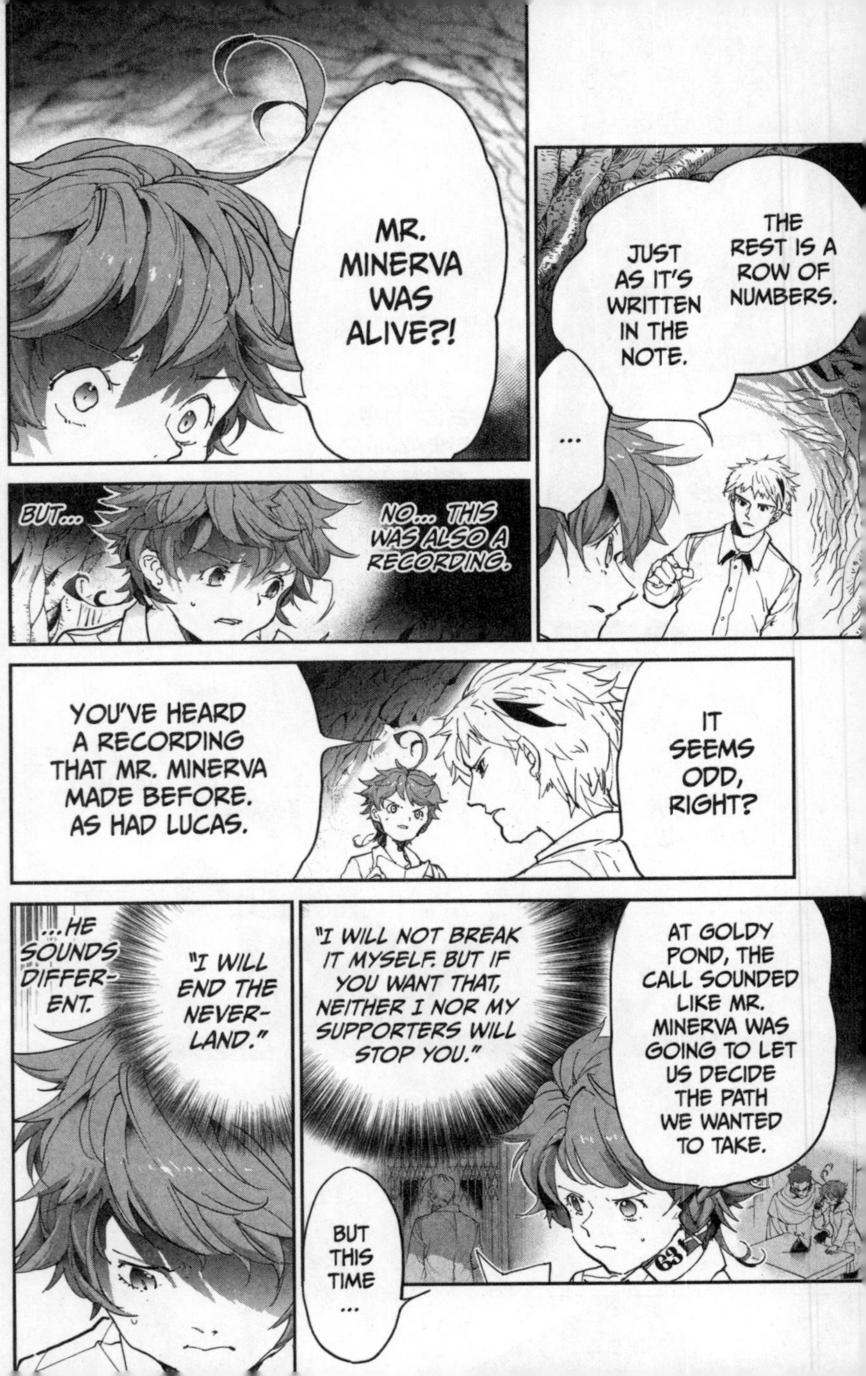
JUST AS IT'S WRITTEN IN THE NOTE. THE REST IS A ROW OF NUMBERS.
...
MR. MINERVA WAS ALIVE?!
NO... THIS WAS ALSO A RECORDING.
BUT...
IT SEEMS ODD, RIGHT?
YOU'VE HEARD A RECORDING THAT MR. MINERVA MADE BEFORE. AS HAD LUCAS.
AT GOLDY POND, THE CALL SOUNDED LIKE MR. MINERVA WAS GOING TO LET US DECIDE THE PATH WE WANTED TO TAKE.
BUT THIS TIME ...
"I WILL NOT BREAK IT MYSELF. BUT IF YOU WANT THAT, NEITHER I NOR MY SUPPORTERS WILL STOP YOU."
"I WILL END THE NEVER-LAND."
...HE SOUNDS DIFFER-ENT.

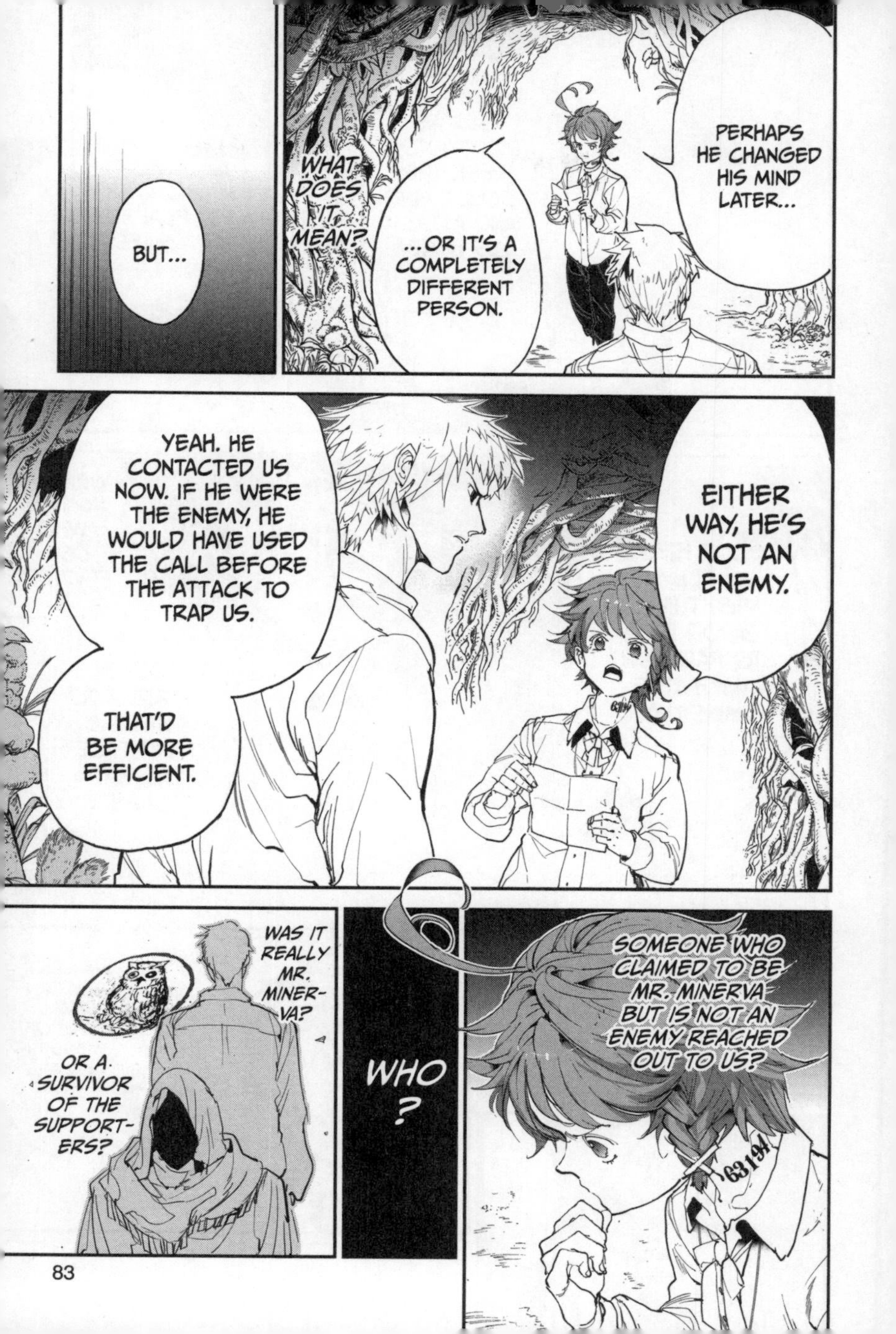
PERHAPS HE CHANGED HIS MIND LATER...
...OR IT'S A COMPLETELY DIFFERENT PERSON.
WHAT DOES IT MEAN?
BUT...
EITHER WAY, HE'S NOT AN ENEMY.
YEAH. HE CONTACTED US NOW. IF HE WERE THE ENEMY, HE WOULD HAVE USED THE CALL BEFORE THE ATTACK TO TRAP US.
THAT'D BE MORE EFFICIENT.
SOMEONE WHO CLAIMED TO BE MR. MINERVA BUT IS NOT AN ENEMY REACHED OUT TO US?
WHO?
WAS IT REALLY MR. MINER-VA?
OR A SURVIVOR OF THE SUPPORT-ERS?

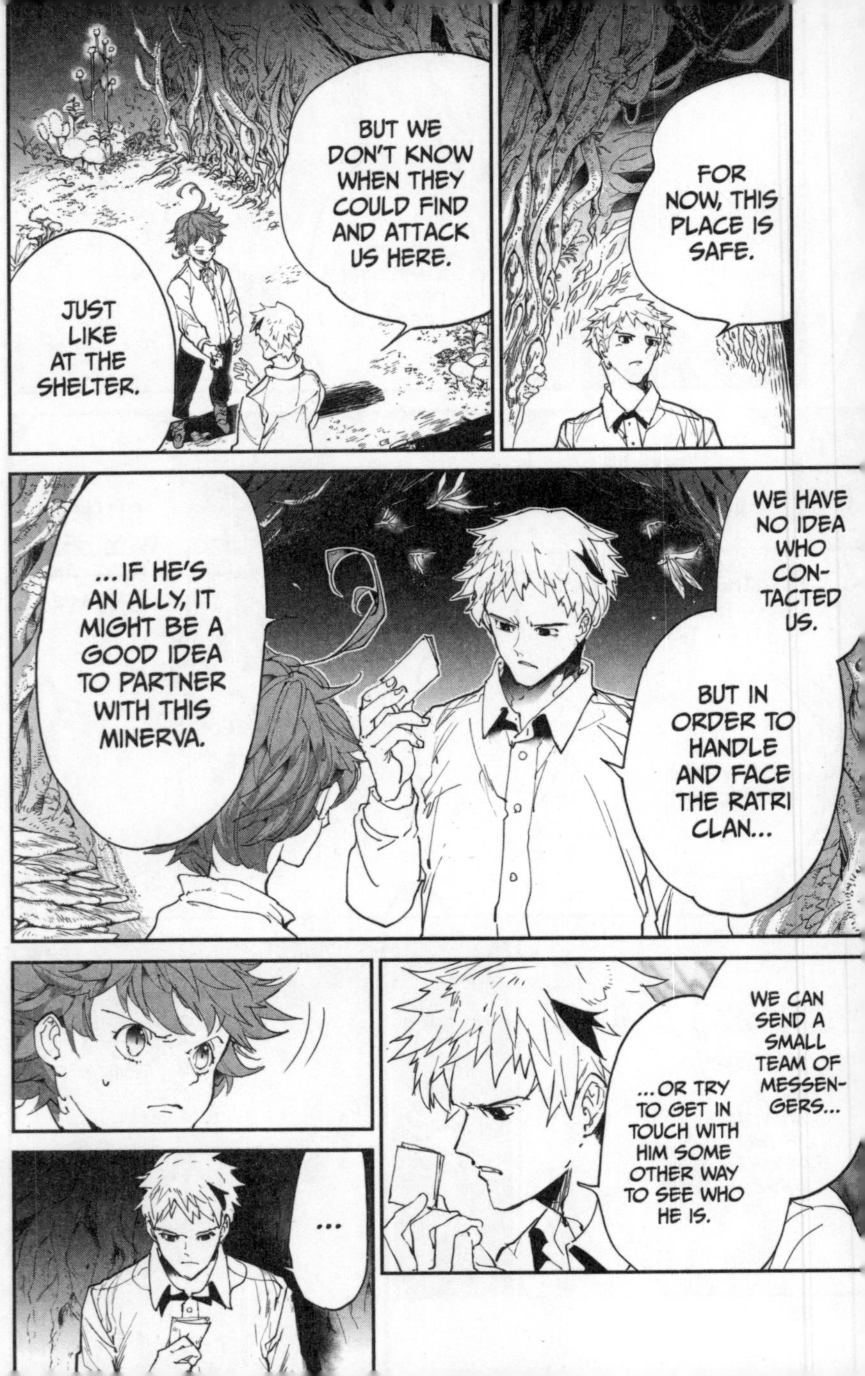
FOR NOW, THIS PLACE IS SAFE.
BUT WE DON'T KNOW WHEN THEY COULD FIND AND ATTACK US HERE.
JUST LIKE AT THE SHELTER.
WE HAVE NO IDEA WHO CON-TACTED US.
BUT IN ORDER TO HANDLE AND FACE THE RATRI CLAN...
...IF HE'S AN ALLY, IT MIGHT BE A GOOD IDEA TO PARTNER WITH THIS MINERVA.
WE CAN SEND A SMALL TEAM OF MESSEN-GERS...
...OR TRY TO GET IN TOUCH WITH HIM SOME OTHER WAY TO SEE WHO HE IS.
...

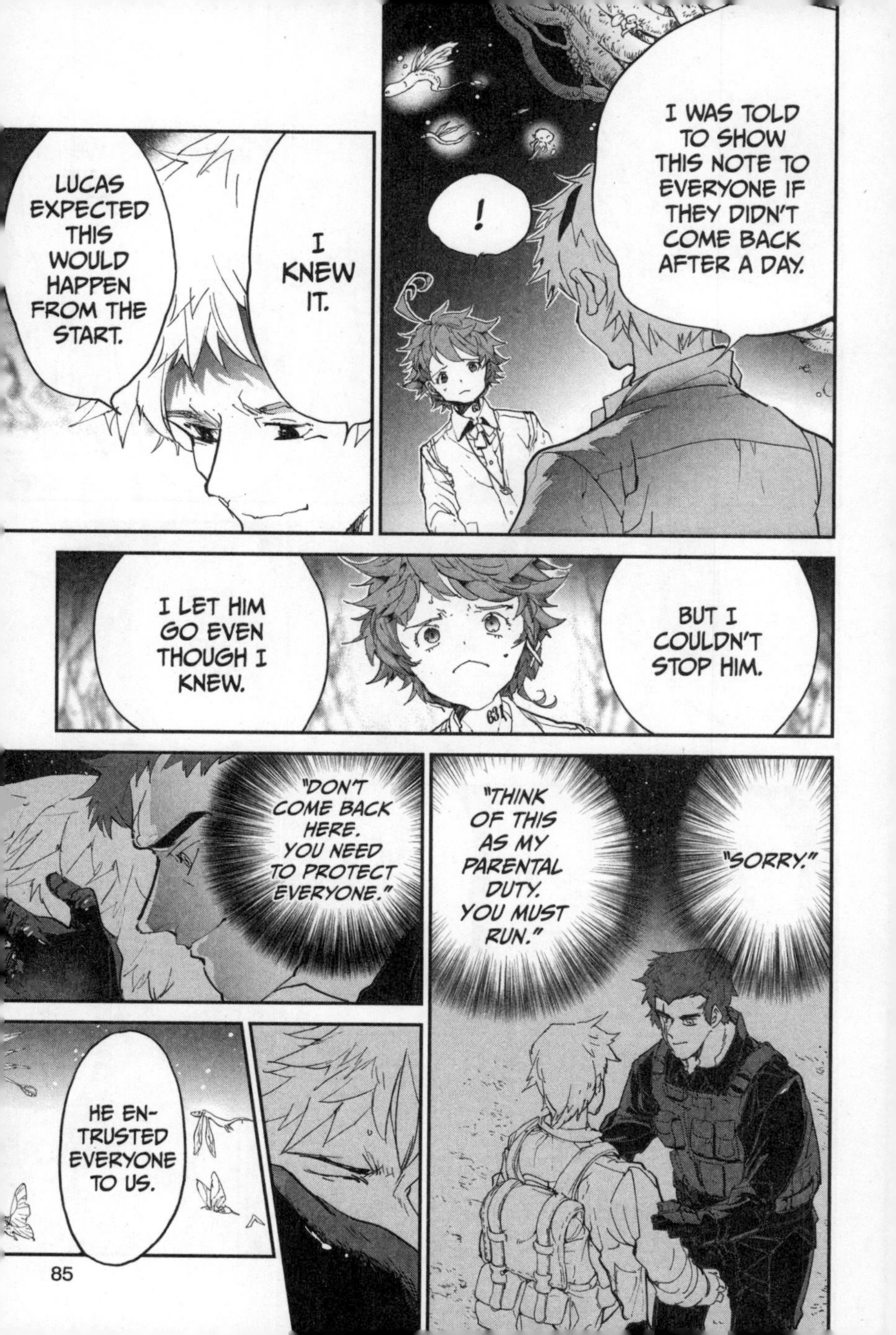
I WAS TOLD TO SHOW THIS NOTE TO EVERYONE IF THEY DIDN'T COME BACK AFTER A DAY.
!
I KNEW IT.
LUCAS EXPECTED THIS WOULD HAPPEN FROM THE START.
BUT I COULDN'T STOP HIM.
I LET HIM GO EVEN THOUGH I KNEW.
"SORRY."
"THINK OF THIS AS MY PARENTAL DUTY. YOU MUST RUN."
"DON'T COME BACK HERE. YOU NEED TO PROTECT EVERYONE."
HE EN-TRUSTED EVERYONE TO US.

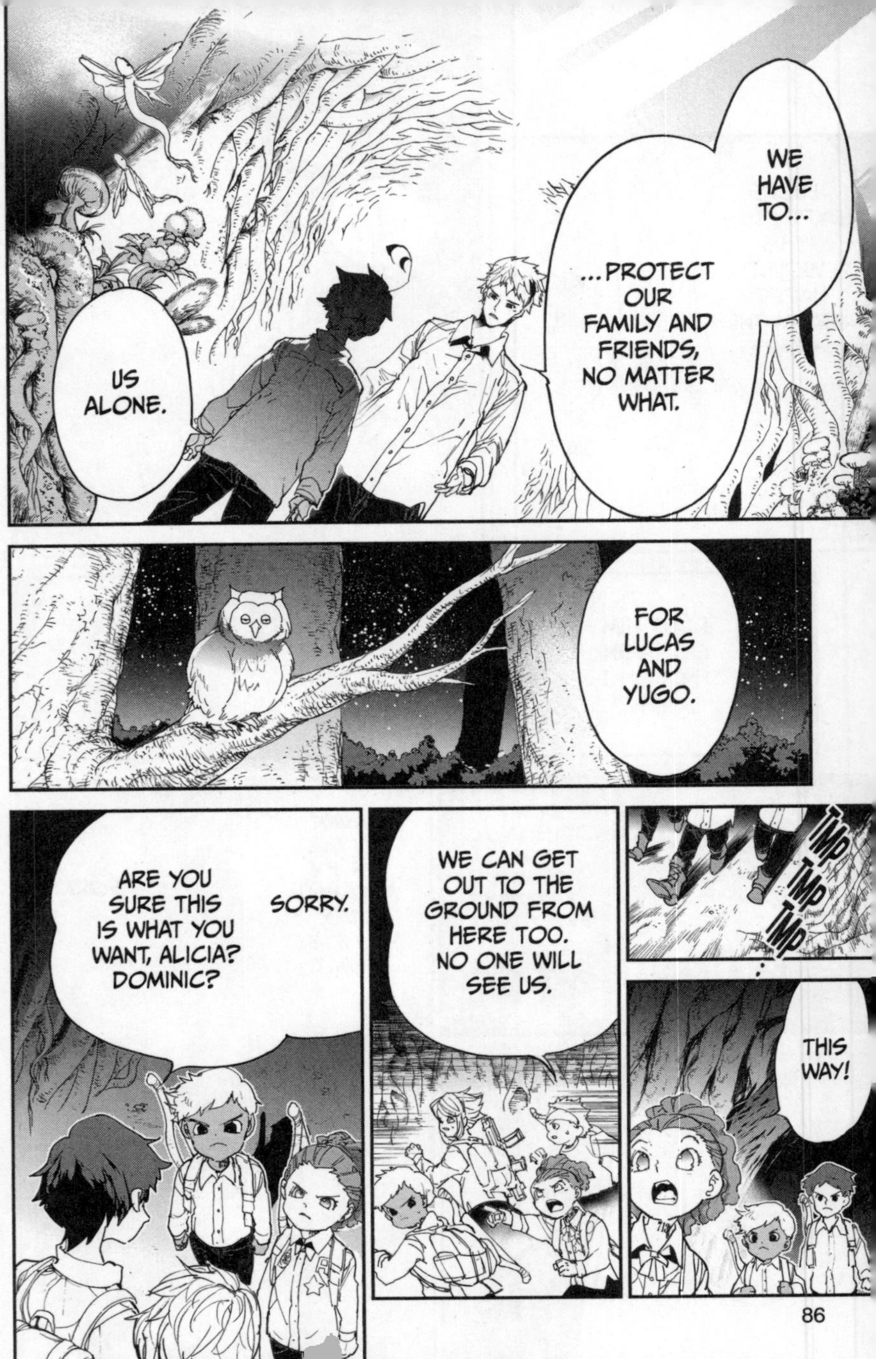
WE HAVE TO...
...PROTECT OUR FAMILY AND FRIENDS, NO MATTER WHAT.
US ALONE.
FOR LUCAS AND YUGO.
TMP TMP TMP
THIS WAY!
WE CAN GET OUT TO THE GROUND FROM HERE TOO. NO ONE WILL SEE US.
SORRY.
ARE YOU SURE THIS IS WHAT YOU WANT, ALICIA? DOMINIC?

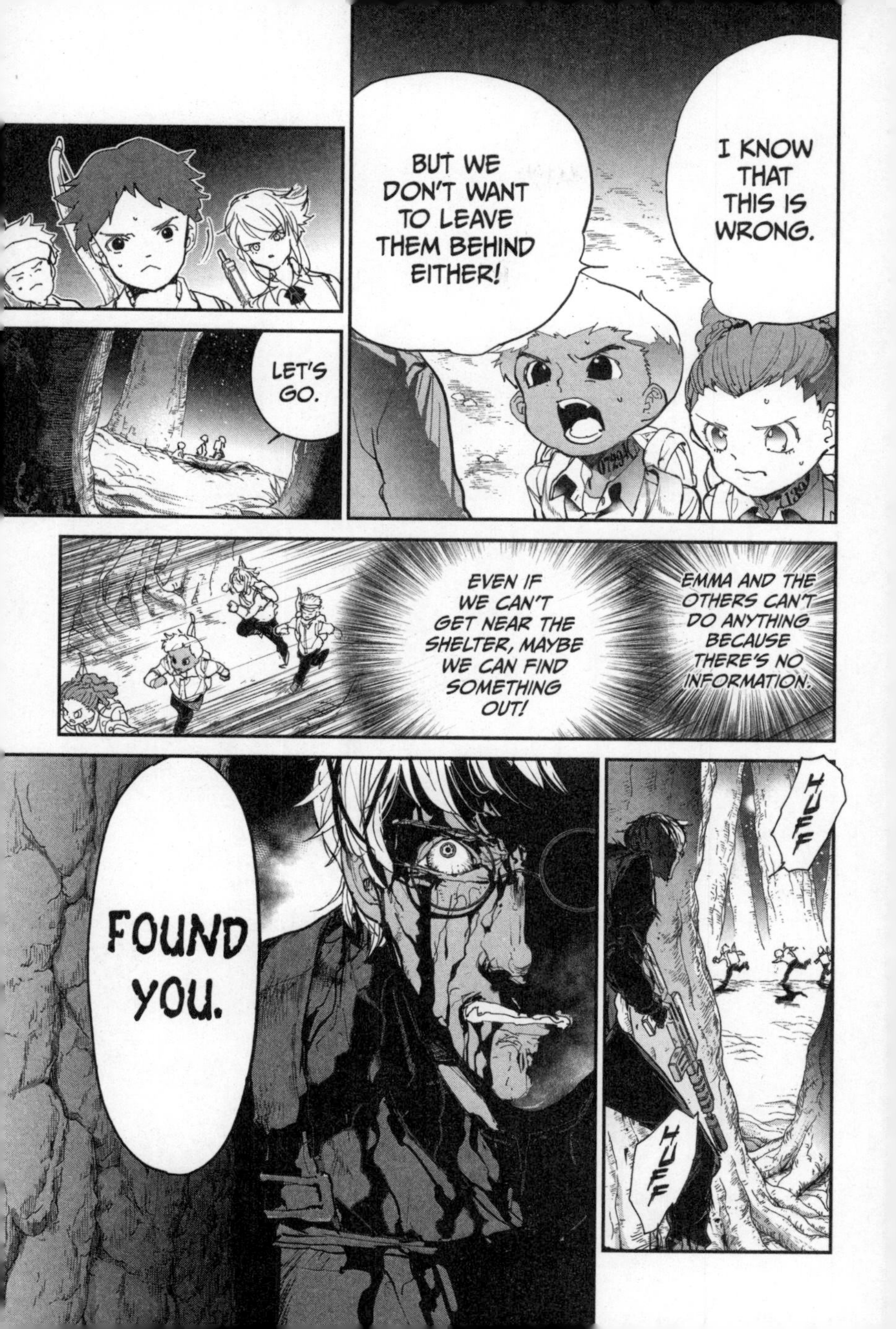
I KNOW THAT THIS IS WRONG.
BUT WE DON'T WANT TO LEAVE THEM BEHIND EITHER!
LET'S GO.
EMMA AND THE OTHERS CAN'T DO ANYTHING BECAUSE THERE'S NO INFORMATION.
EVEN IF WE CAN'T GET NEAR THE SHELTER, MAYBE WE CAN FIND SOMETHING OUT!
HUFF
HUFF
FOUND YOU.

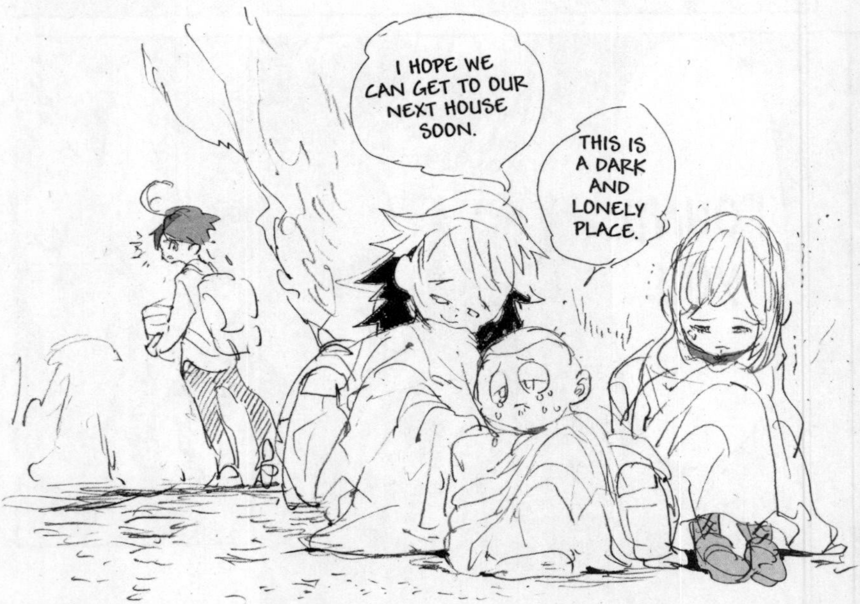

THIS IS A DARK AND LONELY PLACE.
I HOPE WE CAN GET TO OUR NEXT HOUSE SOON.

CHAPTER 111: UNWANTED GUEST

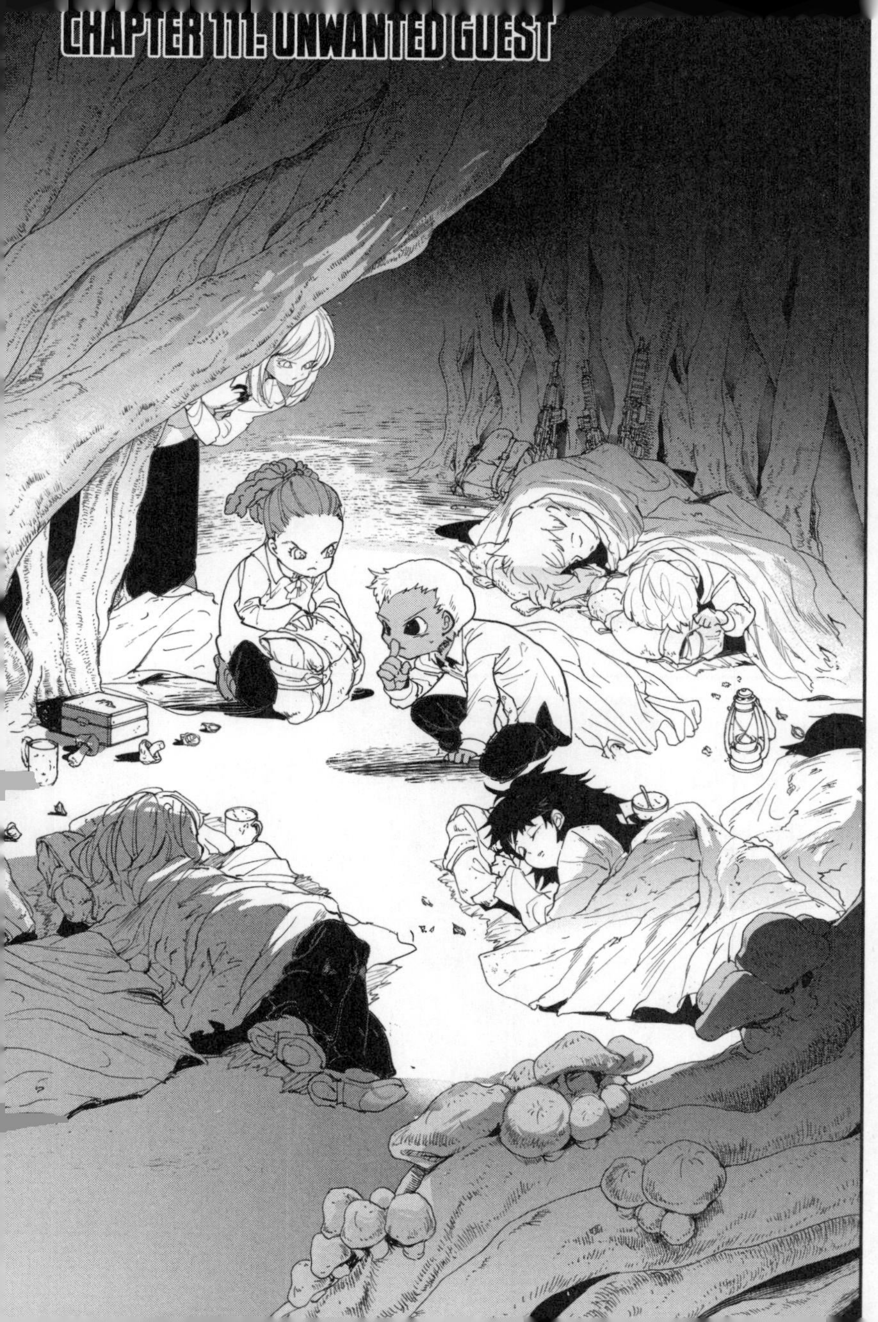

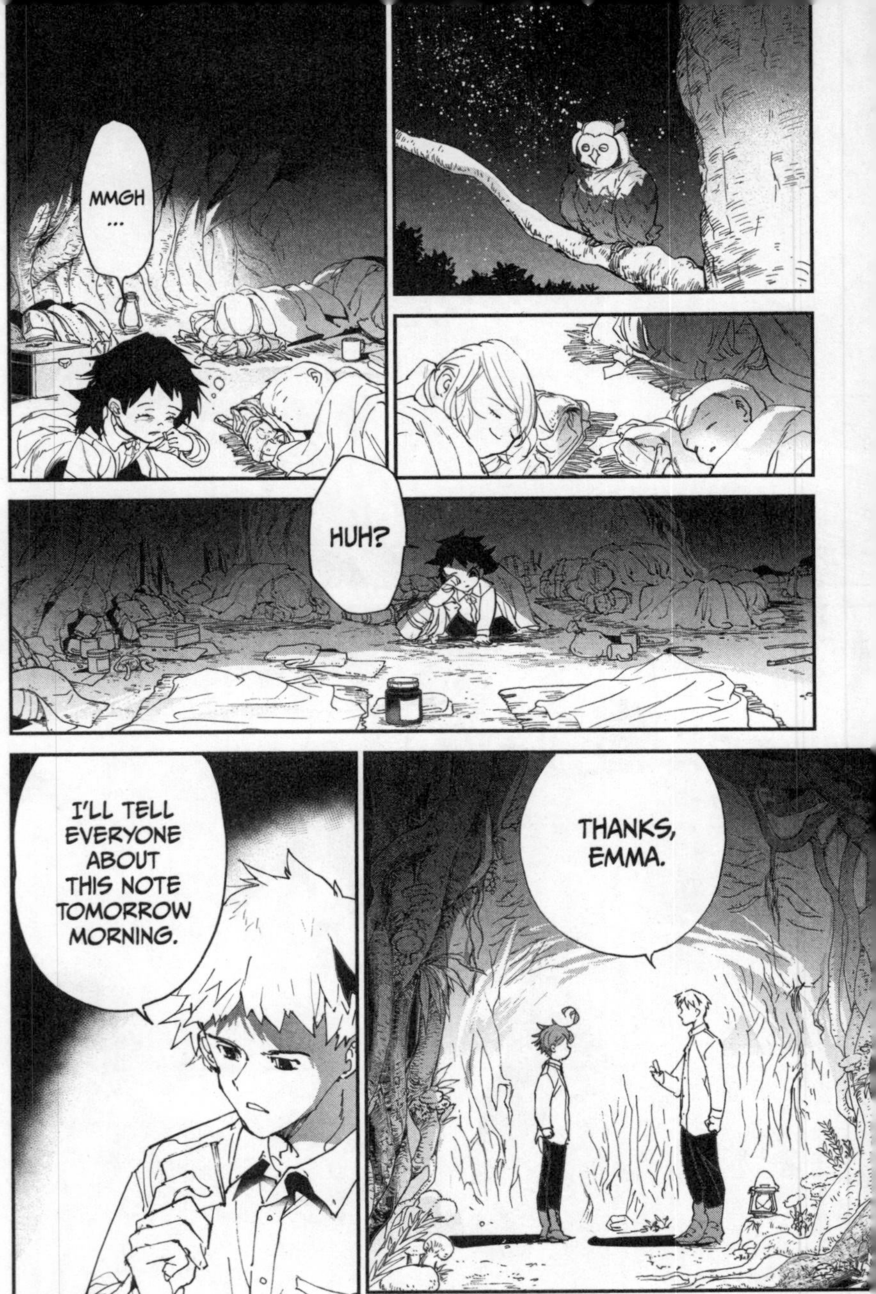
MMGH ...
HUH?
THANKS, EMMA.
I'LL TELL EVERYONE ABOUT THIS NOTE TOMORROW MORNING.

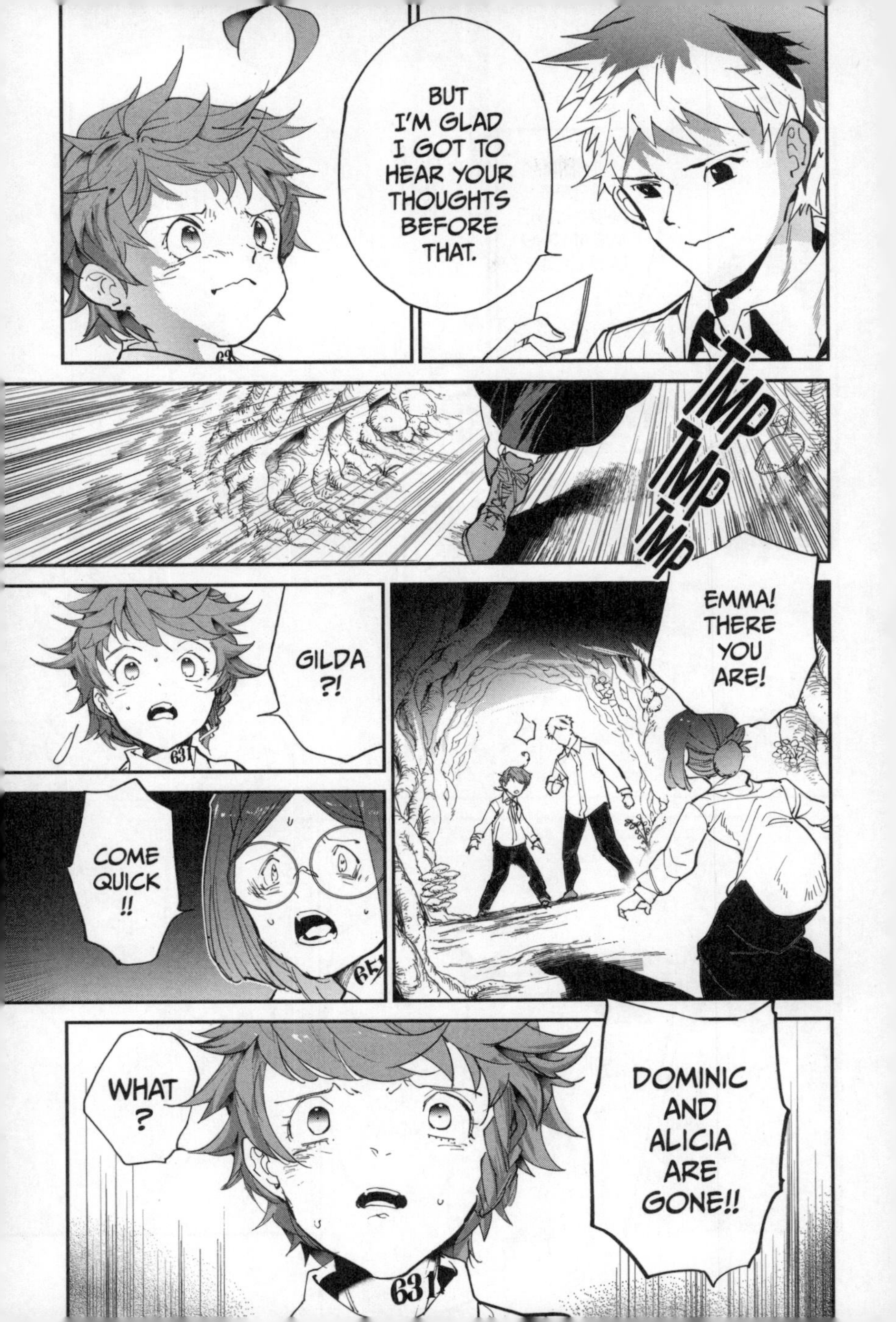
BUT I'M GLAD I GOT TO HEAR YOUR THOUGHTS BEFORE THAT.
TMP TMP TMP
EMMA! THERE YOU ARE!
GILDA ?!
COME QUICK !!
DOMINIC AND ALICIA ARE GONE!!
WHAT ?

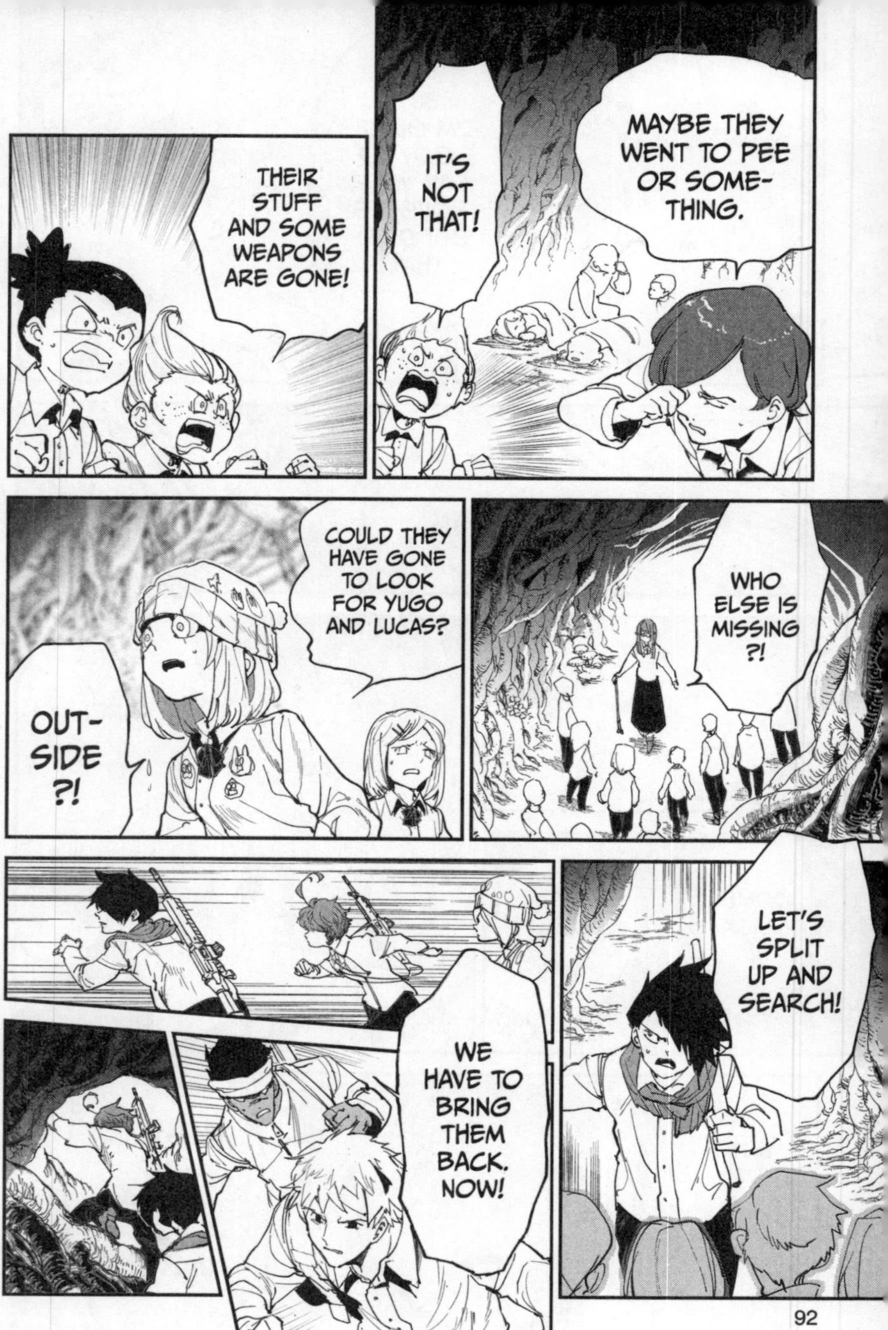
MAYBE THEY WENT TO PEE OR SOME-THING.
IT'S NOT THAT!
THEIR STUFF AND SOME WEAPONS ARE GONE!
WHO ELSE IS MISSING?!
COULD THEY HAVE GONE TO LOOK FOR YUGO AND LUCAS?
OUT-SIDE?!
LET'S SPLIT UP AND SEARCH!
WE HAVE TO BRING THEM BACK. NOW!

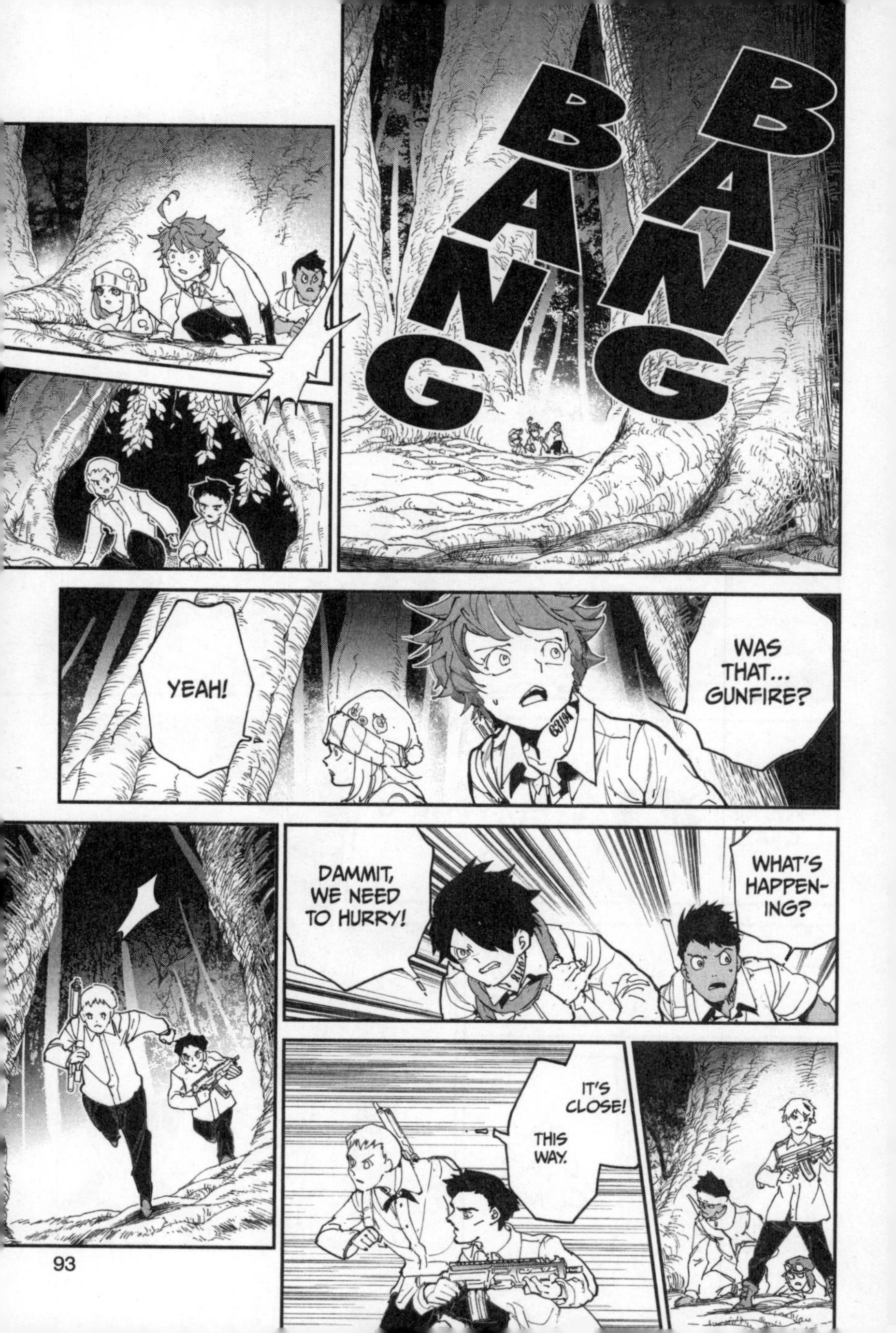
BANG
BANG
WAS THAT... GUNFIRE?
YEAH!
WHAT'S HAPPEN-ING?
DAMMIT, WE NEED TO HURRY!
IT'S CLOSE!
THIS WAY.

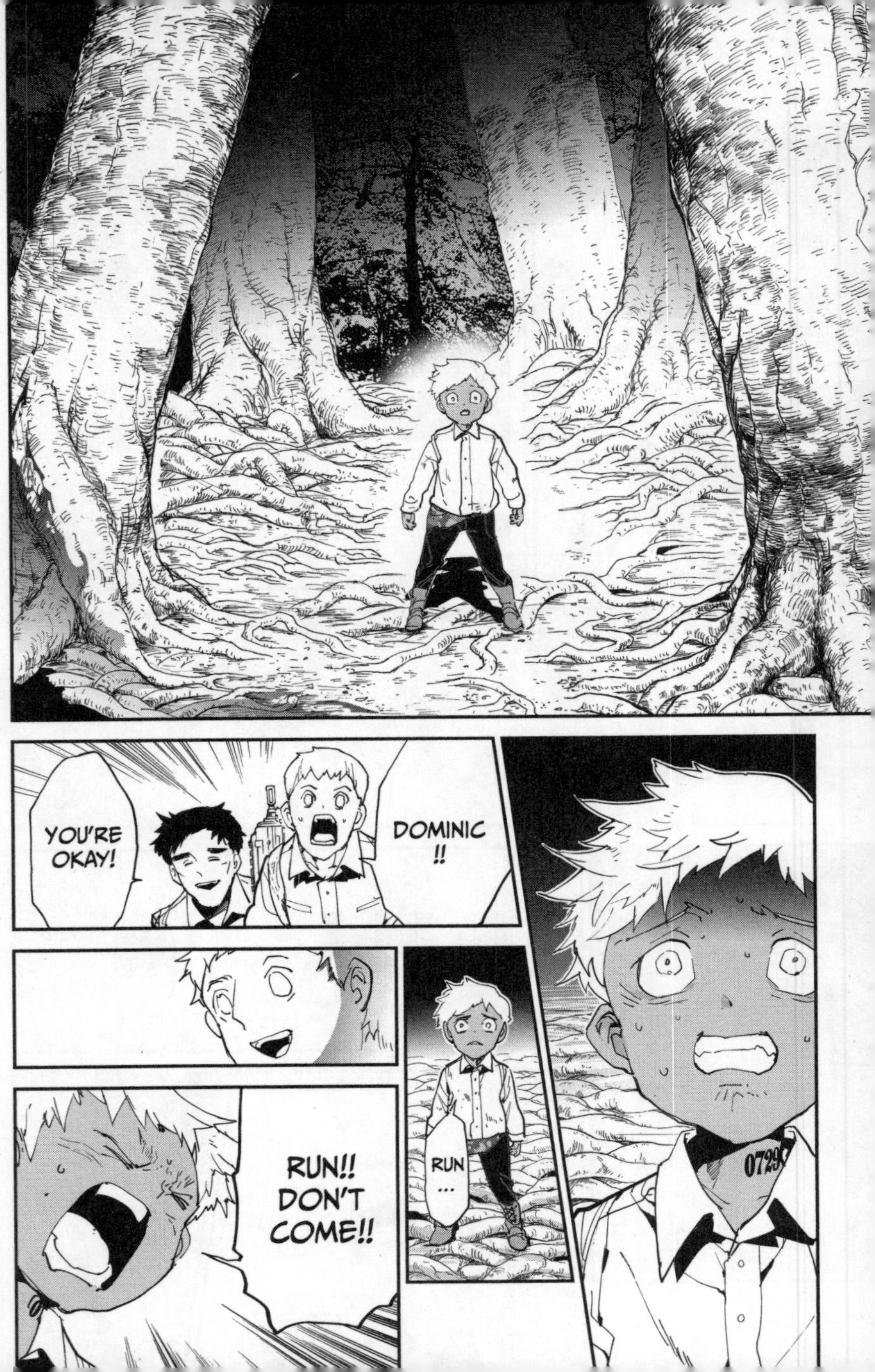
DOMINIC !!
YOU'RE OKAY!
RUN ...
RUN!! DON'T COME!!

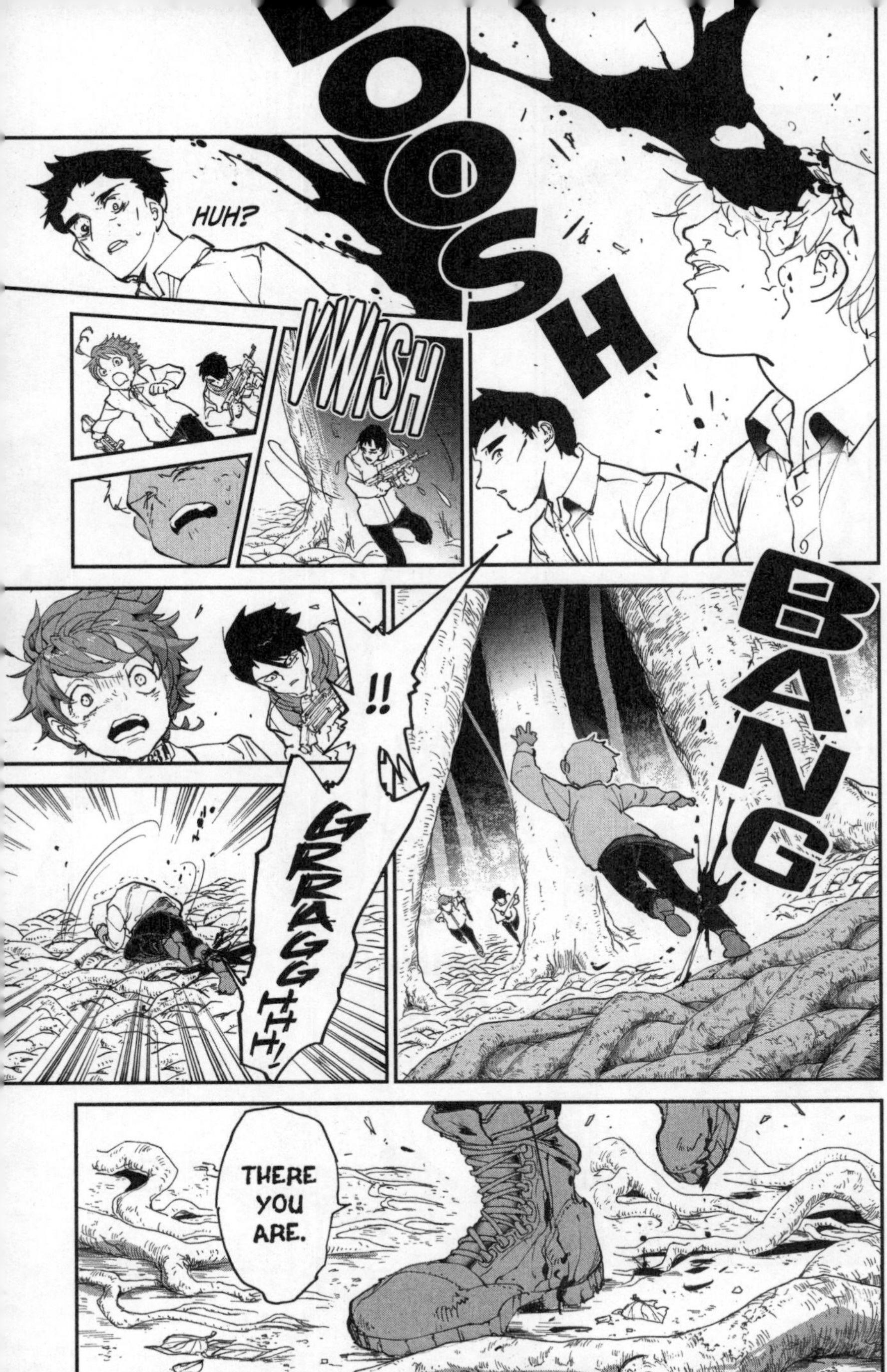
WOOSH
HUH?
VWISH
BANG
!!
GRRAGGHHH!
THERE YOU ARE.

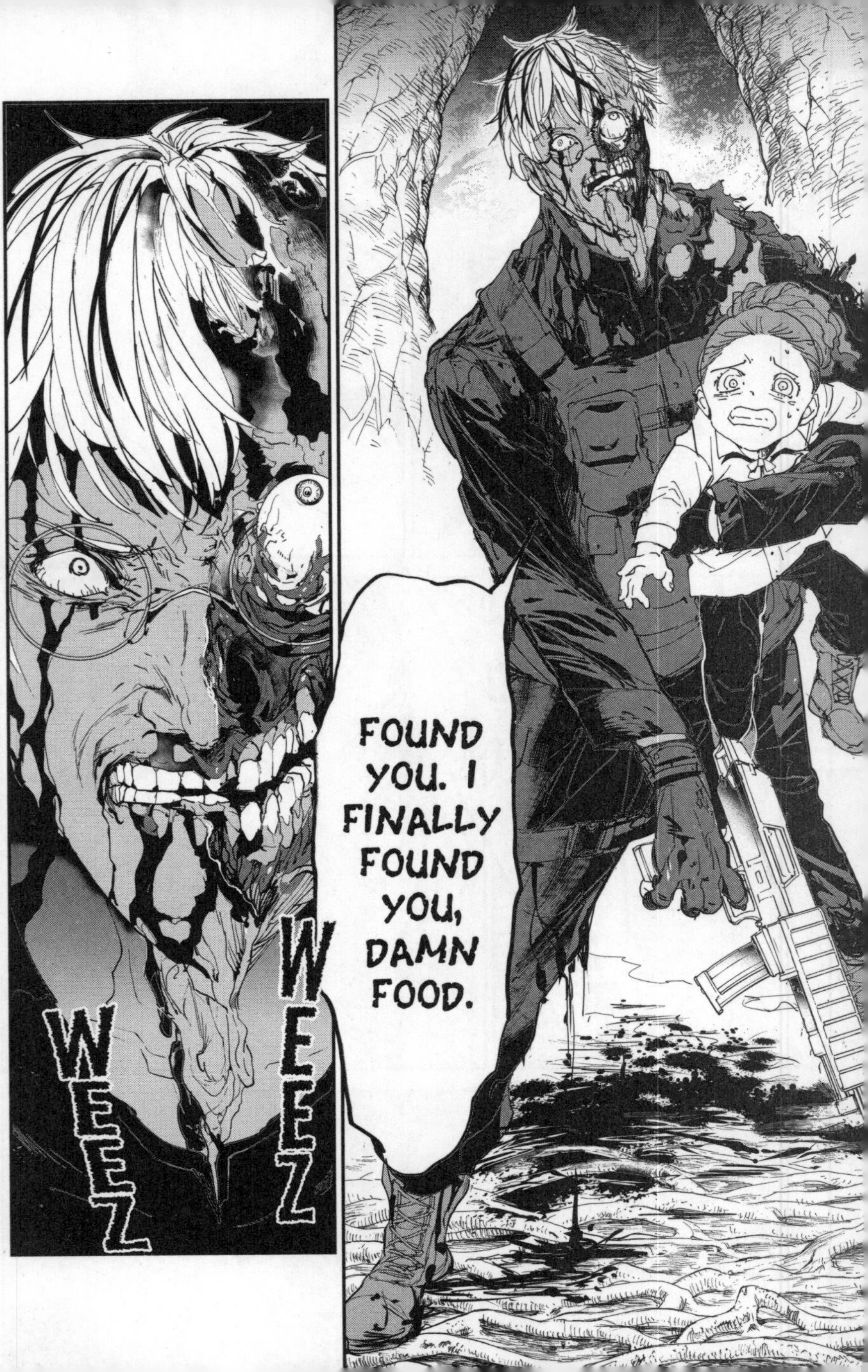
FOUND YOU. I FINALLY FOUND YOU, DAMN FOOD.
WEEZ
WEEZ

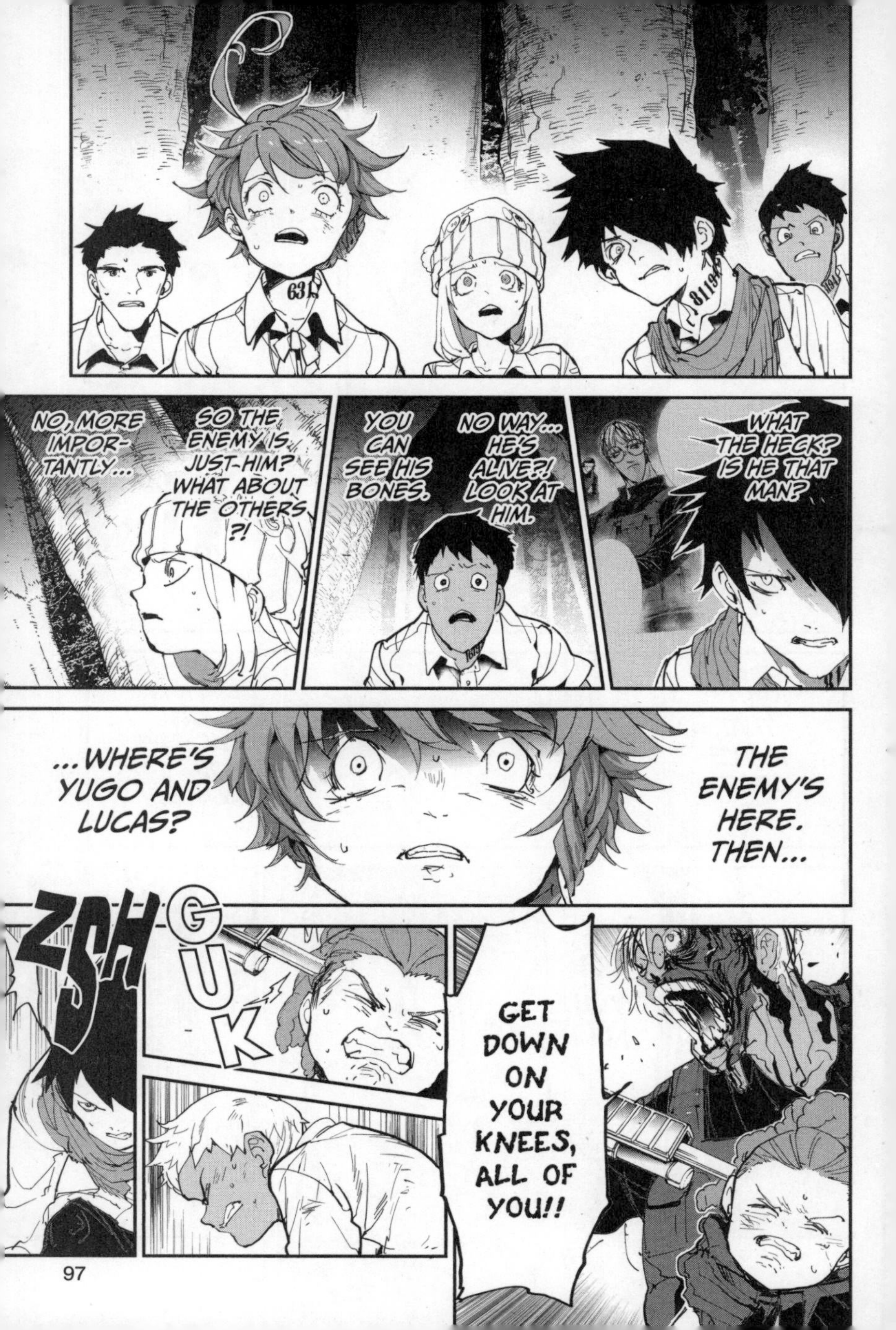
WHAT THE HECK? IS HE THAT MAN?
NO WAY... HE'S ALIVE?! LOOK AT HIM.
YOU CAN SEE HIS BONES.
SO THE ENEMY IS JUST HIM? WHAT ABOUT THE OTHERS?!
NO, MORE IMPORTANTLY...
THE ENEMY'S HERE. THEN...
...WHERE'S YUGO AND LUCAS?
GET DOWN ON YOUR KNEES, ALL OF YOU!!
GUK
ZSH

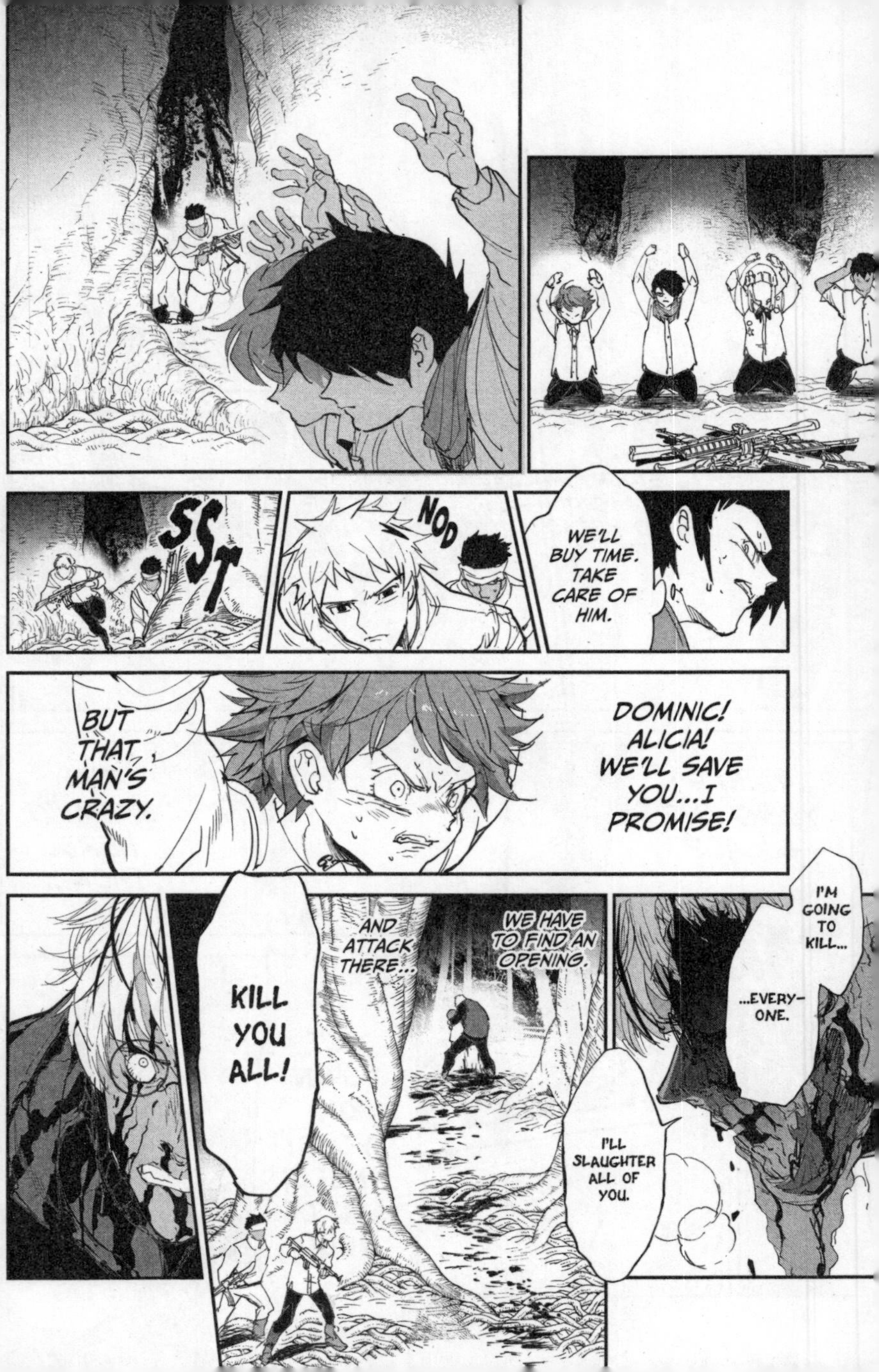
WE'LL BUY TIME. TAKE CARE OF HIM.
NOD
SST
DOMINIC! ALICIA! WE'LL SAVE YOU...I PROMISE!
BUT THAT MAN'S CRAZY.
I'M GOING TO KILL...
...EVERY-ONE.
I'LL SLAUGHTER ALL OF YOU.
WE HAVE TO FIND AN OPENING.
AND ATTACK THERE...
KILL YOU ALL!

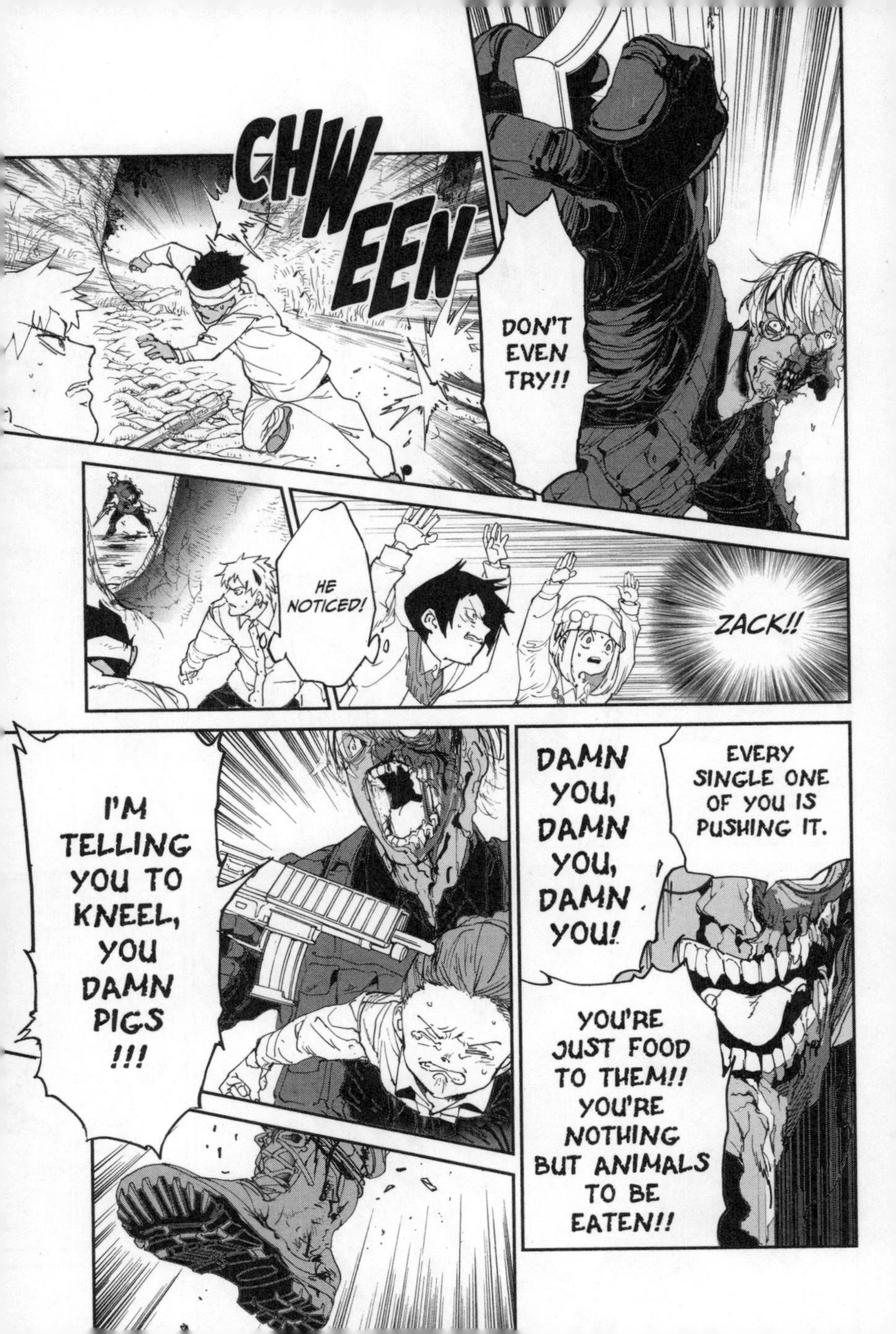
DON'T EVEN TRY!!
CHWEEN
ZACK!!
HE NOTICED!
EVERY SINGLE ONE OF YOU IS PUSHING IT.
DAMN YOU, DAMN YOU, DAMN YOU!
YOU'RE JUST FOOD TO THEM!! YOU'RE NOTHING BUT ANIMALS TO BE EATEN!!
I'M TELLING YOU TO KNEEL, YOU DAMN PIGS!!!

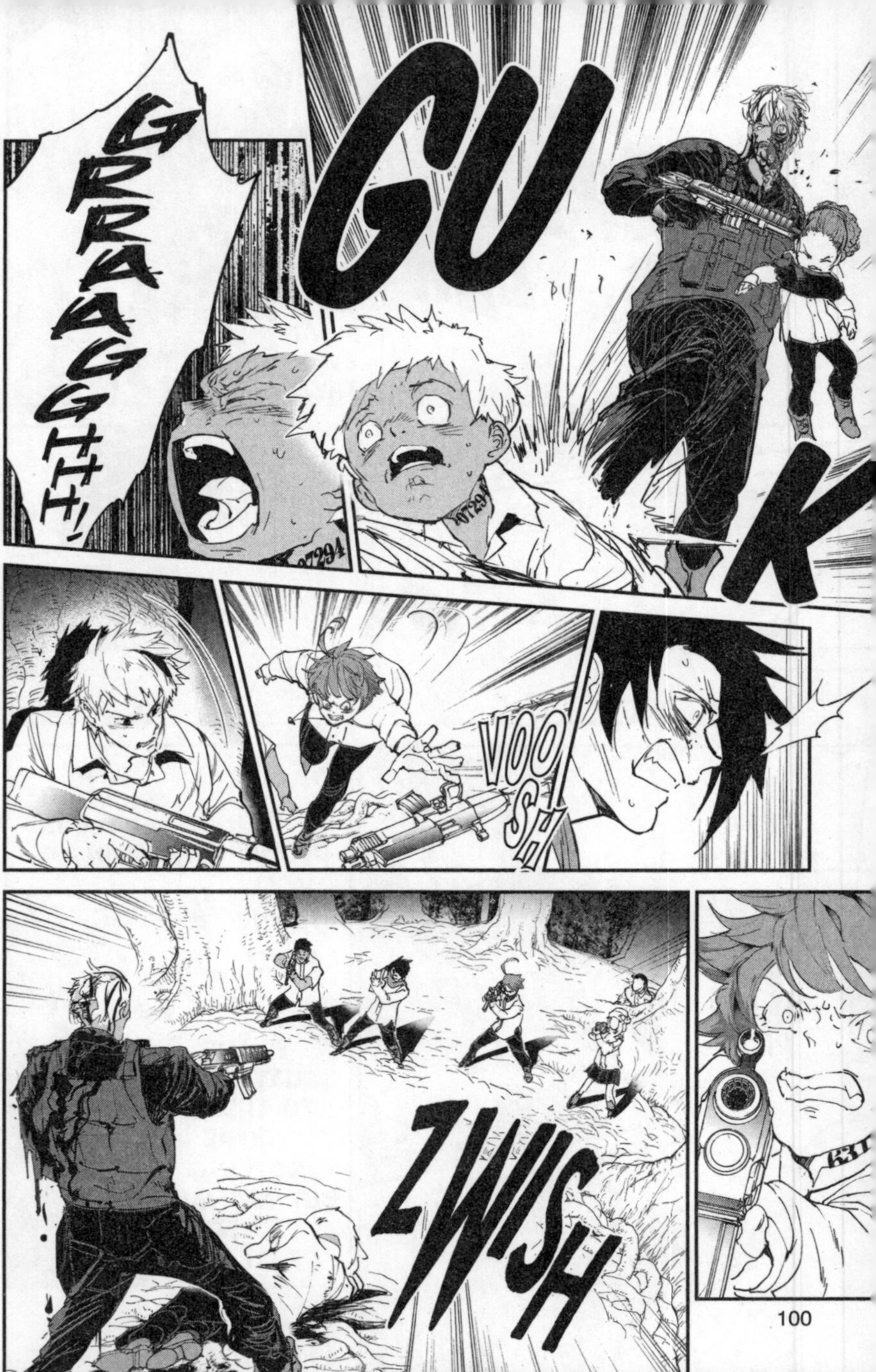
GU
K
GRRAAGGHHH!
VOOSH
ZWISH

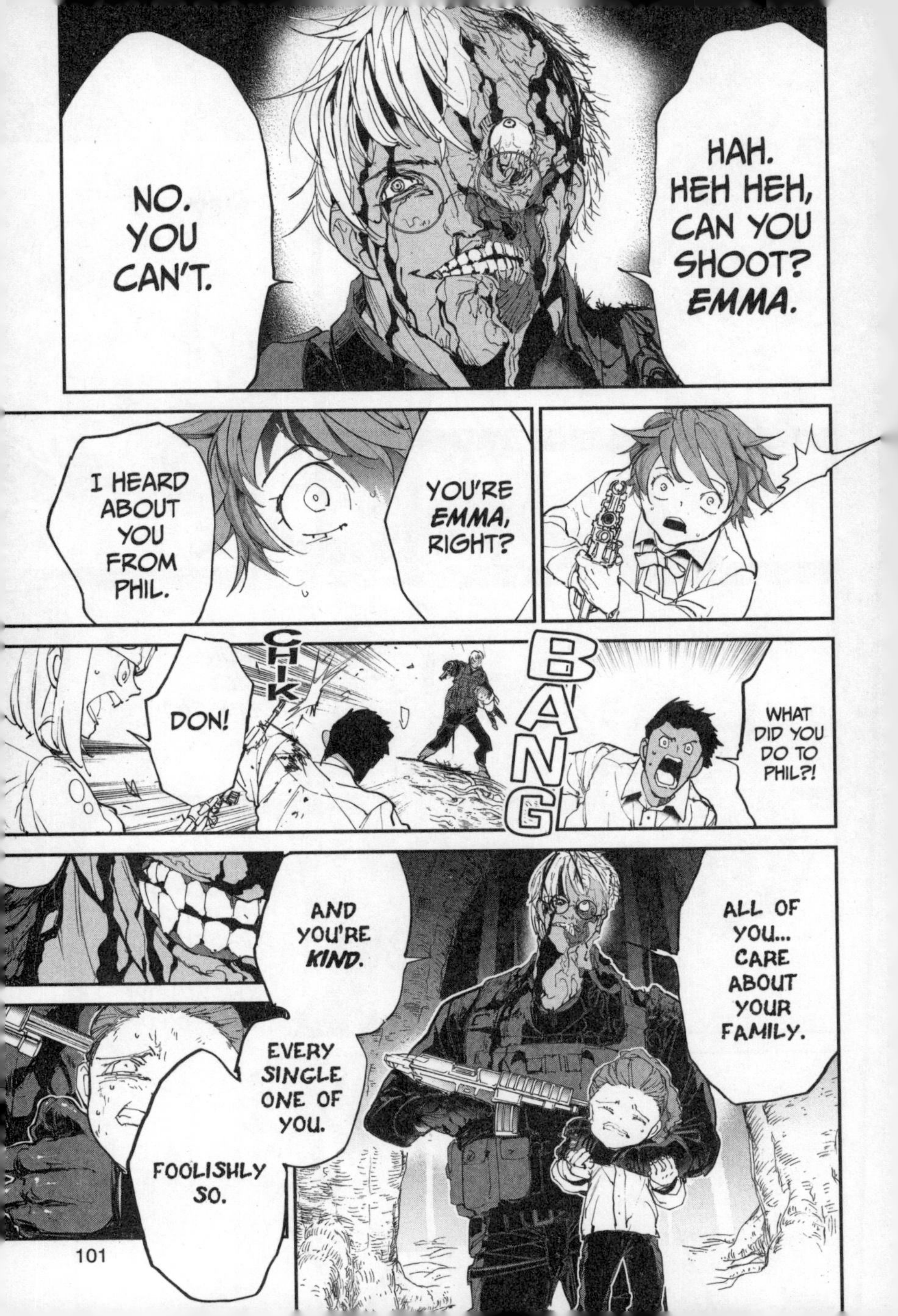
HAH. HEH HEH, CAN YOU SHOOT? EMMA.
NO. YOU CAN'T.
YOU'RE EMMA, RIGHT?
I HEARD ABOUT YOU FROM PHIL.
WHAT DID YOU DO TO PHIL?!
BANG
CHIK
DON!
ALL OF YOU... CARE ABOUT YOUR FAMILY.
AND YOU'RE KIND.
EVERY SINGLE ONE OF YOU.
FOOLISHLY SO.

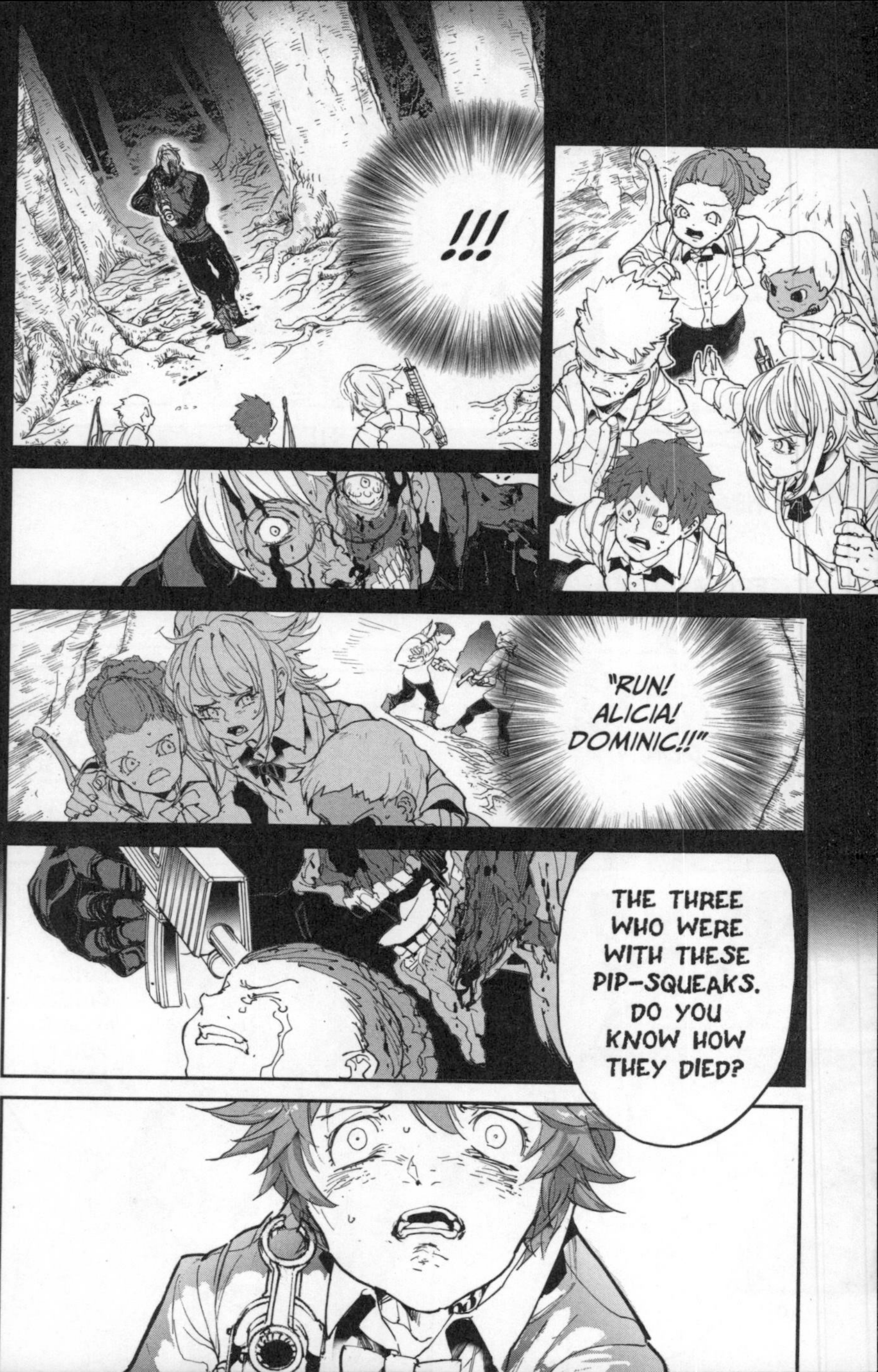
!!!
"RUN! ALICIA! DOMINIC!!"
THE THREE WHO WERE WITH THESE PIP-SQUEAKS. DO YOU KNOW HOW THEY DIED?

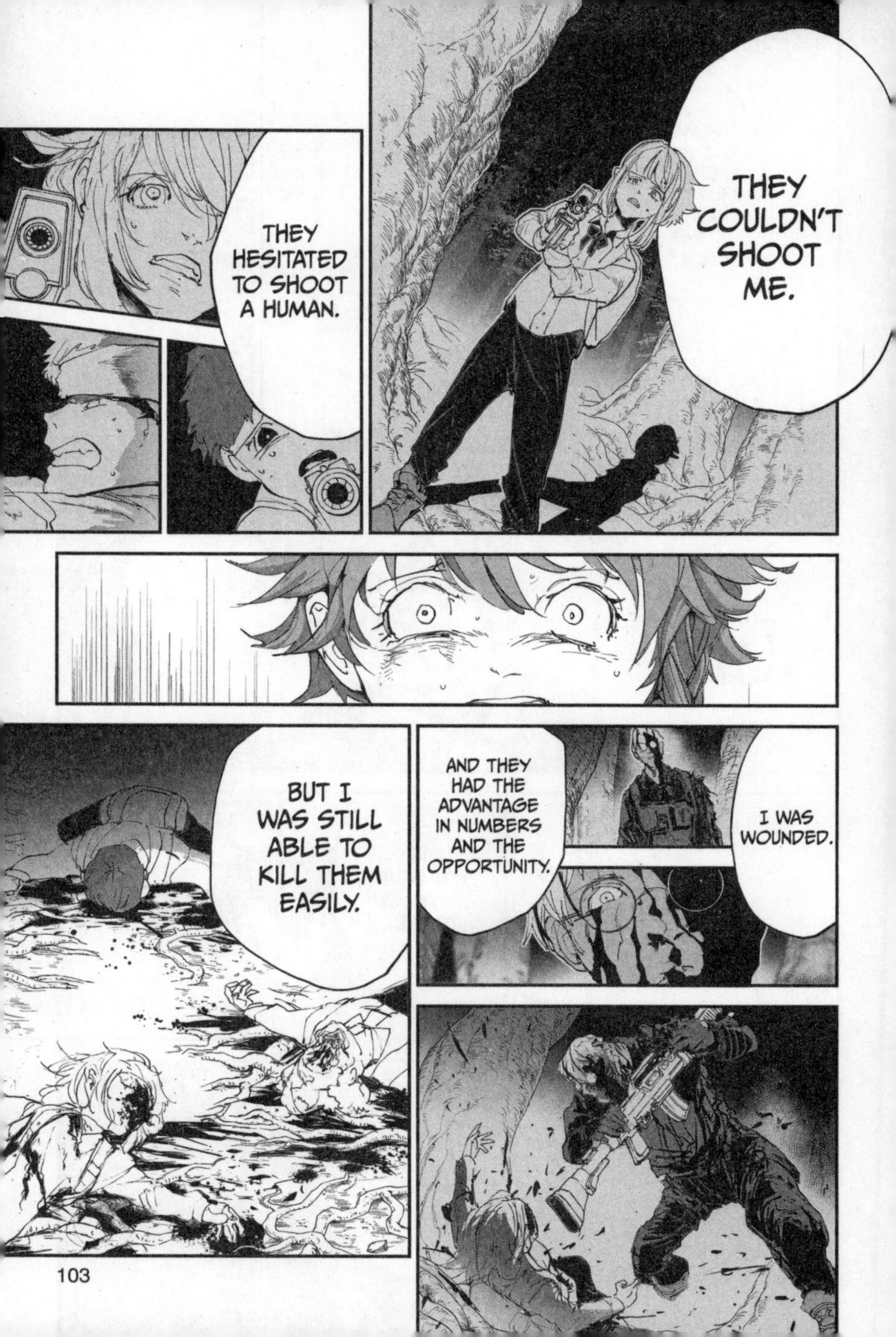
THEY COULDN'T SHOOT ME.
THEY HESITATED TO SHOOT A HUMAN.
I WAS WOUNDED.
AND THEY HAD THE ADVANTAGE IN NUMBERS AND THE OPPORTUNITY.
BUT I WAS STILL ABLE TO KILL THEM EASILY.

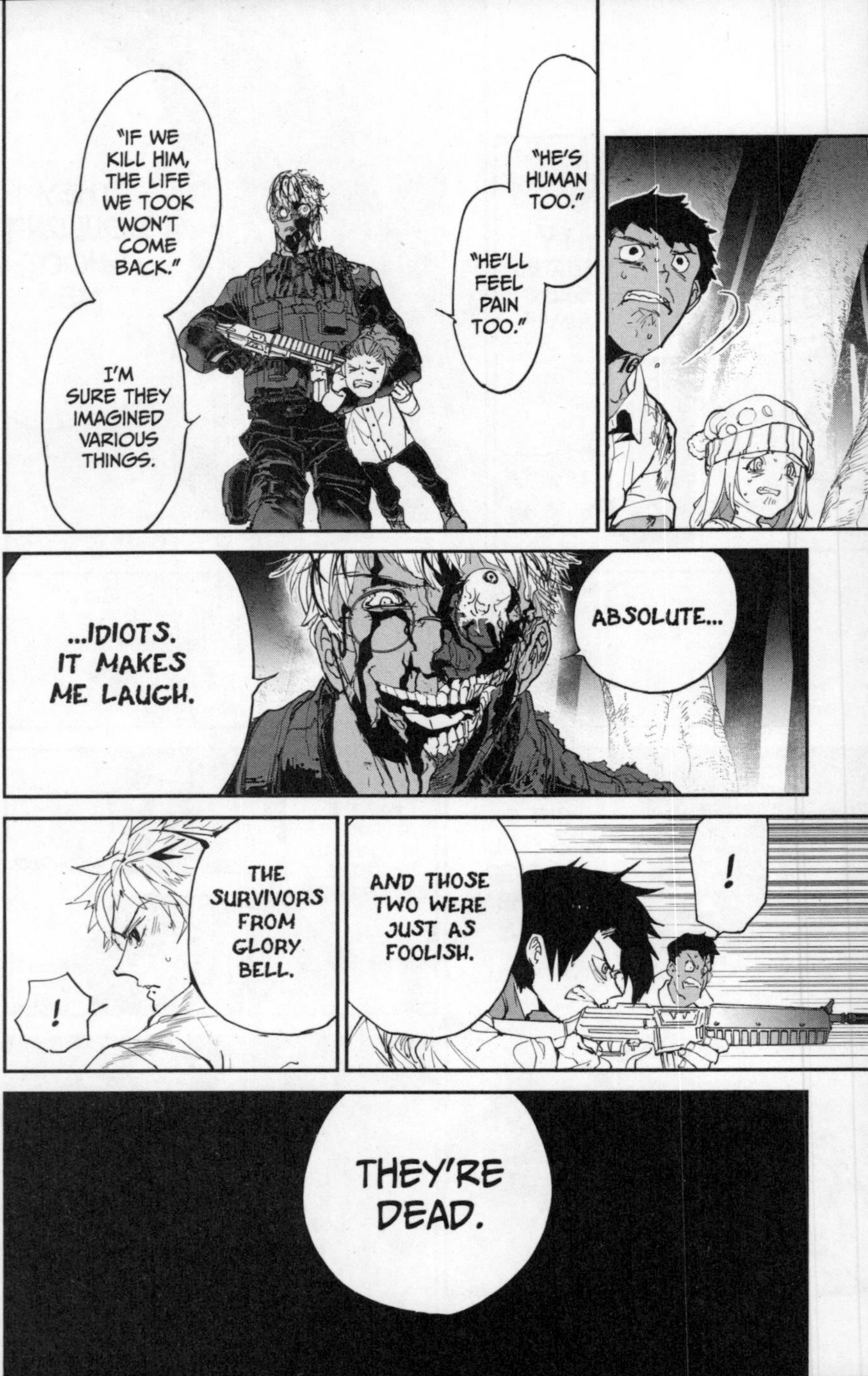
"HE'S HUMAN TOO."
"IF WE KILL HIM, THE LIFE WE TOOK WON'T COME BACK."
"HE'LL FEEL PAIN TOO."
I'M SURE THEY IMAGINED VARIOUS THINGS.
ABSOLUTE...
...IDIOTS. IT MAKES ME LAUGH.
!
AND THOSE TWO WERE JUST AS FOOLISH.
THE SURVIVORS FROM GLORY BELL.
!
THEY'RE DEAD.

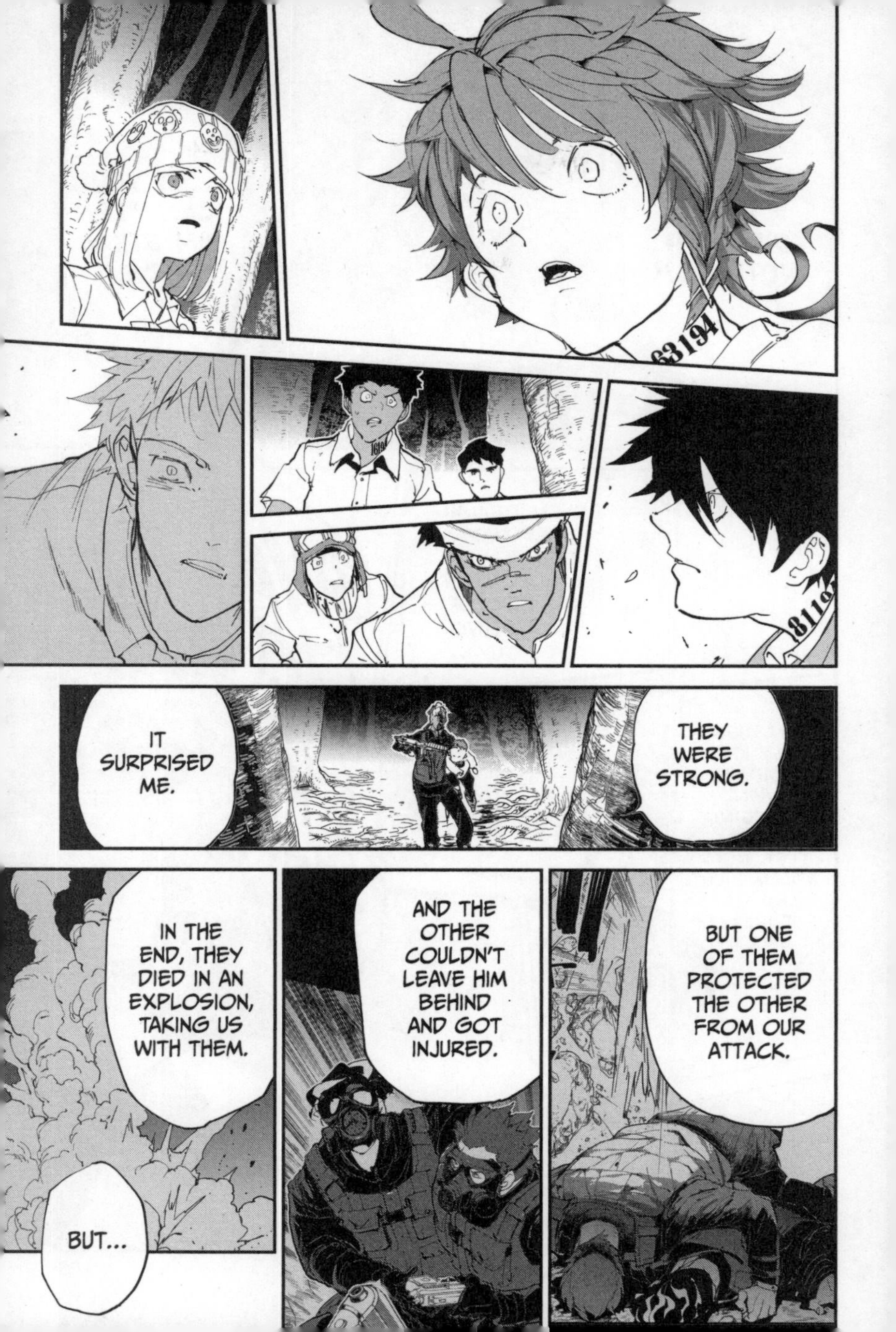
THEY WERE STRONG.
IT SURPRISED ME.
BUT ONE OF THEM PROTECTED THE OTHER FROM OUR ATTACK.
AND THE OTHER COULDN'T LEAVE HIM BEHIND AND GOT INJURED.
IN THE END, THEY DIED IN AN EXPLOSION, TAKING US WITH THEM.
BUT...

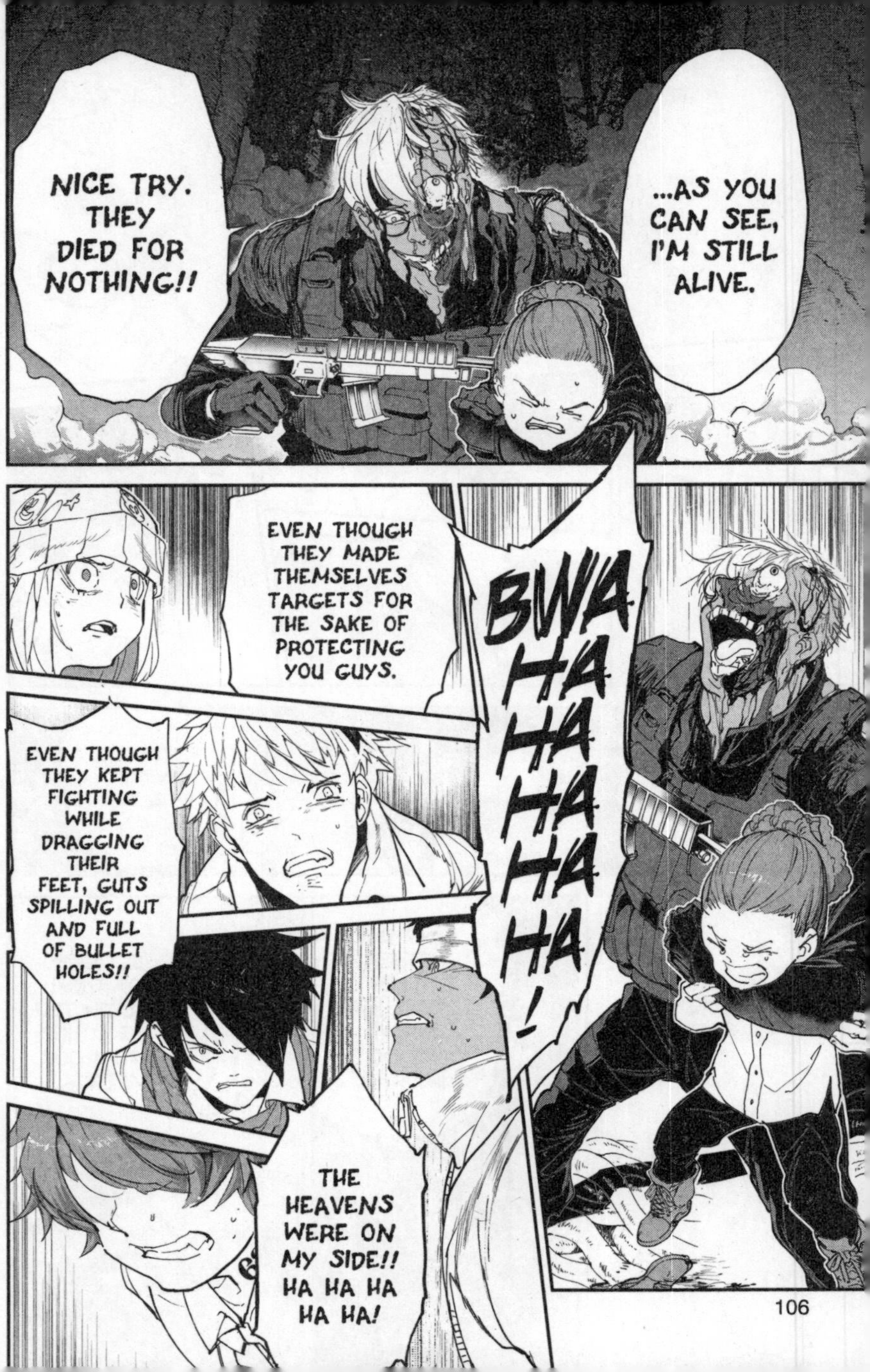
...AS YOU CAN SEE, I'M STILL ALIVE.
NICE TRY. THEY DIED FOR NOTHING!!
BWAHAHAHAHAHAHA!
EVEN THOUGH THEY MADE THEMSELVES TARGETS FOR THE SAKE OF PROTECTING YOU GUYS.
EVEN THOUGH THEY KEPT FIGHTING WHILE DRAGGING THEIR FEET, GUTS SPILLING OUT AND FULL OF BULLET HOLES!!
THE HEAVENS WERE ON MY SIDE!! HA HA HA HA HA!

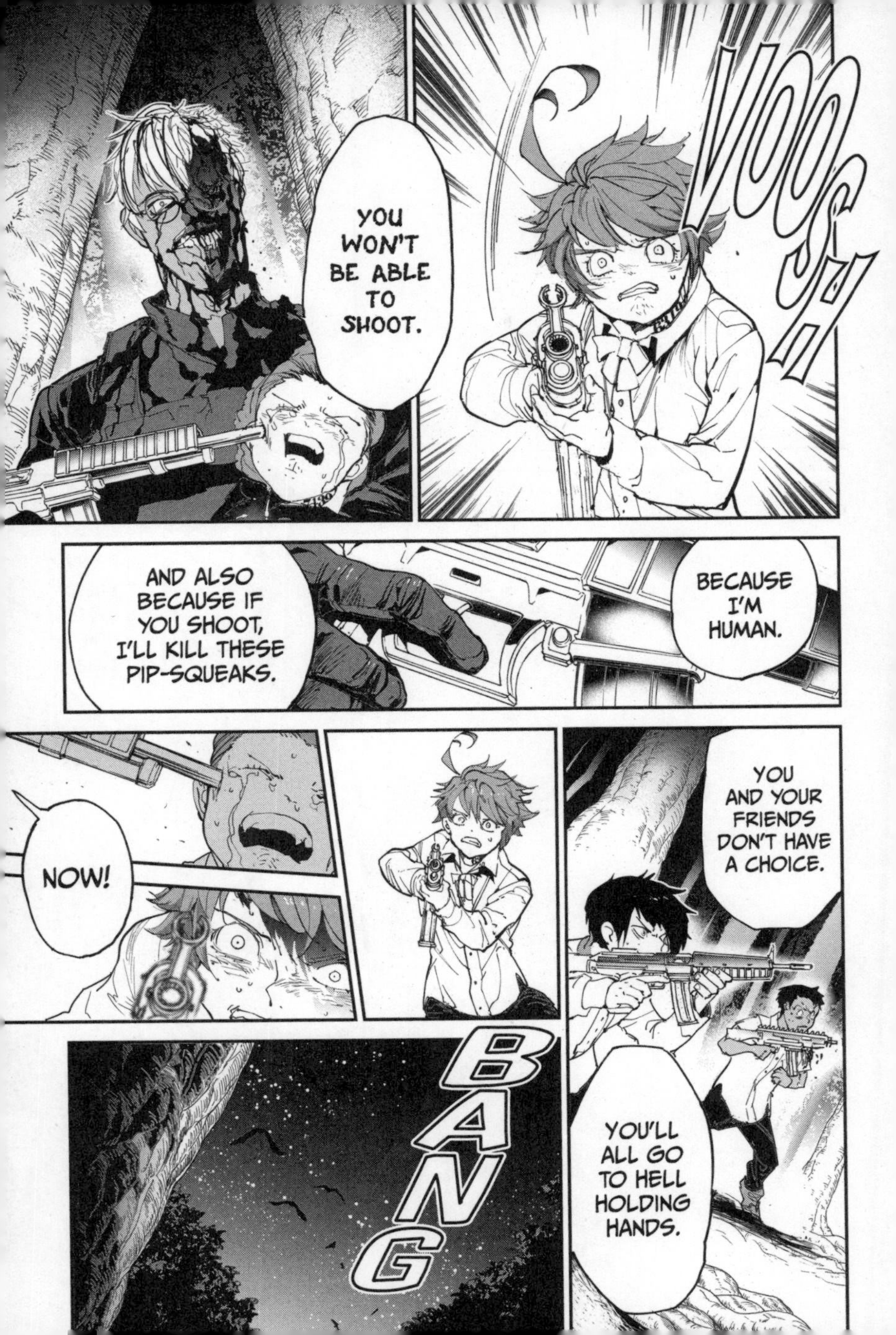
VOOSH!
YOU WON'T BE ABLE TO SHOOT.
BECAUSE I'M HUMAN.
AND ALSO BECAUSE IF YOU SHOOT, I'LL KILL THESE PIP-SQUEAKS.
YOU AND YOUR FRIENDS DON'T HAVE A CHOICE.
YOU'LL ALL GO TO HELL HOLDING HANDS.
NOW!
BANG

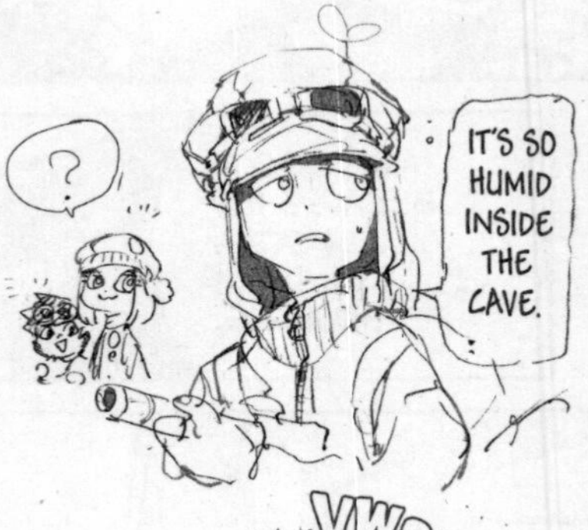
IT'S SO HUMID INSIDE THE CAVE.
?
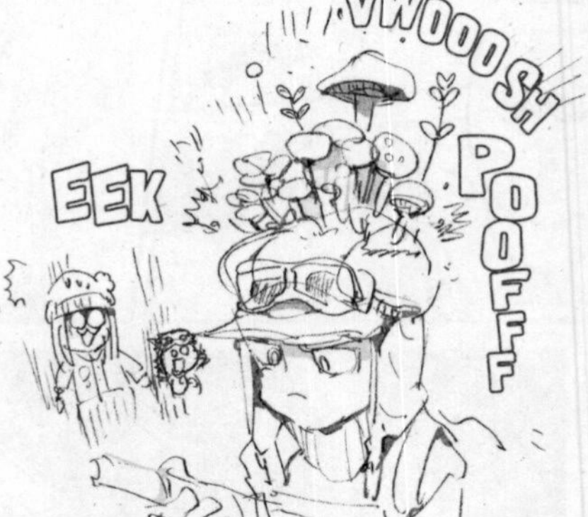
VWOOOSH
POOFFF
EEK
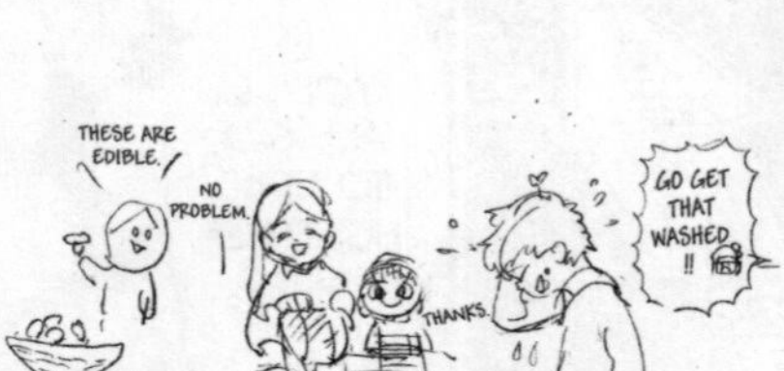
GO GET THAT WASHED !!
THANKS.
NO PROBLEM.
THESE ARE EDIBLE.

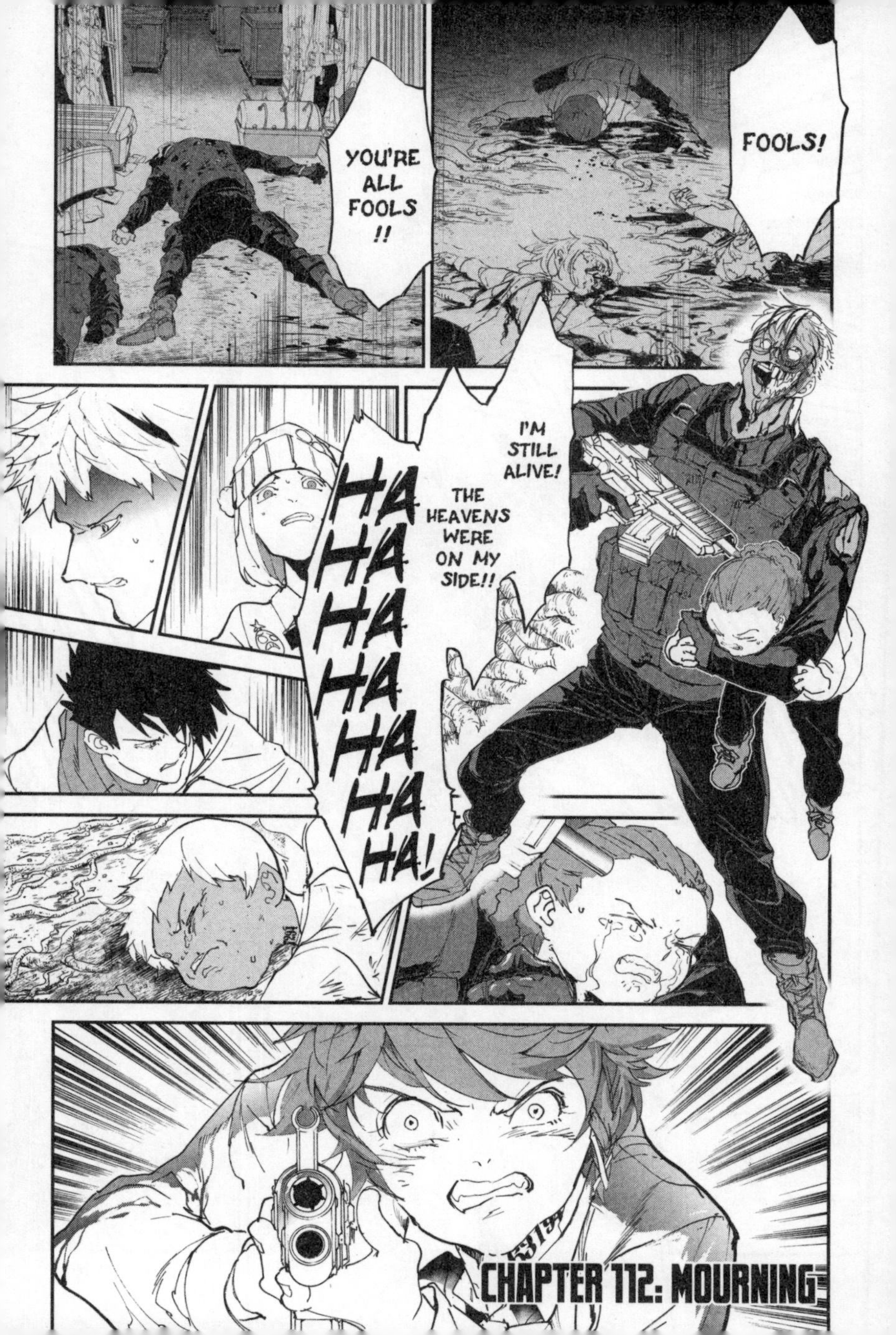
FOOLS!
YOU'RE ALL FOOLS !!
I'M STILL ALIVE!
THE HEAVENS WERE ON MY SIDE!!
HA HA HA HA HA HA HA HA!
CHAPTER 112: MOURNING

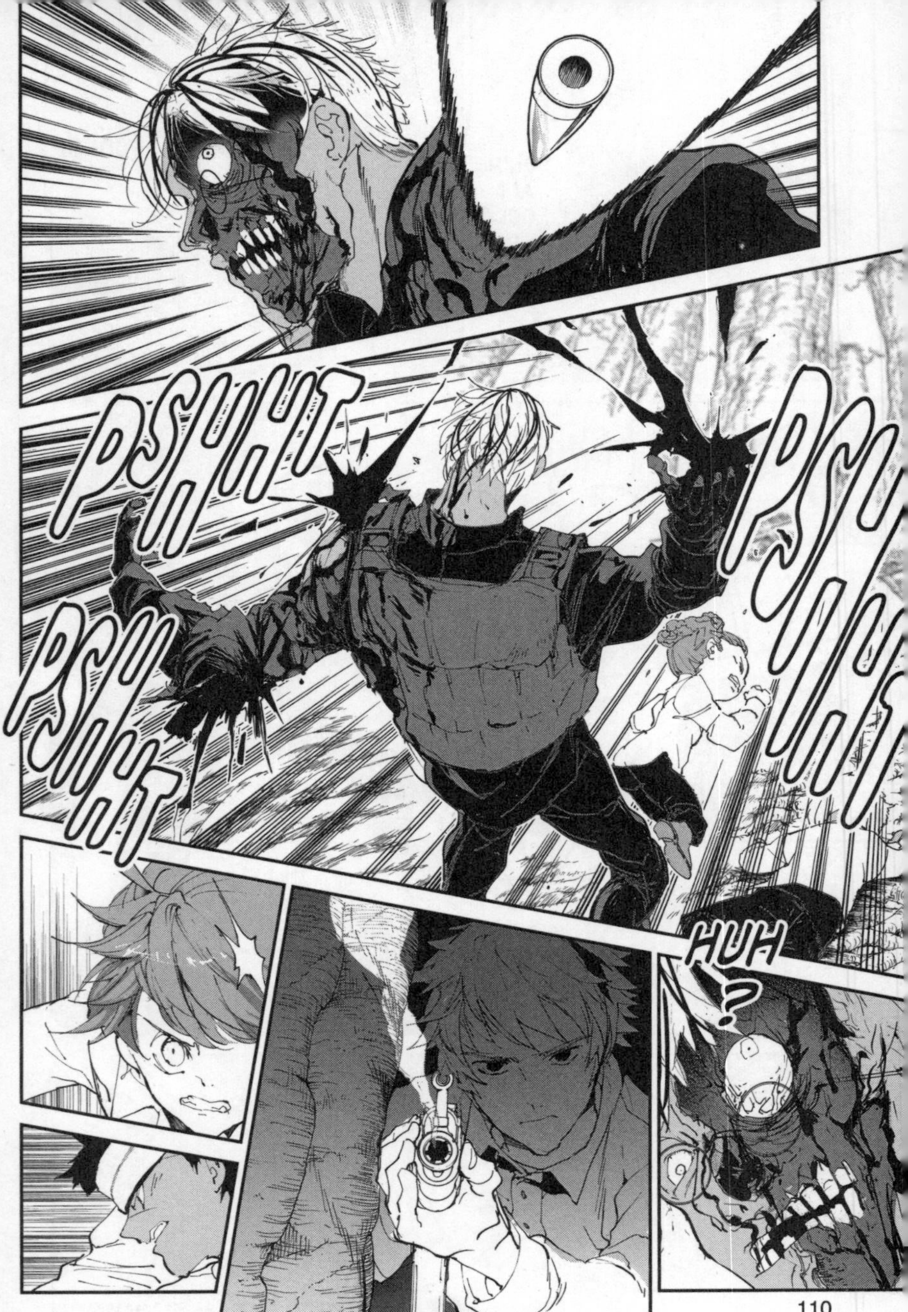
PSHHT
PSHHT
PSHHT
HUH
?

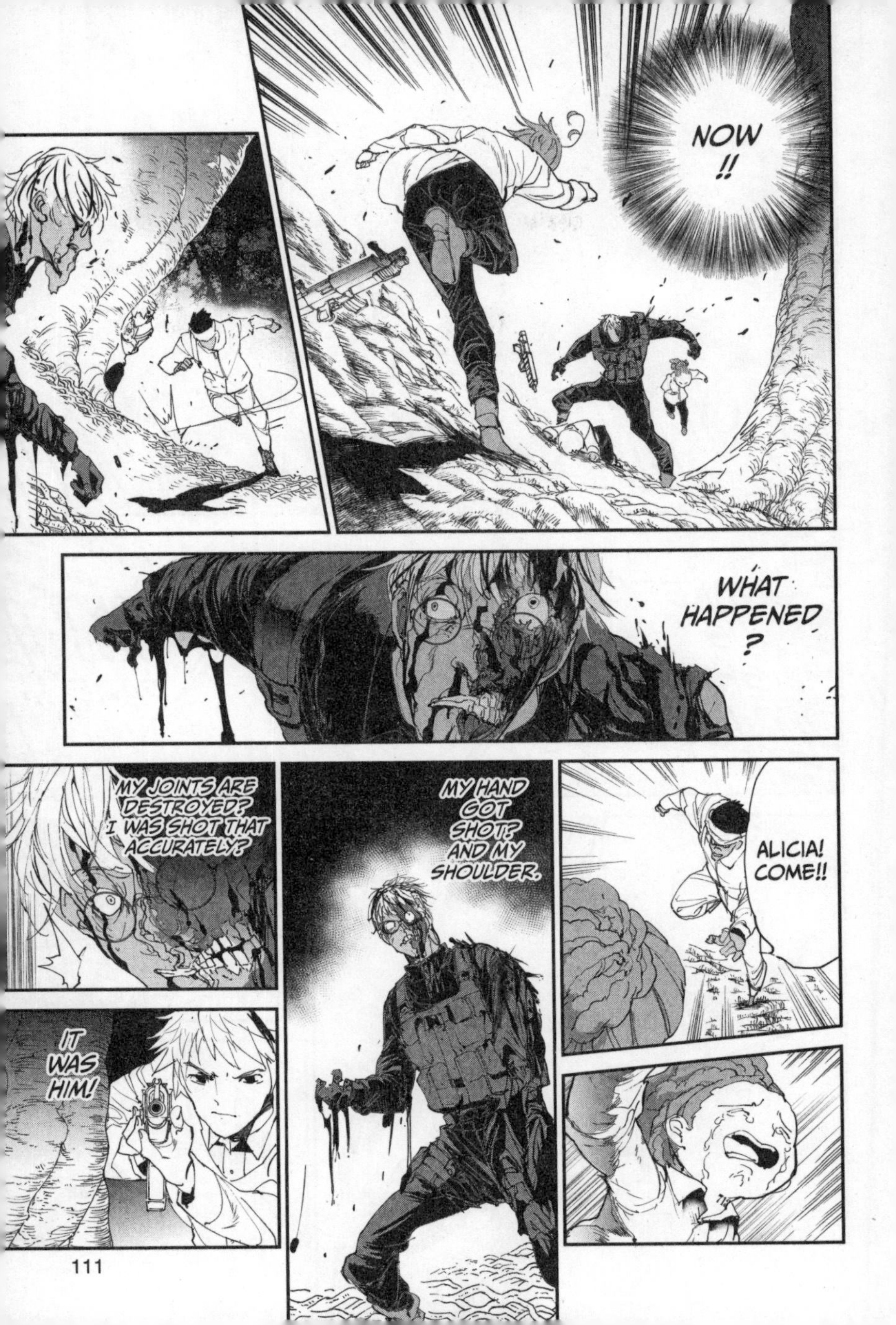
NOW !!
WHAT HAPPENED ?
ALICIA! COME!!
MY HAND GOT SHOT? AND MY SHOULDER.
MY JOINTS ARE DESTROYED? I WAS SHOT THAT ACCURATELY?
IT WAS HIM!

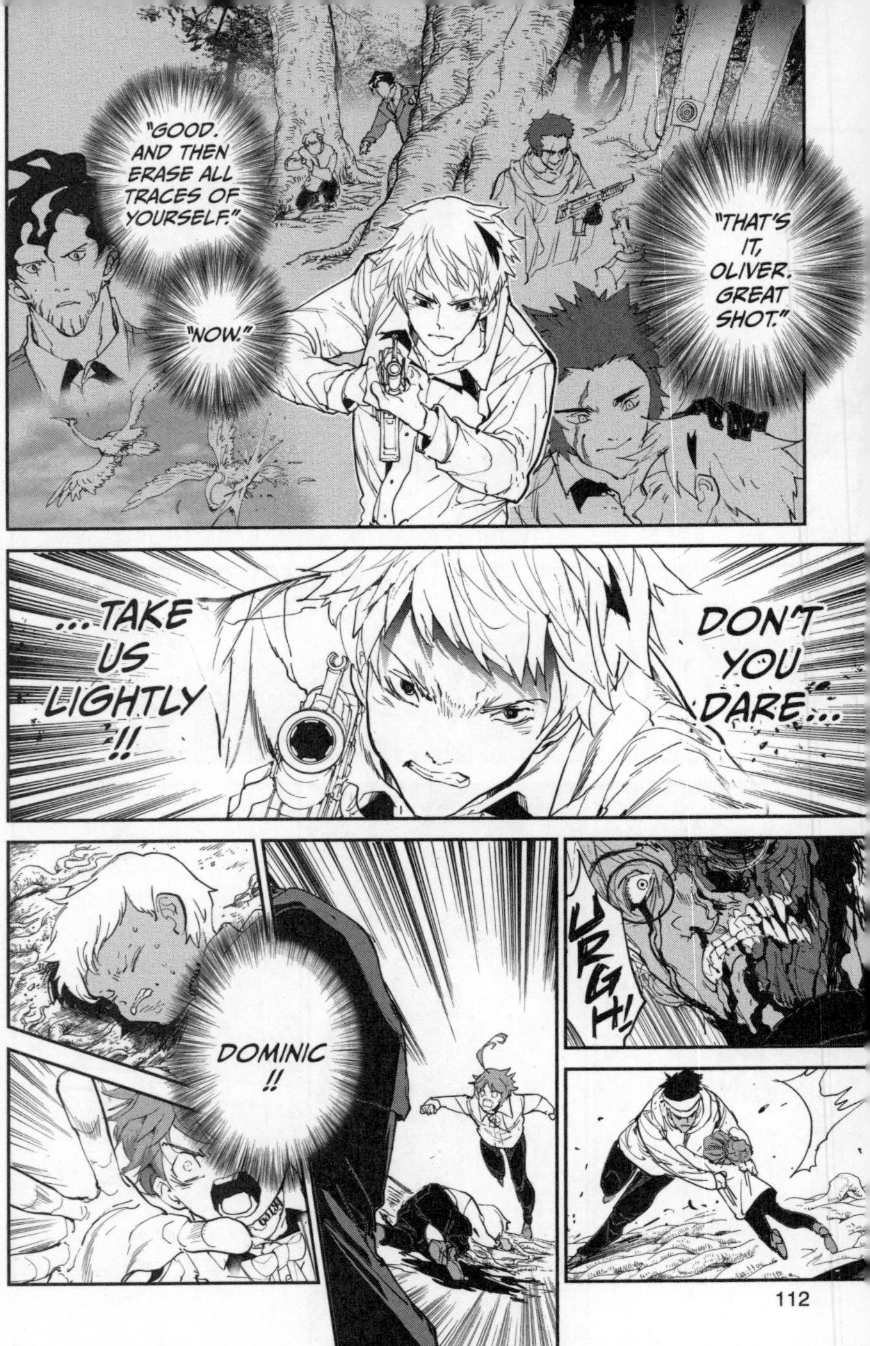
"THAT'S IT, OLIVER. GREAT SHOT."
"GOOD. AND THEN ERASE ALL TRACES OF YOURSELF."
"NOW."
DON'T YOU DARE...
...TAKE US LIGHTLY!!
URGH!
DOMINIC!!

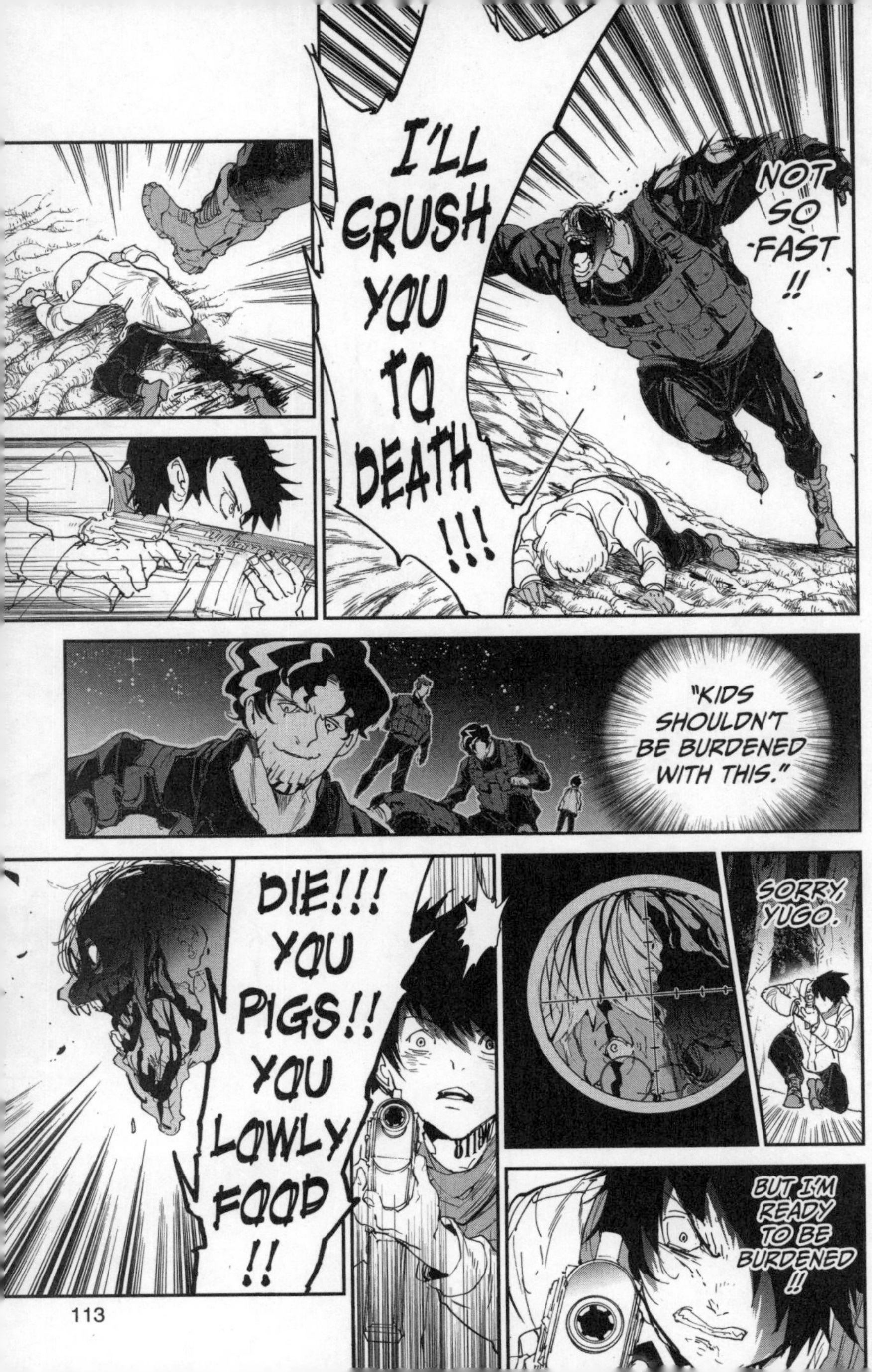
NOT SO FAST!!
I'LL CRUSH YOU TO DEATH!!!
"KIDS SHOULDN'T BE BURDENED WITH THIS."
SORRY, YUGO.
BUT I'M READY TO BE BURDENED!!
DIE!!! YOU PIGS!! YOU LOWLY FOOD!!

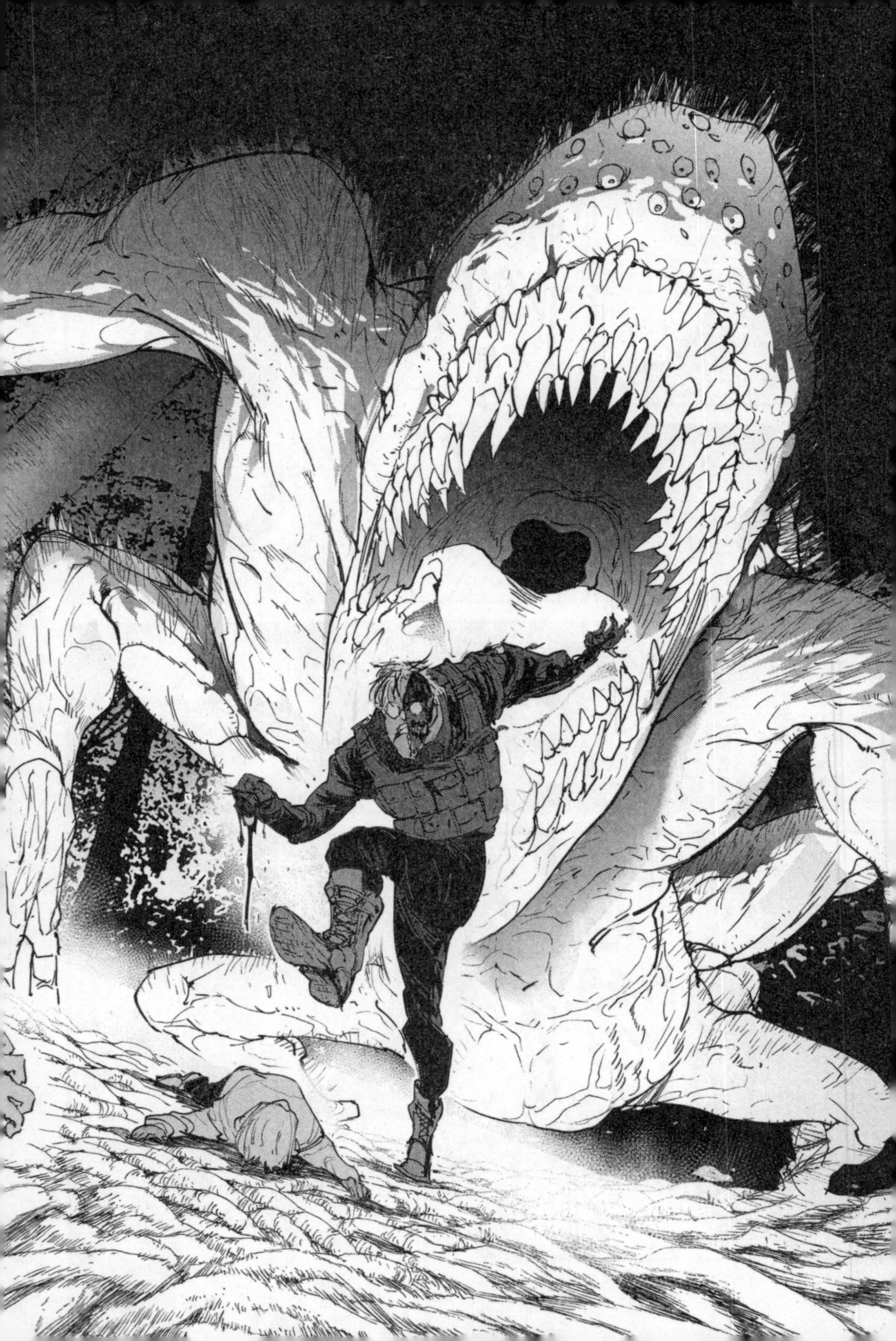

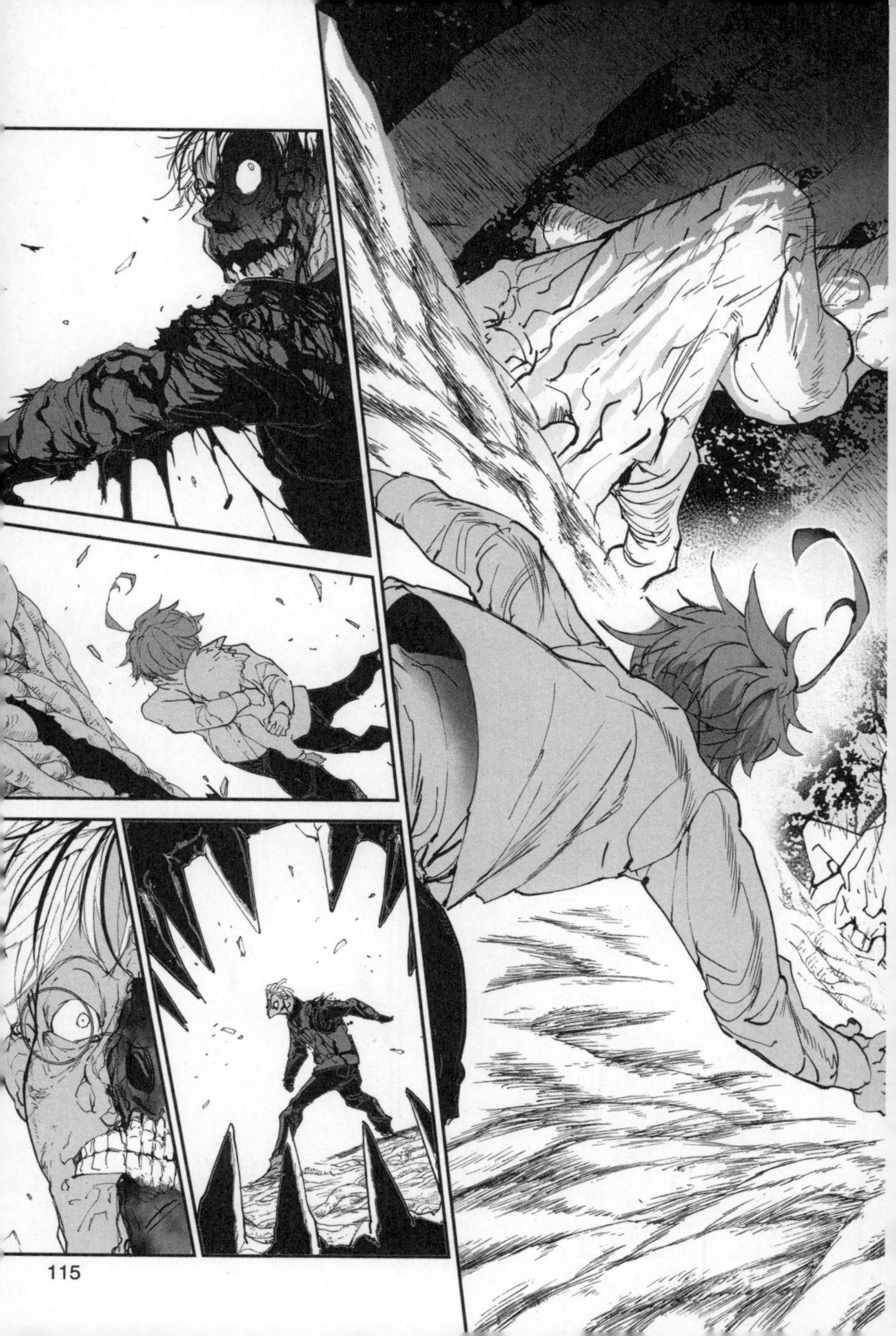

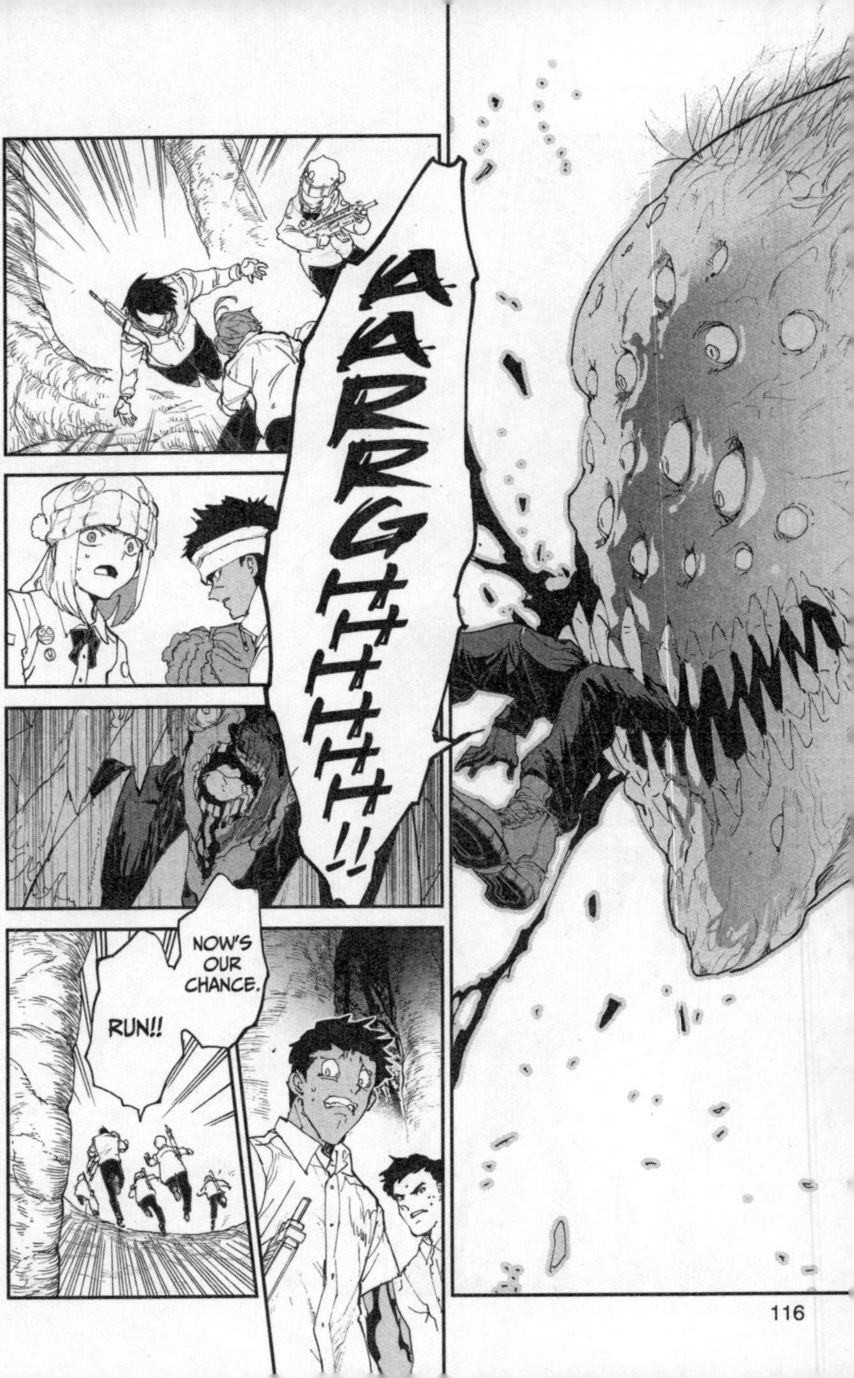
AARRGHHHHH!!
NOW'S OUR CHANCE.
RUN!!

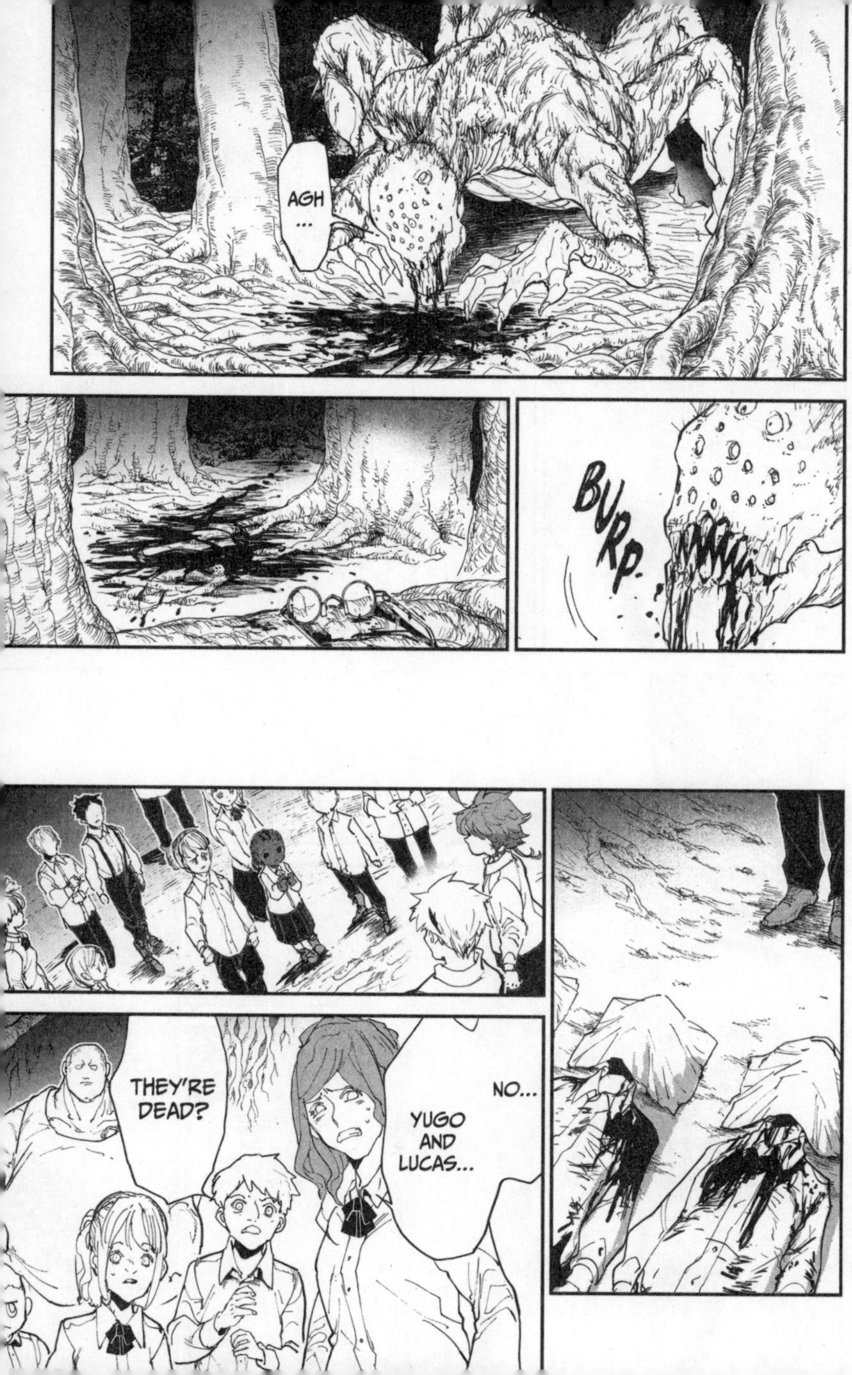
AGH ...
BURP
NO...
YUGO AND LUCAS...
THEY'RE DEAD?

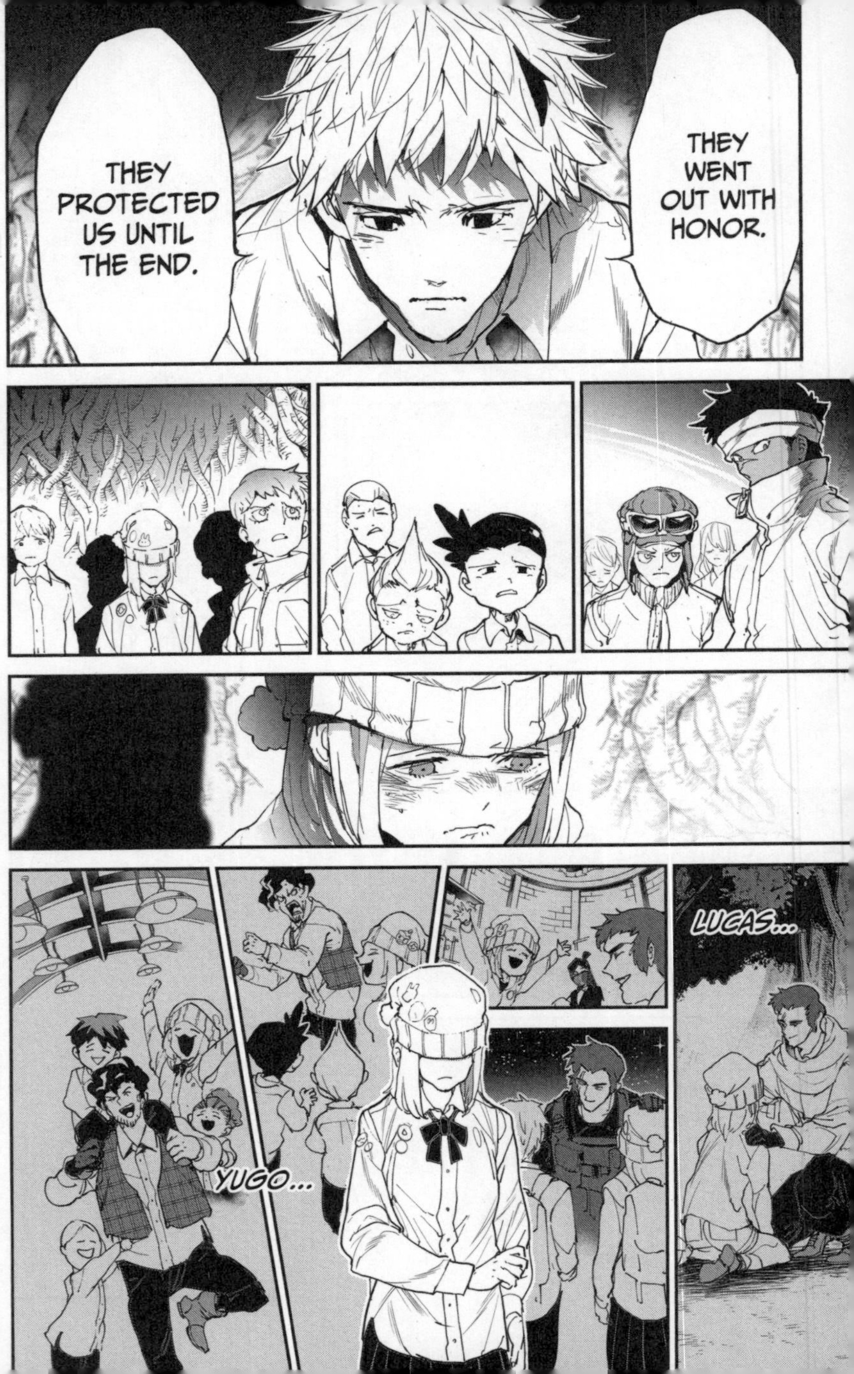
THEY WENT OUT WITH HONOR.
THEY PROTECTED US UNTIL THE END.
LUCAS...
YUGO...

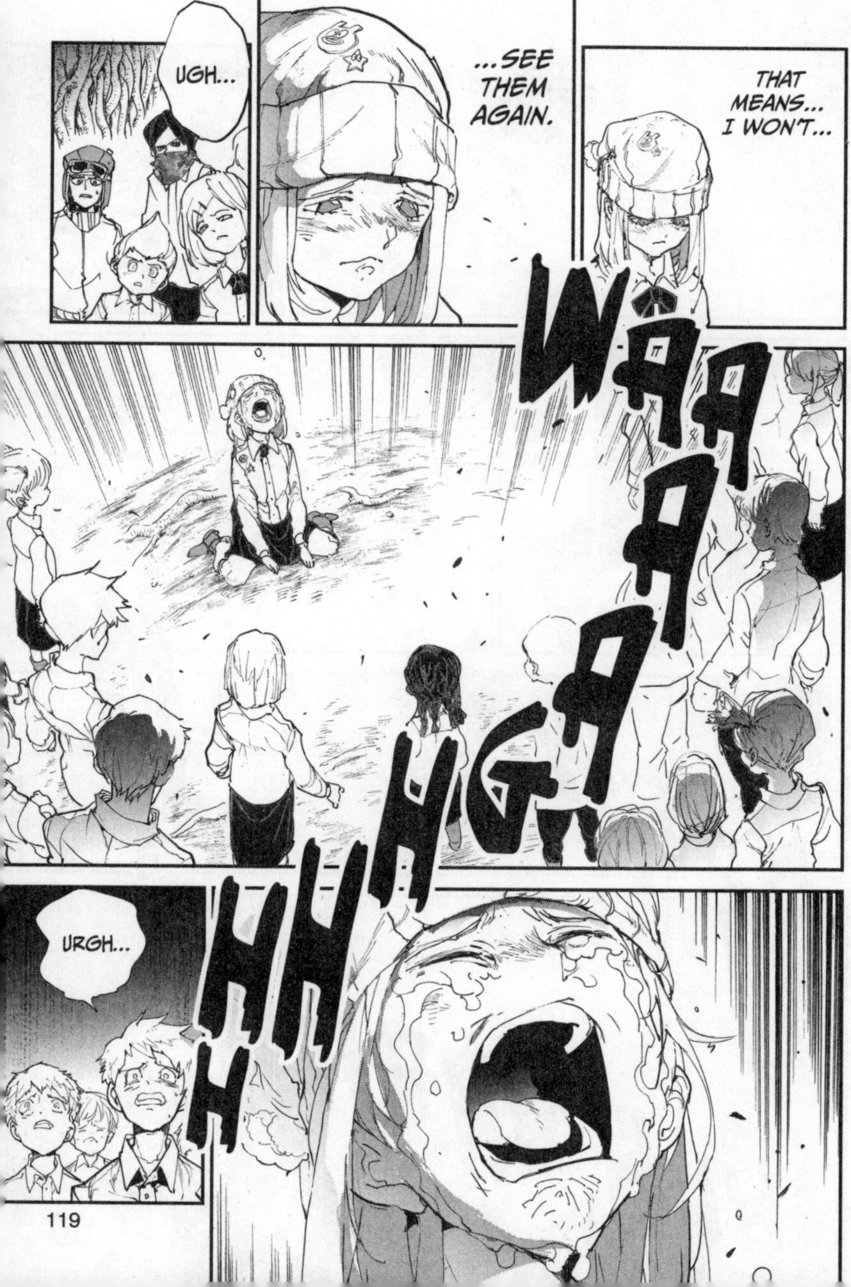
THAT MEANS... I WON'T...
...SEE THEM AGAIN.
UGH...
WAAAAAGHHHH
URGH...

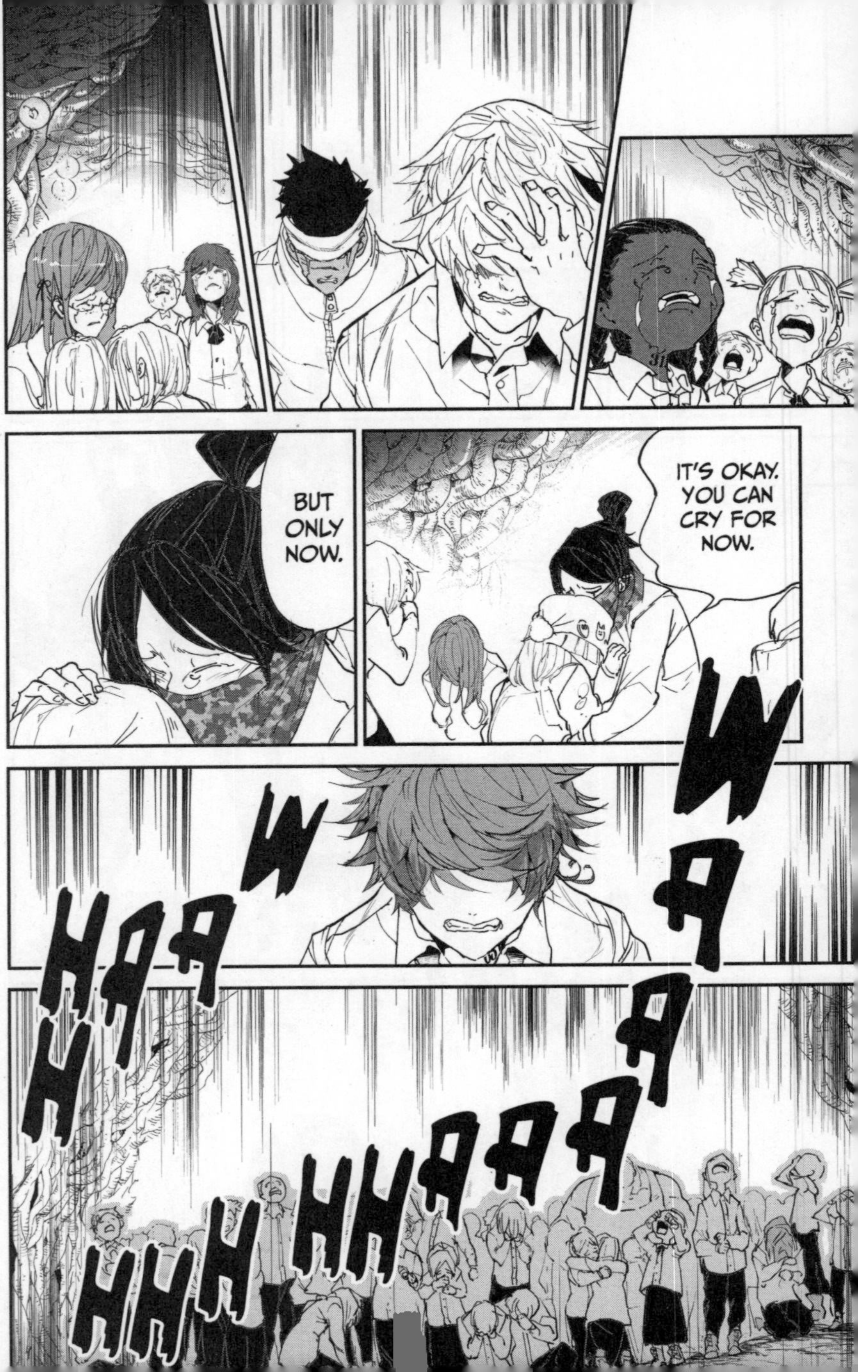
IT'S OKAY. YOU CAN CRY FOR NOW.
BUT ONLY NOW.

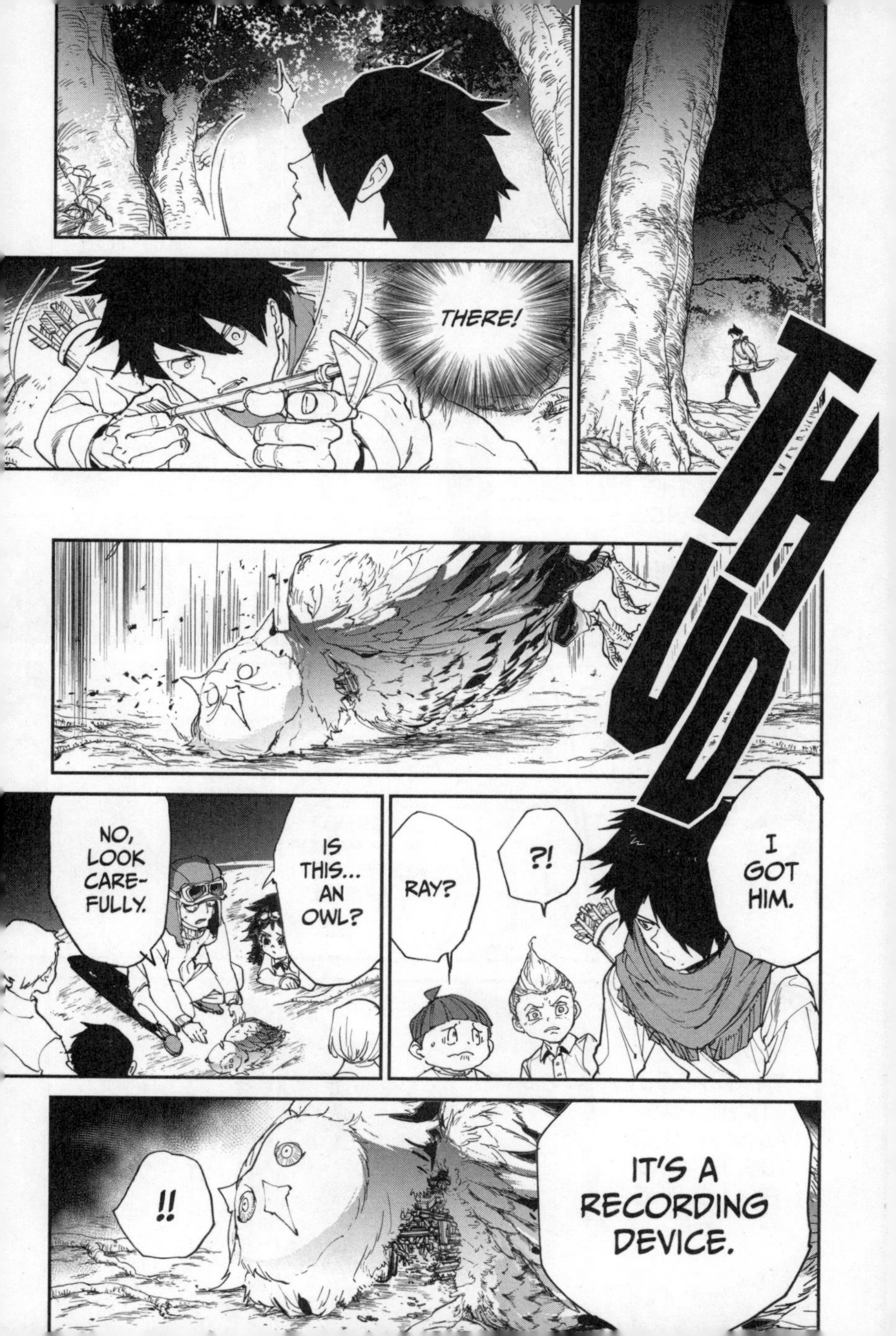
THERE!
THUD
I GOT HIM.
?!
RAY?
IS THIS... AN OWL?
NO, LOOK CAREFULLY.
IT'S A RECORDING DEVICE.
!!

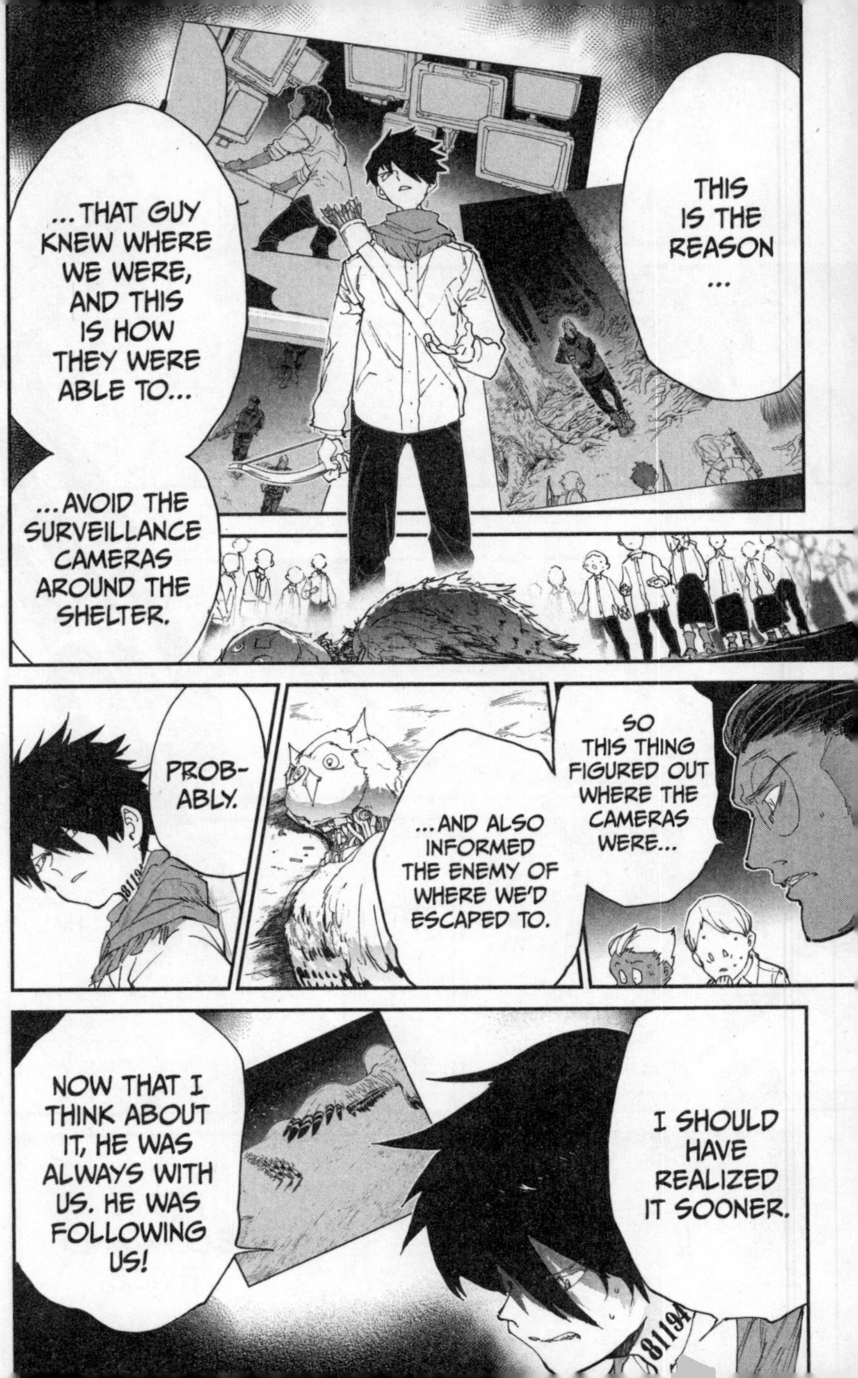
THIS IS THE REASON ...
...THAT GUY KNEW WHERE WE WERE, AND THIS IS HOW THEY WERE ABLE TO...
...AVOID THE SURVEILLANCE CAMERAS AROUND THE SHELTER.
SO THIS THING FIGURED OUT WHERE THE CAMERAS WERE...
...AND ALSO INFORMED THE ENEMY OF WHERE WE'D ESCAPED TO.
PROB- ABLY.
I SHOULD HAVE REALIZED IT SOONER.
NOW THAT I THINK ABOUT IT, HE WAS ALWAYS WITH US. HE WAS FOLLOWING US!
81194

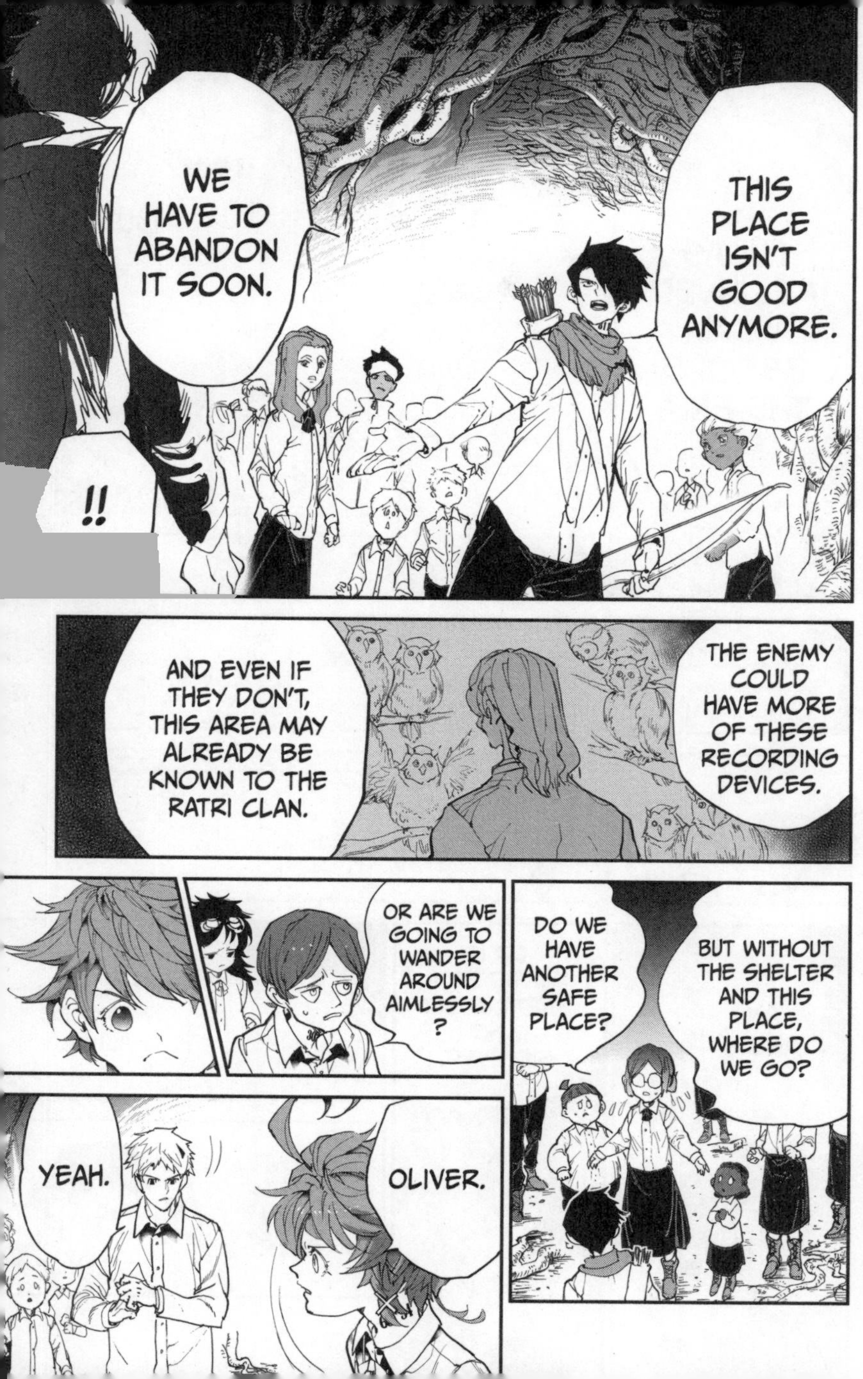
THIS PLACE ISN'T GOOD ANYMORE.
WE HAVE TO ABANDON IT SOON.
!!
THE ENEMY COULD HAVE MORE OF THESE RECORDING DEVICES.
AND EVEN IF THEY DON'T, THIS AREA MAY ALREADY BE KNOWN TO THE RATRI CLAN.
BUT WITHOUT THE SHELTER AND THIS PLACE, WHERE DO WE GO?
DO WE HAVE ANOTHER SAFE PLACE?
OR ARE WE GOING TO WANDER AROUND AIMLESSLY?
OLIVER.
YEAH.

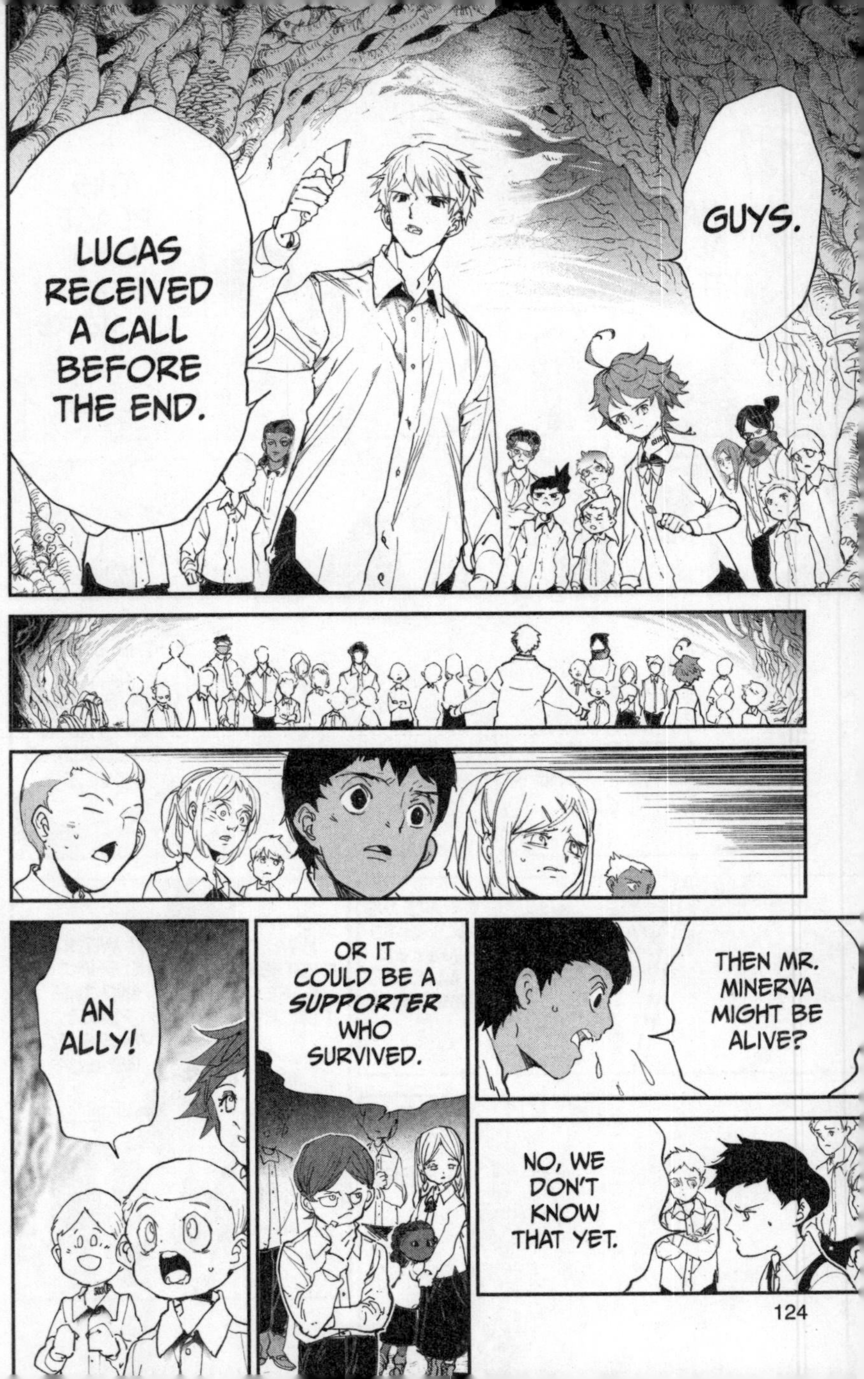
GUYS.
LUCAS RECEIVED A CALL BEFORE THE END.
THEN MR. MINERVA MIGHT BE ALIVE?
NO, WE DON'T KNOW THAT YET.
OR IT COULD BE A *SUPPORTER* WHO SURVIVED.
AN ALLY!

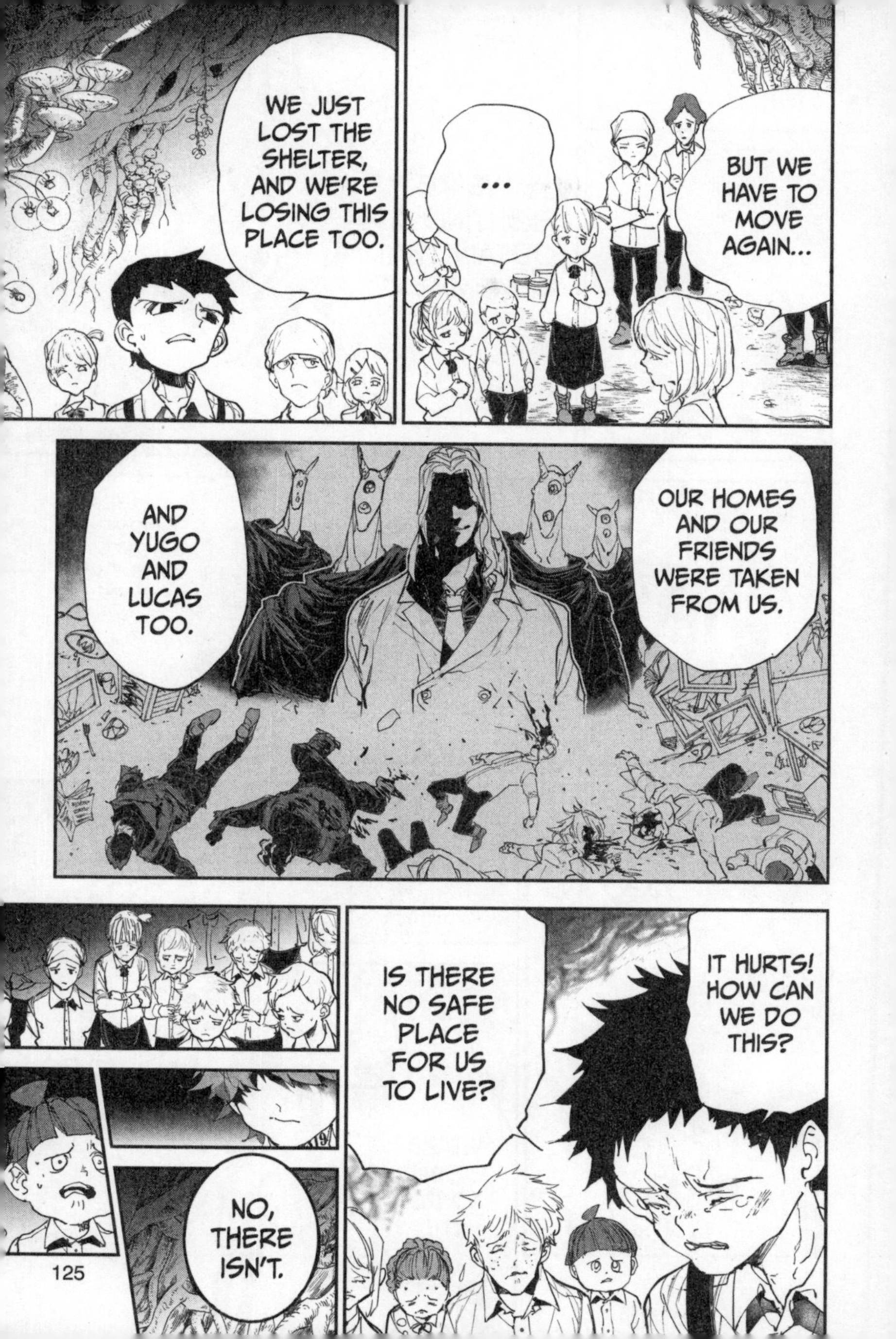
BUT WE HAVE TO MOVE AGAIN...
...
WE JUST LOST THE SHELTER, AND WE'RE LOSING THIS PLACE TOO.
OUR HOMES AND OUR FRIENDS WERE TAKEN FROM US.
AND YUGO AND LUCAS TOO.
IT HURTS! HOW CAN WE DO THIS?
IS THERE NO SAFE PLACE FOR US TO LIVE?
NO, THERE ISN'T.

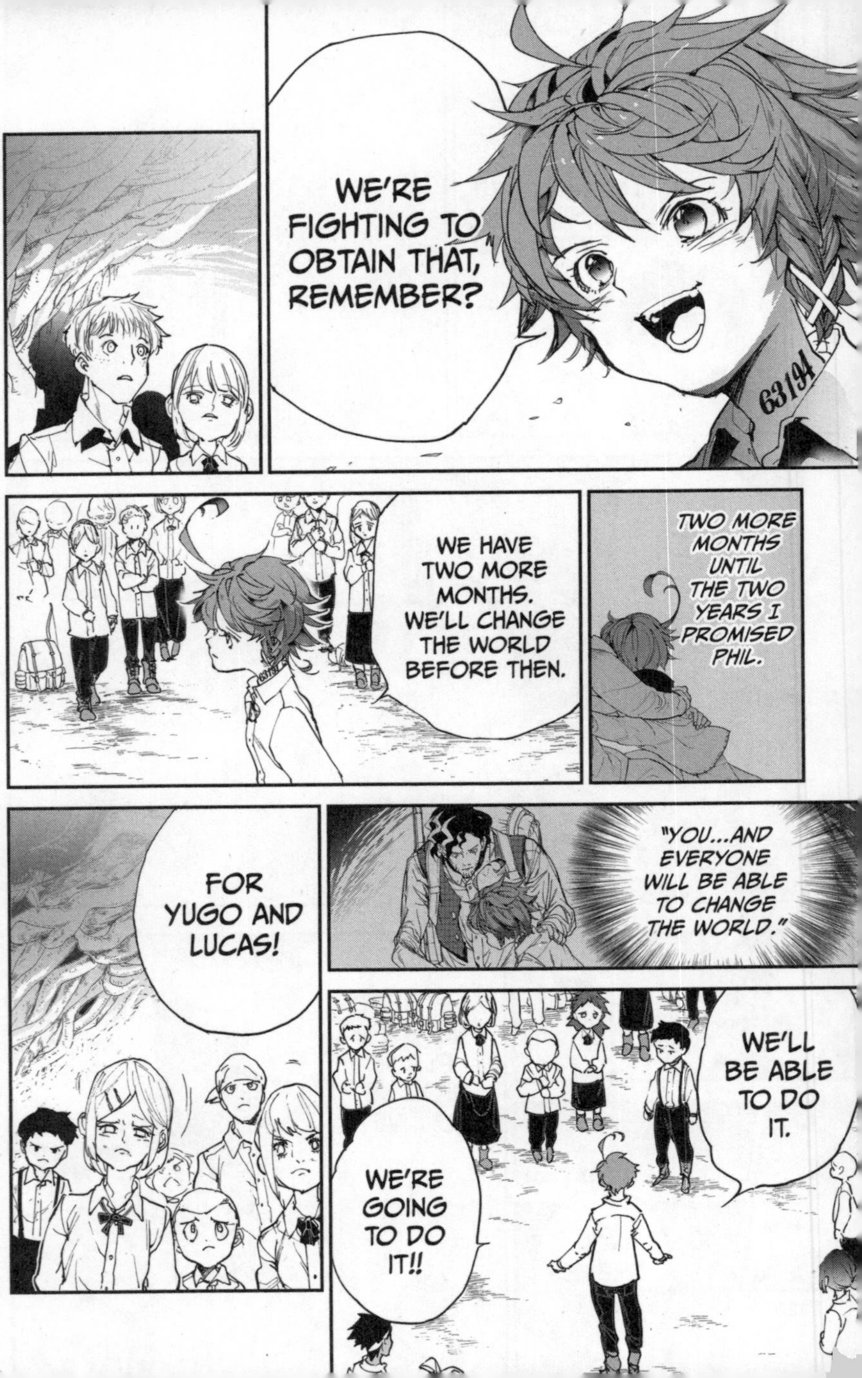
WE'RE FIGHTING TO OBTAIN THAT, REMEMBER?
TWO MORE MONTHS UNTIL THE TWO YEARS I PROMISED PHIL.
WE HAVE TWO MORE MONTHS. WE'LL CHANGE THE WORLD BEFORE THEN.
"YOU...AND EVERYONE WILL BE ABLE TO CHANGE THE WORLD."
WE'LL BE ABLE TO DO IT.
WE'RE GOING TO DO IT!!
FOR YUGO AND LUCAS!

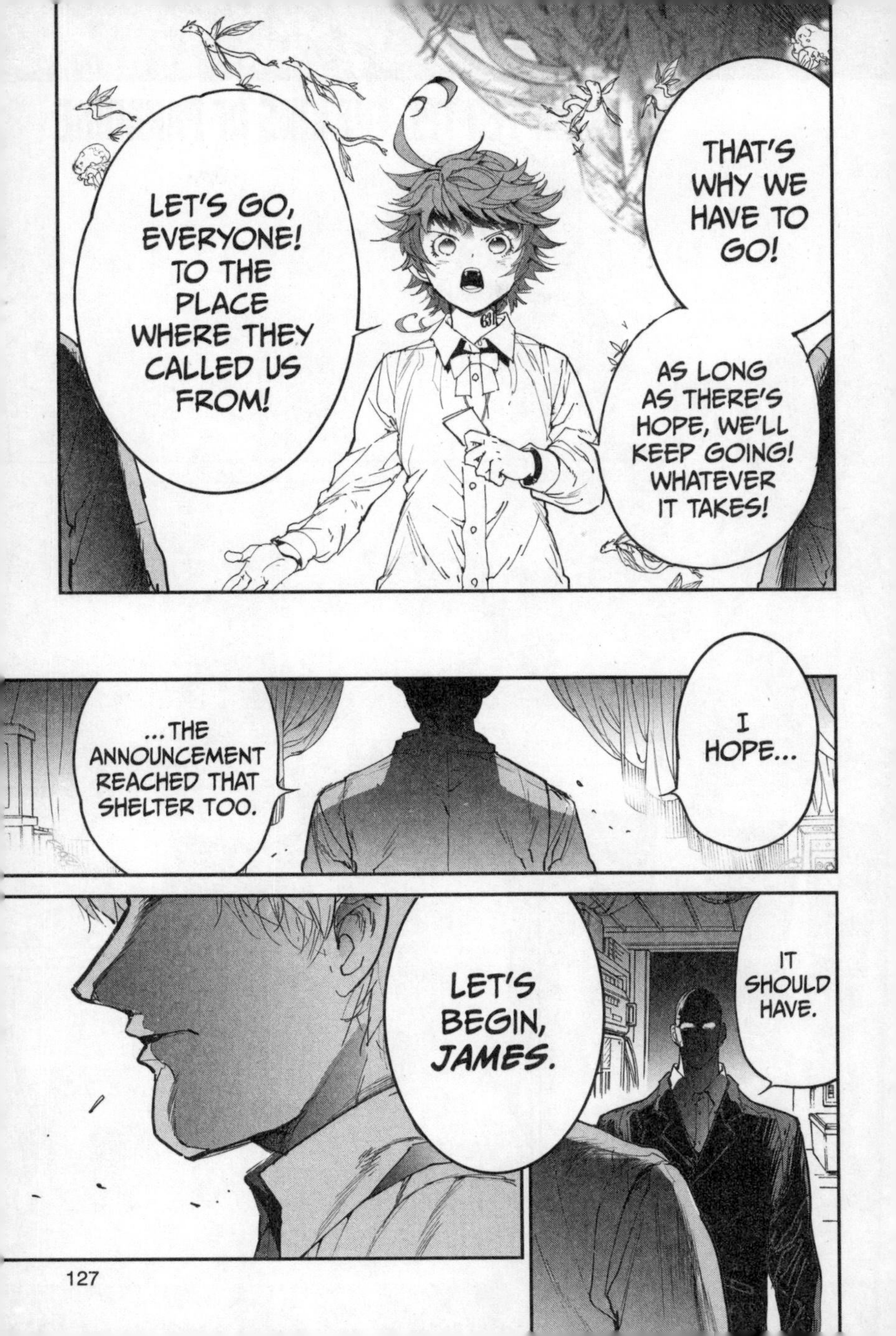
THAT'S WHY WE HAVE TO GO!
AS LONG AS THERE'S HOPE, WE'LL KEEP GOING! WHATEVER IT TAKES!
LET'S GO, EVERYONE! TO THE PLACE WHERE THEY CALLED US FROM!
I HOPE...
...THE ANNOUNCEMENT REACHED THAT SHELTER TOO.
IT SHOULD HAVE.
LET'S BEGIN, *JAMES*.

CHAPTER 113: THE KING OF PARADISE

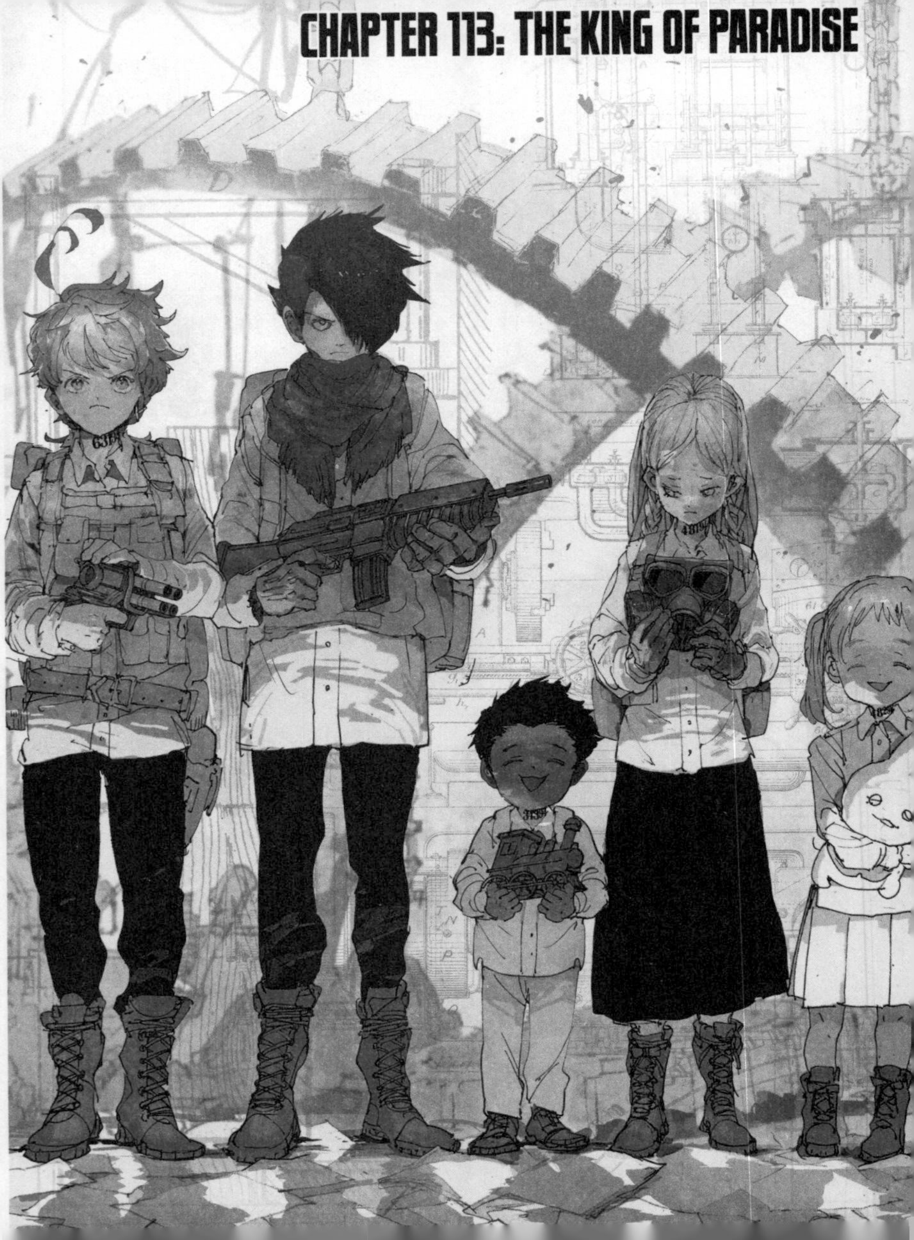

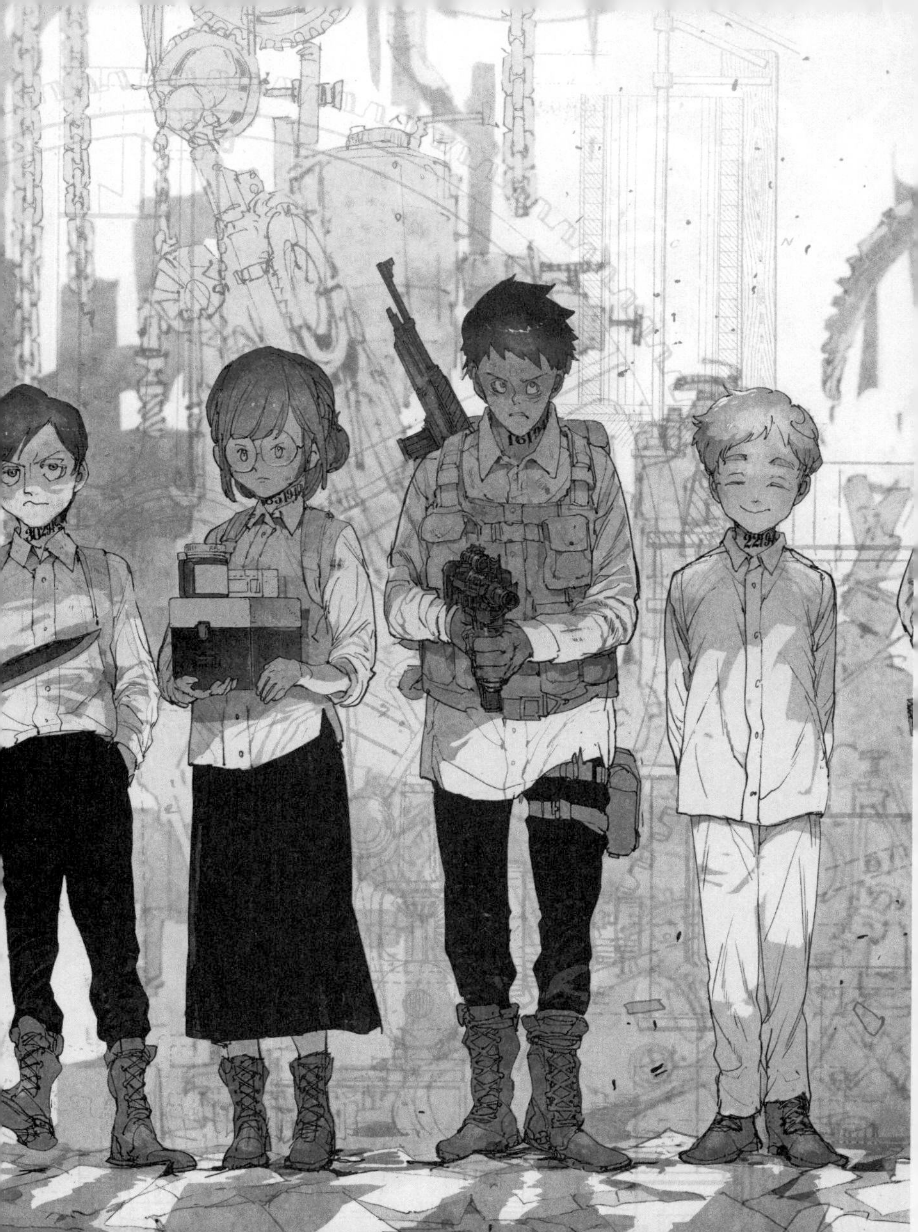

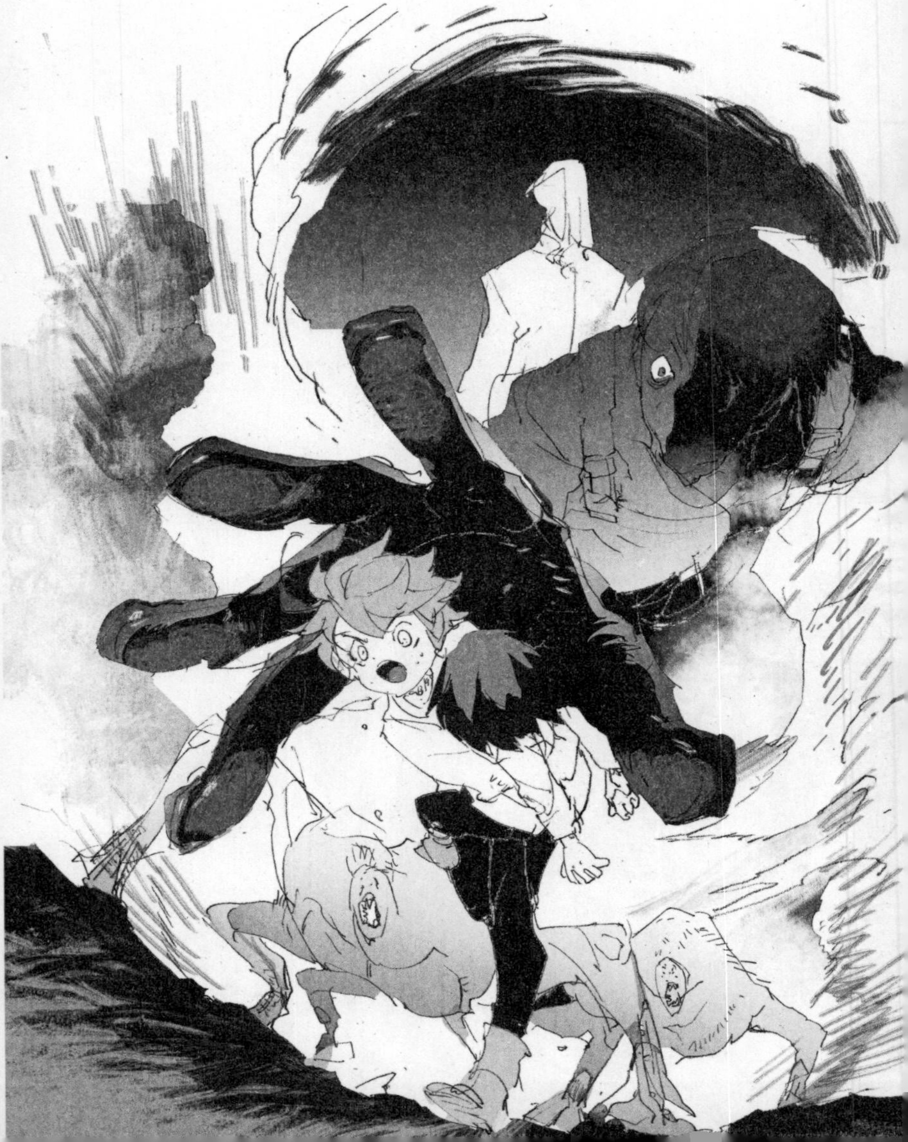

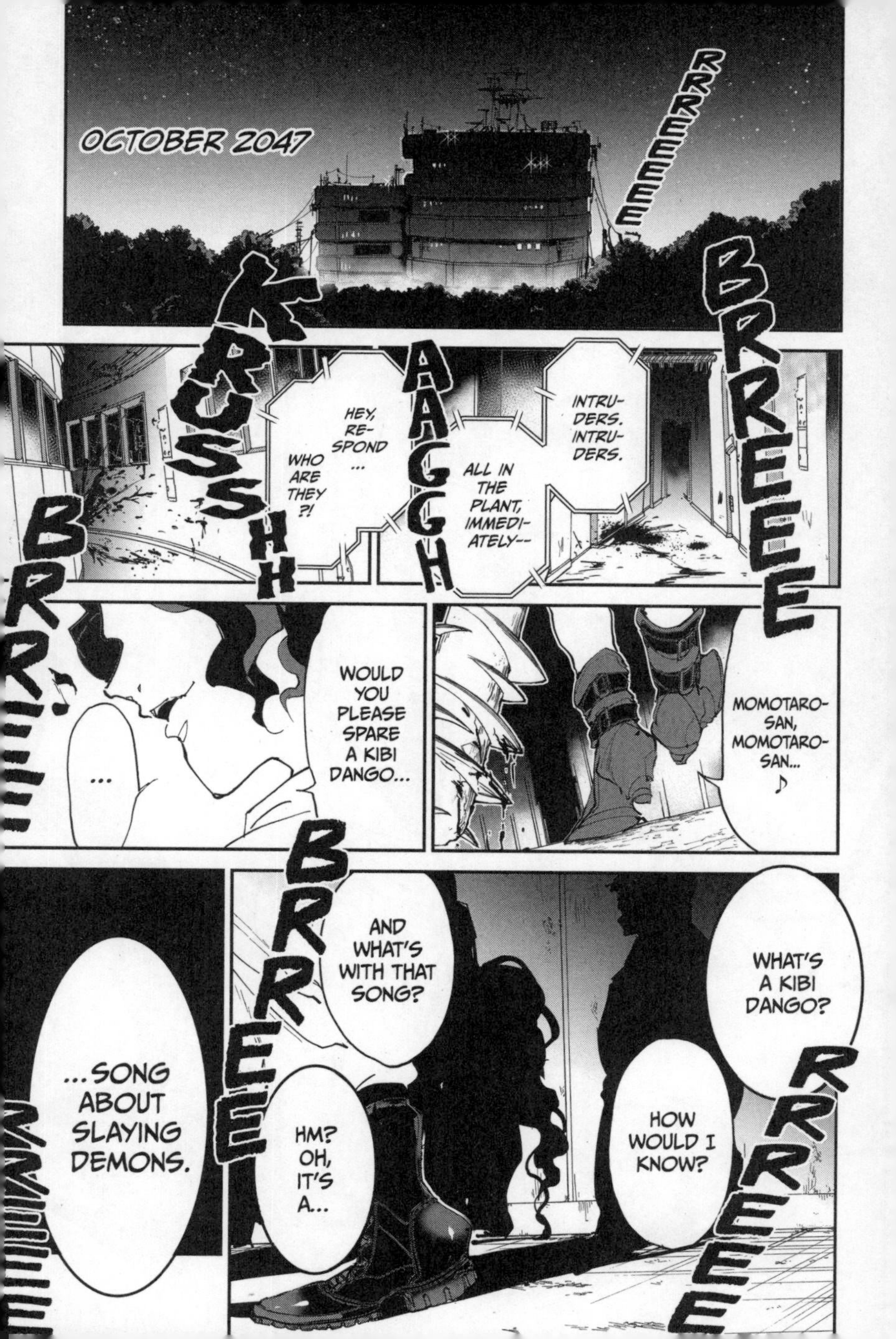

OCTOBER 2047
RRREEEEE
BRREEEE
KRUSSHH
AAGGH
INTRU-DERS. INTRU-DERS.
ALL IN THE PLANT, IMMEDI-ATELY--
HEY, RE-SPOND ...
WHO ARE THEY ?!
MOMOTARO-SAN, MOMOTARO-SAN... ♪
WOULD YOU PLEASE SPARE A KIBI DANGO...
...
WHAT'S A KIBI DANGO?
HOW WOULD I KNOW?
AND WHAT'S WITH THAT SONG?
HM? OH, IT'S A...
...SONG ABOUT SLAYING DEMONS.
BRREE
RRREEEE

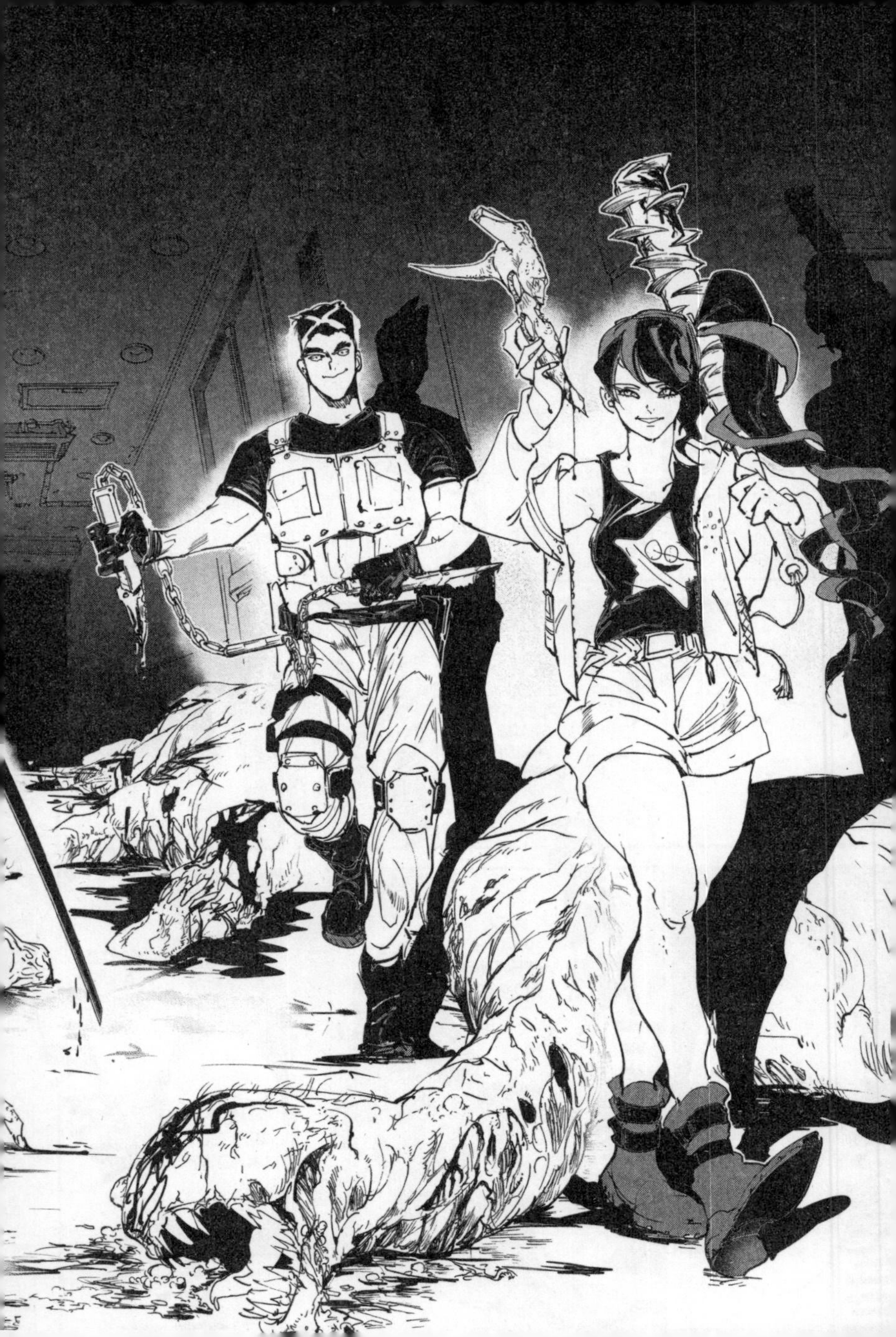

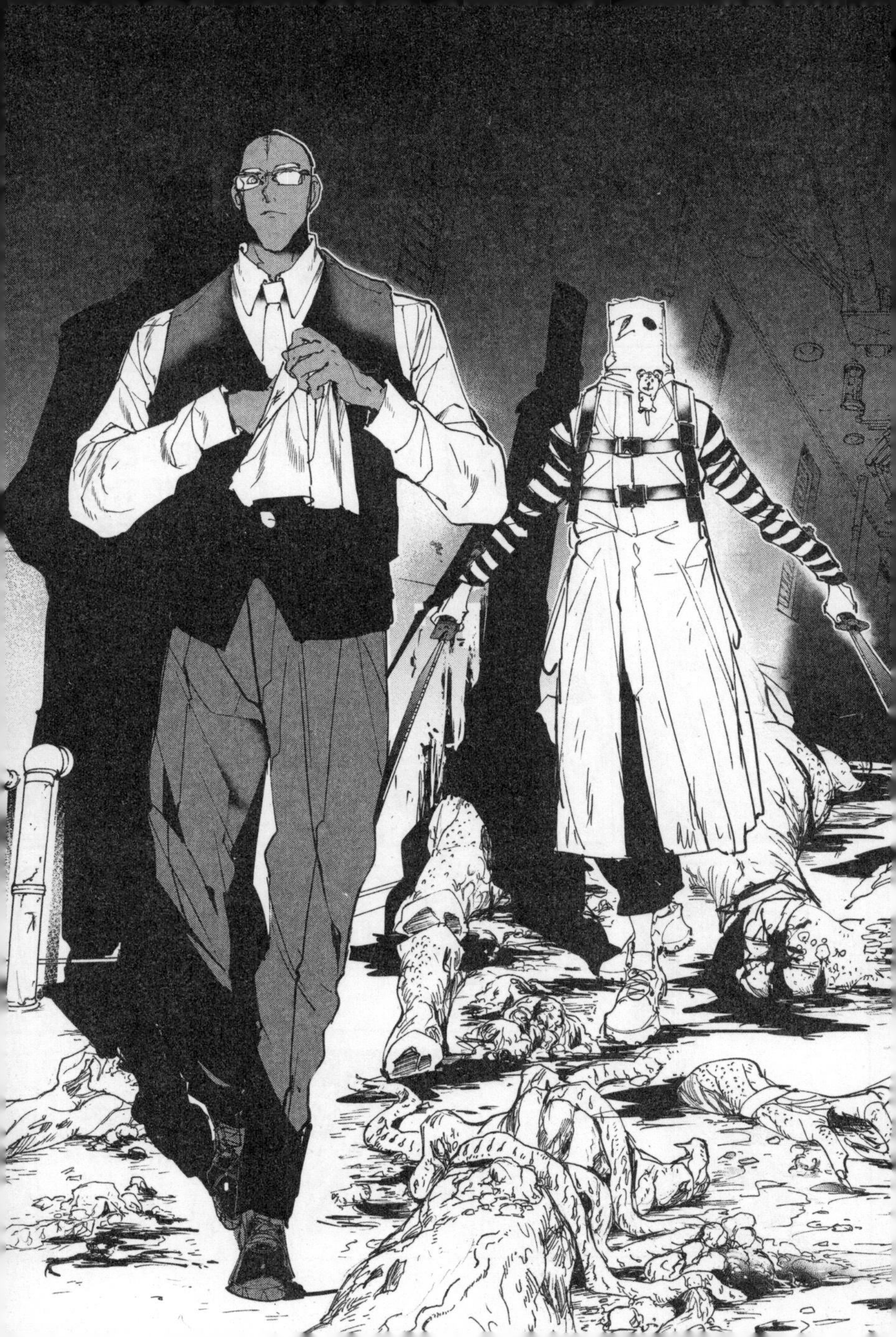

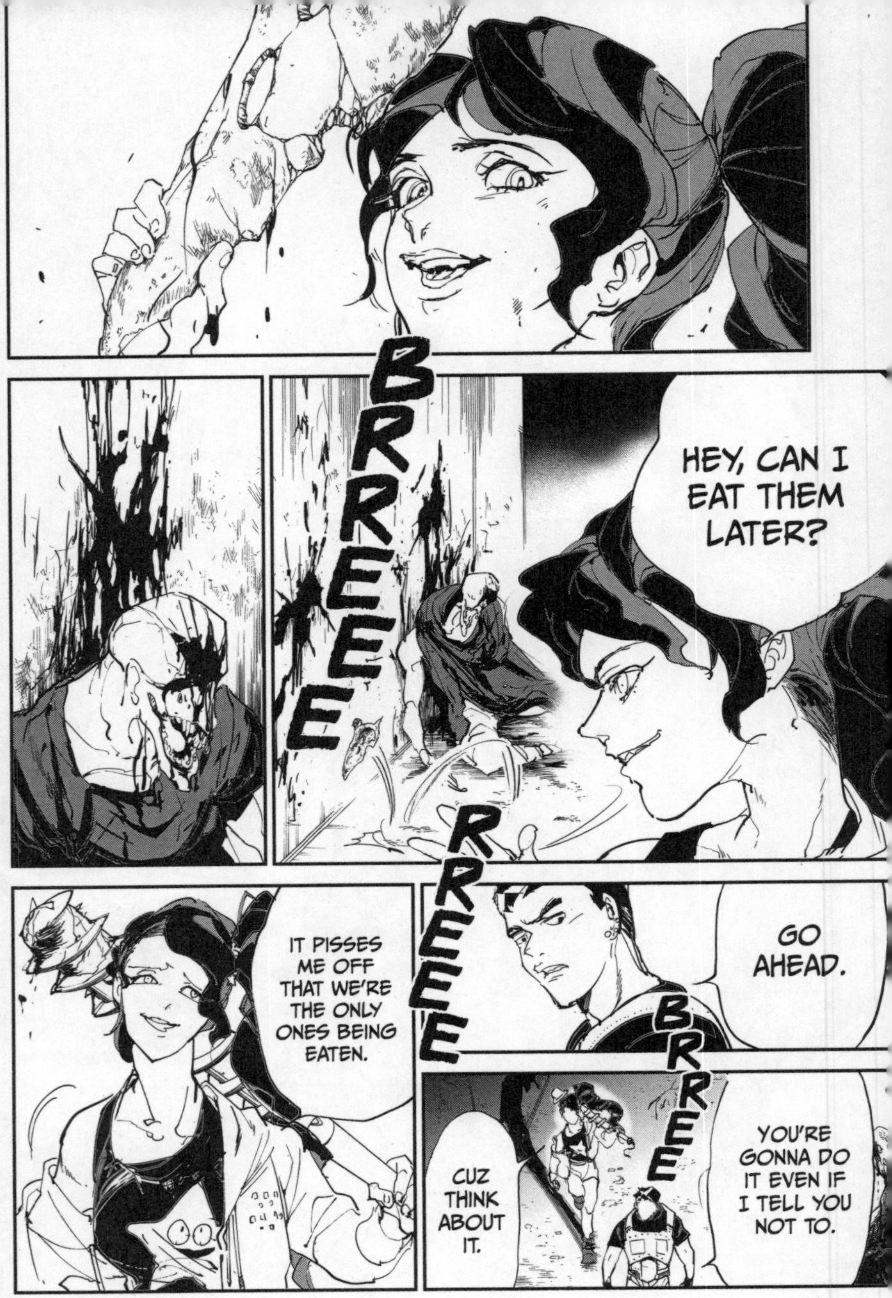
BRREEEE
HEY, CAN I EAT THEM LATER?
RREEEE
GO AHEAD.
BRREE
YOU'RE GONNA DO IT EVEN IF I TELL YOU NOT TO.
CUZ THINK ABOUT IT.
IT PISSES ME OFF THAT WE'RE THE ONLY ONES BEING EATEN.

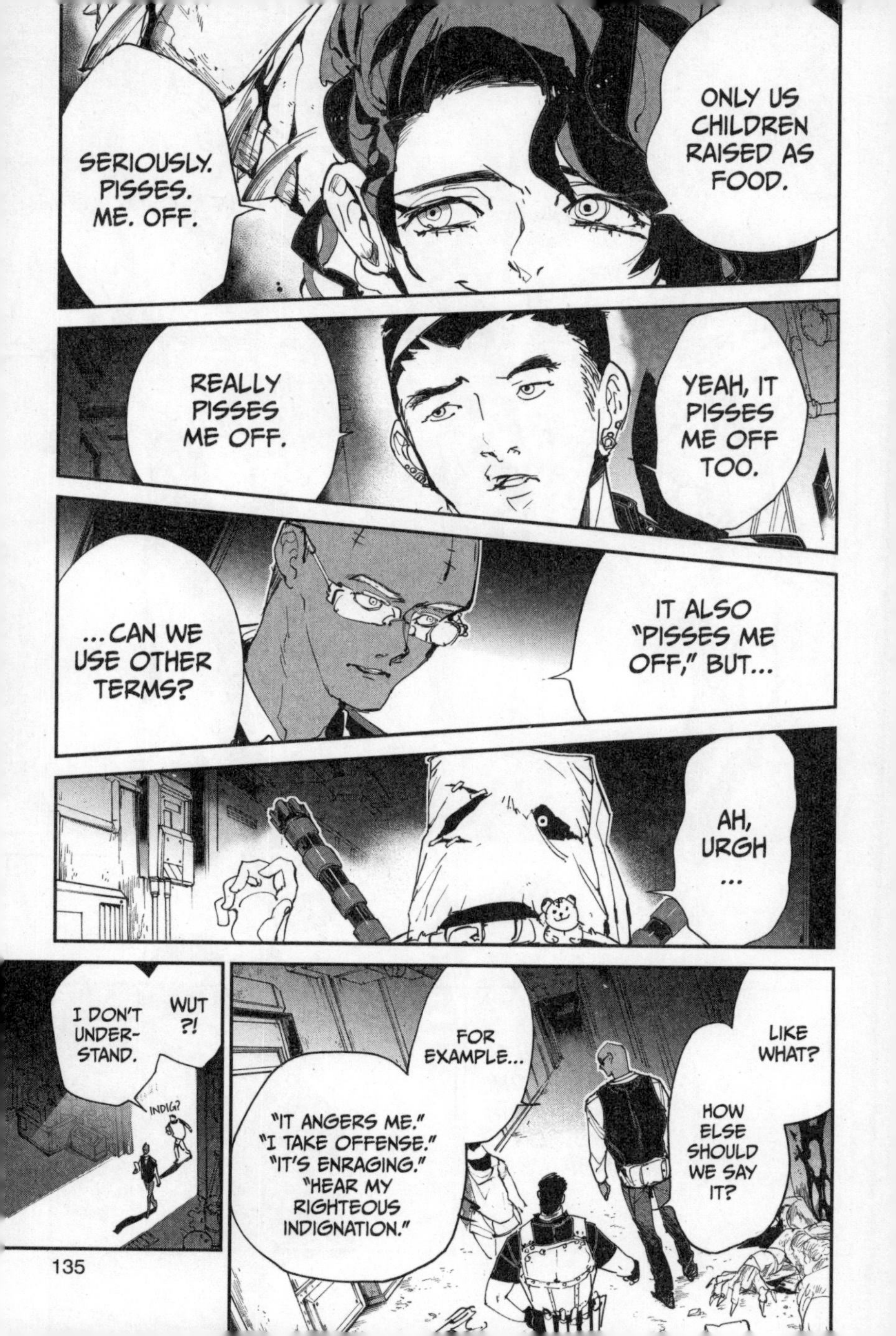
ONLY US CHILDREN RAISED AS FOOD.
SERIOUSLY. PISSES. ME. OFF.
YEAH, IT PISSES ME OFF TOO.
REALLY PISSES ME OFF.
IT ALSO "PISSES ME OFF," BUT...
...CAN WE USE OTHER TERMS?
AH, URGH ...
LIKE WHAT?
HOW ELSE SHOULD WE SAY IT?
FOR EXAMPLE...
"IT ANGERS ME." "I TAKE OFFENSE." "IT'S ENRAGING." "HEAR MY RIGHTEOUS INDIGNATION."
WUT ?!
I DON'T UNDER-STAND.
INDIG?

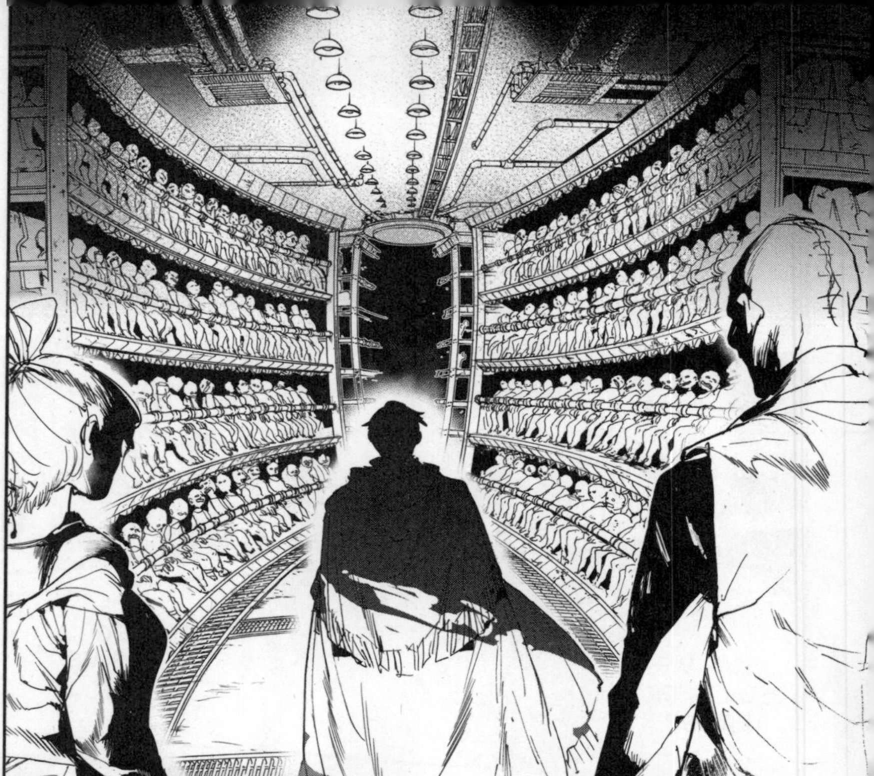

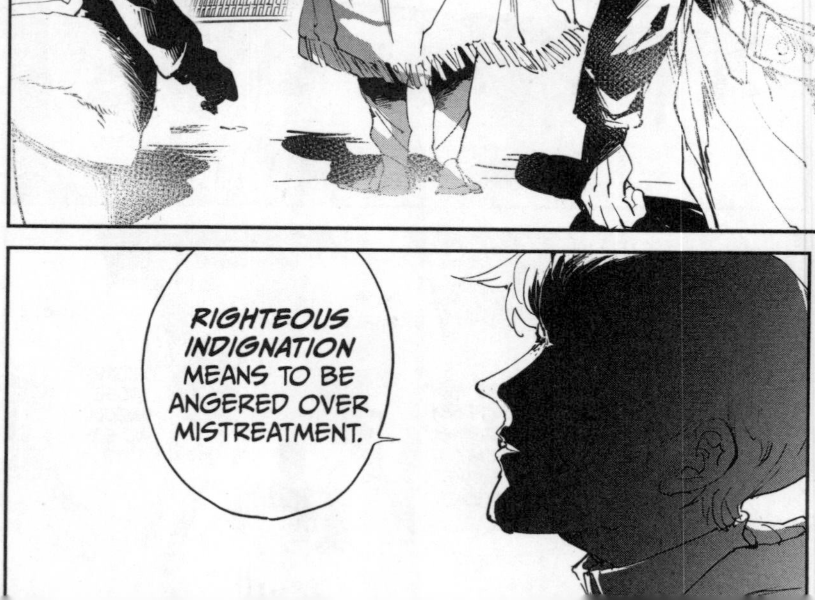
RIGHTEOUS INDIGNATION MEANS TO BE ANGERED OVER MISTREATMENT.

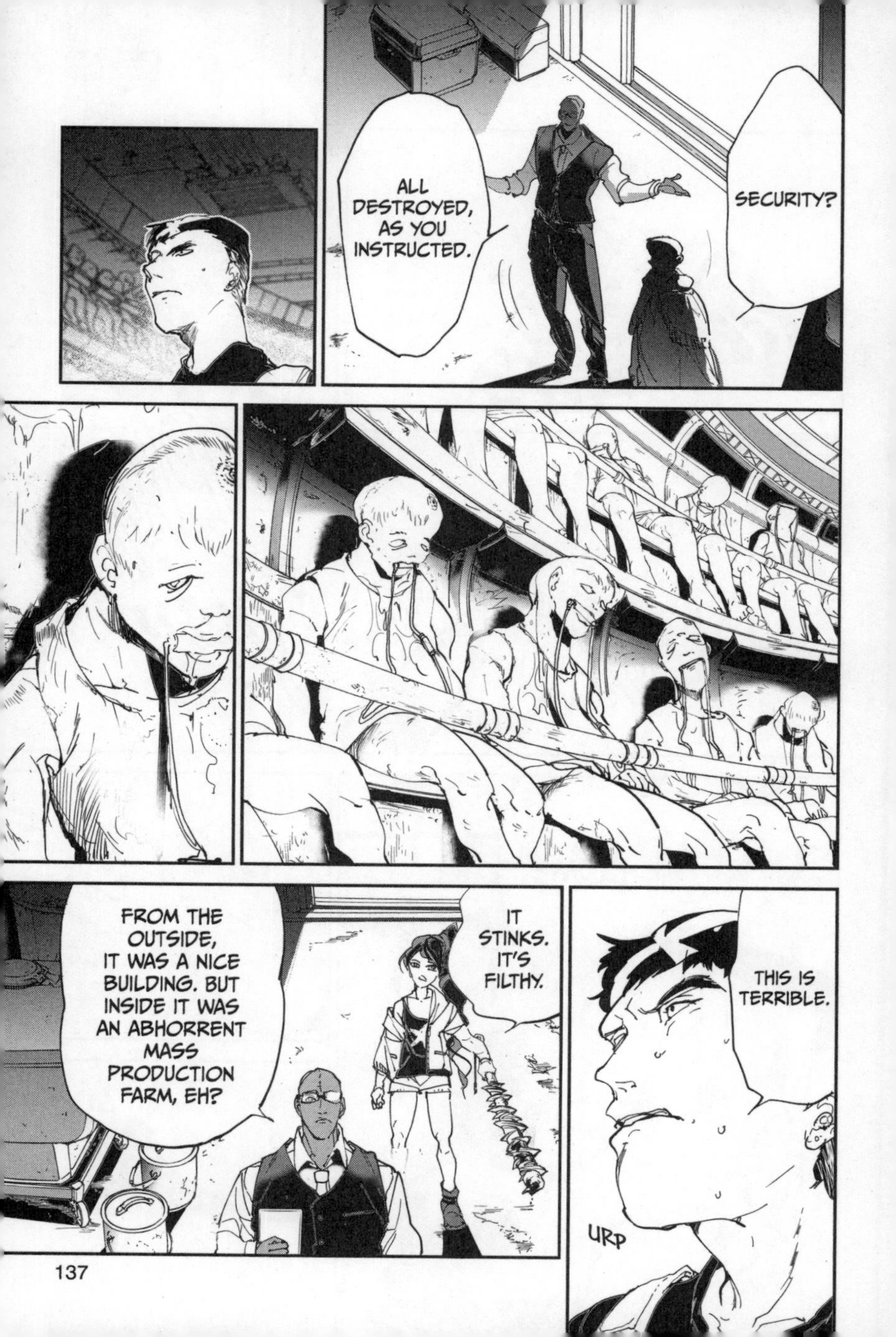
SECURITY?
ALL DESTROYED, AS YOU INSTRUCTED.
THIS IS TERRIBLE.
URP
IT STINKS. IT'S FILTHY.
FROM THE OUTSIDE, IT WAS A NICE BUILDING. BUT INSIDE IT WAS AN ABHORRENT MASS PRODUCTION FARM, EH?

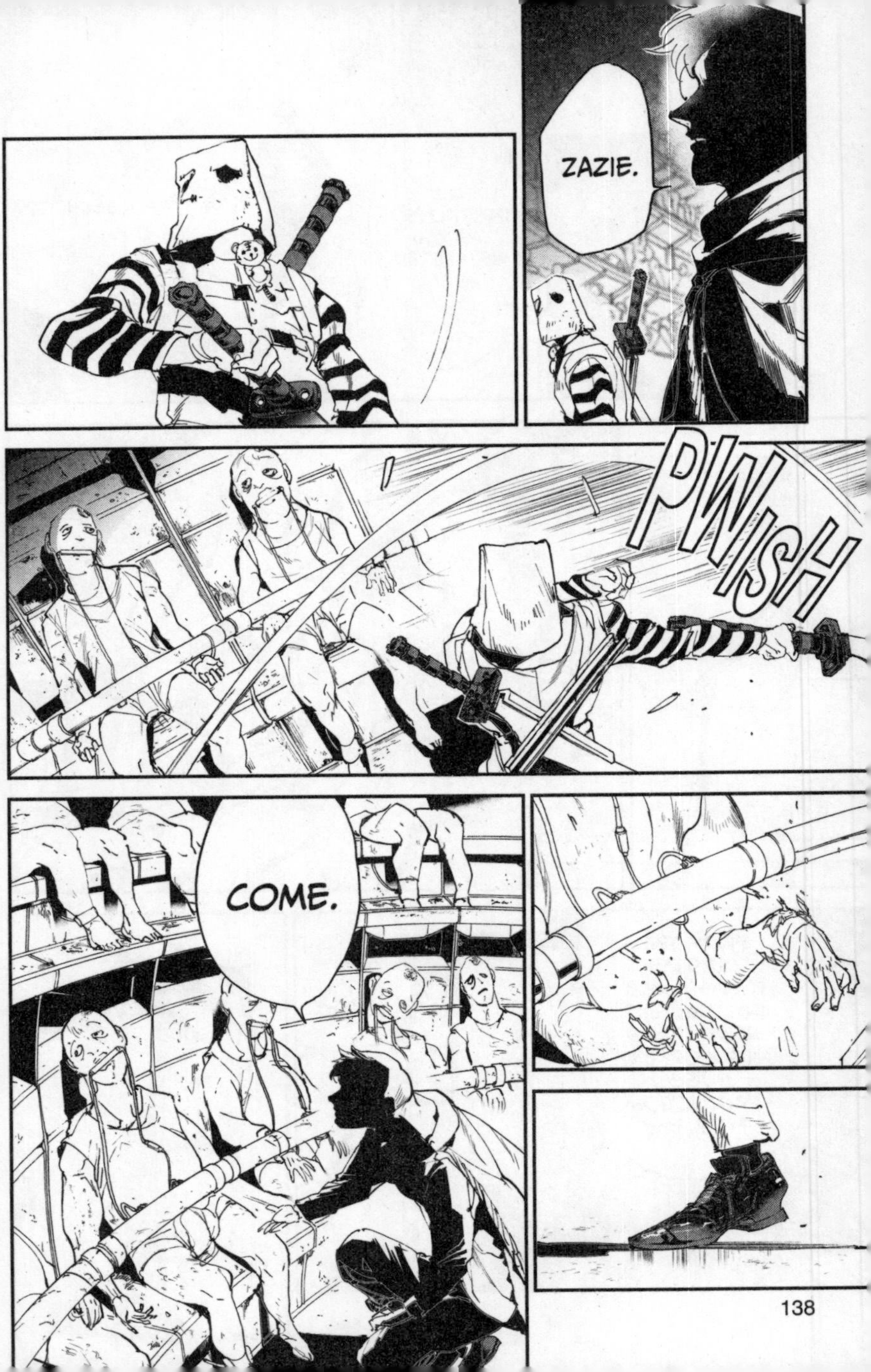
ZAZIE.
PWISH
COME.

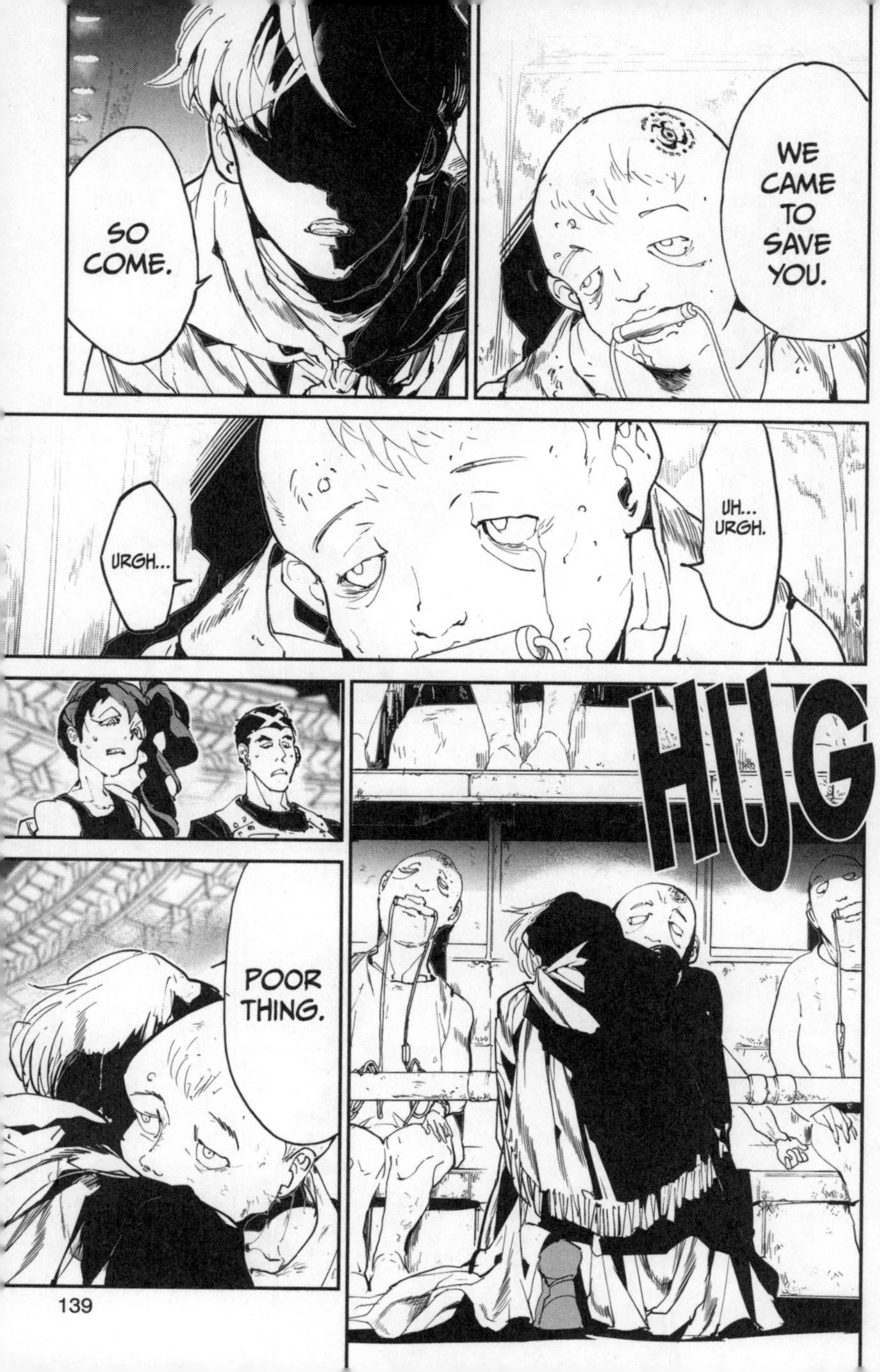
WE CAME TO SAVE YOU.
SO COME.
UH... URGH.
URGH...
HUG
POOR THING.

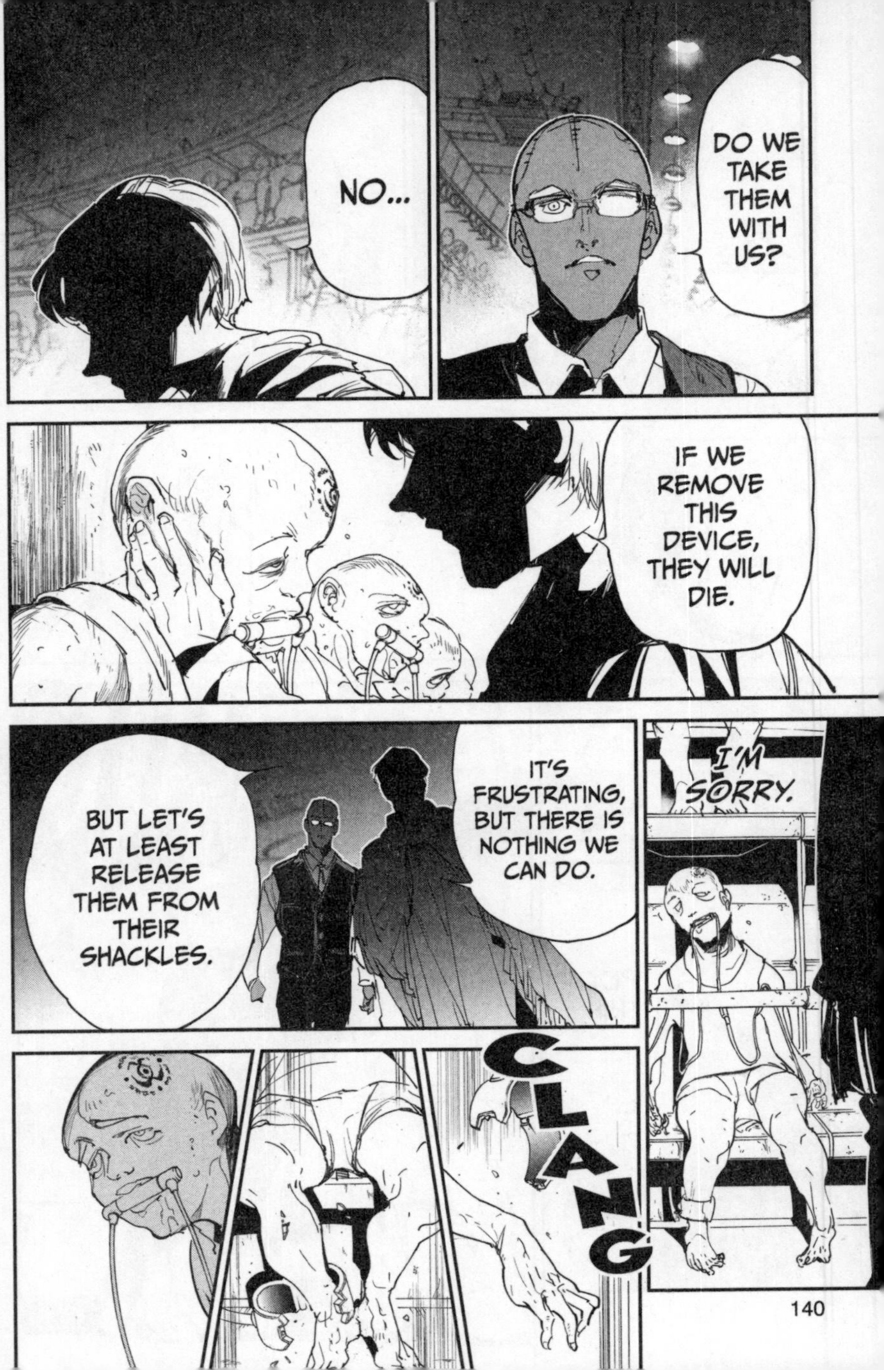
DO WE TAKE THEM WITH US?
NO...
IF WE REMOVE THIS DEVICE, THEY WILL DIE.
I'M SORRY.
IT'S FRUSTRATING, BUT THERE IS NOTHING WE CAN DO.
BUT LET'S AT LEAST RELEASE THEM FROM THEIR SHACKLES.
CLANG

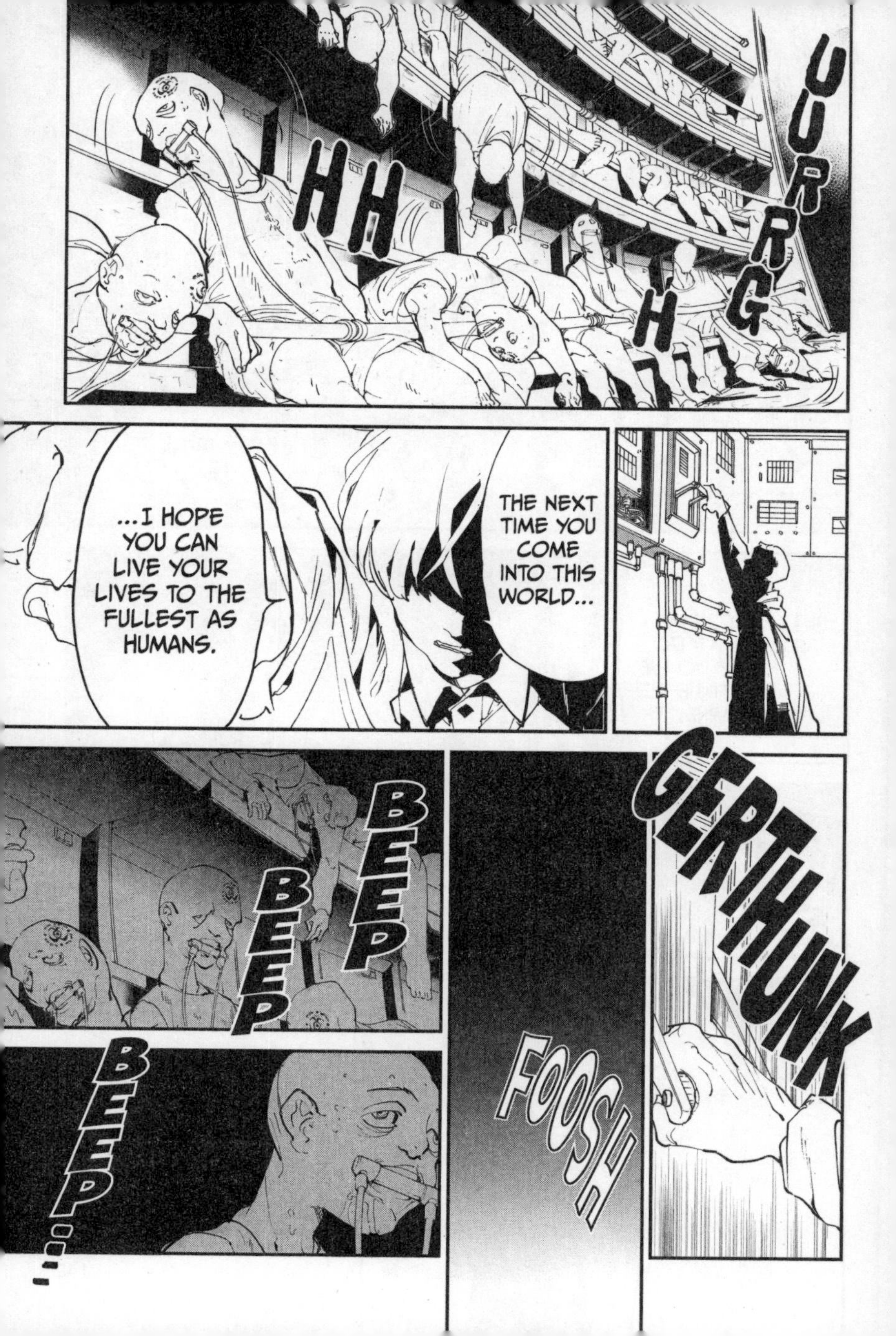
UURRG
H
HH
THE NEXT TIME YOU COME INTO THIS WORLD...
...I HOPE YOU CAN LIVE YOUR LIVES TO THE FULLEST AS HUMANS.
GERTHUNK
FOOSH
BEEP
BEEP
BEEP......

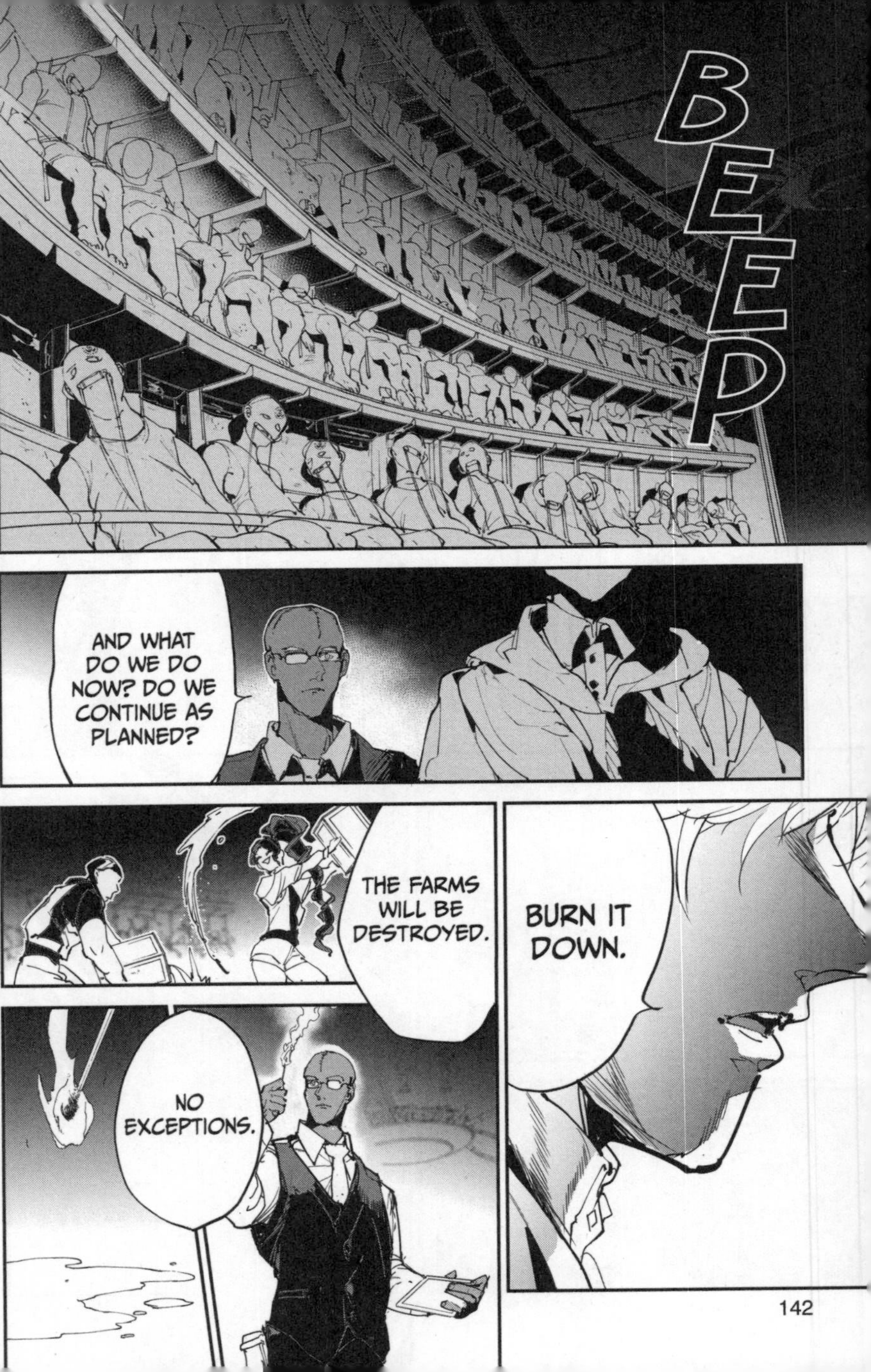
BEEP
AND WHAT DO WE DO NOW? DO WE CONTINUE AS PLANNED?
BURN IT DOWN.
THE FARMS WILL BE DESTROYED.
NO EXCEPTIONS.

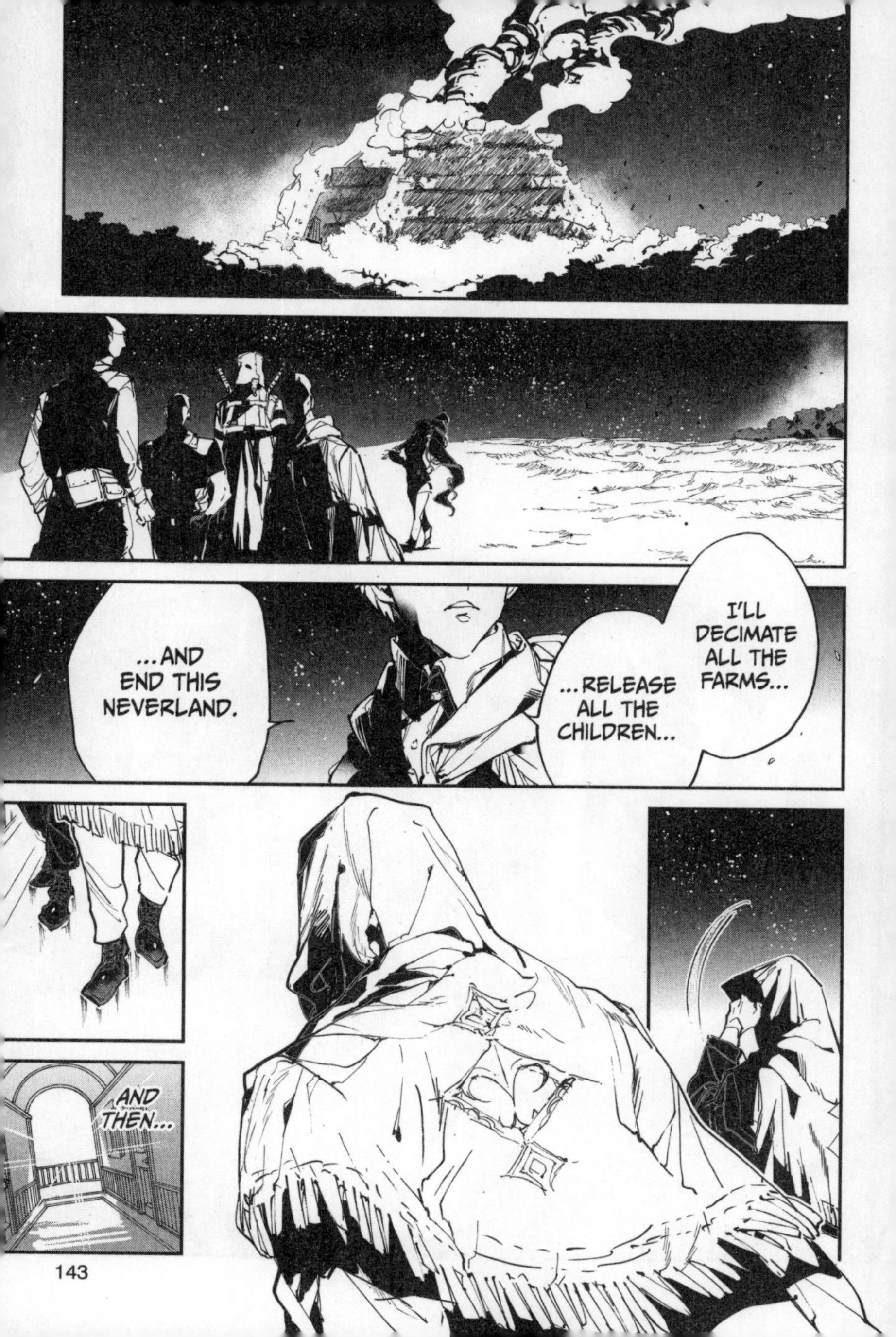
I'LL DECIMATE ALL THE FARMS...
...RELEASE ALL THE CHILDREN...
...AND END THIS NEVERLAND.
AND THEN...

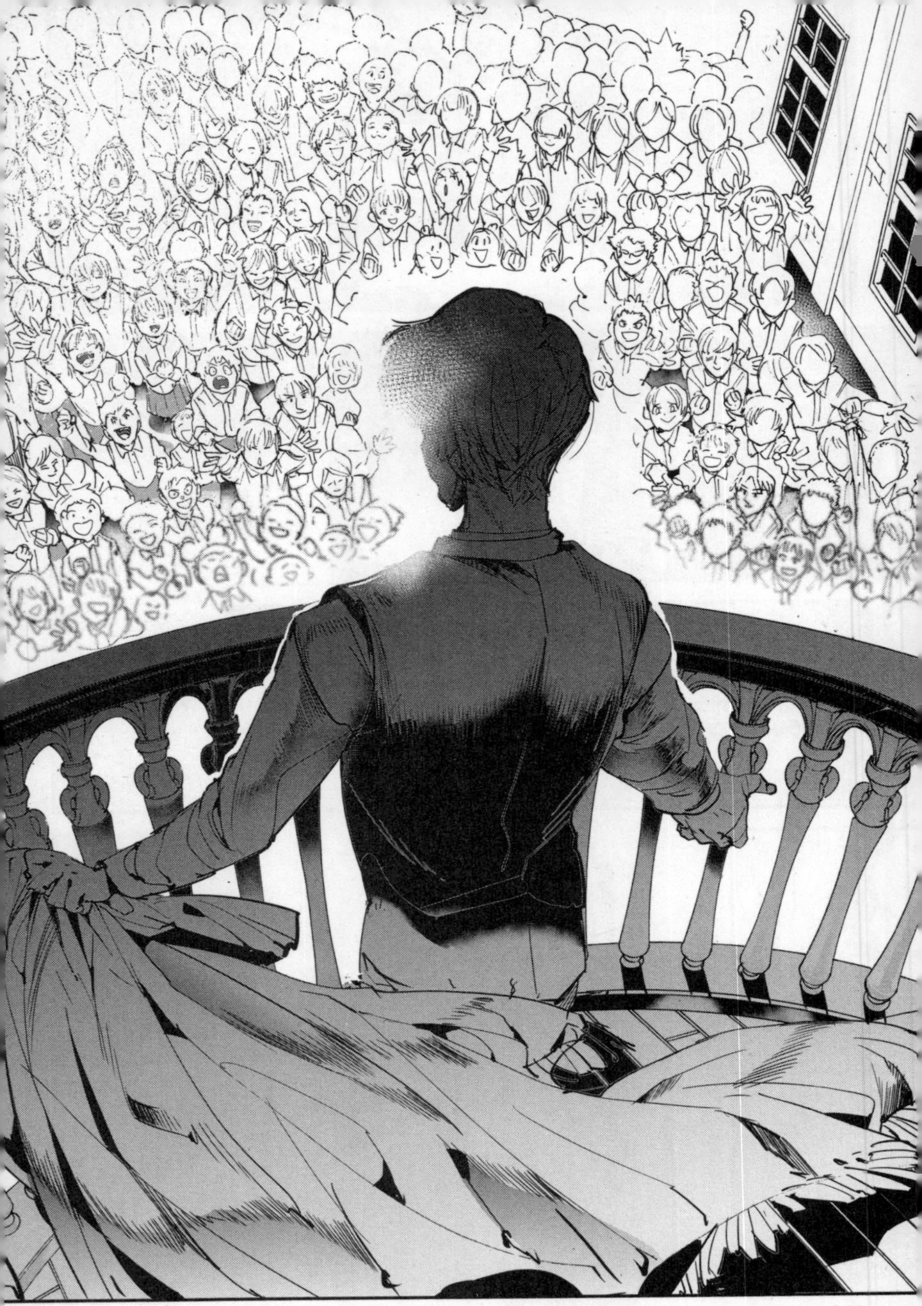

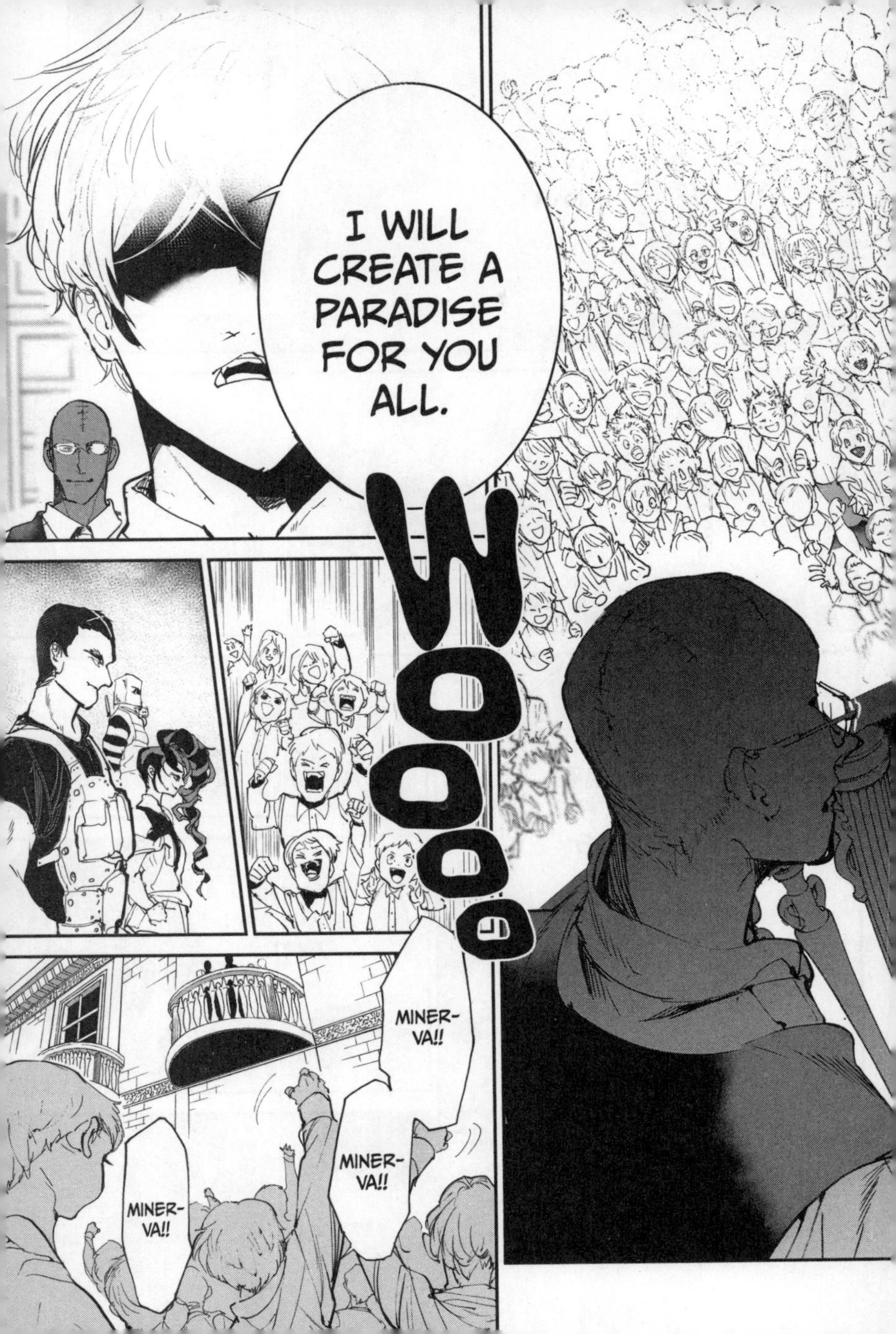
I WILL CREATE A PARADISE FOR YOU ALL.
WOOOO
MINER-VA!!
MINER-VA!!
MINER-VA!!

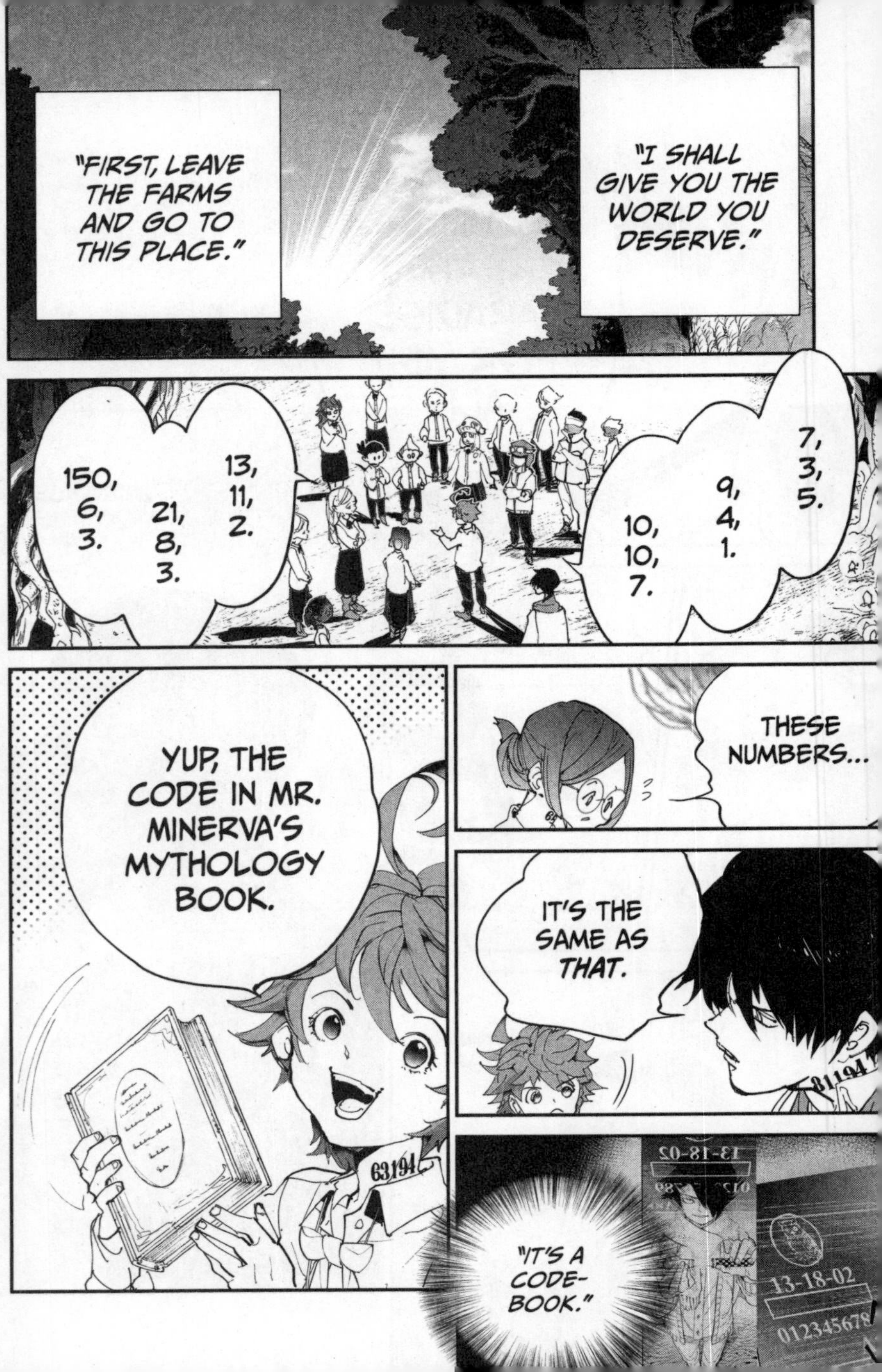
"I SHALL GIVE YOU THE WORLD YOU DESERVE."
"FIRST, LEAVE THE FARMS AND GO TO THIS PLACE."
7, 3, 5. 9, 4, 1. 10, 10, 7.
13, 11, 2. 21, 8, 3. 150, 6, 3.
THESE NUMBERS...
IT'S THE SAME AS THAT.
81194
13-18-02
012345678
"IT'S A CODE-BOOK."
YUP, THE CODE IN MR. MINERVA'S MYTHOLOGY BOOK.
63194

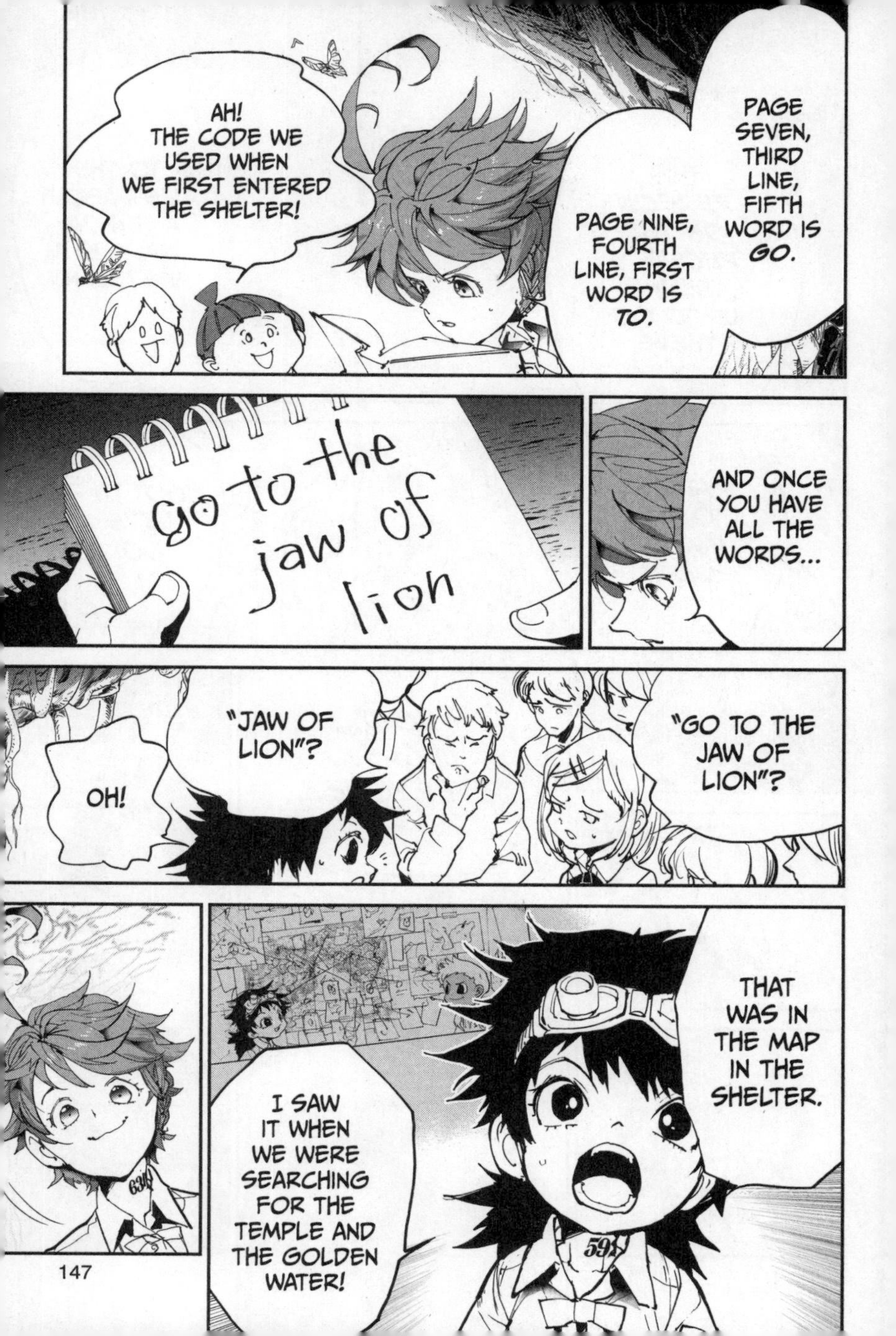
PAGE SEVEN, THIRD LINE, FIFTH WORD IS GO.
PAGE NINE, FOURTH LINE, FIRST WORD IS TO.
AH! THE CODE WE USED WHEN WE FIRST ENTERED THE SHELTER!
AND ONCE YOU HAVE ALL THE WORDS...
go to the jaw of lion
"GO TO THE JAW OF LION"?
"JAW OF LION"?
OH!
THAT WAS IN THE MAP IN THE SHELTER.
I SAW IT WHEN WE WERE SEARCHING FOR THE TEMPLE AND THE GOLDEN WATER!

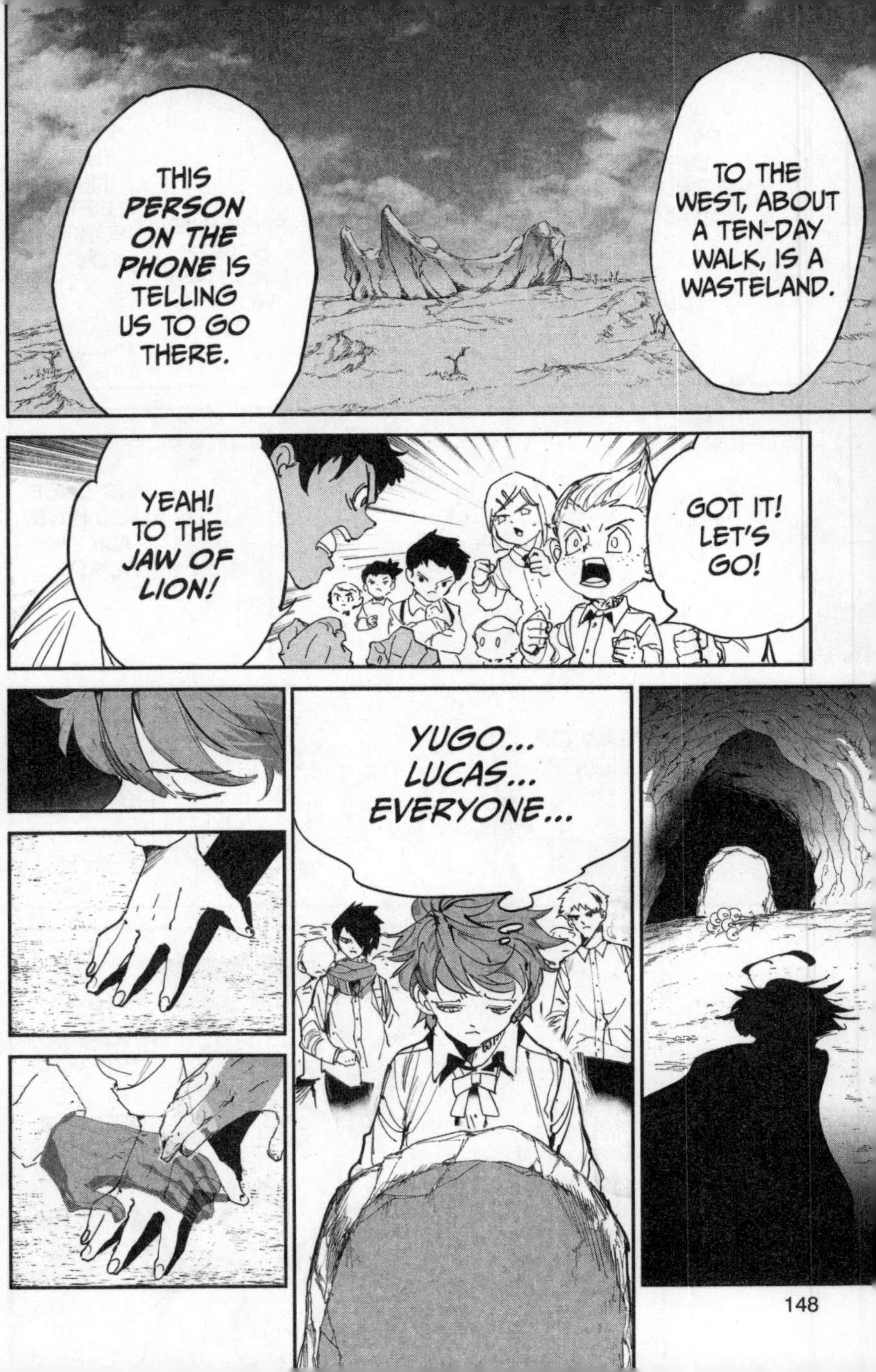
TO THE WEST, ABOUT A TEN-DAY WALK, IS A WASTELAND.
THIS PERSON ON THE PHONE IS TELLING US TO GO THERE.
GOT IT! LET'S GO!
YEAH! TO THE JAW OF LION!
YUGO... LUCAS... EVERYONE...

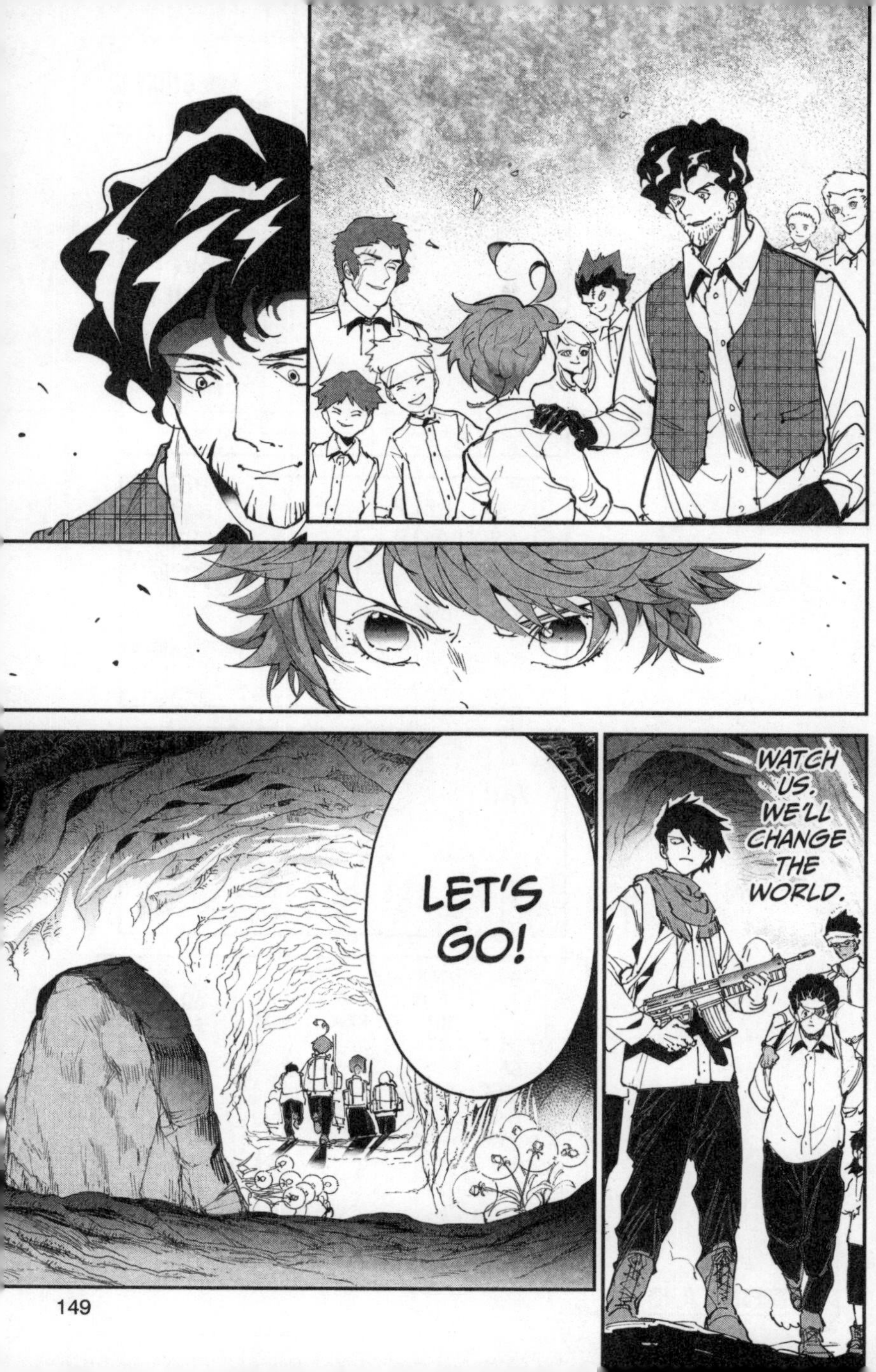
WATCH US. WE'LL CHANGE THE WORLD.
LET'S GO!

SIDE STORY 10

THE RATRI BROTHERS

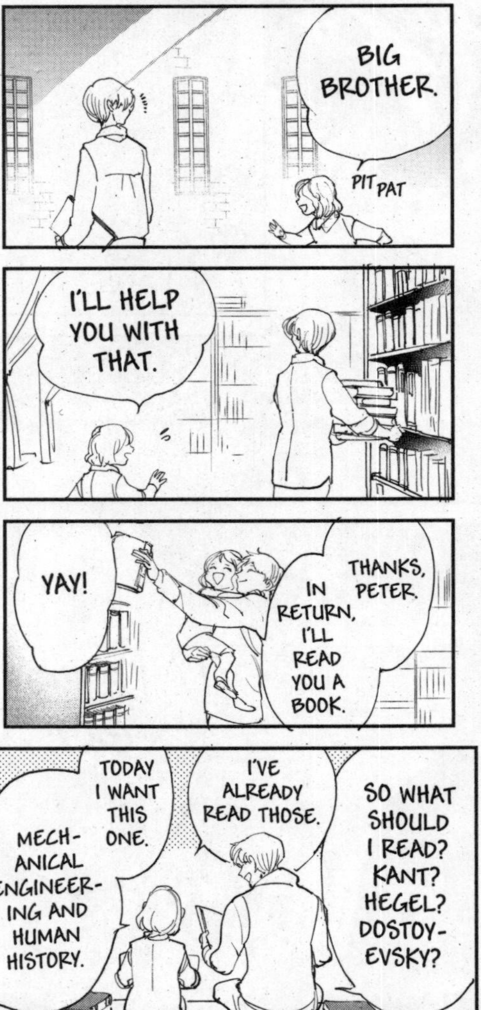
BIG BROTHER.
PIT PAT
I'LL HELP YOU WITH THAT.
THANKS, PETER.
IN RETURN, I'LL READ YOU A BOOK.
YAY!
SO WHAT SHOULD I READ? KANT? HEGEL? DOSTOY-EVSKY?
I'VE ALREADY READ THOSE.
TODAY I WANT THIS ONE.
MECH-ANICAL ENGINEER-ING AND HUMAN HISTORY.

SIDE STORY 10...FIN

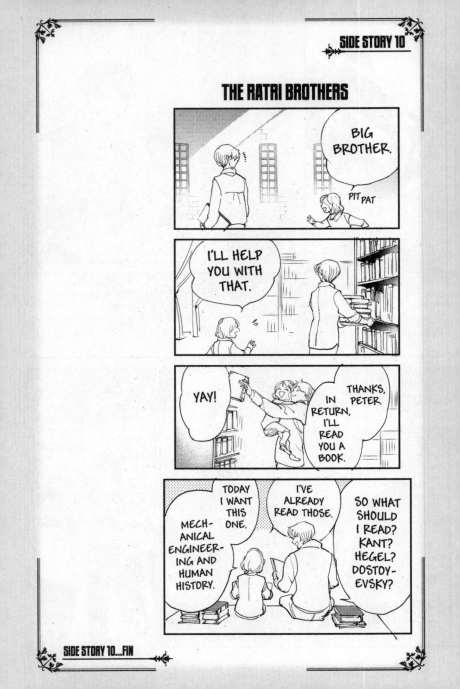

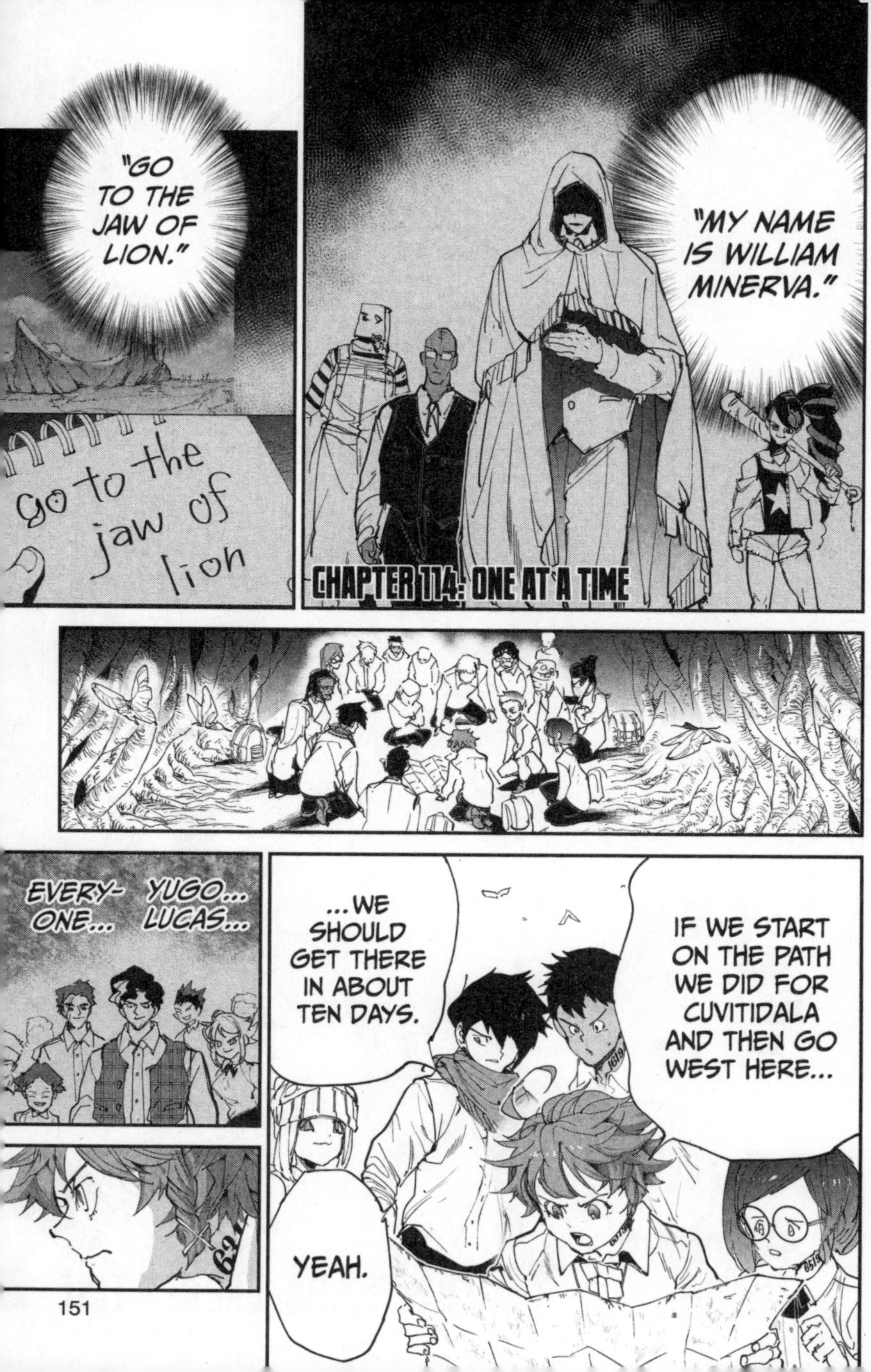
"MY NAME IS WILLIAM MINERVA."
CHAPTER 114: ONE AT A TIME
"GO TO THE JAW OF LION."
go to the jaw of lion
IF WE START ON THE PATH WE DID FOR CUVITIDALA AND THEN GO WEST HERE...
...WE SHOULD GET THERE IN ABOUT TEN DAYS.
YEAH.
YUGO... LUCAS...
EVERY-ONE...

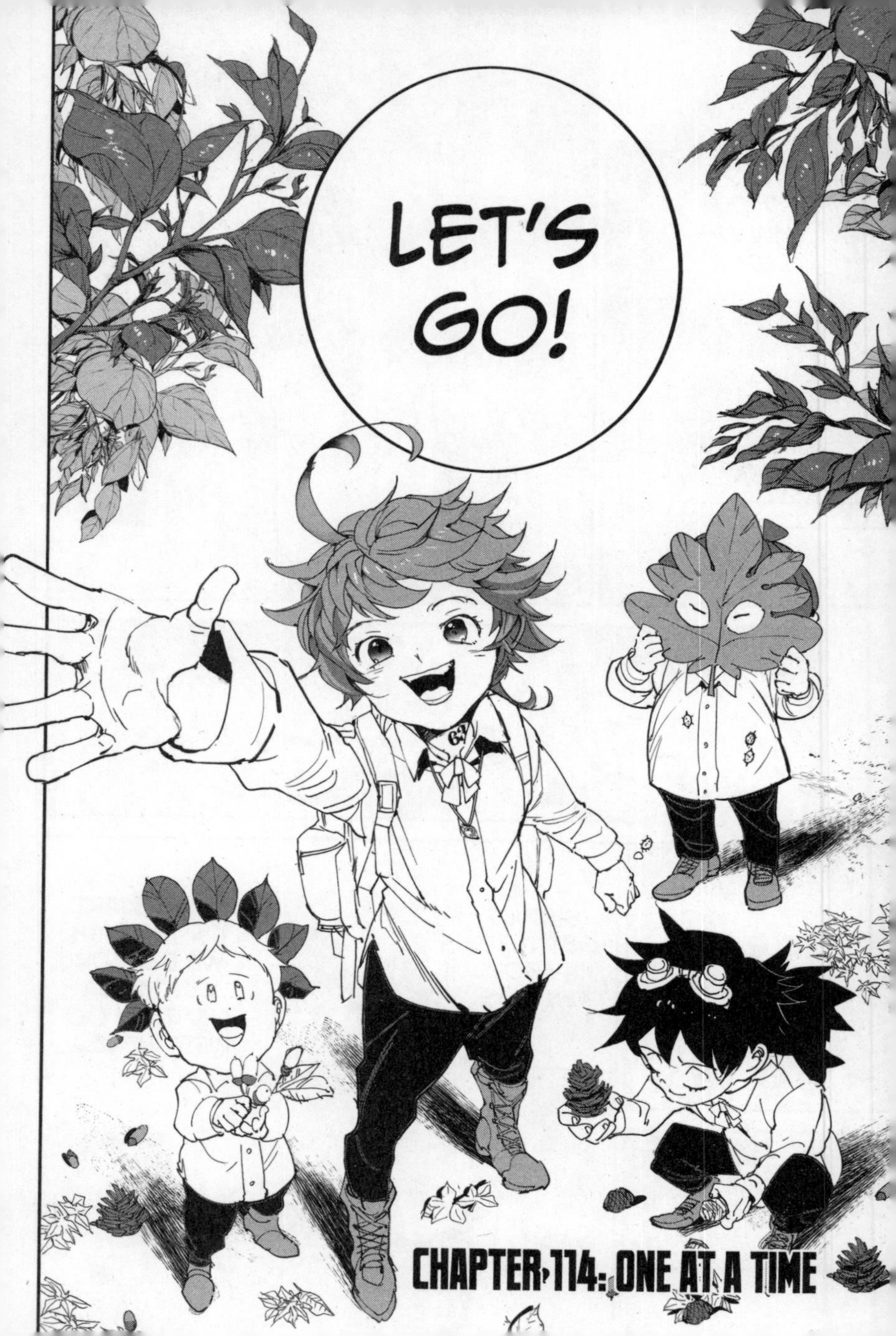
LET'S GO!
CHAPTER 114: ONE AT A TIME

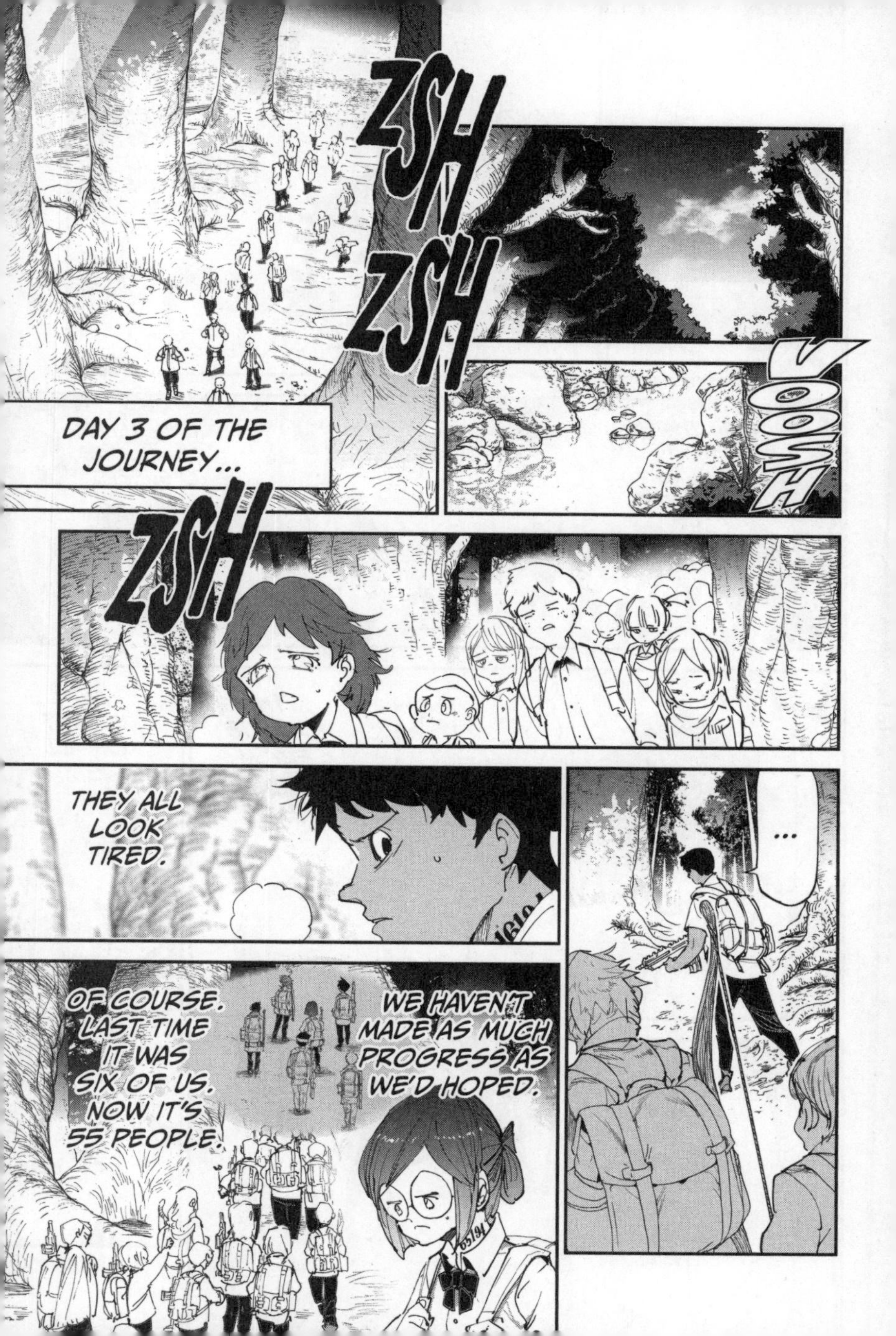
ZSH
ZSH
VOOSH
DAY 3 OF THE JOURNEY...
ZSH
...
THEY ALL LOOK TIRED.
WE HAVEN'T MADE AS MUCH PROGRESS AS WE'D HOPED.
OF COURSE. LAST TIME IT WAS SIX OF US. NOW IT'S 55 PEOPLE.

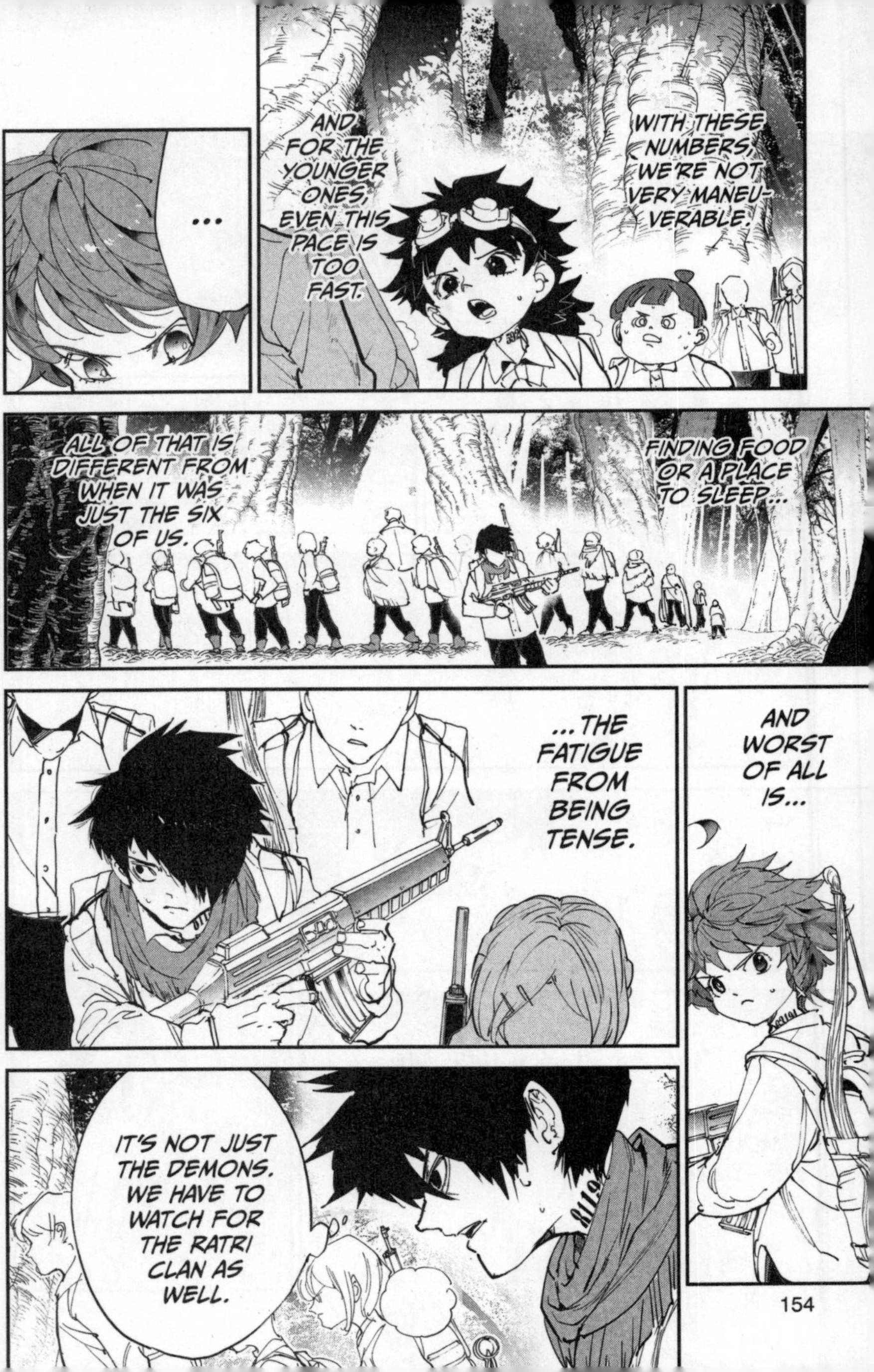
WITH THESE NUMBERS, WE'RE NOT VERY MANEU-VERABLE.
AND FOR THE YOUNGER ONES, EVEN THIS PACE IS TOO FAST.
...
FINDING FOOD OR A PLACE TO SLEEP...
ALL OF THAT IS DIFFERENT FROM WHEN IT WAS JUST THE SIX OF US.
AND WORST OF ALL IS...
...THE FATIGUE FROM BEING TENSE.
IT'S NOT JUST THE DEMONS. WE HAVE TO WATCH FOR THE RATRI CLAN AS WELL.

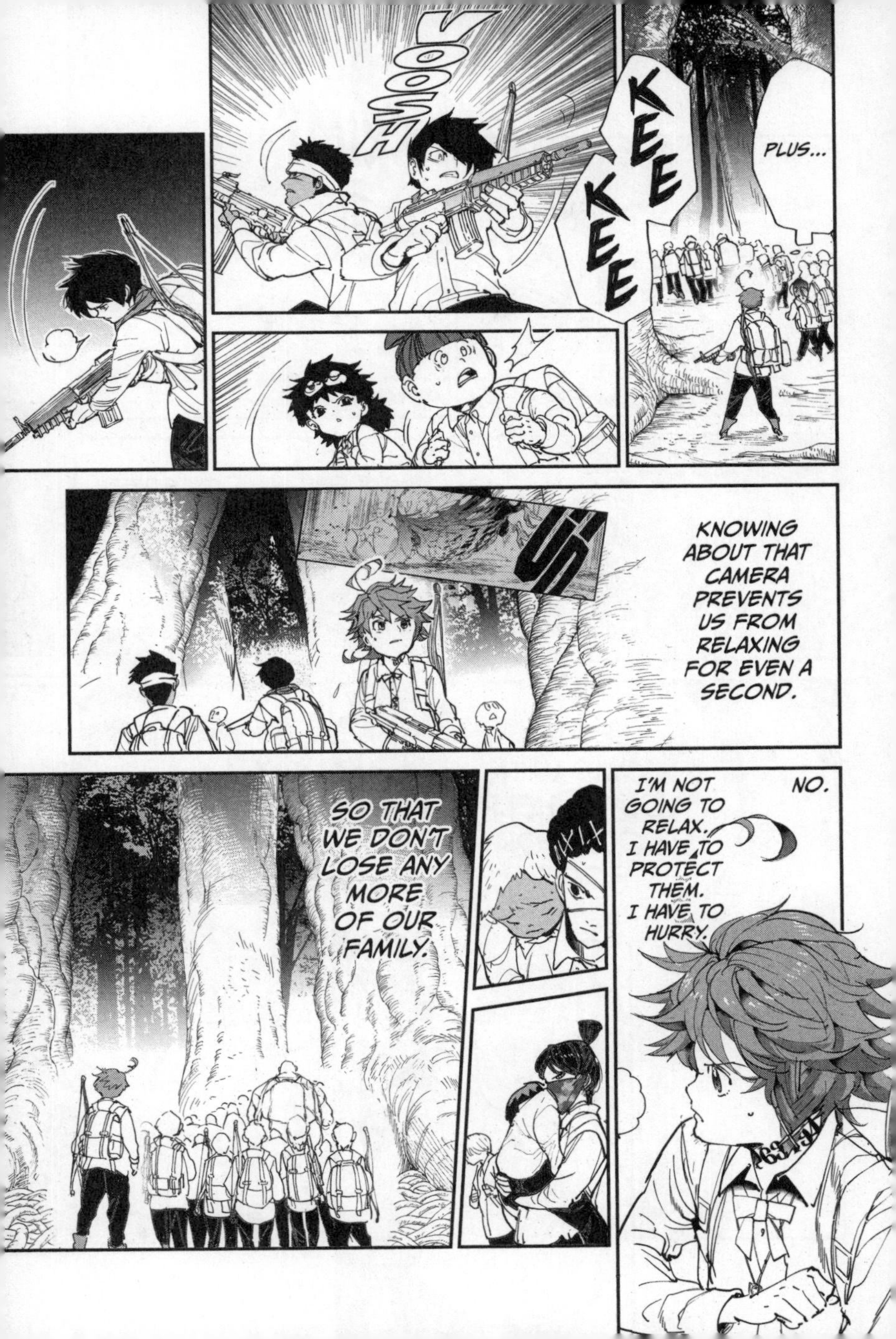
PLUS...
KEE KEE
KEE KEE
VOOSH
KNOWING ABOUT THAT CAMERA PREVENTS US FROM RELAXING FOR EVEN A SECOND.
NO.
I'M NOT GOING TO RELAX. I HAVE TO PROTECT THEM. I HAVE TO HURRY.
SO THAT WE DON'T LOSE ANY MORE OF OUR FAMILY.

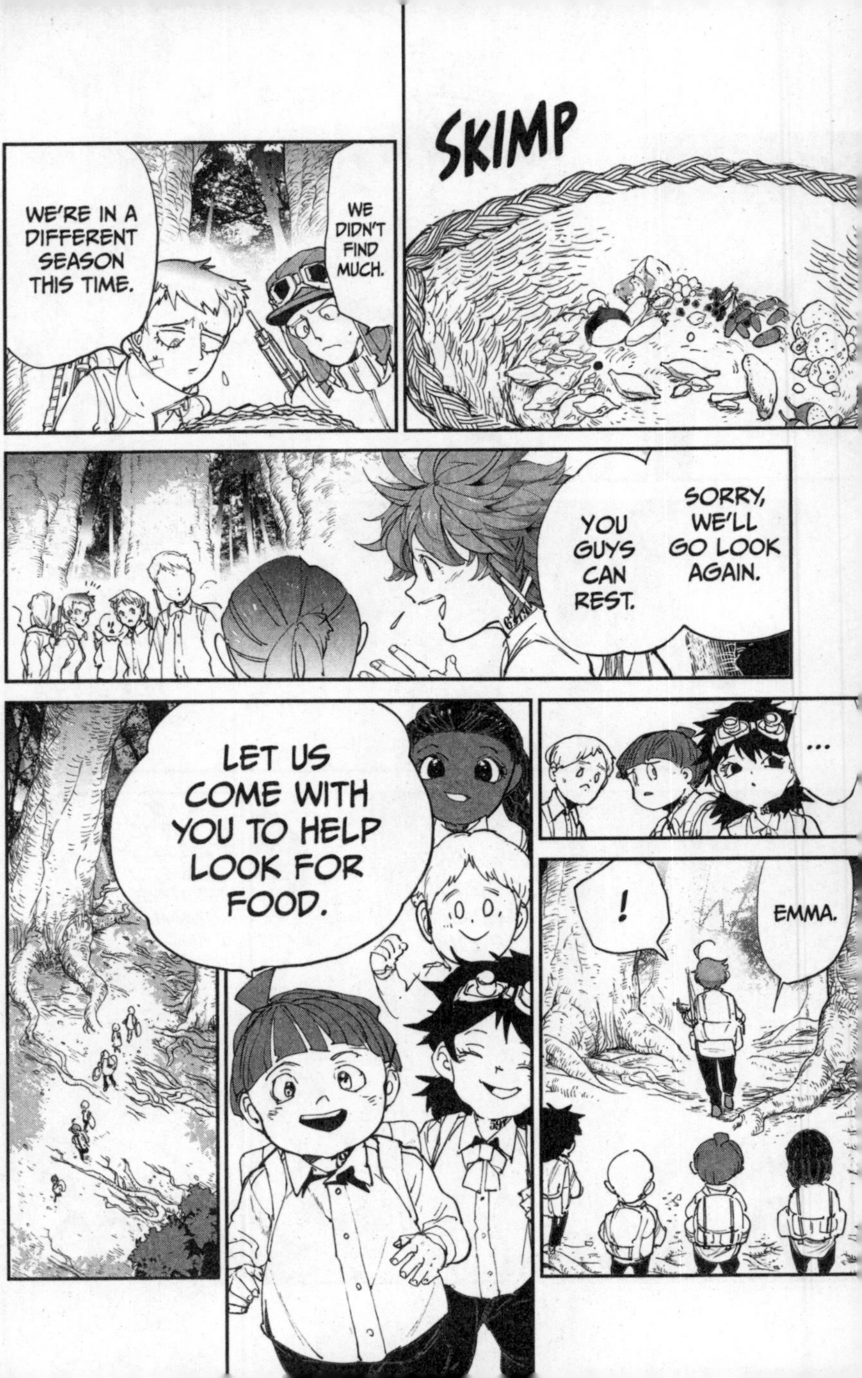
SKIMP
WE DIDN'T FIND MUCH.
WE'RE IN A DIFFERENT SEASON THIS TIME.
SORRY, WE'LL GO LOOK AGAIN.
YOU GUYS CAN REST.
...
EMMA.
!
LET US COME WITH YOU TO HELP LOOK FOR FOOD.

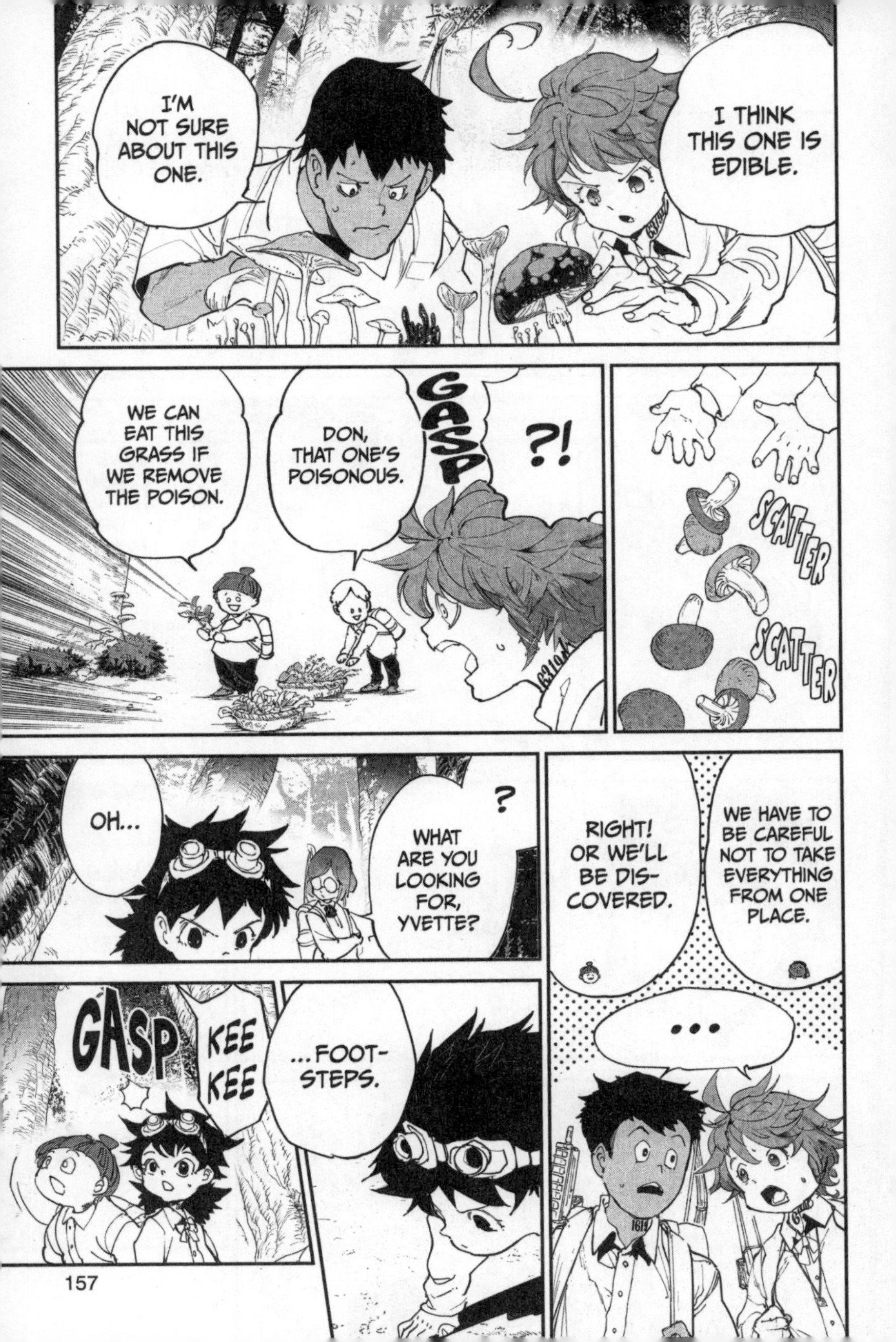
I THINK THIS ONE IS EDIBLE.
I'M NOT SURE ABOUT THIS ONE.
SCATTER
SCATTER
?!
GASP
DON, THAT ONE'S POISONOUS.
WE CAN EAT THIS GRASS IF WE REMOVE THE POISON.
WE HAVE TO BE CAREFUL NOT TO TAKE EVERYTHING FROM ONE PLACE.
RIGHT! OR WE'LL BE DIS- COVERED.
...
?
WHAT ARE YOU LOOKING FOR, YVETTE?
OH...
...FOOT- STEPS.
KEE KEE
GASP

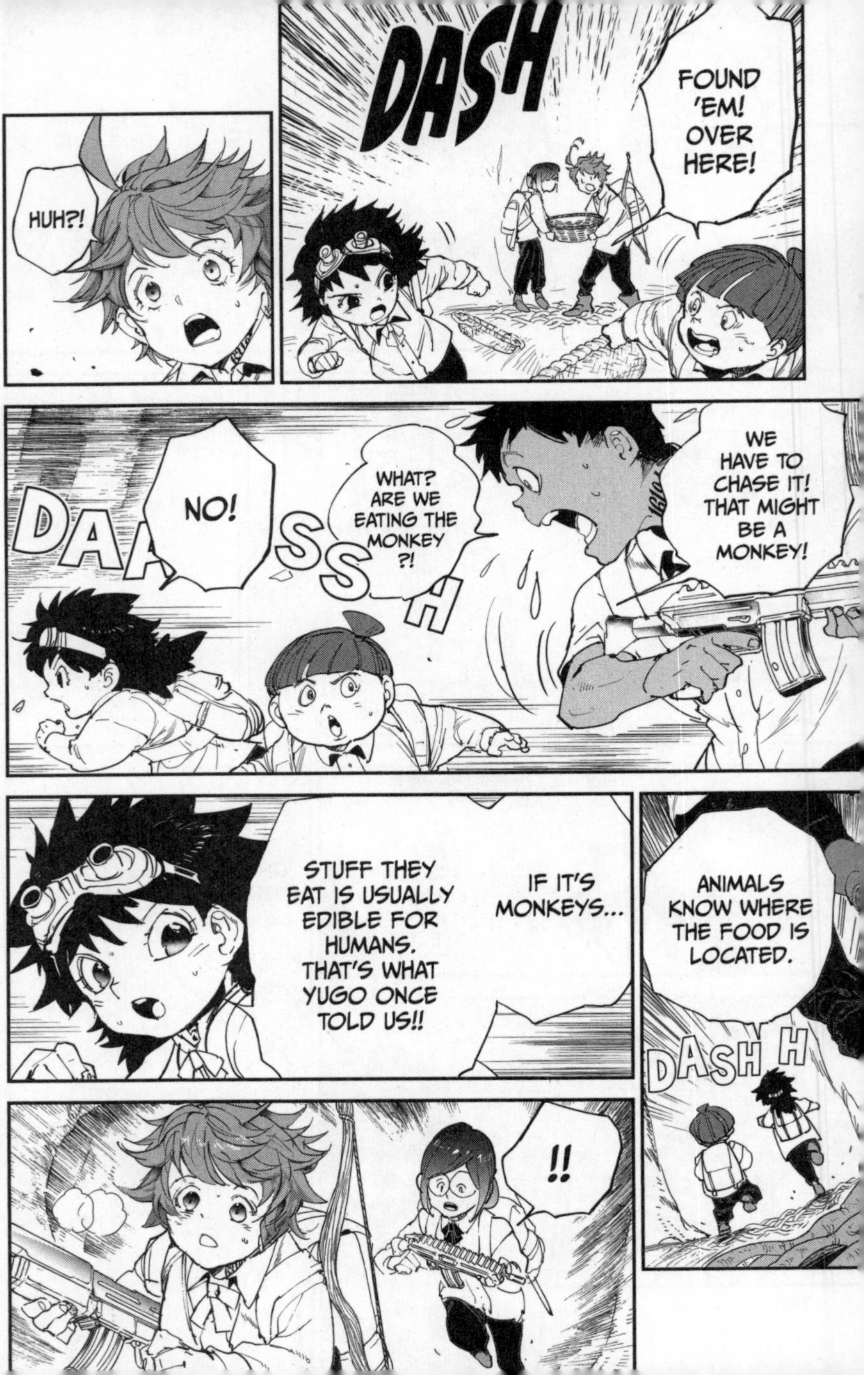
DASH
FOUND 'EM! OVER HERE!
HUH?!
WE HAVE TO CHASE IT! THAT MIGHT BE A MONKEY!
WHAT? ARE WE EATING THE MONKEY?!
NO!
DAASSH
ANIMALS KNOW WHERE THE FOOD IS LOCATED.
DASH H
IF IT'S MONKEYS...
STUFF THEY EAT IS USUALLY EDIBLE FOR HUMANS. THAT'S WHAT YUGO ONCE TOLD US!!
!!

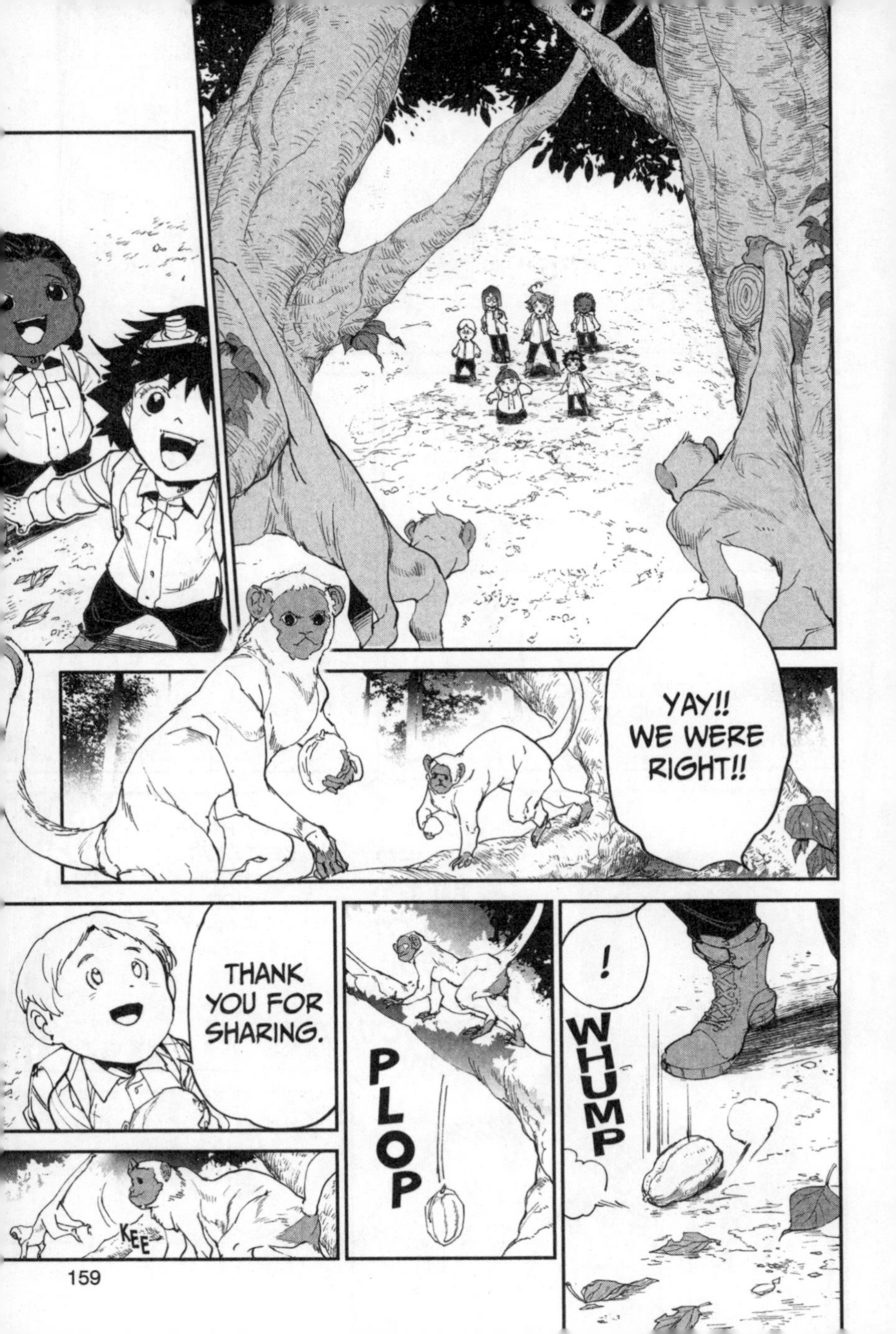
YAY!! WE WERE RIGHT!!
!
WHUMP
PLOP
THANK YOU FOR SHARING.
KEE

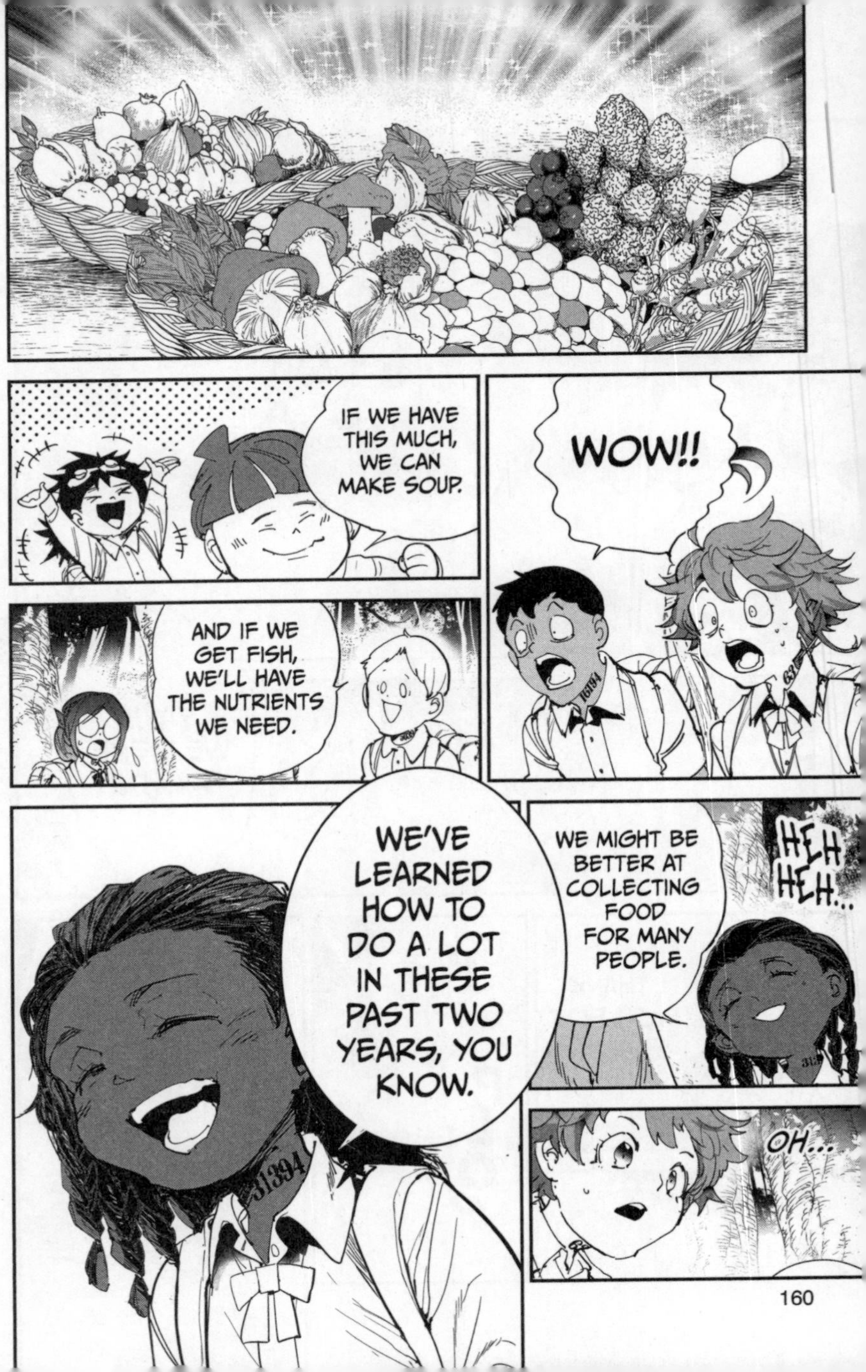
WOW!!
IF WE HAVE THIS MUCH, WE CAN MAKE SOUP.
AND IF WE GET FISH, WE'LL HAVE THE NUTRIENTS WE NEED.
HEH HEH...
WE MIGHT BE BETTER AT COLLECTING FOOD FOR MANY PEOPLE.
OH...
WE'VE LEARNED HOW TO DO A LOT IN THESE PAST TWO YEARS, YOU KNOW.

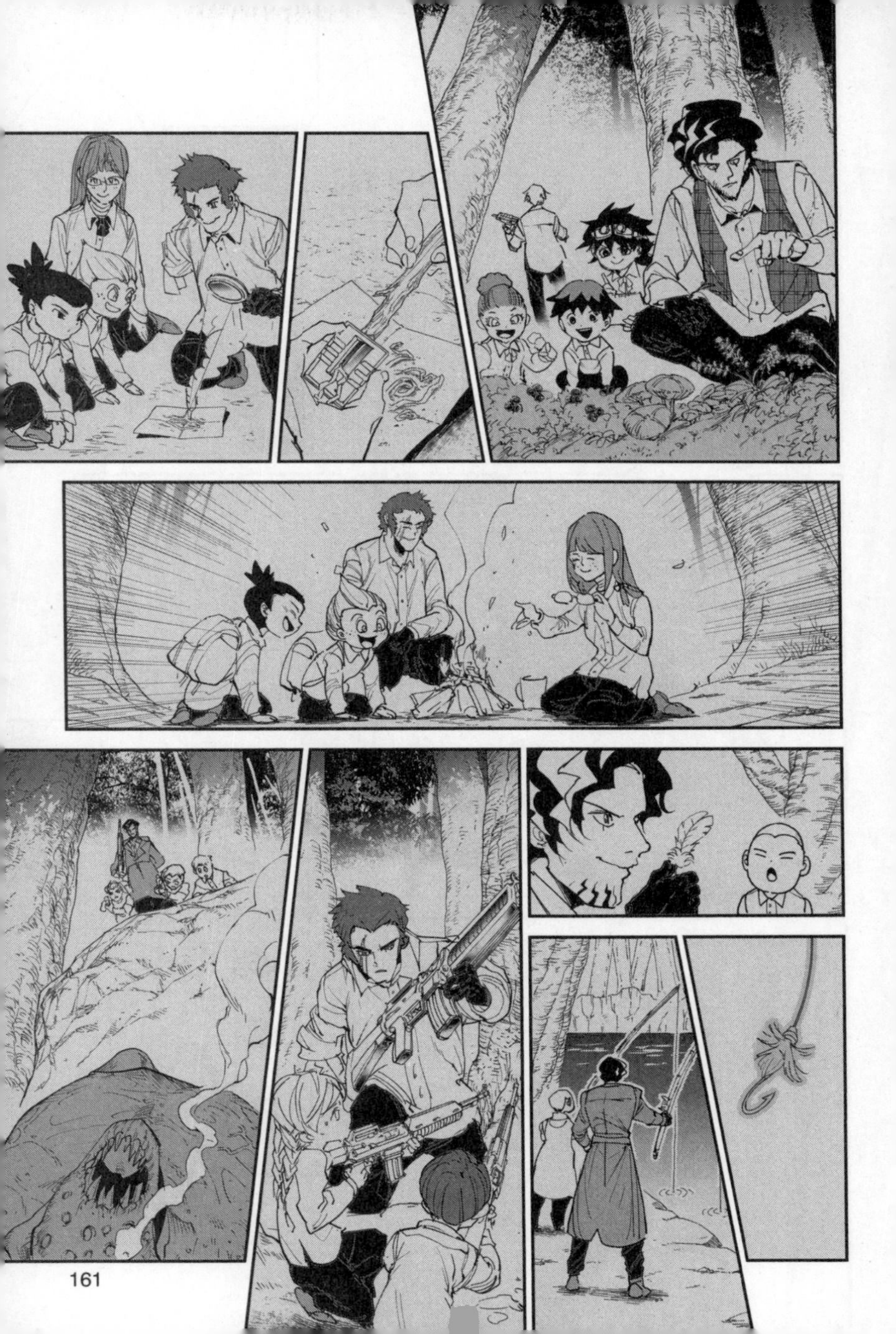

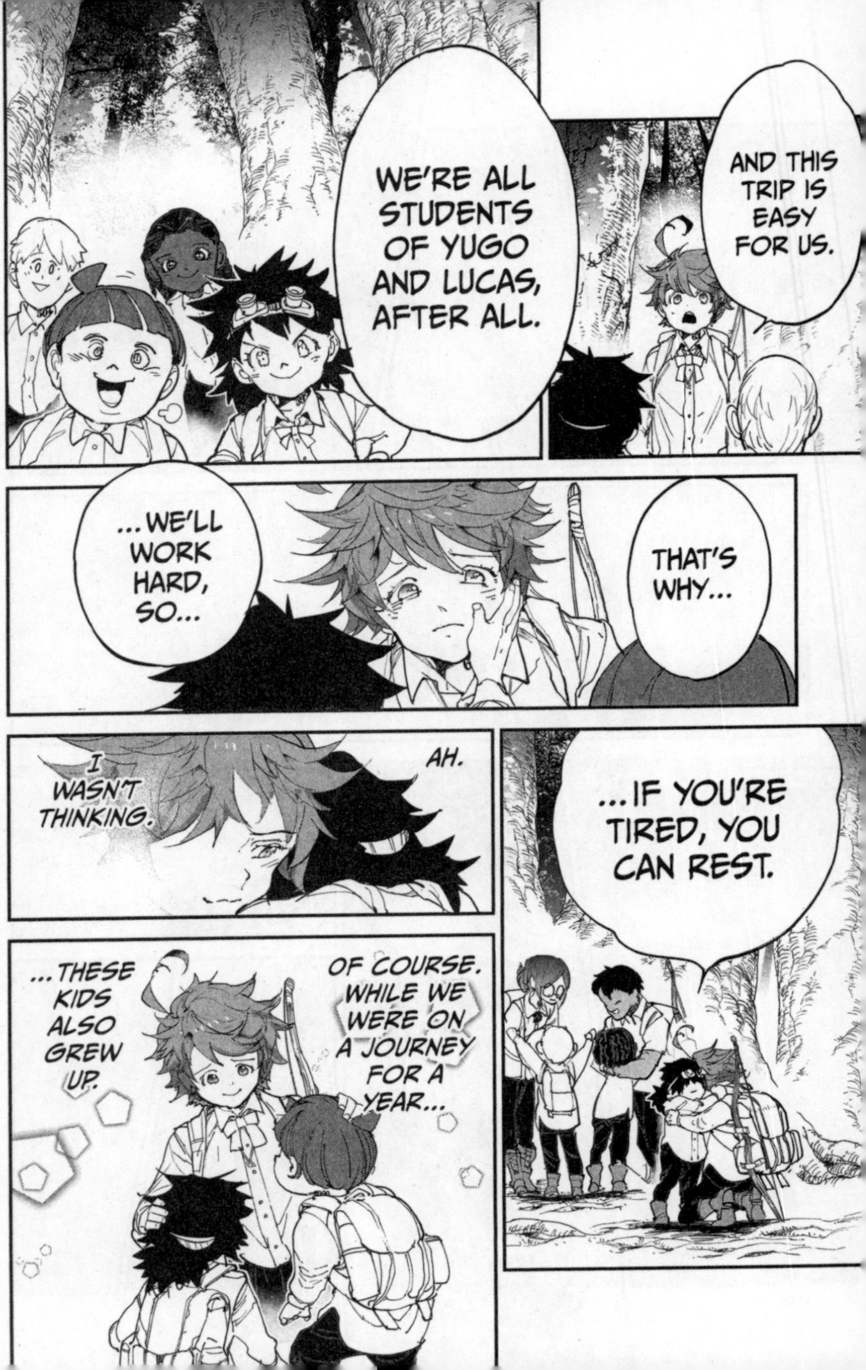
AND THIS TRIP IS EASY FOR US.
WE'RE ALL STUDENTS OF YUGO AND LUCAS, AFTER ALL.
THAT'S WHY...
...WE'LL WORK HARD, SO...
...IF YOU'RE TIRED, YOU CAN REST.
AH.
I WASN'T THINKING.
OF COURSE. WHILE WE WERE ON A JOURNEY FOR A YEAR...
...THESE KIDS ALSO GREW UP.

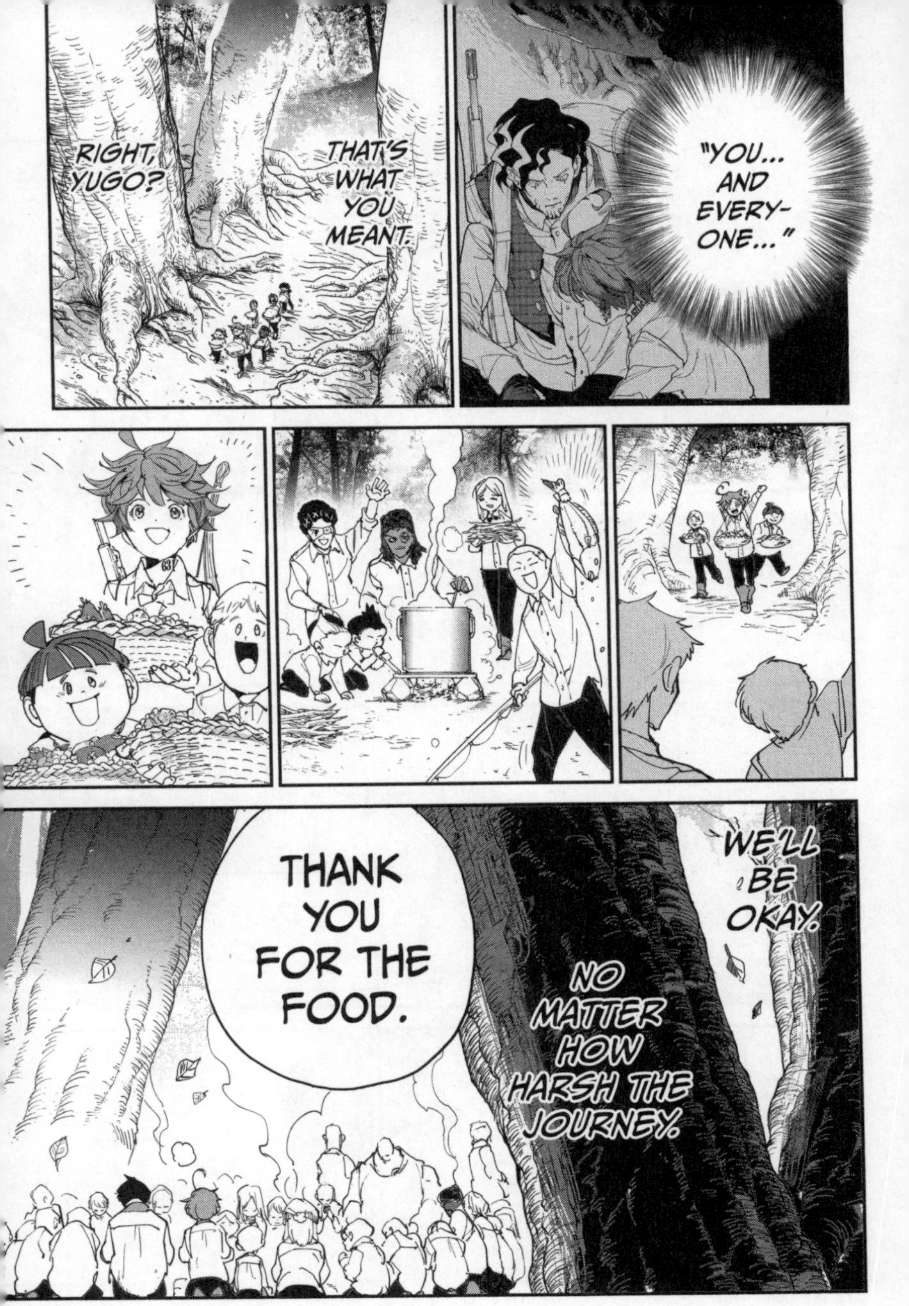
"YOU... AND EVERY-ONE..."
THAT'S WHAT YOU MEANT.
RIGHT, YUGO?
WE'LL BE OKAY.
NO MATTER HOW HARSH THE JOURNEY.
THANK YOU FOR THE FOOD.

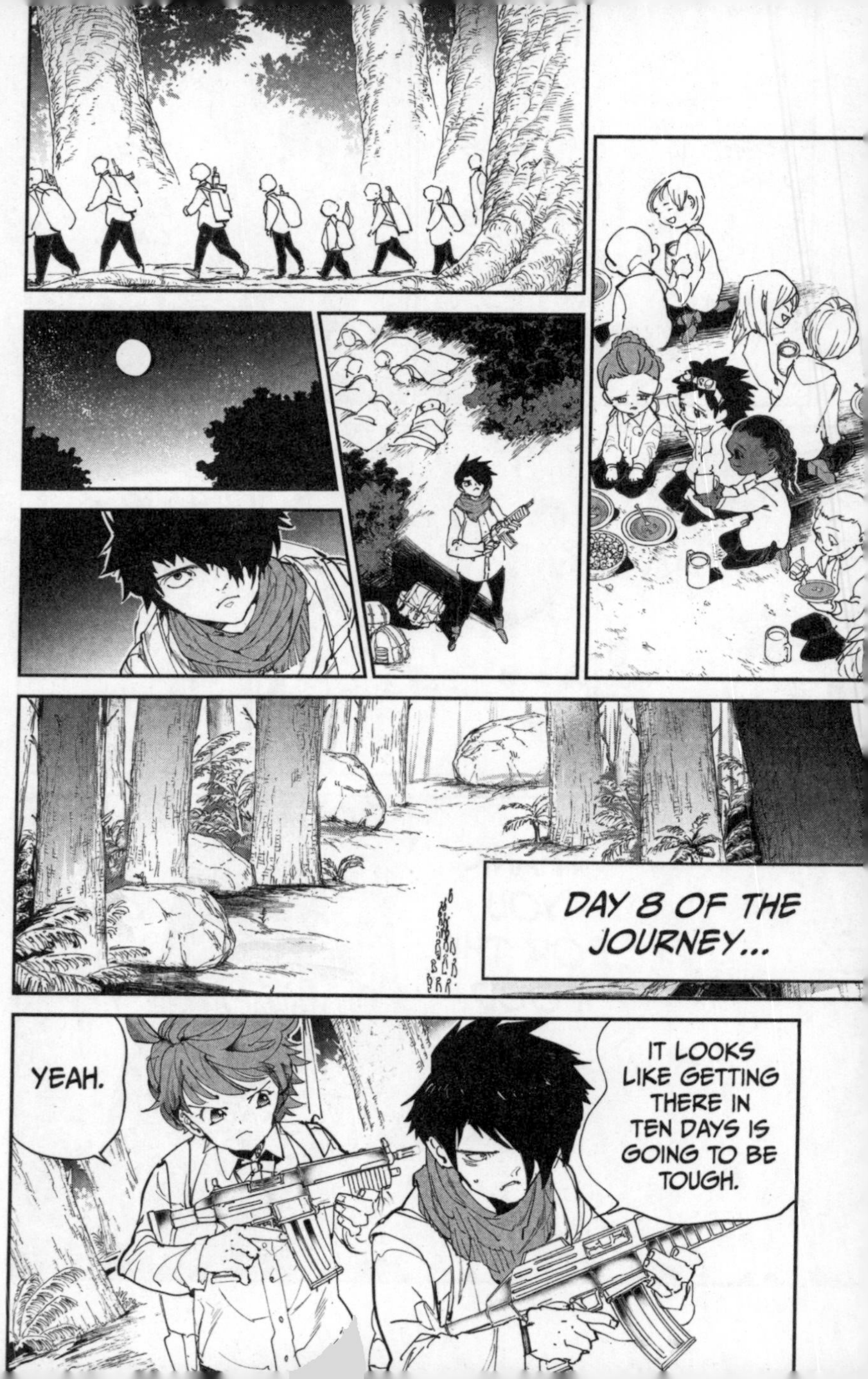
DAY 8 OF THE JOURNEY...
IT LOOKS LIKE GETTING THERE IN TEN DAYS IS GOING TO BE TOUGH.
YEAH.

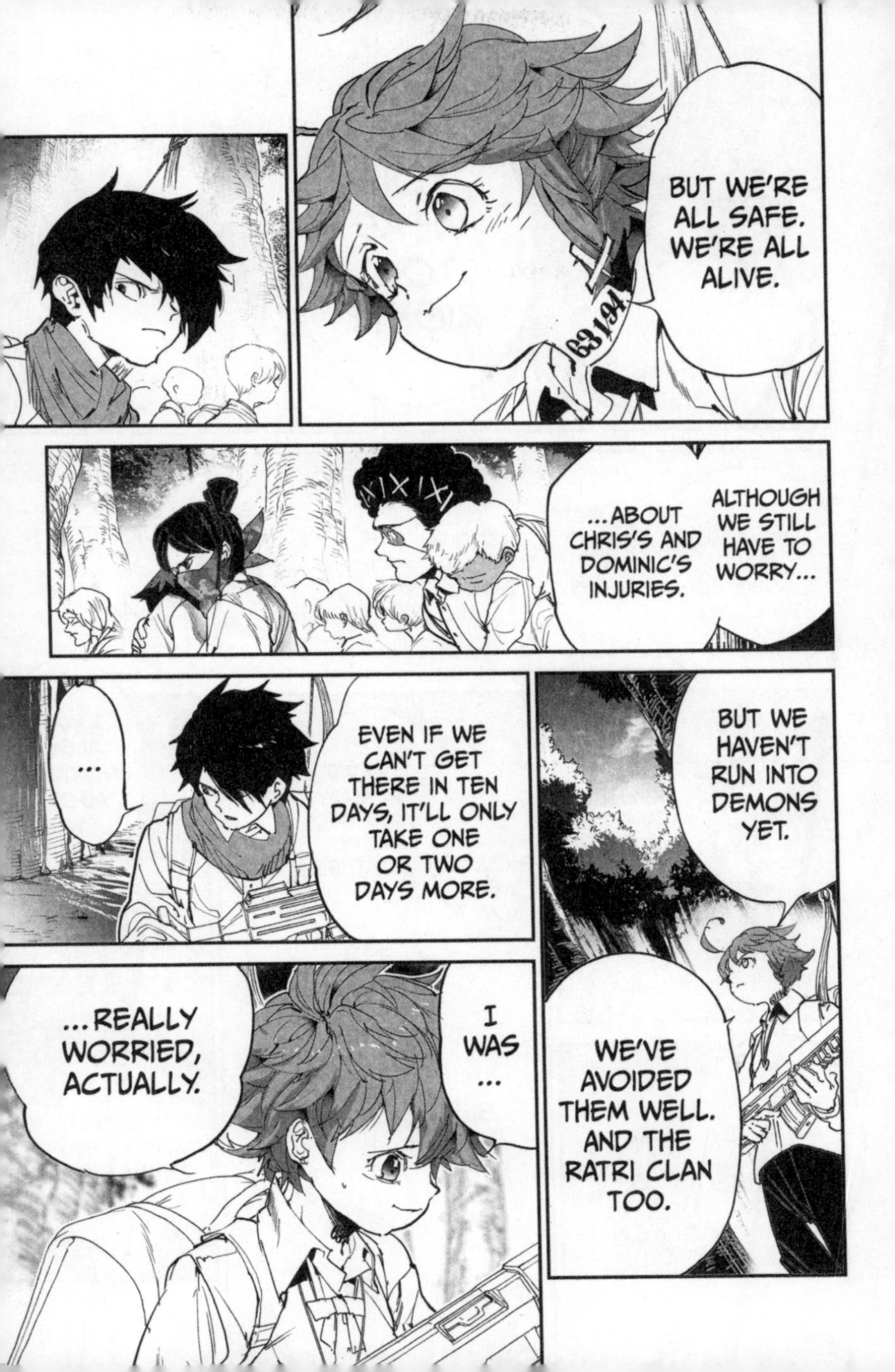
BUT WE'RE ALL SAFE. WE'RE ALL ALIVE.
63194
ALTHOUGH WE STILL HAVE TO WORRY...
...ABOUT CHRIS'S AND DOMINIC'S INJURIES.
BUT WE HAVEN'T RUN INTO DEMONS YET.
WE'VE AVOIDED THEM WELL. AND THE RATRI CLAN TOO.
EVEN IF WE CAN'T GET THERE IN TEN DAYS, IT'LL ONLY TAKE ONE OR TWO DAYS MORE.
...
I WAS ...
...REALLY WORRIED, ACTUALLY.

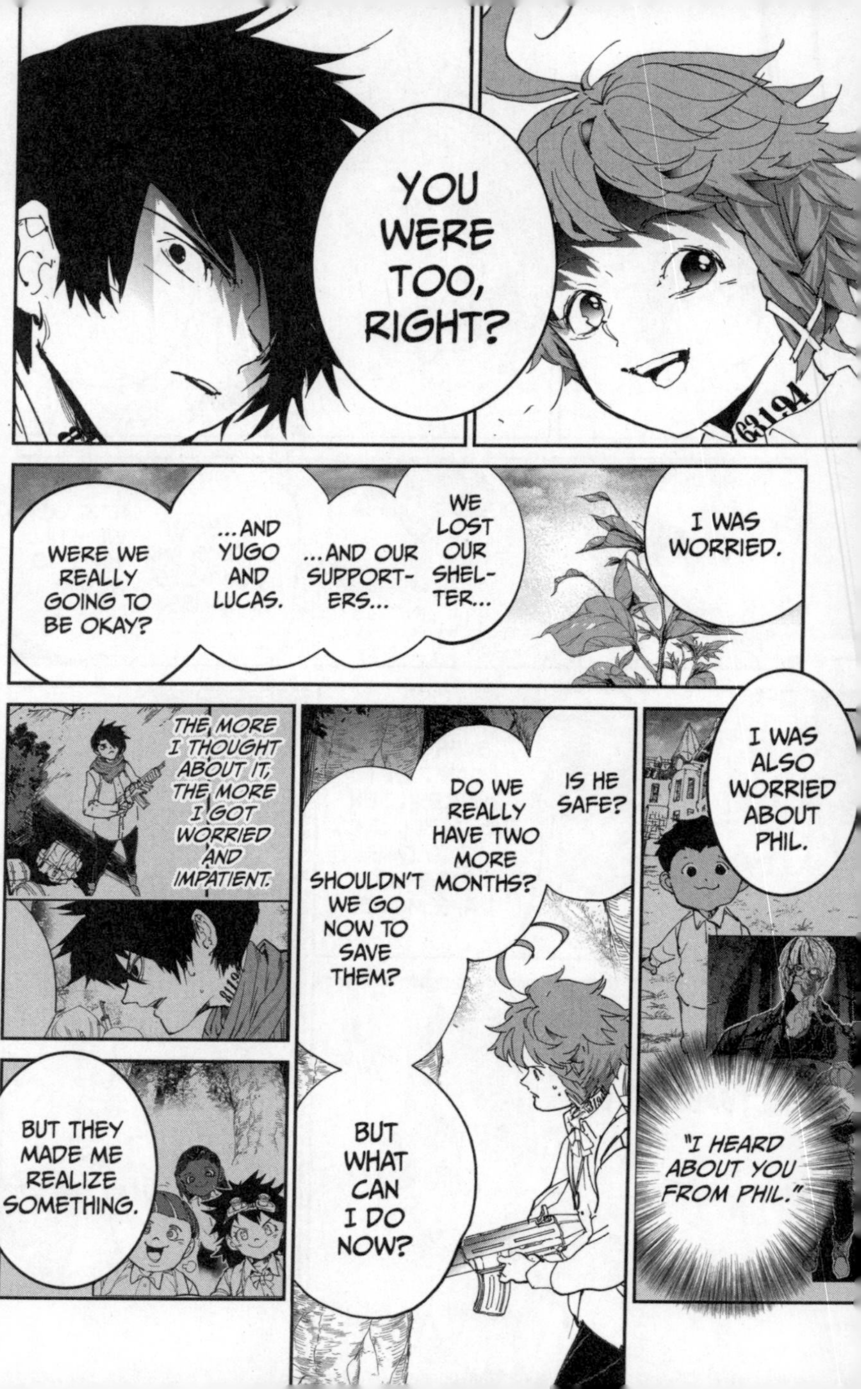
YOU WERE TOO, RIGHT?
I WAS WORRIED.
WE LOST OUR SHELTER...
...AND OUR SUPPORTERS...
...AND YUGO AND LUCAS.
WERE WE REALLY GOING TO BE OKAY?
I WAS ALSO WORRIED ABOUT PHIL.
"I HEARD ABOUT YOU FROM PHIL."
IS HE SAFE?
DO WE REALLY HAVE TWO MORE MONTHS?
SHOULDN'T WE GO NOW TO SAVE THEM?
BUT WHAT CAN I DO NOW?
THE MORE I THOUGHT ABOUT IT, THE MORE I GOT WORRIED AND IMPATIENT.
BUT THEY MADE ME REALIZE SOMETHING.

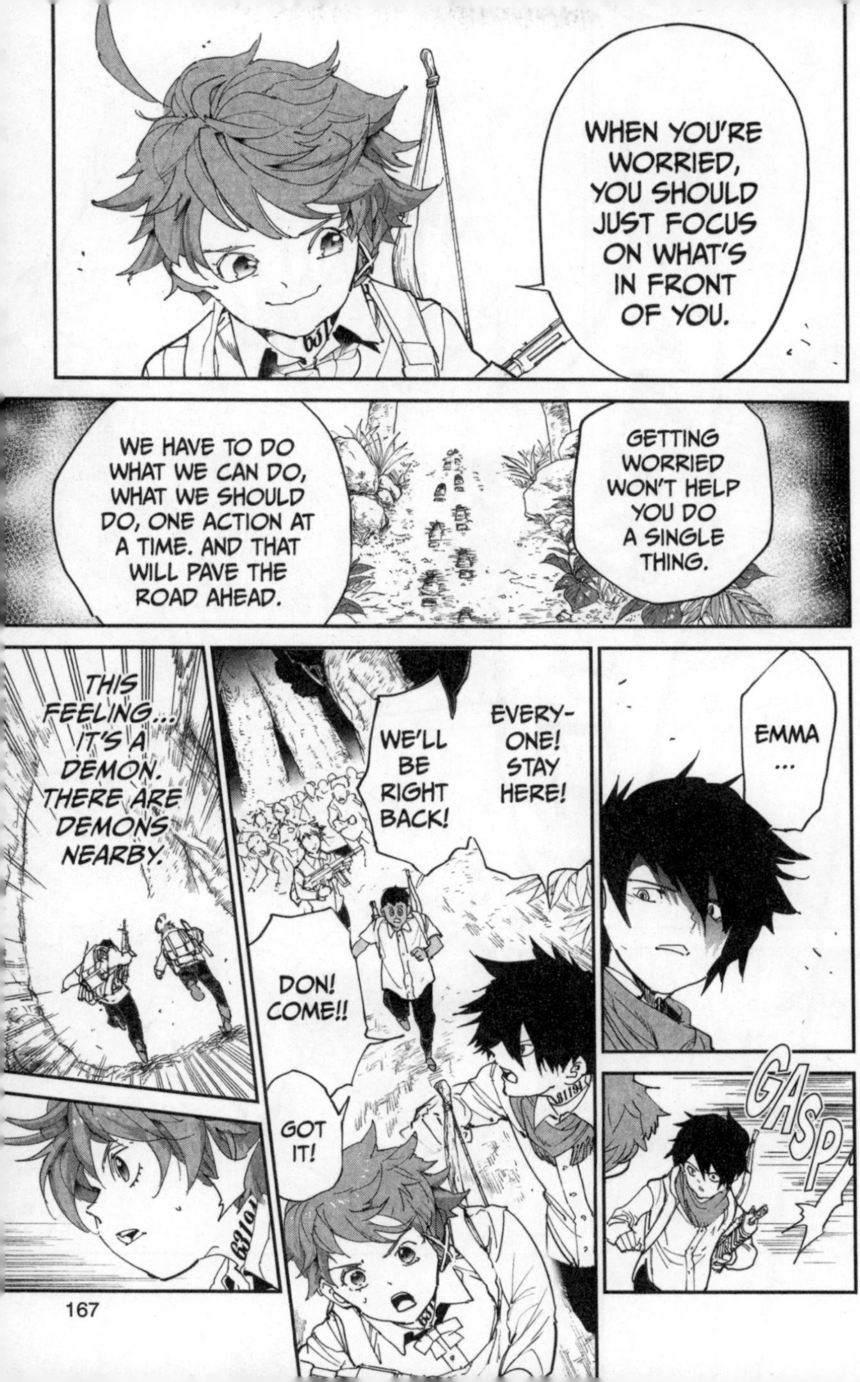
WHEN YOU'RE WORRIED, YOU SHOULD JUST FOCUS ON WHAT'S IN FRONT OF YOU.
GETTING WORRIED WON'T HELP YOU DO A SINGLE THING.
WE HAVE TO DO WHAT WE CAN DO, WHAT WE SHOULD DO, ONE ACTION AT A TIME. AND THAT WILL PAVE THE ROAD AHEAD.
EMMA ...
GASP
EVERY-ONE! STAY HERE!
WE'LL BE RIGHT BACK!
DON! COME!!
GOT IT!
THIS FEELING... IT'S A DEMON. THERE ARE DEMONS NEARBY.

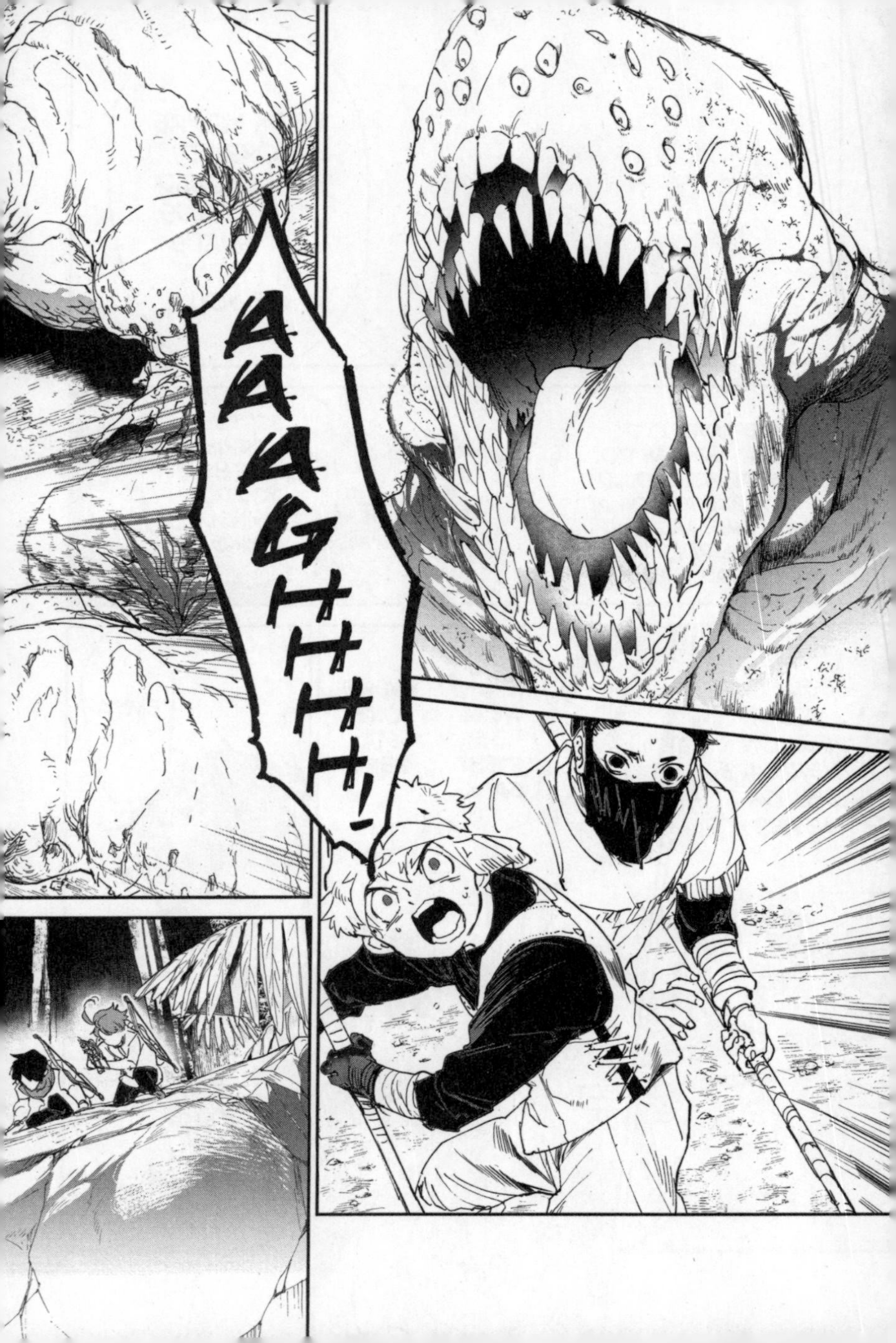
AAAGHHHH!

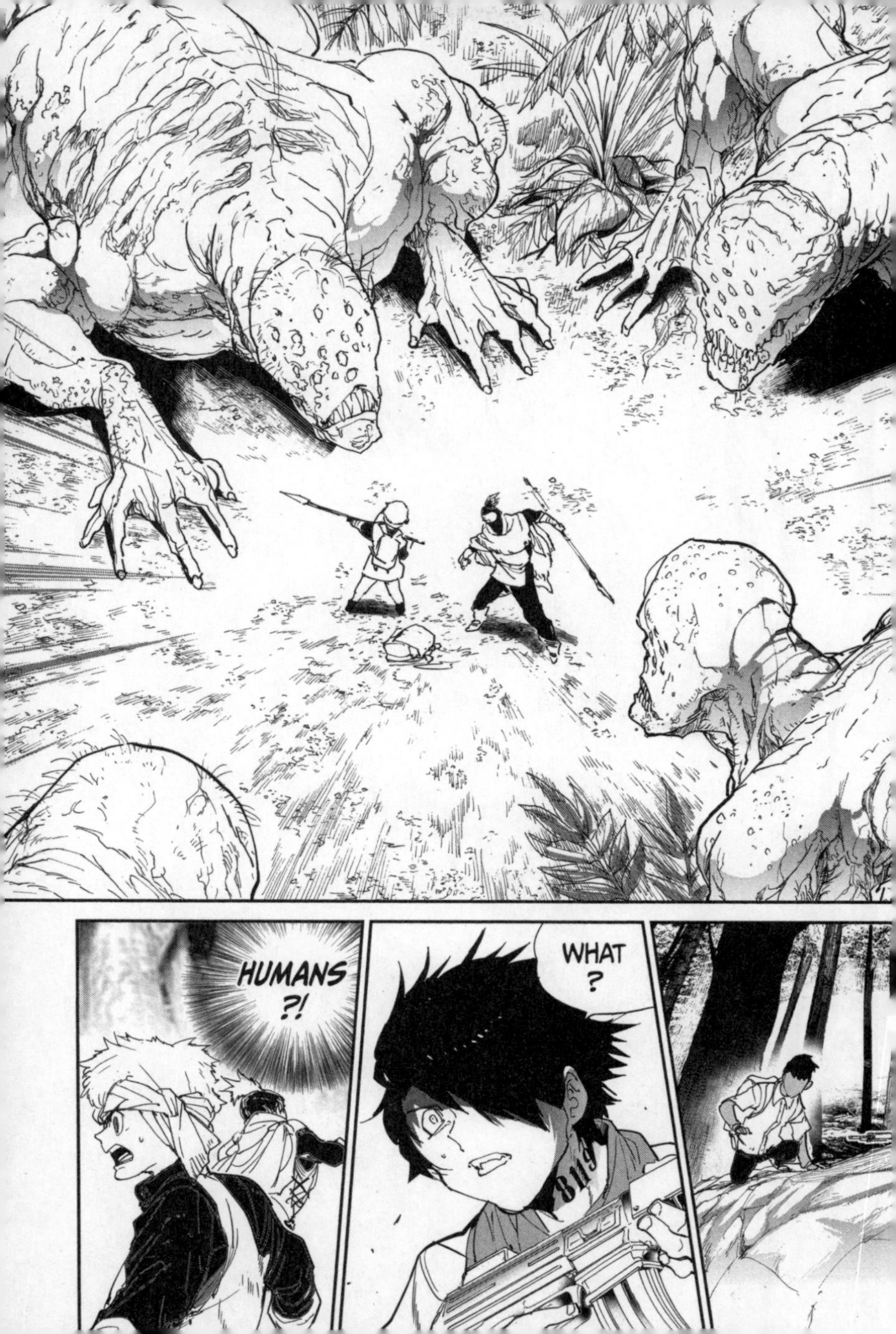
WHAT ?
HUMANS ?!

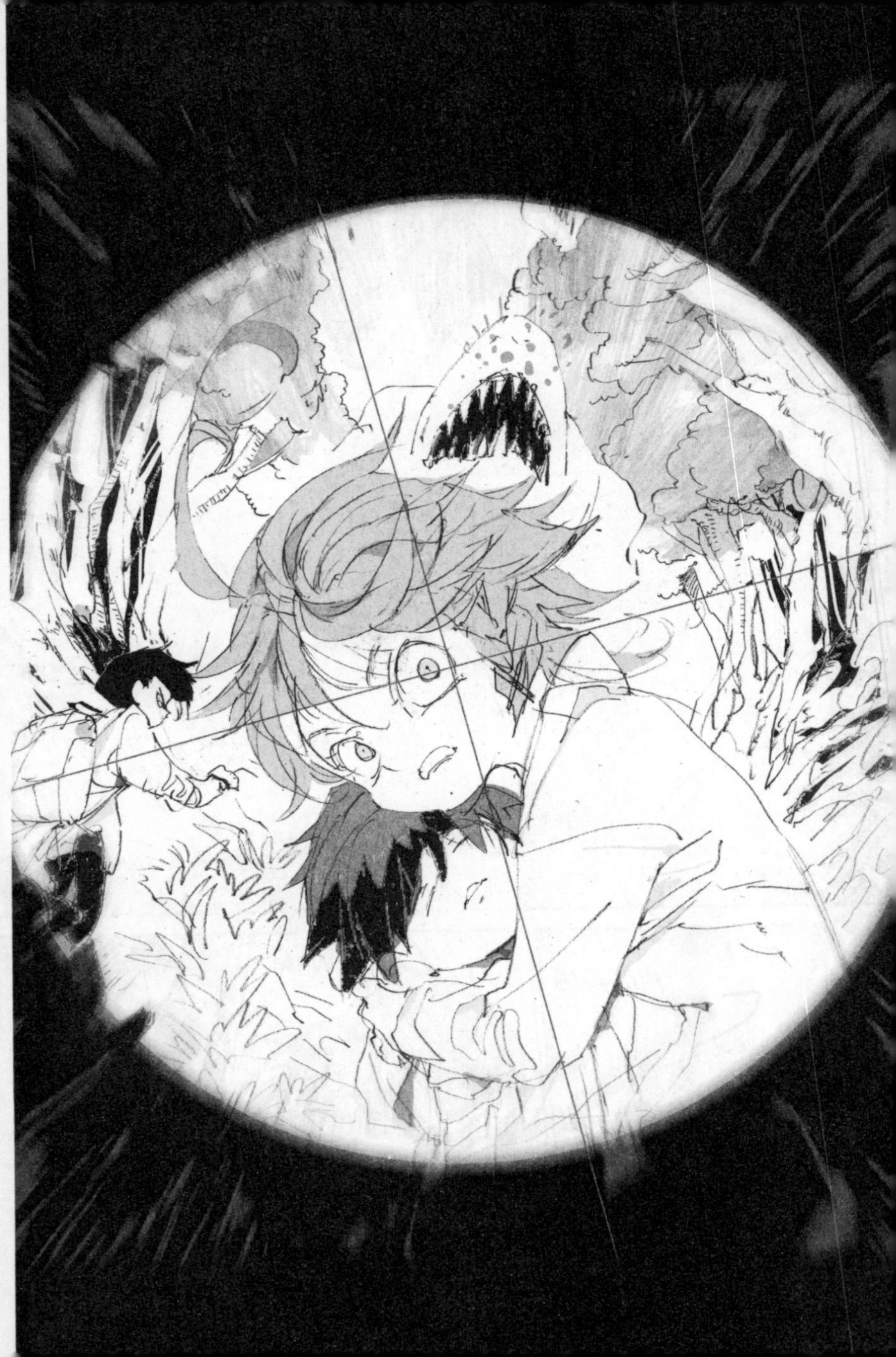

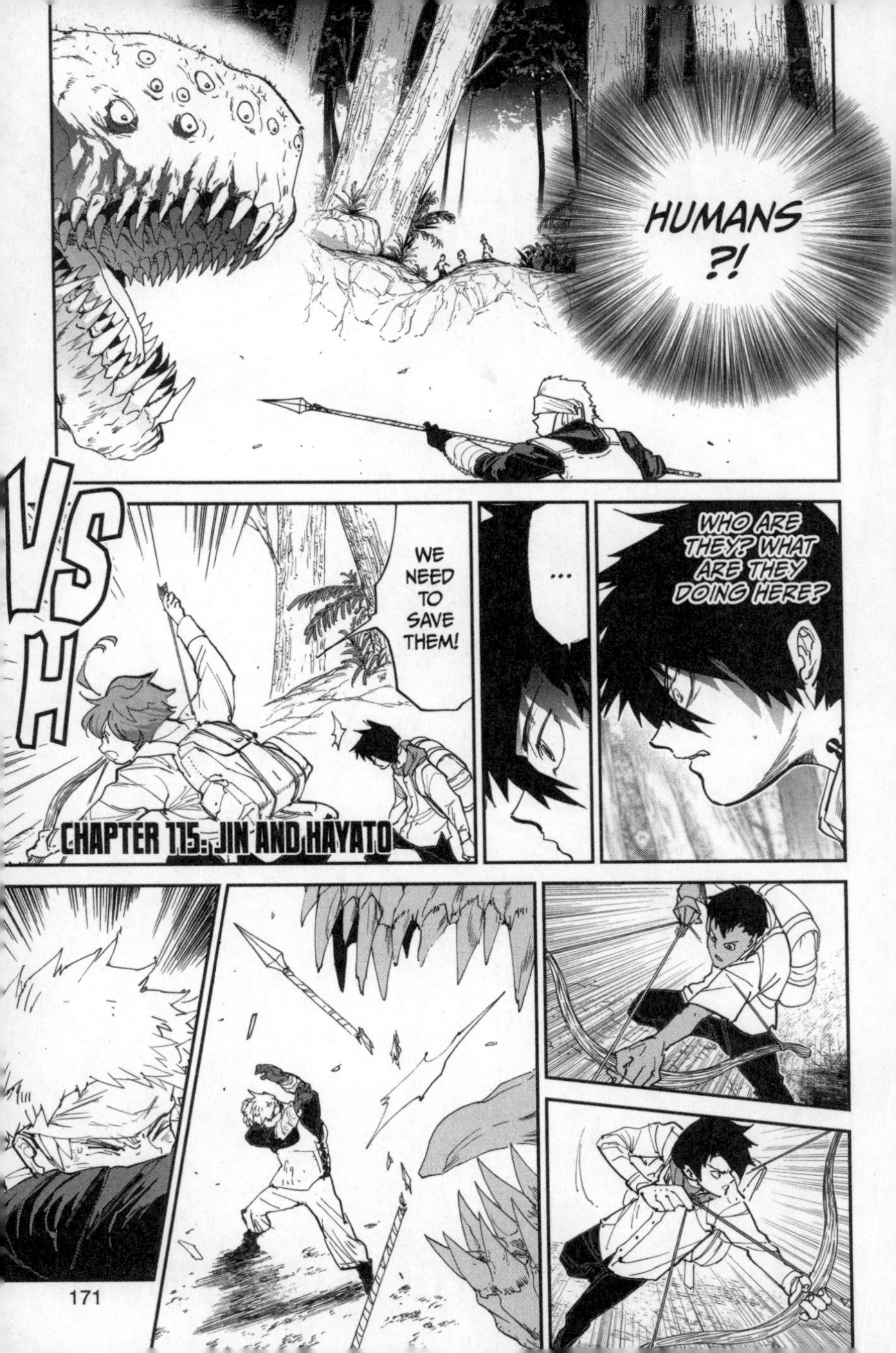
HUMANS ?!
WHO ARE THEY? WHAT ARE THEY DOING HERE?
...
WE NEED TO SAVE THEM!
VS
H
CHAPTER 115: JIN AND HAYATO

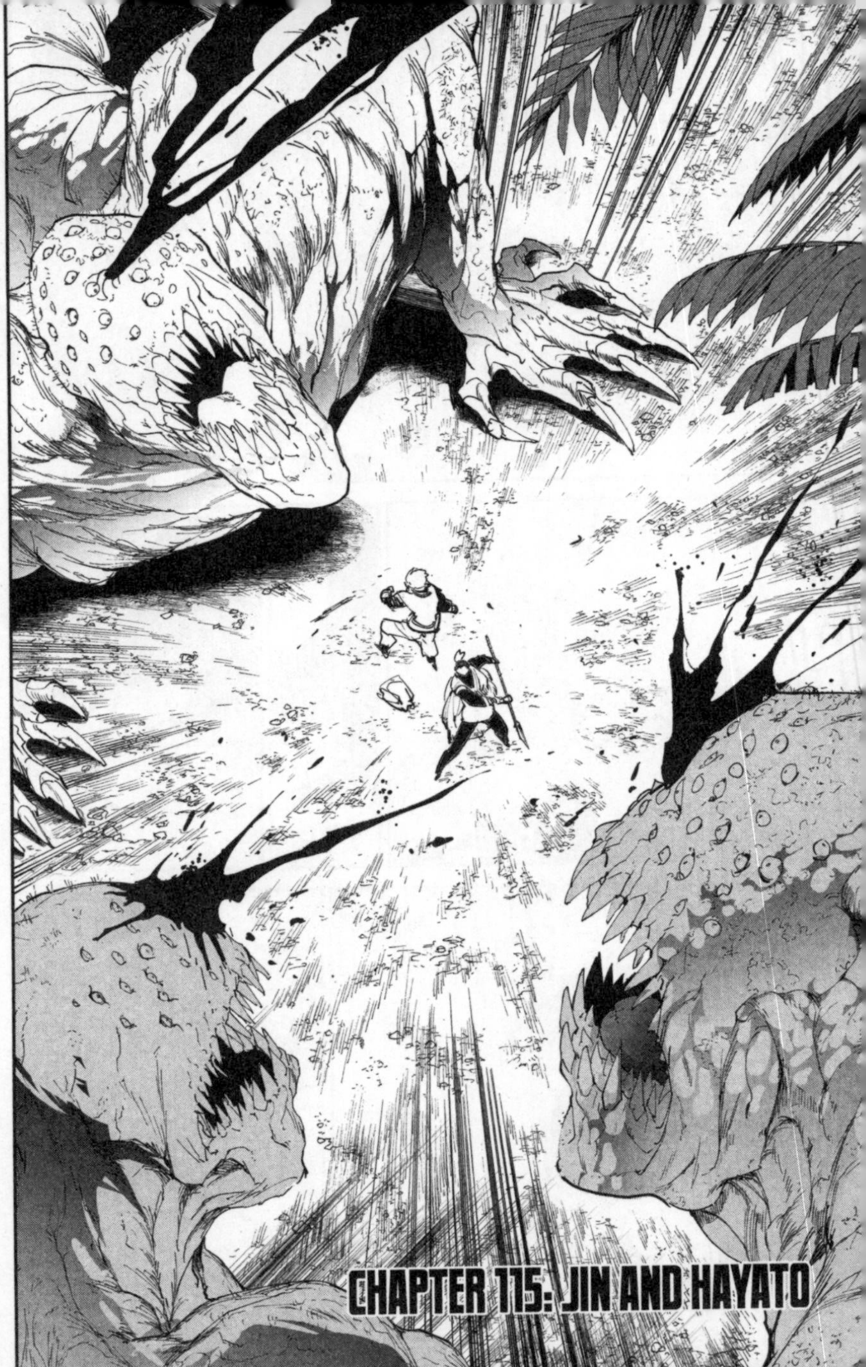
CHAPTER 115: JIN AND HAYATO

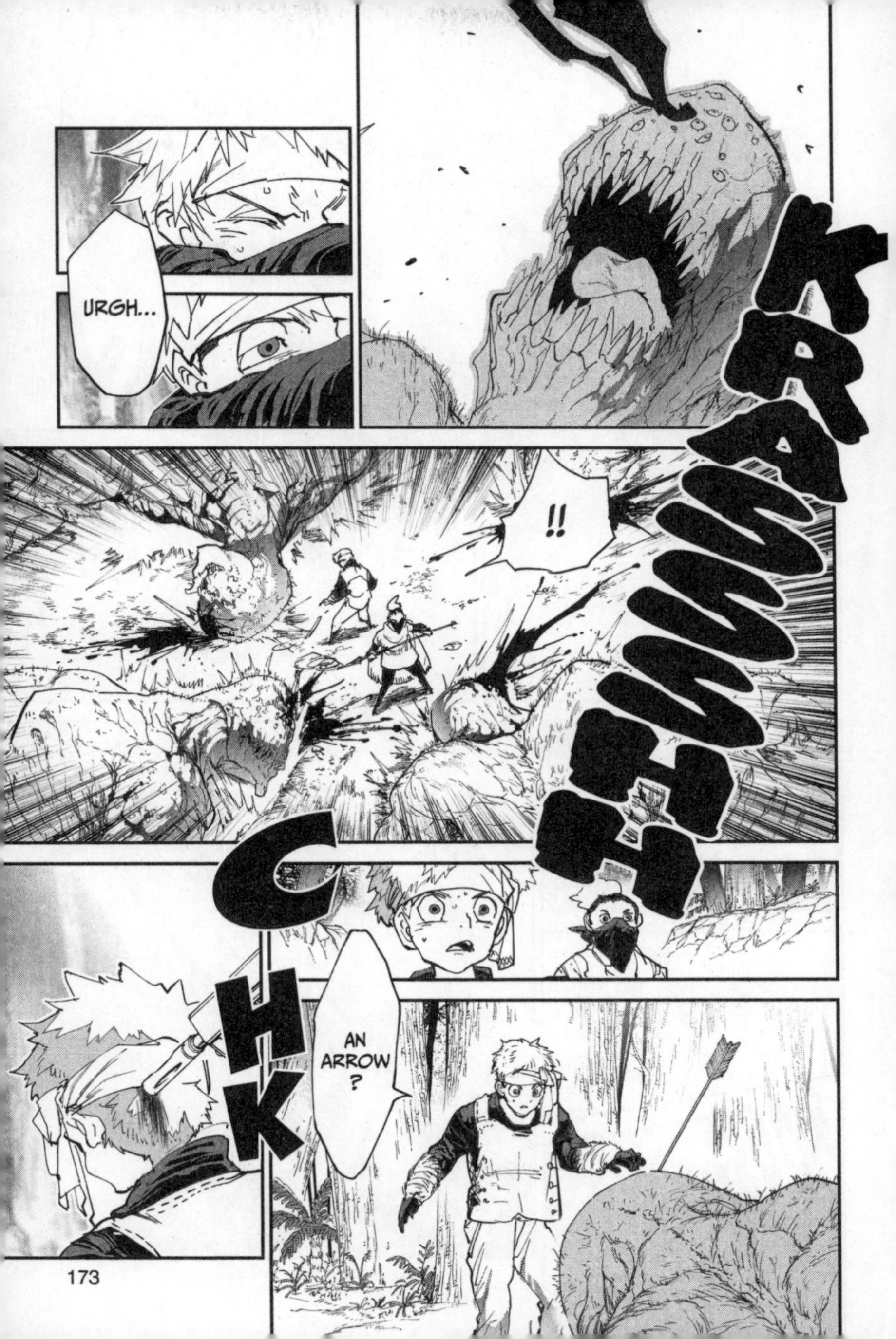

KRASSSSHH
URGH...
!!
CHK
AN ARROW ?

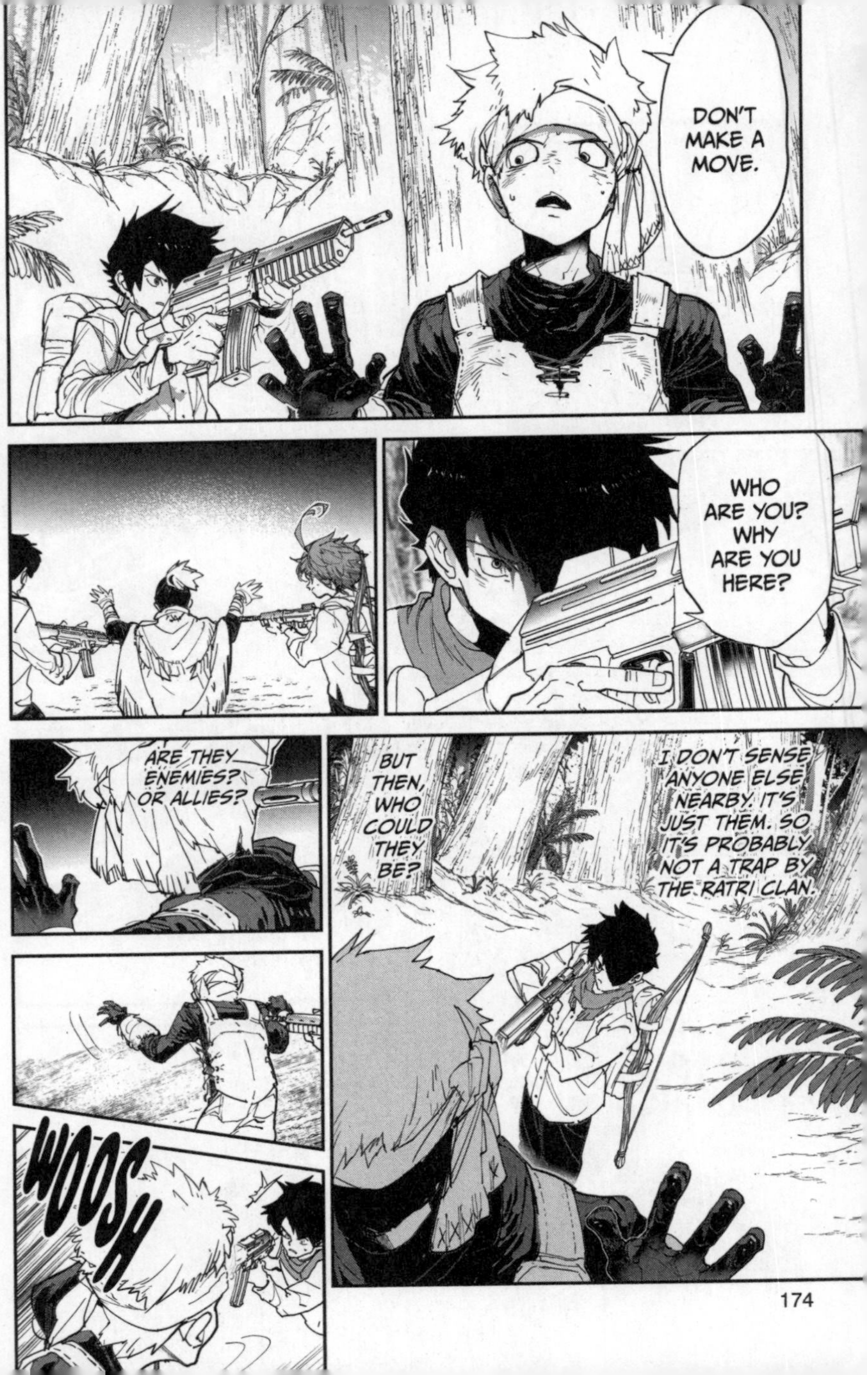
DON'T MAKE A MOVE.
WHO ARE YOU? WHY ARE YOU HERE?
I DON'T SENSE ANYONE ELSE NEARBY. IT'S JUST THEM. SO IT'S PROBABLY NOT A TRAP BY THE RATRI CLAN.
BUT THEN, WHO COULD THEY BE?
ARE THEY ENEMIES? OR ALLIES?
WOOSH

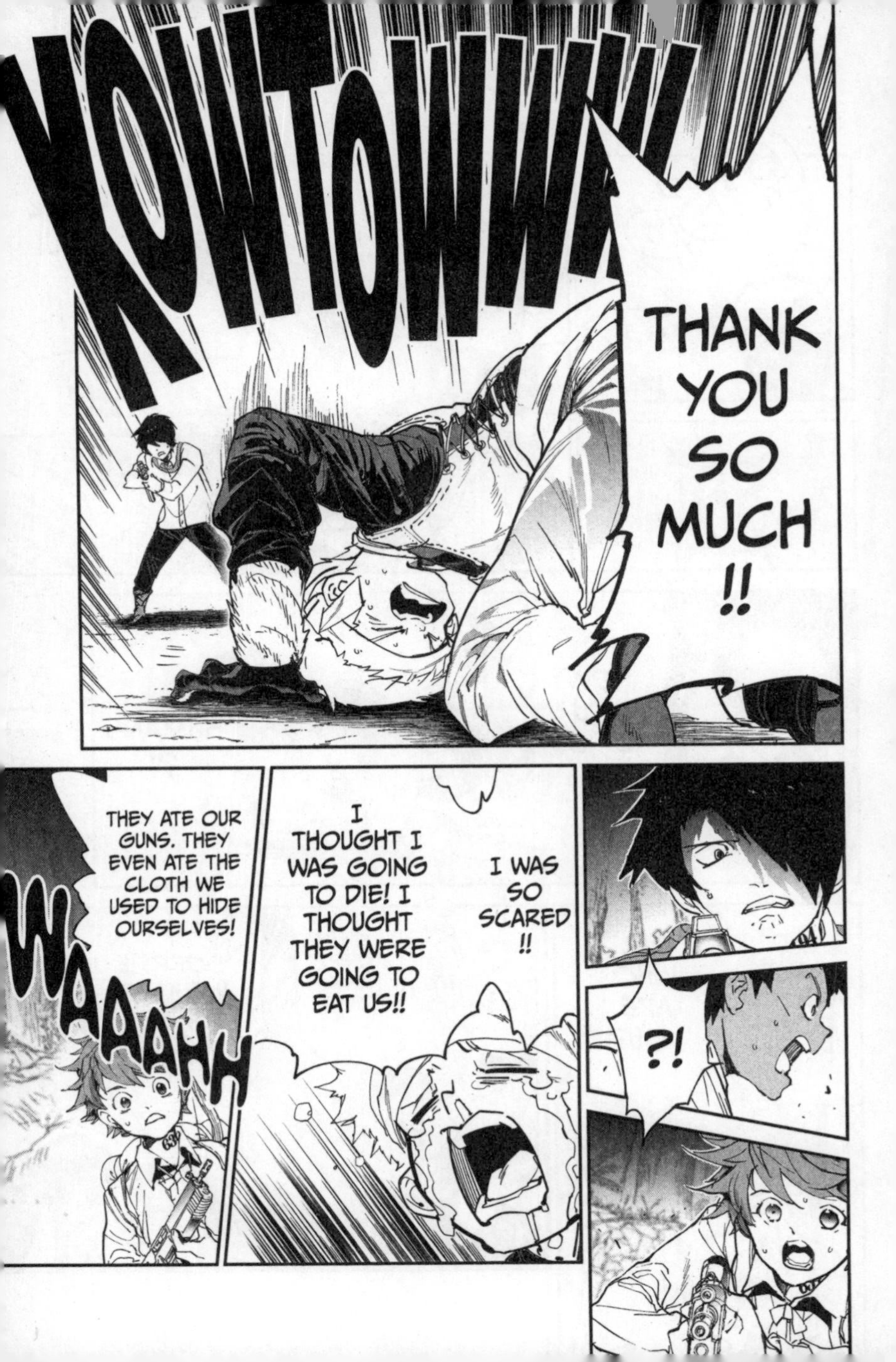
KOWTOWWW
THANK YOU SO MUCH!!
?!
I WAS SO SCARED!!
I THOUGHT I WAS GOING TO DIE! I THOUGHT THEY WERE GOING TO EAT US!!
THEY ATE OUR GUNS. THEY EVEN ATE THE CLOTH WE USED TO HIDE OURSELVES!
WAAAAHH

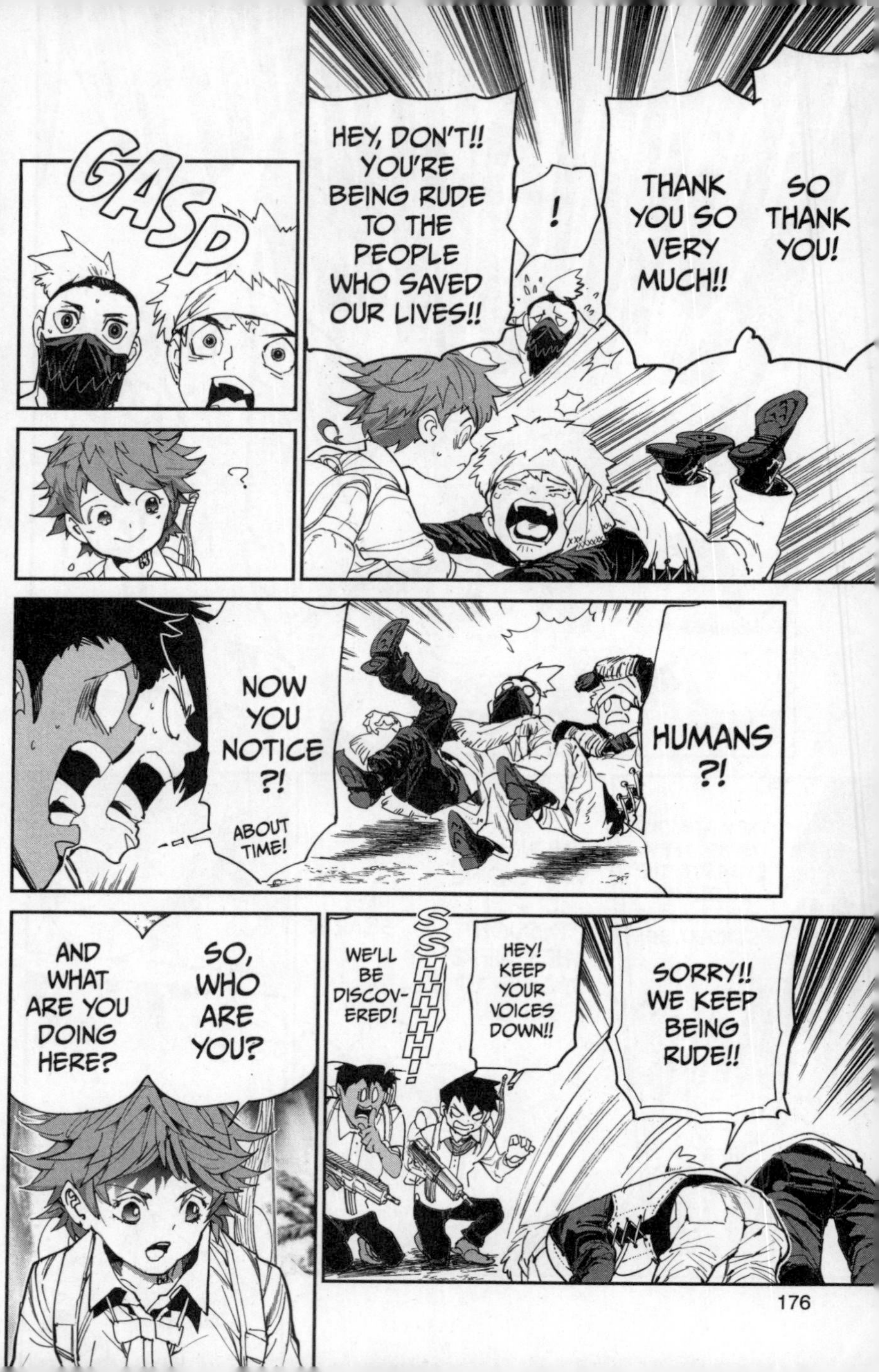
SO THANK YOU!
THANK YOU SO VERY MUCH!!
!
HEY, DON'T!! YOU'RE BEING RUDE TO THE PEOPLE WHO SAVED OUR LIVES!!
GASP
?
HUMANS?!
NOW YOU NOTICE?!
ABOUT TIME!
SORRY!! WE KEEP BEING RUDE!!
HEY! KEEP YOUR VOICES DOWN!!
SSHHHHH!
WE'LL BE DISCOV-ERED!
SO, WHO ARE YOU?
AND WHAT ARE YOU DOING HERE?

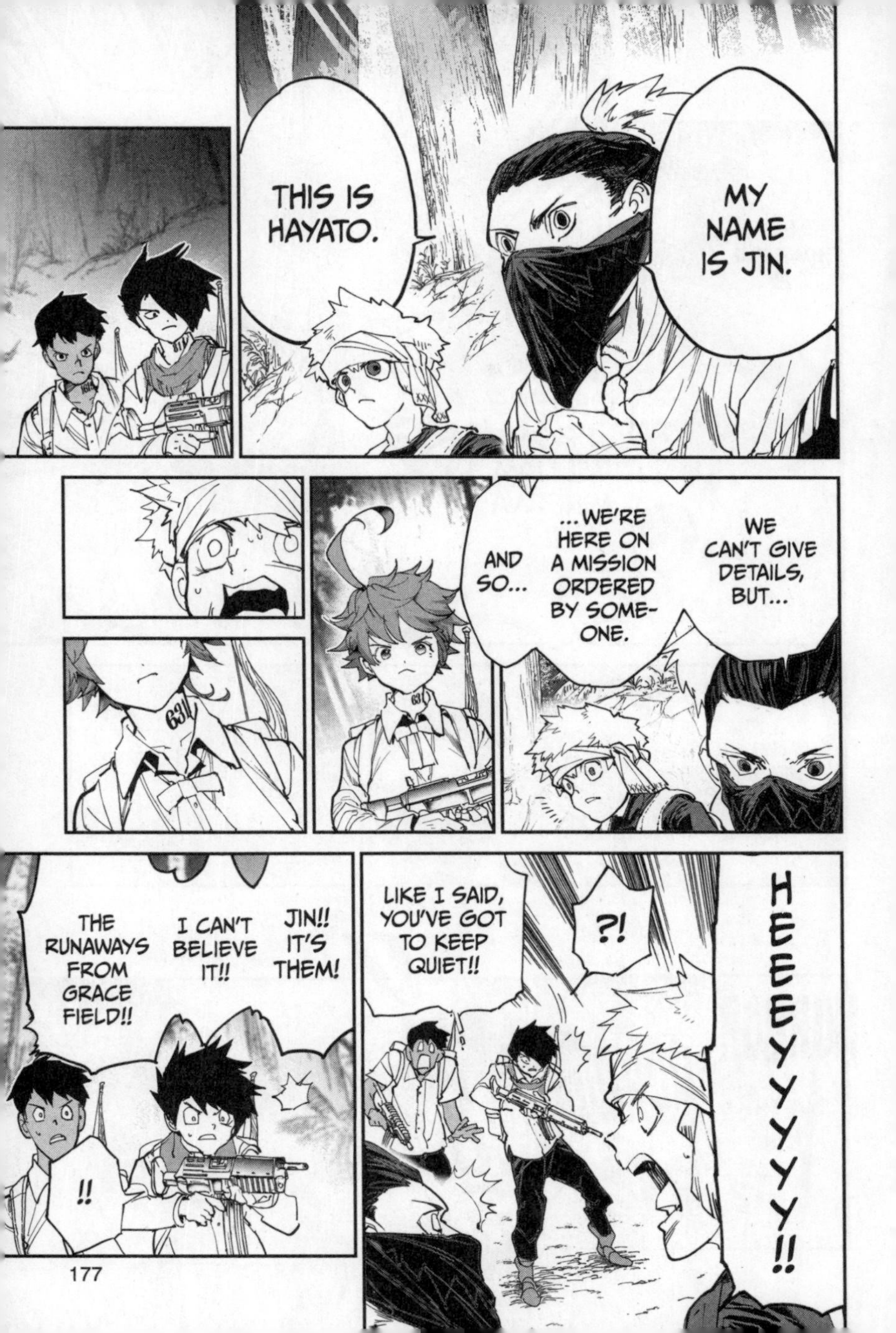
MY NAME IS JIN.
THIS IS HAYATO.
WE CAN'T GIVE DETAILS, BUT...
...WE'RE HERE ON A MISSION ORDERED BY SOME-ONE.
AND SO...
HEEEYYYYYY!!
?!
LIKE I SAID, YOU'VE GOT TO KEEP QUIET!!
JIN!! IT'S THEM!
I CAN'T BELIEVE IT!!
THE RUNAWAYS FROM GRACE FIELD!!
!!

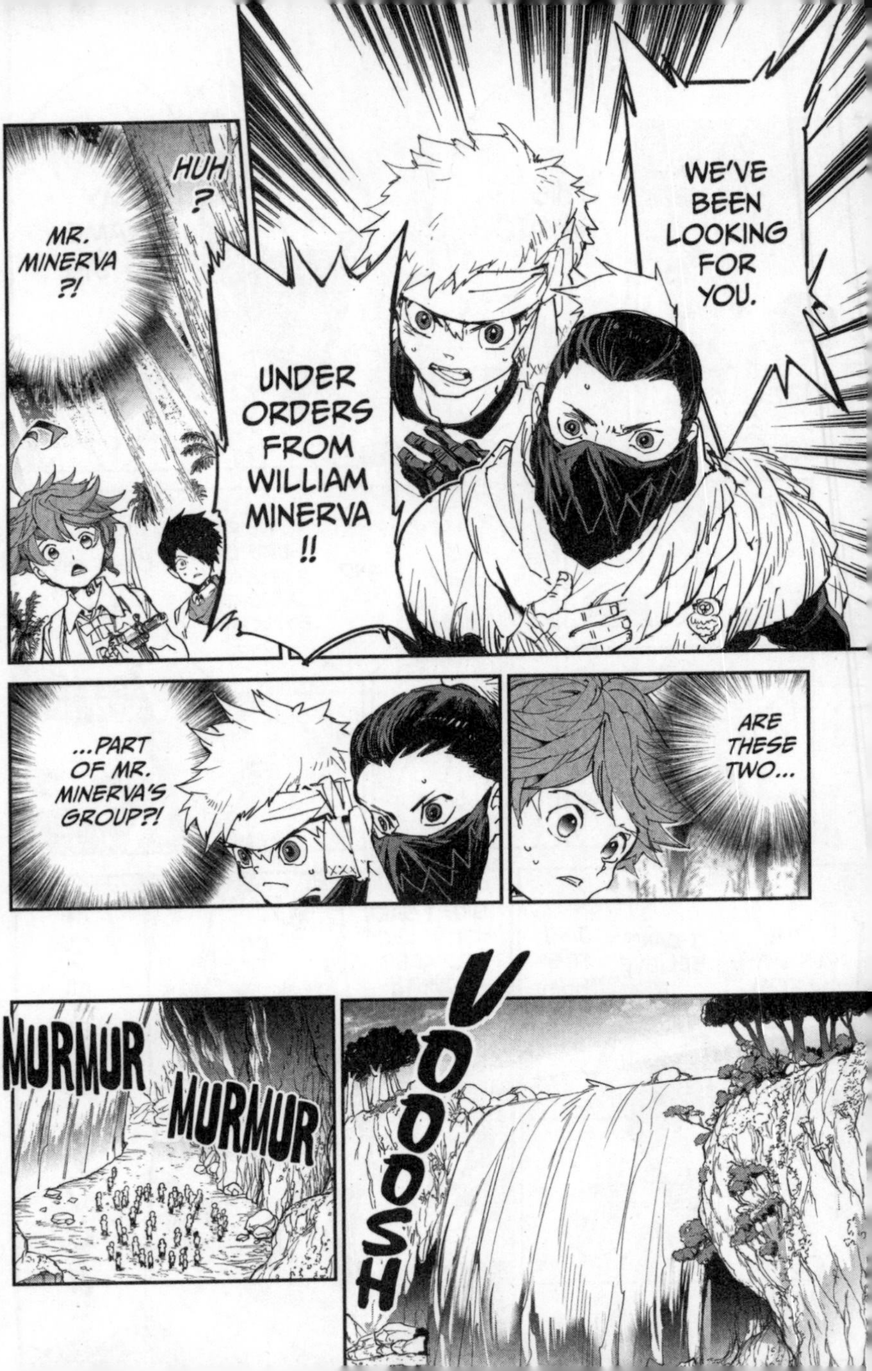
WE'VE BEEN LOOKING FOR YOU.
UNDER ORDERS FROM WILLIAM MINERVA!!
HUH?
MR. MINERVA?!
ARE THESE TWO...
...PART OF MR. MINERVA'S GROUP?!
VOOOOOSH
MURMUR
MURMUR

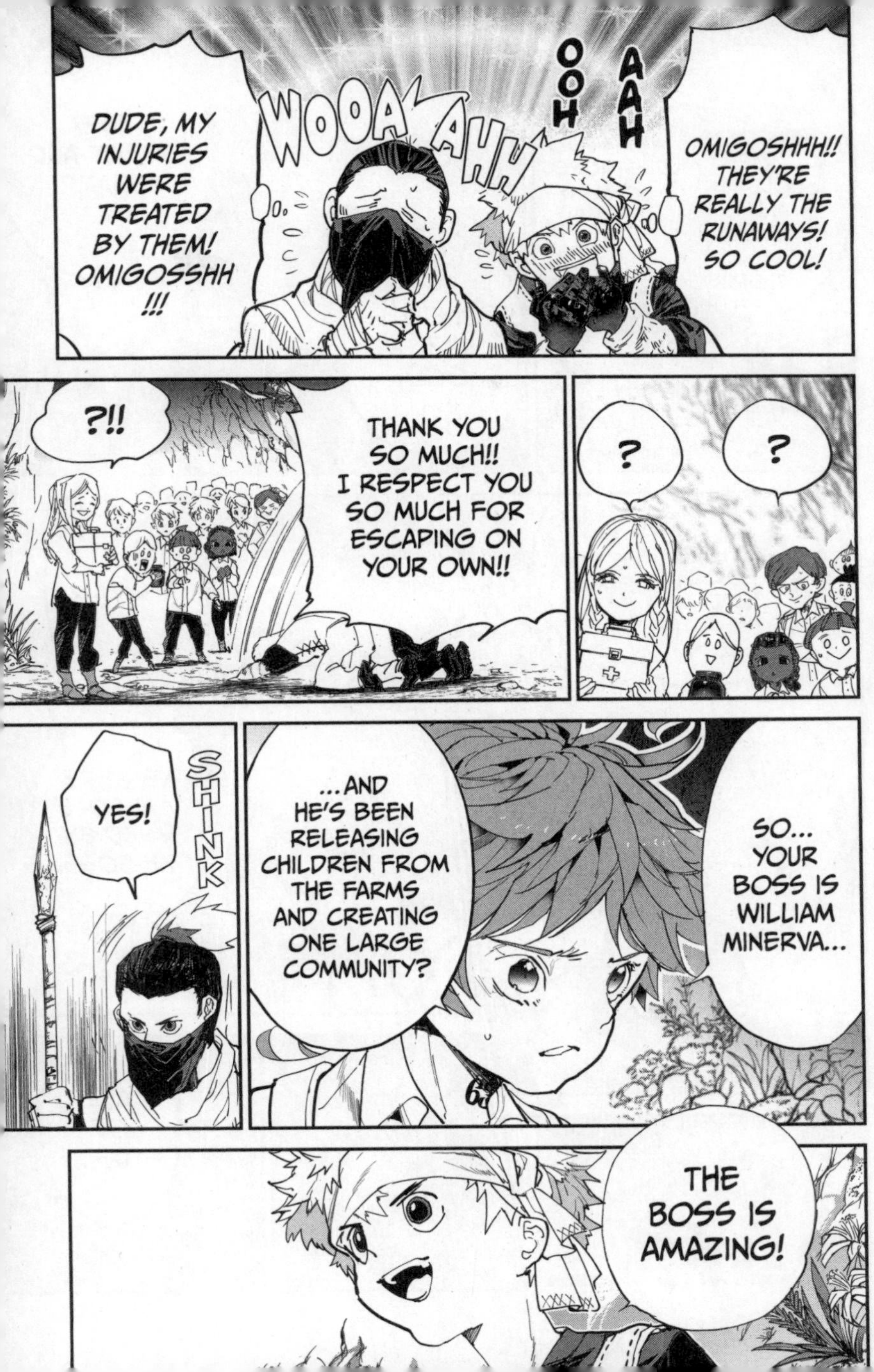
AAH
OOH
OMIGOSHHH!! THEY'RE REALLY THE RUNAWAYS! SO COOL!
WOOAAHH
DUDE, MY INJURIES WERE TREATED BY THEM! OMIGOSSHH!!!
?
?
THANK YOU SO MUCH!! I RESPECT YOU SO MUCH FOR ESCAPING ON YOUR OWN!!
?!!
SO... YOUR BOSS IS WILLIAM MINERVA...
...AND HE'S BEEN RELEASING CHILDREN FROM THE FARMS AND CREATING ONE LARGE COMMUNITY?
SHINK
YES!
THE BOSS IS AMAZING!

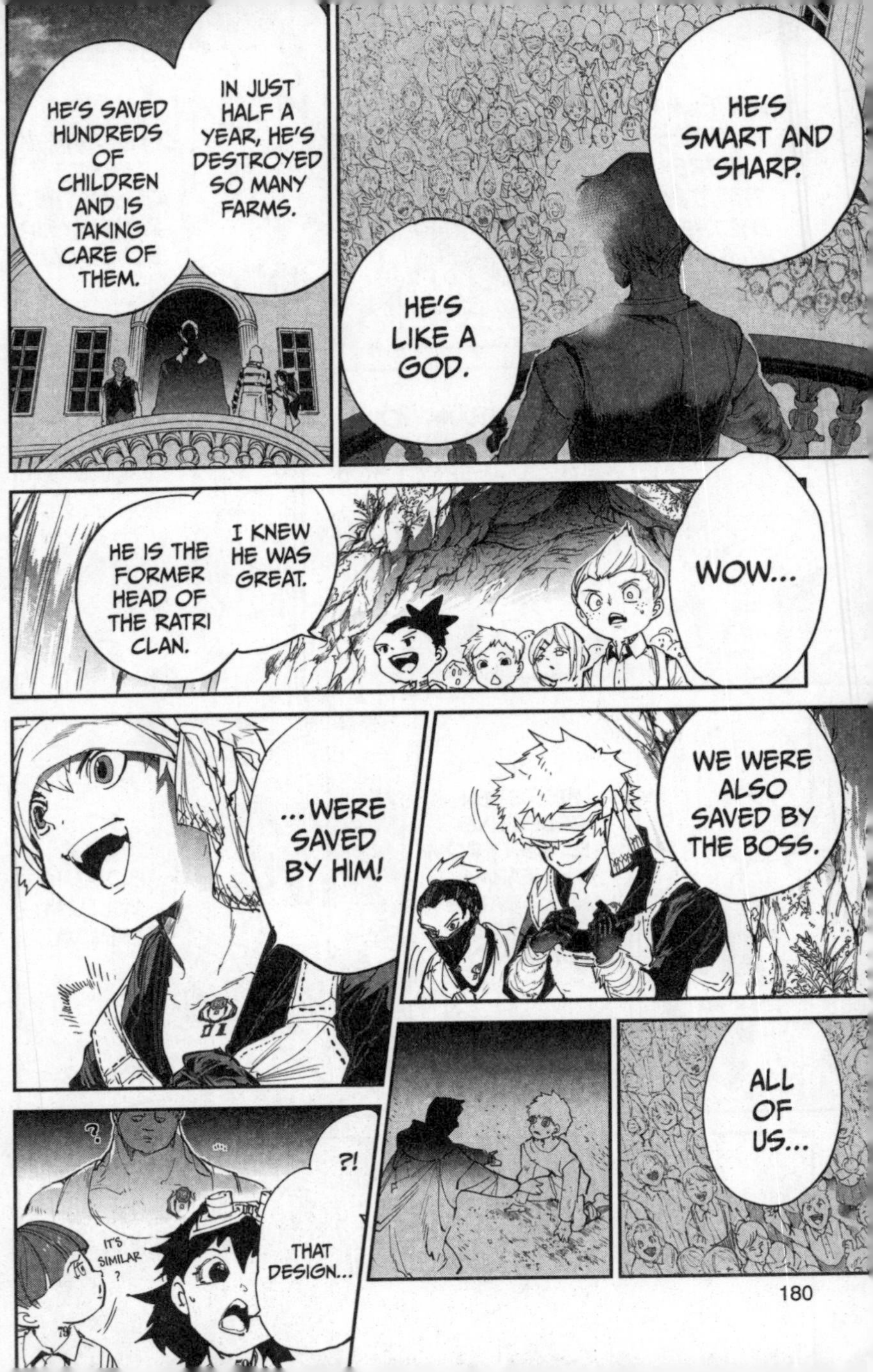
HE'S SMART AND SHARP.
HE'S LIKE A GOD.
IN JUST HALF A YEAR, HE'S DESTROYED SO MANY FARMS.
HE'S SAVED HUNDREDS OF CHILDREN AND IS TAKING CARE OF THEM.
WOW...
I KNEW HE WAS GREAT.
HE IS THE FORMER HEAD OF THE RATRI CLAN.
WE WERE ALSO SAVED BY THE BOSS.
...WERE SAVED BY HIM!
01
ALL OF US...
?!
THAT DESIGN...
IT'S SIMILAR ?

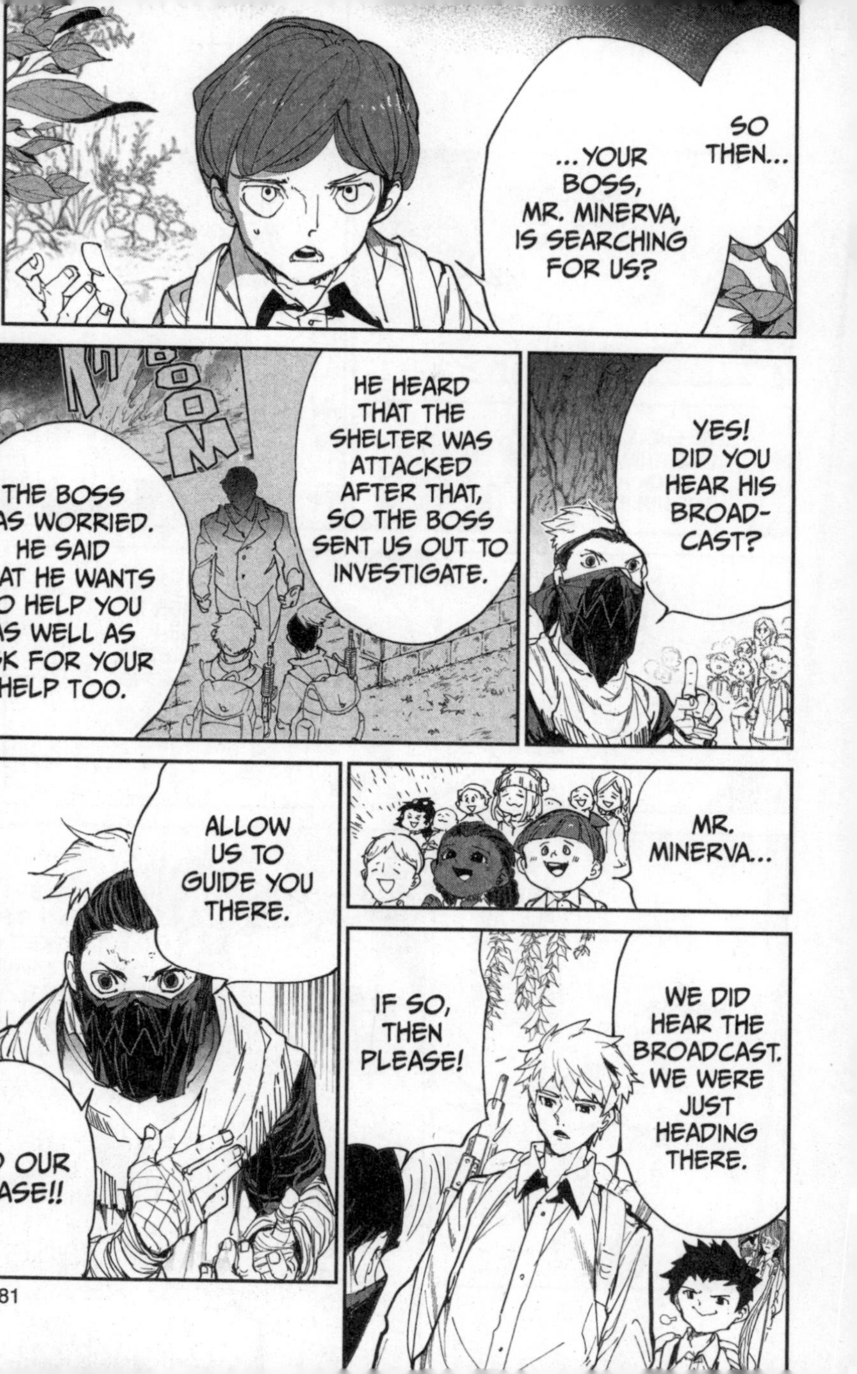
SO THEN...
...YOUR BOSS, MR. MINERVA, IS SEARCHING FOR US?
YES! DID YOU HEAR HIS BROAD-CAST?
HE HEARD THAT THE SHELTER WAS ATTACKED AFTER THAT, SO THE BOSS SENT US OUT TO INVESTIGATE.
BOOM
THE BOSS WAS WORRIED. HE SAID THAT HE WANTS TO HELP YOU AS WELL AS ASK FOR YOUR HELP TOO.
MR. MINERVA...
WE DID HEAR THE BROADCAST. WE WERE JUST HEADING THERE.
IF SO, THEN PLEASE!
ALLOW US TO GUIDE YOU THERE.
TO OUR BASE!!

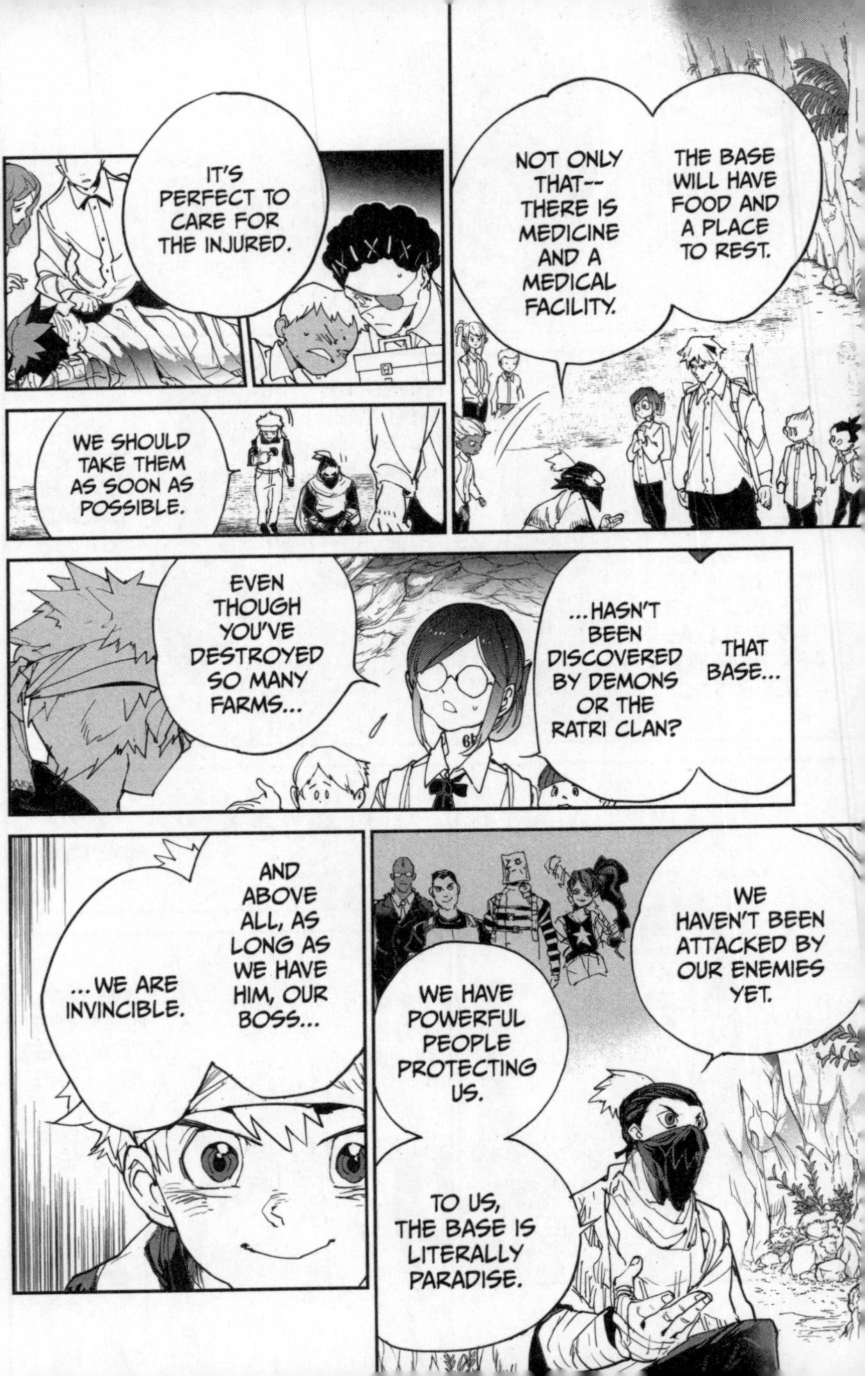
THE BASE WILL HAVE FOOD AND A PLACE TO REST.
NOT ONLY THAT-- THERE IS MEDICINE AND A MEDICAL FACILITY.
IT'S PERFECT TO CARE FOR THE INJURED.
WE SHOULD TAKE THEM AS SOON AS POSSIBLE.
THAT BASE...
...HASN'T BEEN DISCOVERED BY DEMONS OR THE RATRI CLAN?
EVEN THOUGH YOU'VE DESTROYED SO MANY FARMS...
WE HAVEN'T BEEN ATTACKED BY OUR ENEMIES YET.
WE HAVE POWERFUL PEOPLE PROTECTING US.
TO US, THE BASE IS LITERALLY PARADISE.
AND ABOVE ALL, AS LONG AS WE HAVE HIM, OUR BOSS...
...WE ARE INVINCIBLE.

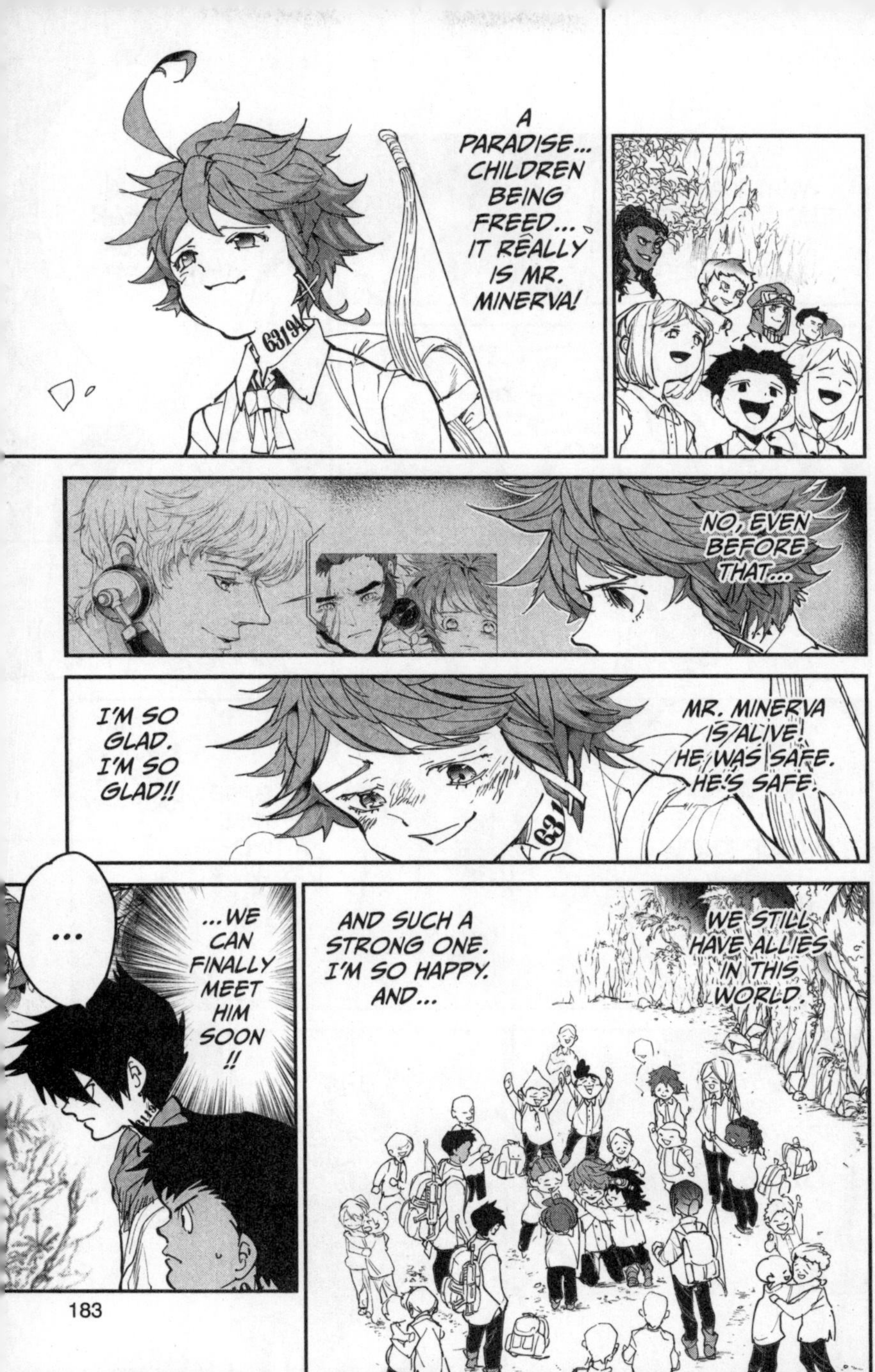
A PARADISE... CHILDREN BEING FREED... IT REALLY IS MR. MINERVA!
NO, EVEN BEFORE THAT...
MR. MINERVA IS ALIVE! HE WAS SAFE. HE'S SAFE.
I'M SO GLAD. I'M SO GLAD!!
WE STILL HAVE ALLIES IN THIS WORLD.
AND SUCH A STRONG ONE. I'M SO HAPPY. AND...
...WE CAN FINALLY MEET HIM SOON!!
...

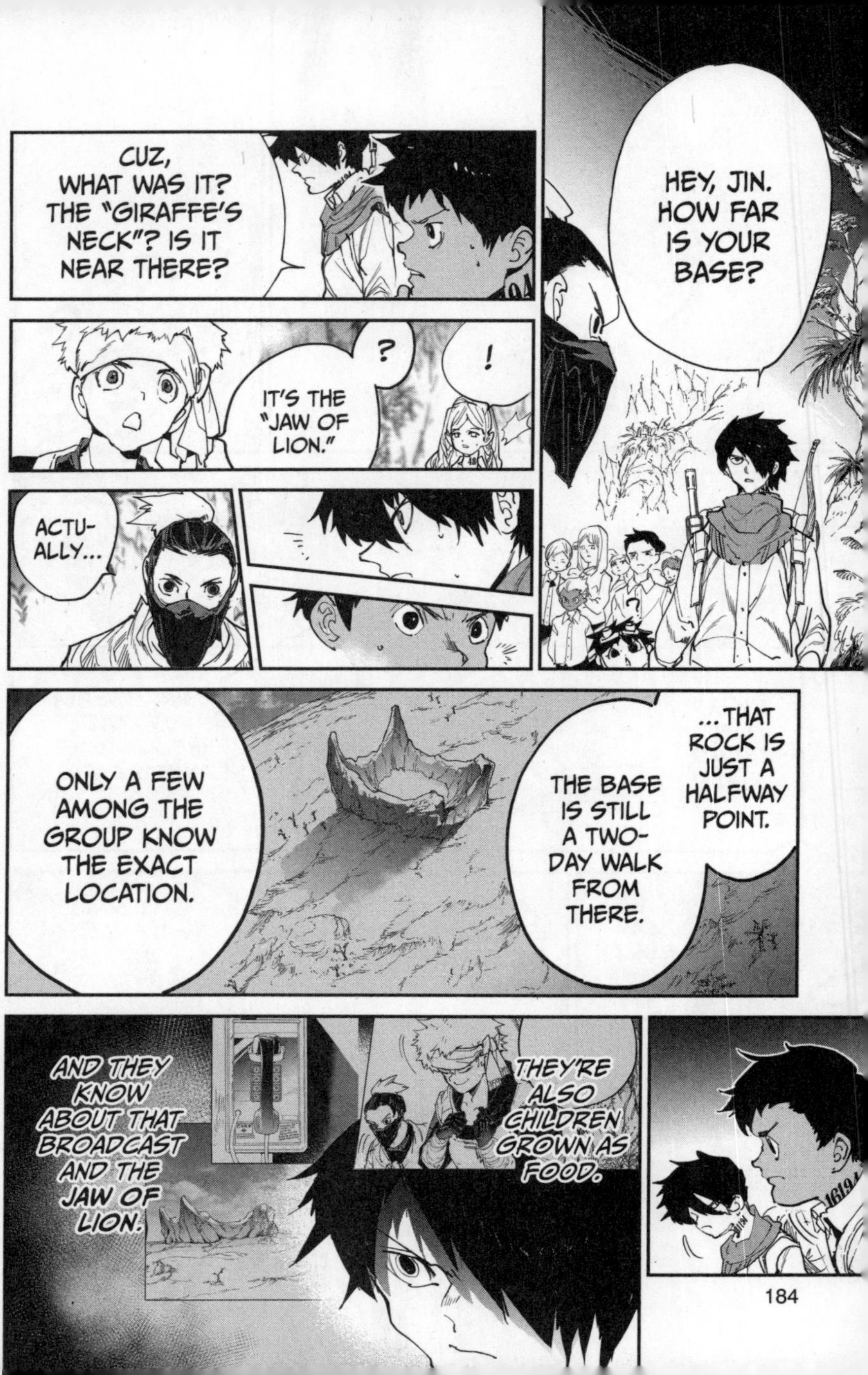
HEY, JIN. HOW FAR IS YOUR BASE?
CUZ, WHAT WAS IT? THE "GIRAFFE'S NECK"? IS IT NEAR THERE?
!
?
IT'S THE "JAW OF LION."
ACTU-ALLY...
...THAT ROCK IS JUST A HALFWAY POINT.
THE BASE IS STILL A TWO-DAY WALK FROM THERE.
ONLY A FEW AMONG THE GROUP KNOW THE EXACT LOCATION.
THEY'RE ALSO CHILDREN GROWN AS FOOD.
AND THEY KNOW ABOUT THAT BROADCAST AND THE JAW OF LION.

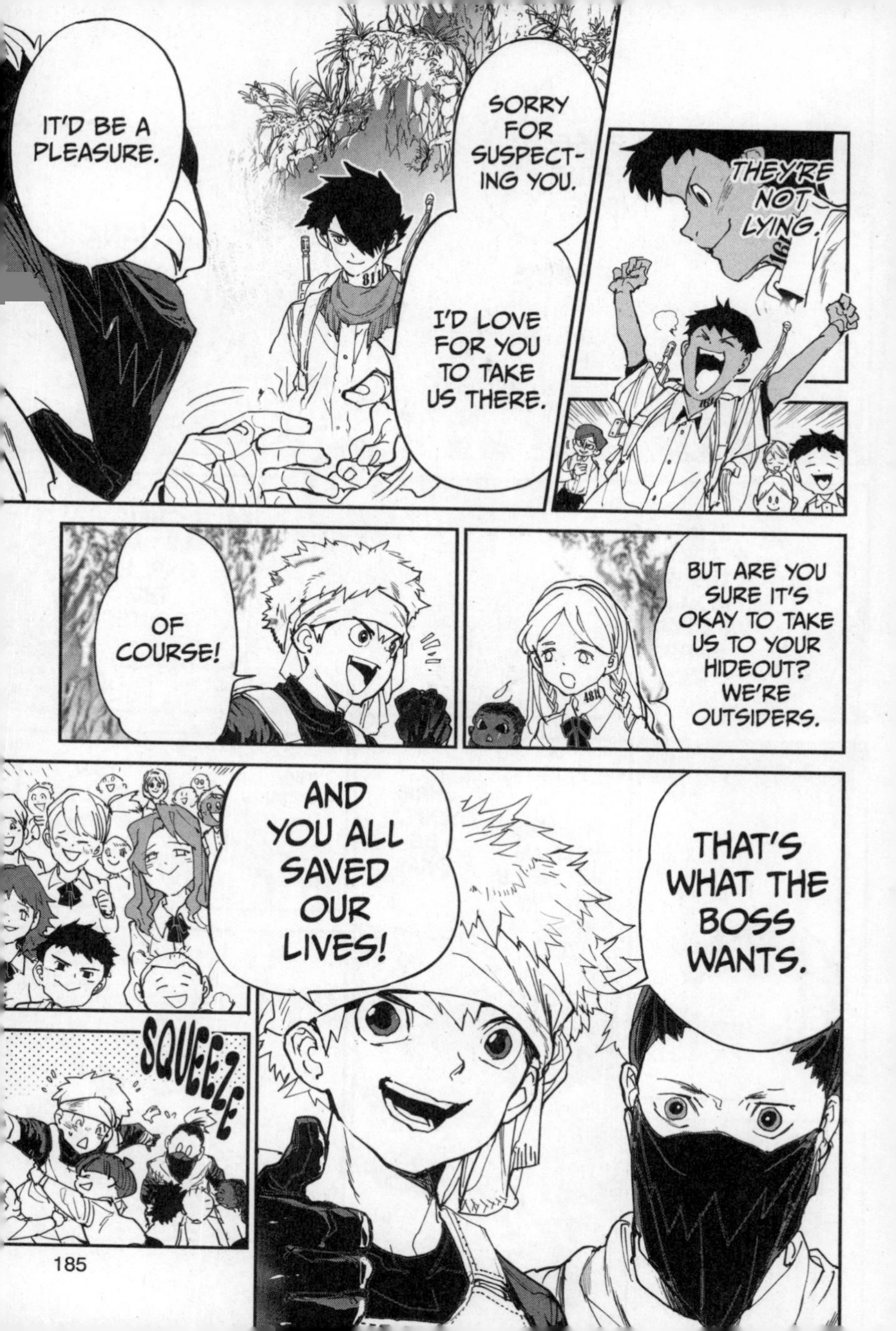
THEY'RE NOT LYING.
SORRY FOR SUSPECTING YOU.
I'D LOVE FOR YOU TO TAKE US THERE.
IT'D BE A PLEASURE.
BUT ARE YOU SURE IT'S OKAY TO TAKE US TO YOUR HIDEOUT? WE'RE OUTSIDERS.
OF COURSE!
THAT'S WHAT THE BOSS WANTS.
AND YOU ALL SAVED OUR LIVES!
SQUEEZE

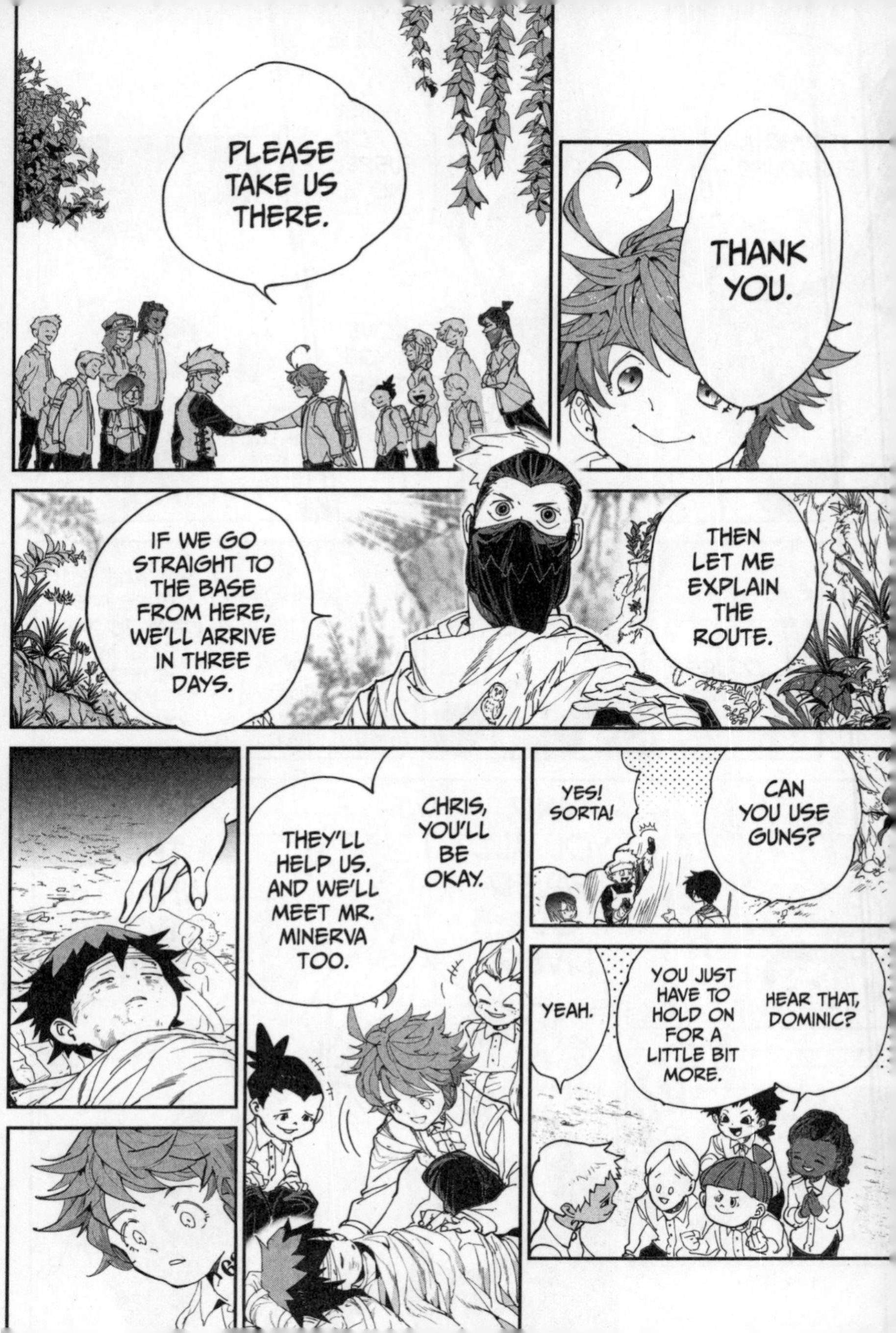
THANK YOU.
PLEASE TAKE US THERE.
THEN LET ME EXPLAIN THE ROUTE.
IF WE GO STRAIGHT TO THE BASE FROM HERE, WE'LL ARRIVE IN THREE DAYS.
CAN YOU USE GUNS?
YES! SORTA!
HEAR THAT, DOMINIC?
YOU JUST HAVE TO HOLD ON FOR A LITTLE BIT MORE.
YEAH.
CHRIS, YOU'LL BE OKAY.
THEY'LL HELP US. AND WE'LL MEET MR. MINERVA TOO.

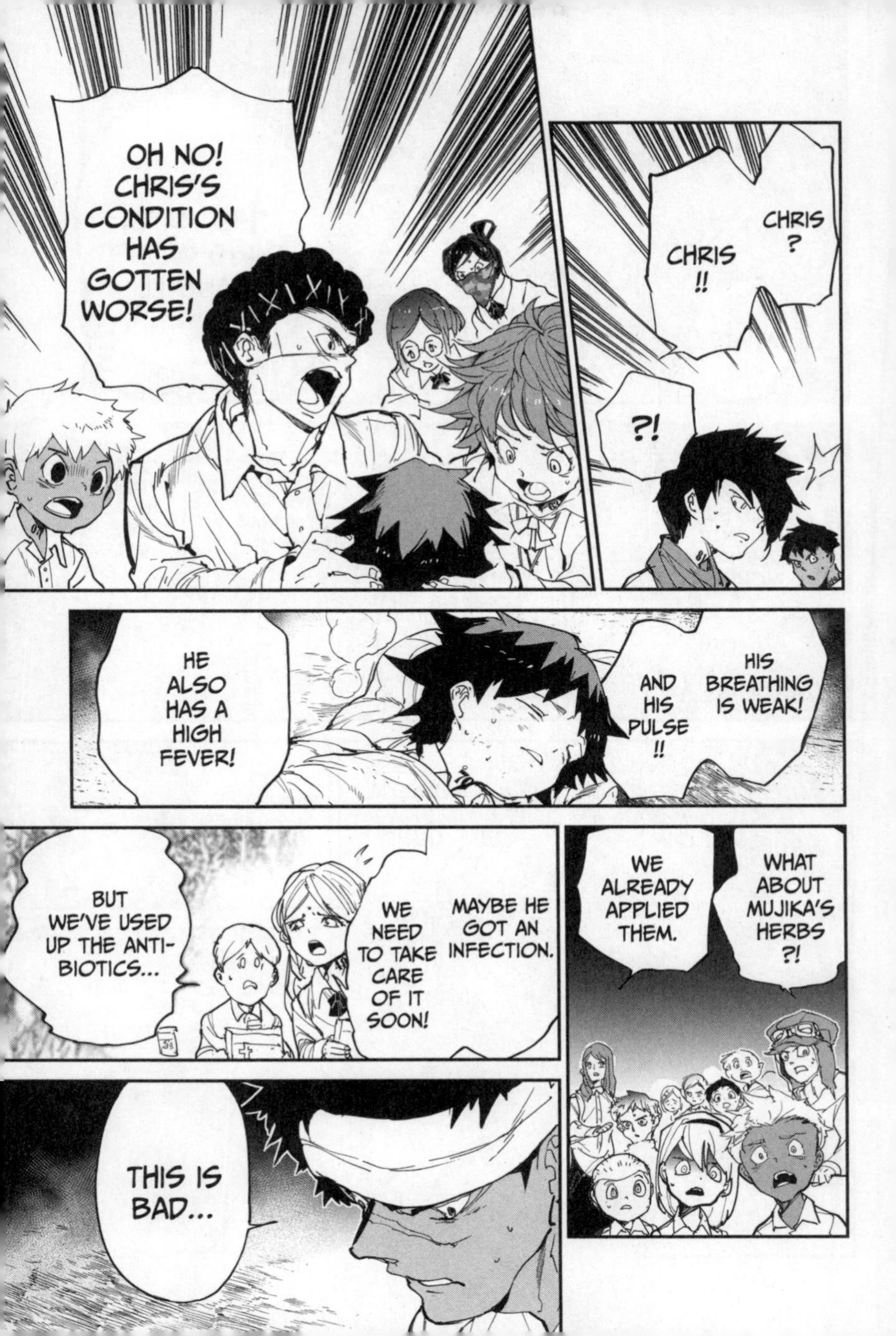
CHRIS?
CHRIS!!
?!
OH NO! CHRIS'S CONDITION HAS GOTTEN WORSE!
HIS BREATHING IS WEAK!
AND HIS PULSE!!
HE ALSO HAS A HIGH FEVER!
WHAT ABOUT MUJIKA'S HERBS?!
WE ALREADY APPLIED THEM.
MAYBE HE GOT AN INFECTION.
WE NEED TO TAKE CARE OF IT SOON!
BUT WE'VE USED UP THE ANTI-BIOTICS...
THIS IS BAD...

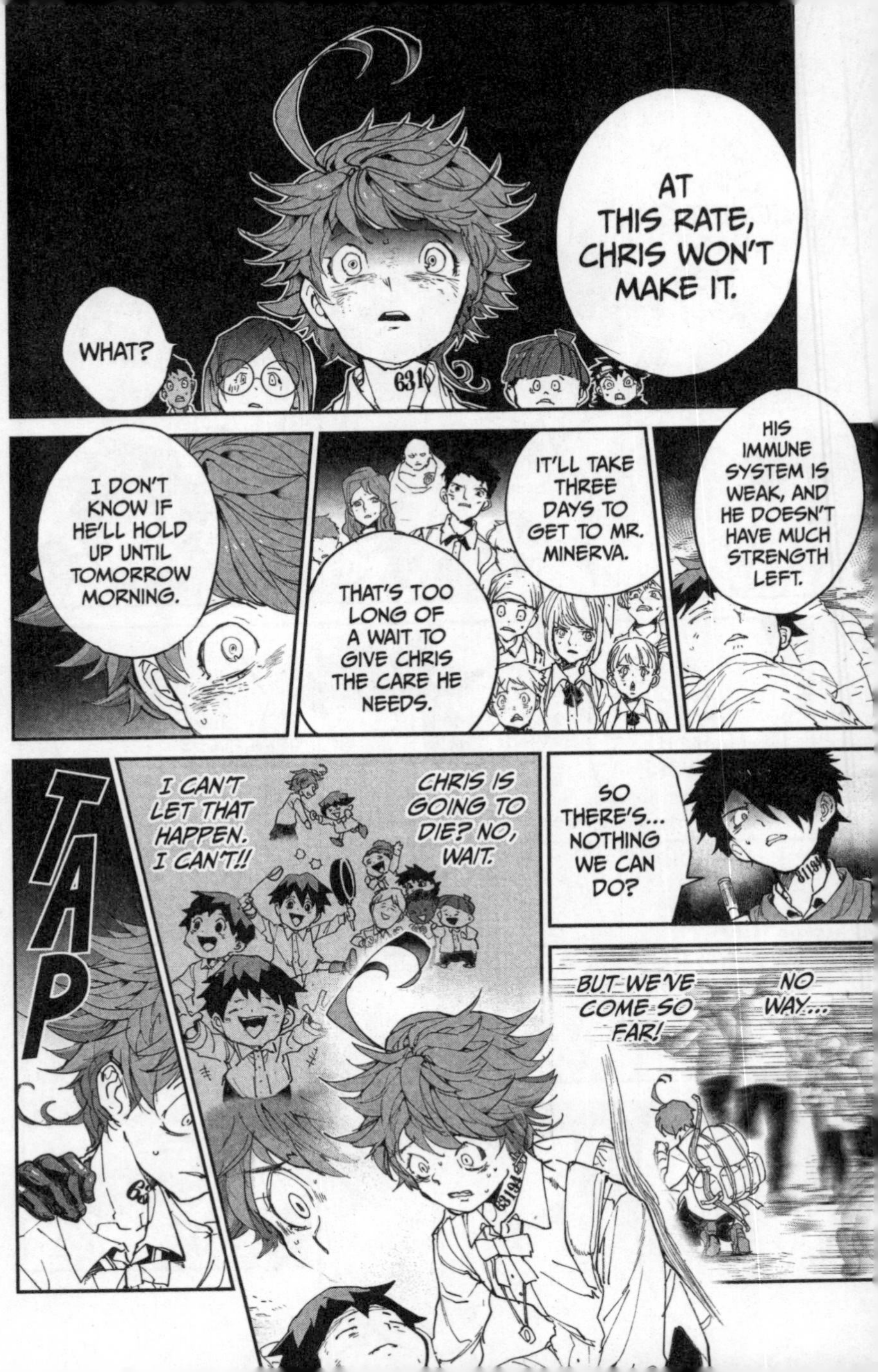
AT THIS RATE, CHRIS WON'T MAKE IT.
WHAT?
HIS IMMUNE SYSTEM IS WEAK, AND HE DOESN'T HAVE MUCH STRENGTH LEFT.
IT'LL TAKE THREE DAYS TO GET TO MR. MINERVA.
THAT'S TOO LONG OF A WAIT TO GIVE CHRIS THE CARE HE NEEDS.
I DON'T KNOW IF HE'LL HOLD UP UNTIL TOMORROW MORNING.
SO THERE'S... NOTHING WE CAN DO?
NO WAY...
BUT WE'VE COME SO FAR!
CHRIS IS GOING TO DIE? NO, WAIT.
I CAN'T LET THAT HAPPEN. I CAN'T!!
TAP

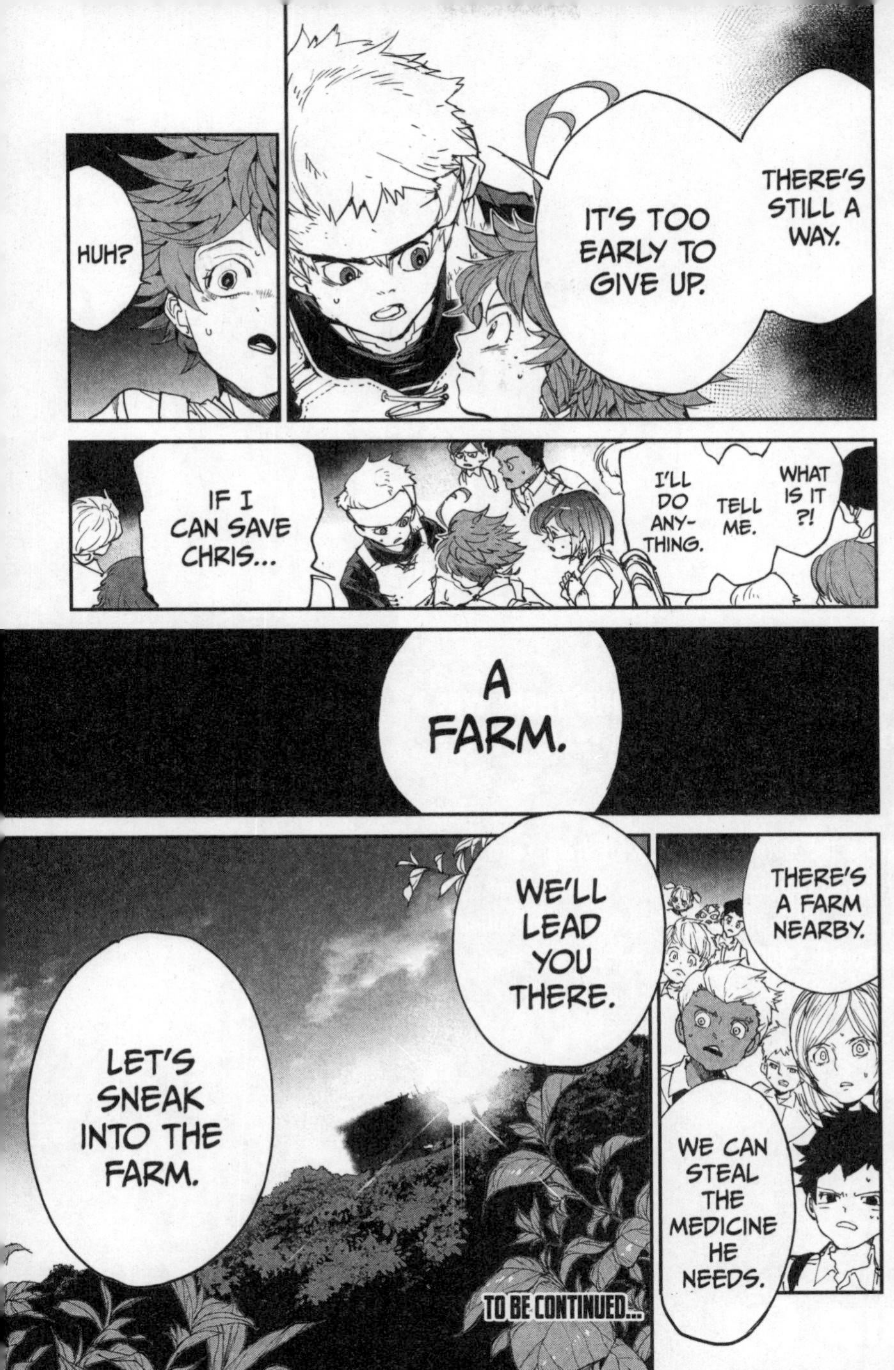
THERE'S STILL A WAY.
IT'S TOO EARLY TO GIVE UP.
HUH?
WHAT IS IT ?!
TELL ME.
I'LL DO ANY-THING.
IF I CAN SAVE CHRIS...
A FARM.
THERE'S A FARM NEARBY.
WE CAN STEAL THE MEDICINE HE NEEDS.
WE'LL LEAD YOU THERE.
LET'S SNEAK INTO THE FARM.
TO BE CONTINUED...

ASTRA
LOST IN SPACE

CAN EIGHT TEENAGERS FIND THEIR WAY HOME FROM 5,000 LIGHT-YEARS AWAY?

It's the year 2063, and interstellar space travel has become the norm. Eight students from Caird High School and one child set out on a routine planet camp excursion. While there, the students are mysteriously transported 5,000 light-years away to the middle of nowhere! Will they ever make it back home?!

ASTRA
LOST IN SPACE
Story and Art by KENTA SHINOHARA

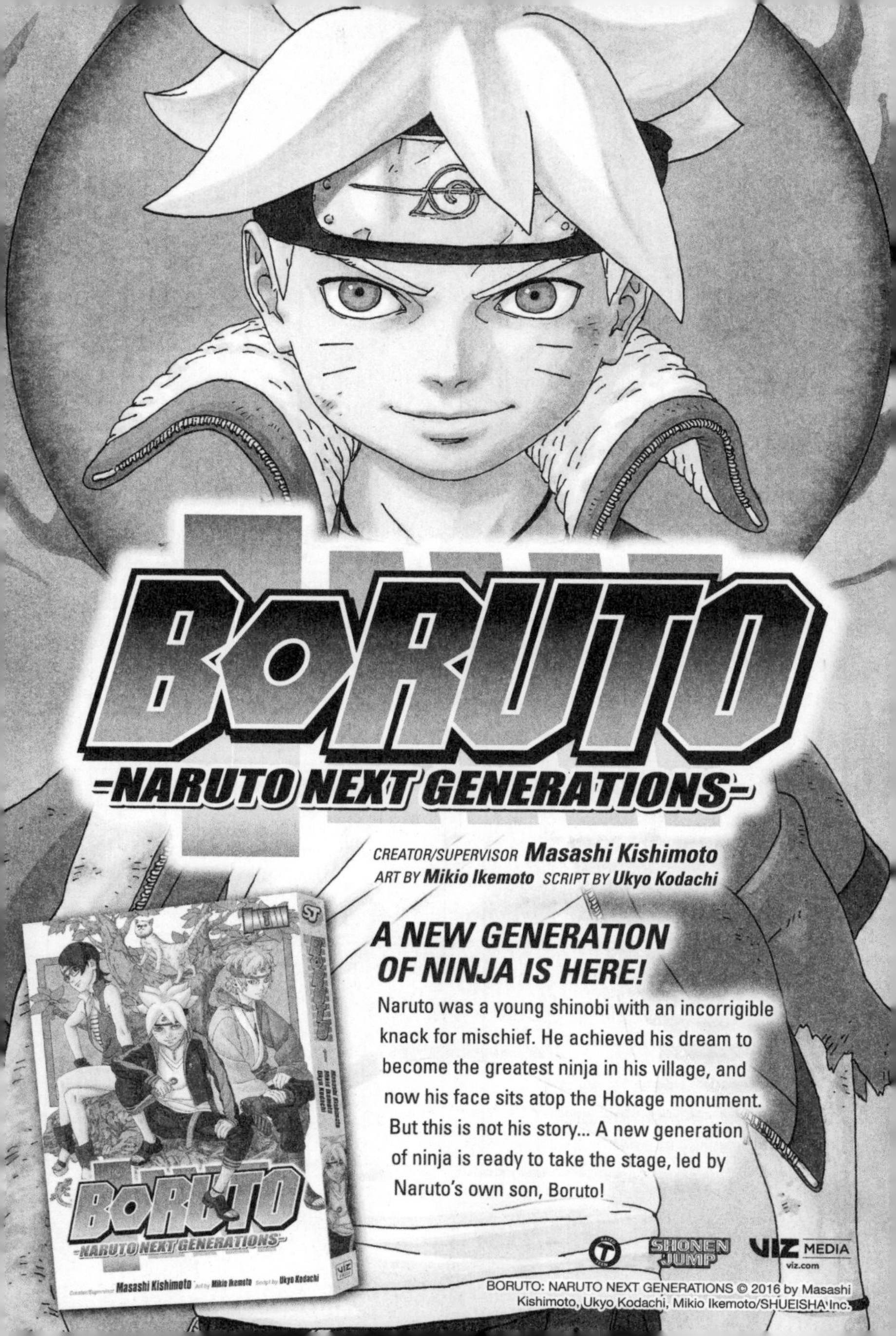
BORUTO
-NARUTO NEXT GENERATIONS-
CREATOR/SUPERVISOR Masashi Kishimoto
ART BY Mikio Ikemoto SCRIPT BY Ukyo Kodachi
A NEW GENERATION OF NINJA IS HERE!
Naruto was a young shinobi with an incorrigible knack for mischief. He achieved his dream to become the greatest ninja in his village, and now his face sits atop the Hokage monument. But this is not his story... A new generation of ninja is ready to take the stage, led by Naruto's own son, Boruto!
BORUTO
-NARUTO NEXT GENERATIONS-
Masashi Kishimoto Mikio Ikemoto Ukyo Kodachi
SHONEN JUMP
VIZ MEDIA
viz.com
BORUTO: NARUTO NEXT GENERATIONS © 2016 by Masashi Kishimoto, Ukyo Kodachi, Mikio Ikemoto/SHUEISHA Inc.

YOU'RE READING THE **WRONG WAY!**

The Promised Neverland reads from right to left, starting in the upper-right corner. Japanese is read from right to left, meaning that action, sound effects and word-balloon order are completely reversed from English order.